ATTACKS ON THE PRESS IN 2005

Cover: AP/Hussein Mala – Holding pens to symbolize press freedom, Lebanese journalists mourn the death of columnist Samir Qassir. Thousands gathered in Martyrs' Square in Beirut on June 3, the day after Qassir was killed by a bomb placed in his car.

The publication of Attacks on the Press in 2005 *is underwritten by a grant from Bloomberg.*

THE COMMITTEE TO PROTECT JOURNALISTS
330 Seventh Avenue, 11th Fl., New York, NY 10001
t: (212) 465-1004   f: (212) 465-9568   info@cpj.org
visit us online for more information: **www.cpj.org**

Founded in 1981, the Committee to Protect Journalists responds to attacks on the press worldwide. CPJ documents hundreds of cases every year and takes action on behalf of journalists and news organizations without regard to political ideology. Join CPJ and help promote press freedom by defending the people who report the news. To maintain its independence, CPJ accepts no government funding. We depend entirely on the support of individuals, foundations, and corporations.

The Associated Press, Lexis-Nexis, and Reuters provided electronic news and Internet services used to conduct research for this book.

Editorial Director: Bill Sweeney
Senior Editor: Robert Mahoney
Designer: Justin Goldberg
Maps: The Associated Press/Francois Duckett
Copy Editors: Barbara Ross, Robin Lauzon
Proofreader: Joe Sullivan

Printed in the United States of America.

Attacks on the Press in 2005:
A Worldwide Survey by the Committee to Protect Journalists

ISSN: 1078-3334
ISBN: 0-944823-25-4

THE COMMITTEE TO PROTECT JOURNALISTS

ATTACKS ON THE PRESS IN 2005

TABLE OF CONTENTS

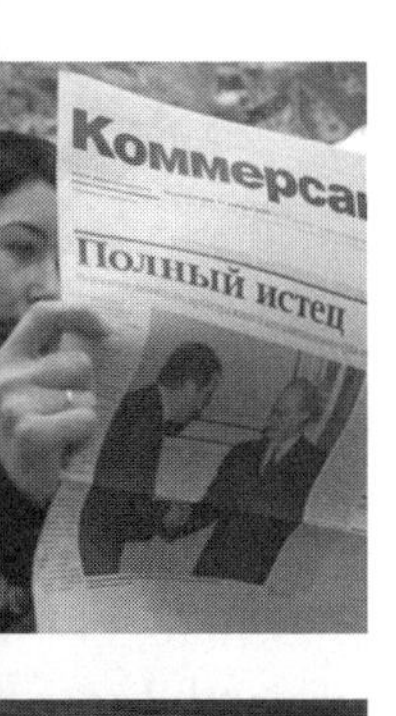

PREFACE

by Paul E. Steiger

For 24 years, the Committee to Protect Journalists has remained steadfast in its mission to defend the press around the world. But in 2005, that mission meant paying unusual attention to what was happening at home.

From Iraq to China, from Uzbekistan to Zimbabwe, 2005 was another terrible year for journalists in much of the world. By CPJ's count, more than 100 journalists were killed doing their jobs over the past two years, the deadliest such period in a decade. Twenty-four countries jailed 125 journalists in 2005, figures that reflect increases from the previous year.

The United States, long a bastion of press freedom, may have contributed to these disturbing trends. With a prominent U.S. reporter jailed for 85 days, new legal threats emerging every day, and the U.S. military stonewalling investigations into the deaths and detentions of journalists in Iraq, the press fared badly at the hands of U.S. authorities. The United States shot up CPJ's list of countries imprisoning journalists, sharing sixth place with Burma.

I strongly suspect that there is a relationship between the rise in deaths and incarcerations abroad and the infringement of press freedom at home.

We journalists in the United States have long embraced an obligation to ourselves, to our colleagues, and, most of all, to the American public to defend press freedom whenever it is under threat in our country. The free flow of information is among the most basic safeguards of our democracy. Moreover, the importance of sustaining those safeguards extends beyond U.S. borders to journalists around the world. When the traditional protections for American reporters and editors are exploded, there is significant fallout in countless places where the basic right to work as a journalist is not protected by law or custom.

To put it simply, repressive governments are delighted when a democracy like the United States imprisons a journalist. It makes it easier for them to justify their own restrictive policies.

So this past year, CPJ met an unusual need to speak out on behalf of journalists put at risk in the United States or because of U.S. actions abroad, particularly in Iraq.

In 2005, CPJ called attention to the carnage at checkpoints in Iraq, reminding the U.S. Department of Defense that its own analysts had called for procedures to minimize accidental casualties among journalists and ordinary citizens. We also sought and received the help of Sen. John Warner, the Virginia Republican who chairs the Armed Services Committee, to intervene with the Pentagon on behalf of jailed Iraqi journalists. These journalists, employed by global news organizations such as CBS and Reuters, have been held incommunicado and without charge for months, apparently under suspicion of aiding insurgents in Iraq. As of this writing, we have yet to see a resolution of this situation, which exacts a toll on each individual and interferes with important coverage.

We also spoke out against the incarceration of *New York Times* reporter Judith Miller, who was imprisoned for nearly three months in an effort to force her disclosure of the source who talked to her confidentially about CIA operative Valerie Plame and her husband, former diplomat Joseph Wilson. While recognizing that Miller's journalism has generated some controversy among those who believe she was too trusting of her sources, CPJ called for her immediate release from jail. It seems clear to me that only extreme circumstances such as a clear and present danger to innocent people could justify using the threat of jail to gain the name of a confidential informant.

Amid all of these concerns for journalists worldwide, there were two signal successes for CPJ in 2005 that I found particularly inspiring. One was in Cuba, and the other was in the Philippines.

The Philippines case is described in some detail by Ann Cooper, CPJ's superbly able executive director, in her introduction to this volume. A shocking string of unsolved murders caused CPJ to brand the Philippines the world's most murderous country for journalists. The Manila government initially disputed the designation but then conceded that the facts were as CPJ had described; it went on to launch a successful prosecution in a particularly heinous assassination. This could mark a significant turnaround in favor of Philippine journalists, and CPJ's staff deserves some of the credit.

The power of CPJ's work on behalf of beleaguered journalists came home to me with particular poignancy at November's annual International Press Freedom Awards dinner in New York. In addition to the inspiring 2005 awardees, journalist Manuel Vázquez Portal accepted the honor he could not receive two years earlier because he was in a Cuban jail for expressing his views. He was freed in large part because of CPJ's efforts to spotlight the injustice.

"Today, because of so many generous words, so much effort by so many, I was able to come here to meet you, thank you personally, and ask you to come with me once again to rescue from loneliness, obscurity, and imprisonment more than 20 journalists who are still locked up in Cuban jails," Vázquez Portal said that night. "It is on their behalf and for them that I accept this award. They need it. May it reach them and set them free."

• •

Paul E. Steiger is managing editor of *The Wall Street Journal*, a vice president of Dow Jones & Company, and a member of the Dow Jones executive committee. He was elected chairman of the Committee to Protect Journalists in 2005.

HEADLINES:
The top developments of 2005

January 11: A killing in Colombia reinforces self-censorship - Gunmen kill radio news host Julio Hernando Palacios Sánchez as he drives to work in Cúcuta. Attacked from all sides, the Colombian press censors itself to an extraordinary degree, CPJ later reports. Probing journalists are killed, detained, or forced to flee. Verified news is suppressed, and investigative reports are abandoned.

February 1: A royal coup in Nepal leads to vast restrictions - King Gyanendra dismisses his multiparty government and declares a state of emergency, curtailing civil rights and instituting broad press restrictions. His forces cut telephone lines, block Internet service, and occupy major media outlets to censor the news line by line. Hundreds are detained.

March 1: In Ukraine, progress and frustration in probe - New President Viktor Yushchenko says investigators have detained suspects in the 2000 murder of Internet reporter Georgy Gongadze—the first real development in the long-stalled probe. Three defendants face trial at year's end, but critics say the government is not pursuing the former high-level officials who plotted the killing.

March 4: A kidnapping, then a shooting in Baghdad - Italian security agent Nicola Calipari is killed and journalist Giuliana Sgrena is wounded when U.S. forces fire on their car near the Baghdad airport. Kidnappers had released Sgrena just hours earlier. CPJ and others urge safety improvements at military checkpoints.

March 16: Solidarity in Latin America for jailed Cubans - More than 100 prominent writers from Latin America join CPJ in calling on Cuban President Fidel Castro to release two dozen imprisoned journalists. Among the petitioners: Mexican novelist Carlos Fuentes, Argentine author Tomás Eloy Martínez, Brazilian journalist Geraldinho Vieira, and Venezuelan editor Teodoro Petkof.

May 13: Massacre in Uzbekistan leads to a clampdown - Uzbek soldiers open fire on demonstrators in the eastern city of Andijan, killing hundreds. The government clamps down on press coverage, blocking foreign news agencies and shutting domestic news outlets. It wages a campaign to persecute independent reporters, driving out more than a dozen foreign correspondents and local reporters working for foreign media.

June 2: Lebanese columnist killed in wave of attacks - Samir Qassir, columnist for the daily *Al-Nahar*, is killed outside his Beirut home by a bomb planted in his car. Violence against Lebanese journalists continues. May Chidiac, a TV news anchor, is wounded when her car explodes in September. Gebran Tueni, *Al-Nahar* columnist and managing director, is murdered in a December car bombing.

July 6: U.S. reporter jailed in CIA leak probe - A U.S. judge jails *New York Times* reporter Judith Miller for refusing to reveal a confidential source to a grand jury investigating the leak of a CIA operative's identity. Miller serves 85 days before she agrees to testify. White House aide I. Lewis "Scooter" Libby is later indicted.

July 7: Families of slain Russian journalists seek justice - The families of 12 journalists slain since 2000 gather in Moscow to seek justice in the string of unsolved murders. The families ratify a declaration calling on President Vladimir Putin "to publicly acknowledge these horrible crimes, express sympathy for the families and colleagues of slain journalists, and demonstrate his commitment to implementing the rule of law."

August 15: Lawlessness, impunity threaten Philippine press - Corruption, easy access to guns, and an ineffective justice system threaten the Philippine press, CPJ reports. Rural radio commentators have been killed in record numbers since 2000. Journalists call for higher professional standards for broadcasters.

September 14: U.S. fails to investigate journalist killings in Iraq - Thirteen journalists have been killed in Iraq by U.S. forces, but the military has not fully investigated the killings or followed its own recommendations to improve press safety, CPJ reports.

September 20: A murder in Mosul makes Iraq the deadliest conflict - Firas Maadidi, Mosul bureau chief for the daily *As-Saffir*, is murdered by suspected insurgents in Iraq. He is the 59th journalist killed since hostilities began in March 2003, making Iraq the deadliest conflict in CPJ's 24-year history. Fifty-eight journalists were killed in Algeria in the 1990s.

October 19: Zimbabwean press driven from homeland - Many of the nation's top journalists—at least 90 to date—have fled a systematic and brutal crackdown by the government of President Robert Mugabe, CPJ reports. The exodus has devastated the Zimbabwean media, once one of Africa's most vital.

November 2: After civil unrest, Ethiopia sweeps up journalists - Ethiopia launches a massive crackdown on the press, arresting more than a dozen journalists in an effort to quell dissent amid civil unrest. Police block private newspapers from publishing and issue a "wanted list" of editors, writers, and dissidents.

December 13: With much in common, China and Cuba are top jailers - China and Cuba continue to be the world's top jailers of journalists, CPJ reports. In both countries, the vast majority of cases are brought under vague "antistate" laws. Many are journalists whose work appears on the Internet. China imprisons 32, and Cuba jails 24.

INTRODUCTION

by Ann Cooper

On May 2, when the Committee to Protect Journalists identified the Philippines as the world's most murderous country for journalists, the reaction was swift. "Exaggerated," huffed presidential spokesman Ignacio Bunye, who was practiced at dismissing the mounting evidence. He had called an earlier CPJ analysis of the dangers to Philippine journalists "grossly misplaced and misleading."

Two days after CPJ's May report was issued, another journalist died from gunshot wounds in the Philippines. Klein Cantoneros, a 32-year-old radio broadcaster known for denouncing corruption on his program "People, Wake Up," was murdered in a fashion sadly familiar to CPJ researchers: Gunmen on motorcycles shot him as he returned home from work in Dipolog City.

This time, the message out of the presidential office was dramatically different. The murder of journalists in the Philippines—Cantoneros was the 20th to die since 2000—had reached the level of "collective national shame," acknowledged a senior administration official, Mass Media Secretary Cerge Remonde. Newspaper editorials, one published in red ink, denounced the government's chronic failure to ensure journalist safety. Politicians and police scrambled to respond. President Gloria Macapagal Arroyo assured the country that "the whole criminal justice system has been alerted and put in motion."

Action should be expected in murder cases. But when journalists are killed because of their work, whether in the Philippines or elsewhere, justice is the exception, not the rule. According to CPJ research spanning more than a decade, less than 15 percent of journalist murders are ever solved. In its May report, "Marked for Death," CPJ called this failure of justice the most urgent threat facing journalists worldwide and described it as a terrible deterrent to the free flow of information.

"Marked for Death" identified the world's five most murderous countries as the Philippines, Iraq, Colombia, Bangladesh, and Russia, based on the number of killings from 2000 through early 2005. By year's end, Iraq had displaced the Philippines at the top of that list. Nearly half of the journalists killed in Iraq since the conflict began in March 2003 were murdered by insurgent groups who targeted editors, writers, and photojournalists to silence them or to punish them for working with Western news organizations. It may be some time before violence in Iraq yields to the rule of law.

But in other countries there were promising signs that those who kill journalists could be called to account. Political change in Ukraine brought progress in solving the notorious beheading of online journalist Georgy Gongadze in 2000. President Viktor Yushchenko, swept into office in late 2004 by the peaceful Orange Revolution, made an early pledge to solve the Gongadze case. A year later, prosecutors had arrested three of four suspects, and a parliamentary commission had accused former President Leonid Kuchma and his allies of plotting the crime.

Reuters/Erik de Castro – *This 2004 photo of Philippine journalist Jose Torres Jr., taken at a Manila demonstration, appeared on the cover of last year's edition of* Attacks on the Press. *A year later, the government is more intent on stopping the violence.*

In Brazil, seven members of a criminal gang were convicted in the 2002 murder of television reporter Tim Lopes. While working on an investigative story about the sexual exploitation of minors in Rio de Janeiro, Lopes was tortured and then brutally killed with a sword. The slaying galvanized the Brazilian press and drew international attention.

Putting a spotlight on murder makes a difference. In Mexico, where drug-fueled violence endangers the press, CPJ lobbied vigorously for federal intervention in the cases of several murdered journalists. The investigations had stalled in the hands of state and local authorities, who are prone to corruption and have few resources. President Vicente Fox visited CPJ's New York offices in September and pledged federal support in the prosecution of crimes against free expression.

In countries where political will was lacking, CPJ took other approaches.

This fall, CPJ turned to the United Nations Security Council to intervene in violence against journalists in Lebanon. Newspaper columnist Gebran Tueni was slain in one car bombing and colleague Samir Qassir was killed in another. (Qassir's murder sparked the mass demonstration in Beirut featured on the cover of this edition of *Attacks on the Press.*) The killings were seen as retaliation for politically sensitive coverage.

In October, CPJ highlighted the information vacuum in Colombia created by years of violence against journalists. CPJ's report, "Untold Stories," detailed the many sensitive subjects the Colombian press no longer covers for fear of reprisal. In startlingly frank interviews, journalists described how Colombia's warring factions and criminal gangs had forced them into routine self-censorship, depriving the public of reporting on such vital issues as human rights abuses and drug trafficking.

In Russia, where the government had done little to investigate 12 contract-style murders of journalists since 2000, CPJ gathered the victims' relatives and colleagues at a Moscow conference in July. The meeting ended with a joint appeal for the government to vigorously pursue all 12 cases and a vow by participants to speak out for justice. At year's end, Russian prosecutors were set to open the trial of three suspects in the murder of Paul Klebnikov, an American journalist of Russian descent who was gunned down outside his office in Moscow in 2004. And the European Court of Human Rights agreed to hear charges that Russian authorities had failed to properly investigate and prosecute a much older case, the 1994 murder of Moscow reporter Dmitry Kholodov.

But the most heartening sign came in the Philippines, where the government had long shirked responsibility for investigating brutal attacks against journalists in remote regions. After the May 4 murder of Cantoneros and the killing of yet another journalist less than a week later, Arroyo said the attacks were "frightening and must be stopped." She set up a Press Freedom Fund to provide rewards for information on murder cases, as well as assistance to the families of slain journalists.

Manila's new political will began to yield results. More vigorous investigations led to arrests in several cases—something nearly unheard of in the years of violence against Philippine journalists. In November, the conviction of a former police officer in the 2002 murder of journalist Edgar Damalerio was hailed as a landmark that could help eradicate murder as a weapon against the Philippine press.

For years, the Damalerio case had symbolized everything that had gone wrong in the Philippine justice system. Damalerio, a respected newspaper editor and radio commentator, was shot while driving home from a press conference in Pagadian City. Although eyewitnesses identified the killer as police officer Guillermo Wapile, local authorities allowed him to slip away for more than two years. Two witnesses were slain before the case reached court, and it appeared that justice would be brushed aside as easily as it had been in so many other Philippine cases. Little wonder that Edgar Ongue, the sole remaining witness, told CPJ that he felt "like a flame in the dark."

But something different happened this time. Damalerio's widow, Gemma, petitioned to move the trial out of corrupt Pagadian City, and the Supreme Court granted the venue-change request. Damalerio and Ongue, whose lives had been threatened repeatedly, were placed in a federal witness-protection program. Persistent pressure from local and international press groups had helped to create a climate that compelled Philippine authorities to act.

Ongue testified, and Wapile did not get away with murder. A judge convicted the ex-officer and sentenced him to life in prison. It was the first such conviction since the record-setting wave of journalist murders in the Philippines began in 2000. It's just a start, but it's a reminder of the value of individual courage and international attention. Ask Edgar Ongue, who wanted "to show that it's not right just to kill anyone and then get away with it."

• •

Ann Cooper is executive director of the Committee to Protect Journalists. She led CPJ's Moscow conference on journalist murders.

AFRICA

ANALYSIS

Lessons in Democracy, Pressure, and the Press

Elections in Burundi and Zimbabwe sent clear messages: There can be no democratic progress without a free press, and repression of the media is the first sign of democracy going off the rails.

by Julia Crawford

PHOTOS

Section break: Reuters/James Akena – *A Ugandan journalist runs for cover during November riots in Kampala*. Analysis (next): Reuters/Jean Pierre Aimé Harerimana – *A Burundian casts his vote at a polling center near the capital, Bujumbura, during legislative elections in July.*

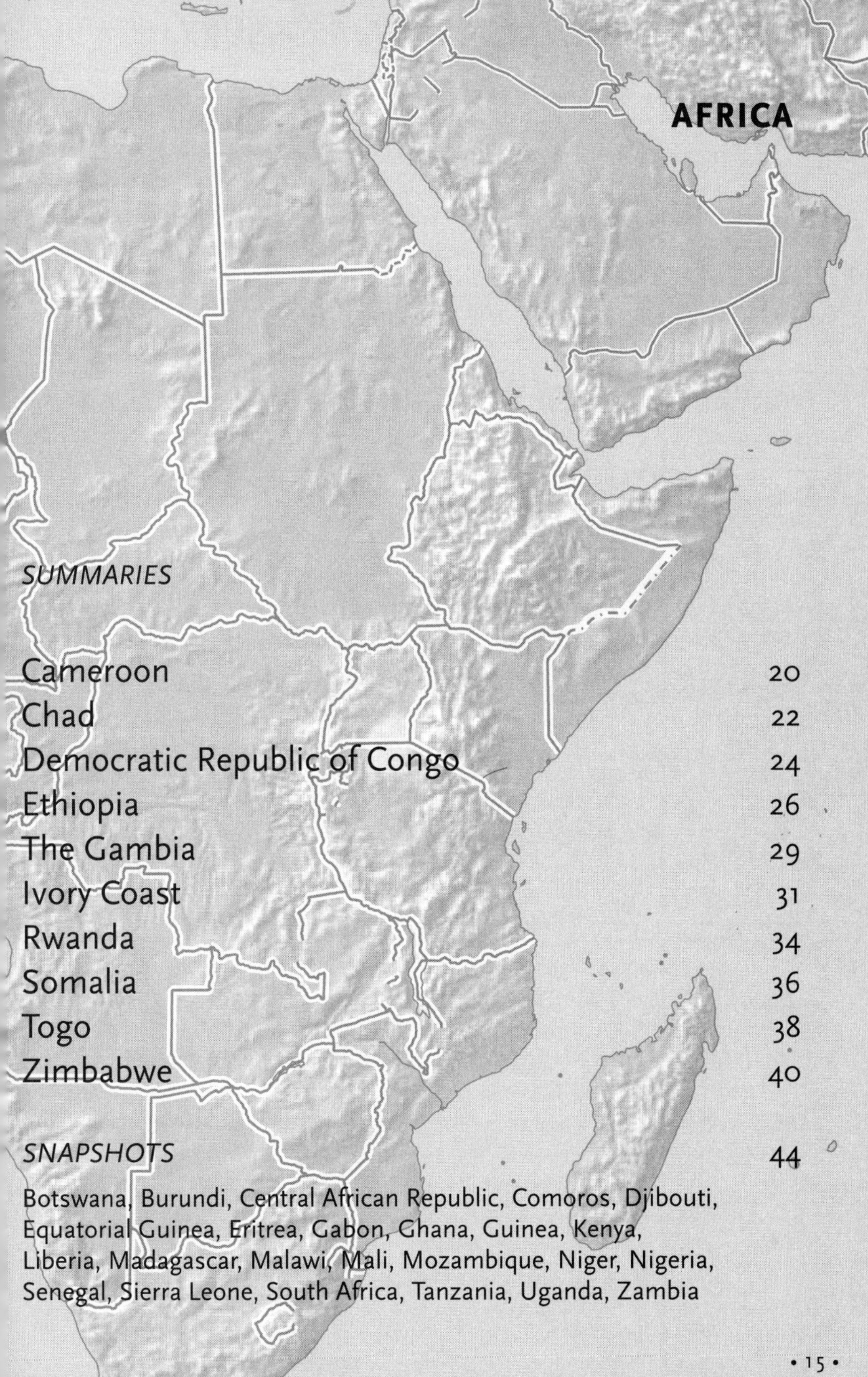

AFRICA

SUMMARIES

LESSONS IN DEMOCRACY, PRESSURE, AND THE PRESS

by Julia Crawford

Zimbabwe and Burundi, countries with very different histories, were among the dozen states in sub-Saharan Africa that held elections this year. In Burundi, the local media played a significant role in informing the public about the democratic process and signaling abuses by those in power. In Zimbabwe, however, the independent media have been so restricted by an increasingly repressive government that elections were no victory for democracy.

The gradual economic and political decline of Zimbabwe was foreshadowed by a clampdown on the media. Burundi's slow emergence from war and ethnic rivalry was heralded by the arrival of independent radio stations, which gradually became a voice for ordinary people and a force for change. No African country is like another, but for a continent trying to shake itself free of oppression, the lessons of Burundi and Zimbabwe are clear: There can be no democratic progress without a free media, and repression of the media is a first sign of democracy going off the rails.

As Burundians voted in a series of crucial elections in 2005, they had access to several independent radio stations informing them about the electoral process, discussing the issues, and allowing ordinary citizens to air their views. Radio stations brought the concerns of the people to the politicians and helped ensure that the elections were transparent.

In Zimbabwe, private radio stations are banned. Since the government closed the only independent daily newspaper, the *Daily News*, in 2003, the propaganda-filled state media dominates domestic news coverage. The government further ensured that the opposition had little access to the media before the March parliamentary election. Zimbabwean media lawyer Beatrice Mtetwa, who received a CPJ International Press Freedom Award in 2005, said she believes government control of information is at the root of her country's problems. "If information cannot flow freely, and if people, whether in business or elsewhere, cannot get that information, I cannot imagine how the economic situation can improve," Mtetwa said.

Not surprisingly, the government of President Robert Mugabe was announced the winner of Zimbabwe's flawed parliamentary vote, with a big enough majority that it could push through changes to the constitution. In Burundi, a former rebel group unseated the transitional authorities, and the country gained its most representative government in more than a decade.

In both nations, journalists have shown remarkable courage in the face of attacks by government authorities and, in the case of Burundi, by rebels as well. In both countries, repressive laws remain on the books, and the courts cannot be relied upon to deliver justice. Weak economies and low media salaries pose a further threat to press freedom, as individual journalists are vulnerable to corruption.

Over the past five years, Mugabe's regime has waged war on the independent press, using repressive legislation to close newspapers and harass journalists. Burundi's leaders have not been friends of the media either.

"Burundi gained its most representative government in more than a decade."

Under former president Pierre Buyoya, media outlets were censored, and independent journalists were frequently harassed and imprisoned. As recently as June, a journalist was imprisoned for nine days and accused of "violating the honor and the privacy of the head of state" for reporting that transitional president Domitien Ndayizeye was depressed by his party's defeat in municipal elections. In July, police shut down Radio Publique Africaine (RPA), whose director, Alexis Sinduhije, won a CPJ International Press Freedom Award in 2004, in a standoff with authorities over election coverage.

So what were the factors at work in the 2005 polls? How did Burundi, an ethnic tinderbox with no history of a reliable independent media, do better than Zimbabwe?

> "Mugabe's historic role as Zimbabwe's liberator from white rule helped him retain regional support."

Ironically, Zimbabwe seemed, until recently, to have the advantage in terms of institutional safeguards, including a strong, unified political opposition and an independent judiciary. Although there was no private radio, there was a professional and influential independent press, which was often critical of the government. But it was precisely the rise of the opposition Movement for Democratic Change (MDC) that sparked a brutal and relentless government backlash against critics of the regime—starting with the independent press. Despite enormous pressure from Western countries, including sanctions, Mugabe's historic role as Zimbabwe's liberator from white rule helped him retain support within the region. Mugabe blamed the West, especially former colonial power Britain, for many of Zimbabwe's problems, and government control of the media helped him do this.

Unlike Mugabe, former Burundian president Pierre Buyoya enjoyed little support as a representative leader, either at home or within the region. Buyoya is a member of the minority Tutsi ethnic group, which makes up only about 14 percent of the Burundian population, and his source of power was mainly the Tutsi-dominated army. When Buyoya took power in a bloodless 1996 coup, neighboring countries imposed sanctions. Faced with a continuing rebellion by ethnic Hutu rebels, growing political opposition, and regional as well as international pressure, Buyoya was finally forced to sign a peace agreement with his political opponents in 2000. In so doing, he promised to reform the army and to help prepare the country for democratic elections. He also promised to step down in favor of a Hutu transitional president. Political crises came and went as deadlines were missed, and Buyoya looked as if he would refuse to implement his promises. But foreign and domestic pressure was sustained, and the peace process lurched painfully forward.

In both Zimbabwe and Burundi, the role of other countries within the region has been pivotal—especially that of South Africa. The regional powerhouse has considerable influence on both its neighbor, Zimbabwe, and Burundi, where former South African president Nelson Mandela mediated the 2000 peace accord.

Mandela helped maintain the pressure necessary to drive the peace process forward, and his country sent the first peacekeepers to Burundi, even before the United Nations would commit forces. This helped create a climate in which the independent media could grow, and the media in turn helped push the peace process forward. Accepting a CPJ award in 2004, RPA director Sinduhije said he believed Burundi was on the path to a future free of dictatorship and mass killings. "This is largely thanks to international pressure and the positive role that all the private radio stations have played in Burundi," he said.

In contrast, current South African President Thabo Mbeki has refused to publicly criticize Mugabe or lead regional efforts to censure Zimbabwe's human rights abuses. Mbeki has also failed to speak out against the relentless attacks on Zimbabwe's independent media.

Burundi's new democracy remains fragile, but the country's independent media—particularly the radio stations that have emerged in recent years—are increasingly self-confident. They have shown courage and solidarity in the face of attacks, and they have won some significant victories. For example, in 2003, when the government banned Radio Isanganiro and RPA for allowing a rebel spokesman on the air, other private stations announced a blackout of government news. The bans were lifted shortly afterward. When authorities closed RPA in July 2005, three media organizations launched a joint mediation attempt and met with the head of state. RPA was allowed to reopen shortly afterward, and a subsequent shakeup of the official regulatory body brought more representation for journalists.

"Burundi's democracy remains fragile, but the media have won significant victories."

As for Zimbabwe, that country's journalists have certainly shown courage, but many have been forced into exile by the brutality of a regime that continues to ride roughshod over the free press. It seems that only a change of heart by the authorities could improve the situation there. More outside pressure is needed if that is to happen any time soon.

• • • • • • • • • • •

Julia Crawford is CPJ's Africa program coordinator.

CAMEROON

President Paul Biya, one of Africa's longest-serving leaders, retained a tight grip on power in his 23rd year in office. While Cameroon boasts diverse media, local independent journalists complain of sophisticated government intimidation, resulting in widespread self-censorship. Local journalists point to a complex web of financial pressures—including the withholding of advertising revenue by government agencies, and the Communications Ministry's policy of providing yearly financial aid to some private media—that can be used to influence coverage. Authorities remained reluctant to repeal harsh criminal defamation laws.

Throughout 2005, government officials and other powerful figures used defamation suits to jail and intimidate critical journalists. For example, a prosecutor in the capital, Yaoundé, ordered Joseph Bessala Ahanda jailed in July pending a judicial investigation into defamation allegations against him. Ahanda, who edits the private weekly *Le Front*, was released without charge after three weeks. The accusations against him stemmed from a series of reports in *Le Front* alleging that the former director of the Cameroon Postal Service had embezzled state funds.

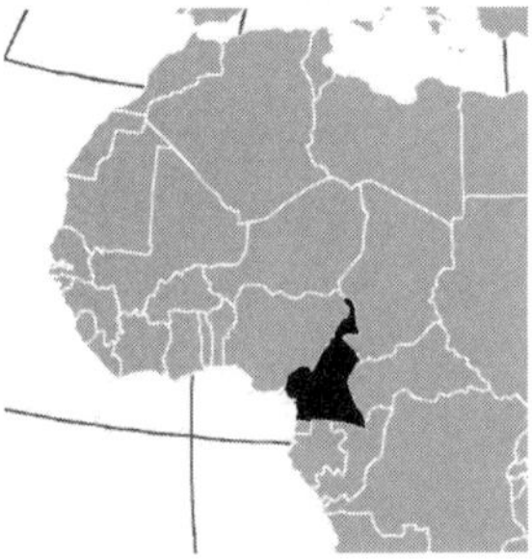

Journalists working in remote rural areas are particularly vulnerable to such suits. Eric Wirkwa Tayu, publisher of the tiny English-language newspaper *Nso Voice*, based in the western town of Kumbo, was freed in March after spending eight months in prison for allegedly defaming the town's mayor. A lack of solidarity among journalists divided by language, region, and political sympathies can prevent such cases from being publicized.

Lawsuits also threatened the financial viability of news outlets. The CPA insurance company filed at least three defamation suits against news staff at the private bimonthly *Le Jeune Observateur* at the beginning of the year, all in connection with an article published in the paper a year earlier. One of the suits sent Publication Director Jules Koum Koum to prison for a month. The resulting cascade of court hearings created severe financial difficulties for the newspaper.

Army officials in northern Cameroon brought at least 12 court cases against the independent weekly *L'Oeil du Sahel* in 2005, in what local journalists said was a campaign of harassment against one of the only publications to cover Cameroon's isolated northern region. The paper frequently reports abuses by security forces in the area, and local officials and soldiers often threaten its journalists, local sources told CPJ. According to

• • • • • • • • • • •

Summaries in this chapter were reported and written by Africa Program Coordinator **Julia Crawford** and Africa Research Associate **Alexis Arieff**.

local journalists, court hearings in the northern city of Maroua were kept secret from the newspaper's staff, and in April publication director Guibaï Gatama and a reporter were sentenced in absentia to five months in jail and a hefty fine for allegedly defaming a local military police commander. The journalists were not arrested, but, by August, the staff was struggling to keep *L'Oeil du Sahel* afloat.

While private radio and television stations have proliferated since Cameroon liberalized broadcasting in the 1990s, local journalists say the government still tries to control content, in part through its licensing system. Rather than issue formal broadcast licenses, the government has long relied on a nebulous system of "provisional authorization," which leaves private broadcasters in a legal limbo where they are liable to be closed down if they anger authorities. Radio's popular appeal and potentially wide reach make it the most influential medium in Cameroon, as in many countries across Africa.

Some good news came in July when authorities unsealed the studios of Freedom FM, a stillborn independent radio station in the southern city of Douala conceived by the veteran journalist Pius Njawé, a 1991 CPJ International Press Freedom Awardee. The Communications Ministry had ordered the station shut in May 2003—one day before Njawé's planned first broadcast—claiming that he had not followed the proper procedures in applying for a broadcasting license. Njawé, who is well-known as the director of the popular newspaper *Le Messager*, maintained that he followed all the necessary steps, and many local journalists saw Freedom FM's closure as a government attempt to censor an influential and critical voice.

Freedom FM's triumph was bittersweet. While the studio was under government seal, neglect and roof leaks left much of the equipment damaged and the station unable to start broadcasting immediately.

After international attention was paid to the Freedom FM case, the Communications Ministry announced in August that a committee drawn from several government ministries, in concert with the official National Communications Council, would begin reviewing applications for official licenses. Communications Minister Pierre Moukoko Mbonjo told CPJ that licenses would be issued in a timely matter, although some local journalists expressed skepticism.

In an attempt to improve the reputation of the private press, which suffers from allegations of corruption and political partisanship, local journalists inaugurated a self-regulatory body in March. The Cameroonian Media Council, organized primarily by a local journalists' union with some financial support from Canada, was given a mandate to improve ethical standards in journalism and to provide a forum for settling complaints against journalists without resorting to the courts. However, financial needs kept the council from becoming active, according to local sources. A national commission to distribute press cards to journalists, which the Communications Ministry set up in 2004 with the cooperation of local journalist associations, was also inactive.

CHAD

President Idriss Déby's government jailed several journalists and closed a community radio station in an unprecedented assault on the media. Equally unprecedented was the response of journalists, who organized protests, a one-week newspaper strike, and a blackout of all radio news bulletins. The protests, together with international pressure, kept the spotlight on the imprisoned journalists, most of whom were freed in September, when an appeals court ruled in their favor.

The government assault on media freedom appeared to be rooted in Déby's attempt to remain in power. Faced with ethnic divisions, rebellion in the provinces, and a refugee spillover from the conflict in the neighboring Darfur region of Sudan, Déby's ruling Patriotic Salvation Movement (MPS) organized a referendum in June to amend the constitution to enable the president to run for a third term in 2006. The government said that the public had approved the amendments, despite protests and an opposition boycott. On June 21, the day before results of the referendum were announced, authorities arrested a newspaper editor and a freelance writer on criminal charges of defaming the president and "inciting hatred." The next day, a third journalist was arrested on similar charges.

The charges against Garondé Djarma, a freelance contributor to several newspapers in the capital, N'Djamena, stemmed from an opinion piece he wrote for the private weekly *L'Observateur* that criticized Déby and the referendum. The newspaper's editor, Ngaradoumbé Samory, was arrested in connection with the publication of an open letter to Déby, written under a pseudonym, that accused the government of mistreating a minority ethnic group known as the Kreda. Authorities had previously detained members of the Kreda and accused them of plotting to overthrow the government.

Michaël Didama, managing editor of the private weekly *Le Temps*, was charged in connection with articles describing rebel activity in eastern Chad, near the border with Darfur, and an alleged massacre of civilians there.

The journalists were released within three weeks of their arrest, after authorities acknowledged procedural irregularities in their detentions. However, between July 18 and August 8 the three were convicted of all charges and sentenced to prison terms ranging from three months to three years. A week later, a court convicted *L'Observateur*'s publication director, Sy Koumbo Singa Gali, of inciting hatred, sentencing her to one year in prison for printing an interview with Djarma in which he accused Arab "janjaweed" members of the Chadian government of conspiring to silence him because of his coverage of the conflict between Arab militias, known as janjaweed, and non-Arabs in Darfur. Djarma received an additional one-year sentence in connection with the interview.

Speaking from jail, Didama called the imprisonments illegal and a "crackdown on the press." Local journalists' associations organized sit-ins, demonstrations, and a one-week media strike in August during which private newspapers suspended publication while private radio stations replaced news bulletins with commentary on press freedom.

Officials denied any desire to stifle the press, claiming that the government could not meddle in the courts' independent decision to convict the journalists.

Following sustained local and international pressure, in late September an N'Djamena appeals court overturned the convictions of Sy, Djarma, and Samory, and reduced Didama's sentence to time served. The head of the Union of Chadian Journalists, Evariste Toldé, told CPJ that, by citing procedural grounds in its decision to overturn the convictions, "the appeals court verdict has shown that these were arbitrary detentions." Local journalists told CPJ that the imprisonments had a chilling effect on reporting throughout Chad, with some of them saying that they were now more careful about what they wrote. After the convictions were overturned and the four journalists released, local media associations agreed to submit proposals for legal reform to the government, with the aim of decriminalizing press offenses such as "defaming the president" and revising laws on incitement.

Despite the high level of attention received in the wake of the crackdown, Chad's print press has minimal influence, due to low literacy rates and limited distribution outside of the capital. Radio is the most important medium, and roughly a dozen private and community radio stations operate in Chad, in addition to the state broadcaster.

In May, the regulatory High Council of Communication (HCC) suspended Radio Brakos, a community station in the remote southern town of Moissala, citing "recurring conflicts between Radio Brakos and administrative and military authorities." The station's director, Tchanguis Vatankah, is known for his pointed criticism of local authorities; in 2004, he was detained and severely beaten after Radio Brakos broadcast an interview with an opposition leader as well as programs criticizing the customs service and the police.

According to local sources, the HCC's decision followed complaints against the station from a local traditional leader and threats from a military commander. The ban was lifted in late August, but the station's plan to resume regular programming was interrupted when authorities arrested Vatankah upon his return to Moissala from the capital, where he had been staying. Officials announced that they would deport Vatankah, a native of Iran who had been living in Chad for decades. Vatankah was detained in an N'Djamena prison for more than two months while awaiting expulsion. His health, already compromised by the 2004 beating, deteriorated further in prison, according to his wife, a Chadian national.

Local journalists told CPJ that, in addition to government repression, the private media's severe financial difficulties also threatened press freedom. The HCC cited unpaid broadcasting fees when it ordered the private N'Djamena-based station DJA FM off the air in January. The station was able to begin broadcasting again in February after reaching an agreement with authorities, but, according to station director Zara Yacoub—who also heads the Union of Private Chadian Radios—many local stations are in the same situation, leaving them vulnerable to closure if they offend the government.

DEMOCRATIC REPUBLIC OF CONGO

The murder and attempted murder of journalists in 2005 sent a chill through the independent press in the Democratic Republic of Congo (DRC). Journalists operated in a tense pre-electoral climate, enduring threats and harassment from government officials and other powerful figures. Rampant corruption and a weak judiciary in a country still bearing the scars of civil war gave them little recourse to justice. The situation worsened after President Joseph Kabila postponed June elections for up to a year.

On November 3, unidentified gunmen killed a veteran political affairs journalist with the independent daily *La Référence Plus*. Franck Kangundu was shot dead along with his wife, Hélène Mpaka, outside their home in the capital, Kinshasa. Local journalists feared he had been killed for his work as a journalist. Kangundu covered a variety of topics for the newspaper, including the sometimes acrimonious relations between political parties in the DRC's power-sharing government, as well as business and economic issues. Press freedom and human rights groups protested in Kinshasa on November 7. Vice President Azerias Ruberwa promised the demonstrators an inquiry into the killing.

In May, men in army uniforms shot at reporter Jean Ngandu at his home in Lubumbashi in the troubled southern province of Katanga. Ngandu dropped to the ground and was unharmed. The motive for the attack was unclear, but CPJ sources said it might have been linked to his work as a reporter for Radio Okapi, a station run jointly by the United Nations and the Swiss nongovernmental organization Fondation Hirondelle. Both Radio France Internationale (RFI) and Journaliste en Danger (JED), a press freedom organization based in Kinshasa, noted that Ngandu had reported on an alleged secession attempt in Katanga in late April. Radio Okapi, which is accessible in most of this vast country on FM and shortwave, has become a popular source of independent news.

In the east of the country, where numerous armed groups continued to operate, journalists increased self-censorship after the murder of a prominent human rights activist on July 31, local sources said. Gunmen killed Pascal Kabungulu Kibembi, executive director of Héritiers de la Justice (Heirs of Justice), in Bukavu, near the Rwandan border. The transitional government in Kinshasa, which comprises former combatants, exercised little control in the east.

Journalists reporting on corruption and human rights abuses faced the constant threat of detention without due process, especially under the DRC's archaic defamation laws. Defamation charges were brought by powerful political, military, and business figures. Most cases did not go to trial, although detainees were often kept for weeks in appalling conditions and had to post bail for their release. In one case, editor Jean-Marie Kanku was abducted at the end of October by the national intelligence agency (ANR) in Kinshasa after his newspaper, *L'Alerte*, published articles accusing ANR Director Lando Lurhakumbirwa of corruption. Kanku was held incommunicado for a week and his health deteriorated sharply. After 12 days in detention, he was finally brought before a court, which charged him with publishing false information and granted him bail. Kanku was ordered to report to court twice a week and to remain in the country.

Journalists faced frequent harassment, threats, and censorship, often by government officials. In January, broadcasting at two private television stations and a radio station owned by Vice President Jean-Pierre Bemba, leader of the former rebel MLC party, was suspended after the stations aired a press conference critical of Kabila. The same day, Information Minister Henri Mova Sakanyi tried to restrict broadcast content through a government memorandum that ordered a halt to live phone-in programs. Although the government did not follow through on the ban, Sakanyi said in the memorandum that the president was "sacred," and that "any attack on him in the written press or broadcast media will be sanctioned in accordance with the law." The three stations resumed broadcasts two days later, following strong local and international protests.

In April, a provincial governor shut down community broadcaster Radiotélévision Debout Kasaï (RTDK) in the central diamond-mining town of Mbuji-Mayi for two days, claiming that it had incited antigovernment violence. Station management said it had merely reported the news. In June, the director of a community radio station in the central town of Tshikapa went into hiding after another provincial governor called publicly for his arrest. This came after the journalist, Casimir Ntwite, conducted interviews on the postponement of national elections. Tshikapa authorities also harassed and threatened a number of other journalists.

In Kinshasa, security forces harassed and briefly detained journalists covering June 30 opposition protests against the election postponement. They also closed a television station and two radio stations belonging to the privately owned RAGA group, and briefly detained its director over RAGA's coverage of the demonstrations. On July 1, the High Authority on Media (HAM), an official regulatory body, ordered RAGA's broadcasts suspended for 10 days, saying that its news coverage was "blatantly partial." Several local journalists and JED denounced the suspension as politically motivated.

JED itself was the subject of serious threats in 2005. The organization has become a vital source of news on press freedom across the country. Its president, Donat M'baya Tshimanga, and secretary-general, Tshivis Tshivuadi, received death threats in an e-mail in April. They had previously received anonymous threatening phone calls and been maligned on state television. In November, JED was targeted by the daily newspaper *L'Avenir*, which launched personal attacks on its leaders. *L'Avenir* is considered close to the ruling PPRD party.

Media regulatory bodies have campaigned to improve professional ethics and remove ethnic and political propaganda from the media. The HAM also imposed sanctions on some media outlets, reprimanding them for what it deemed unethical practices. In June, it banned a discussion program on the private Kinshasa TV station Horizon 33, saying it did not give equal time to participants and lacked balance. It suspended a program on another private TV station, Radio-Télévision Kin Malebo (RTKM), for 60 days, saying that the program "often abuses the open phone line, allowing numerous callers to launch gratuitous accusations, violent and defamatory words against third parties who are often not invited onto the program."

The HAM is headed by Modeste Mutinga, winner of a 2000 CPJ International Press Freedom Award. While Mutinga is a well-respected veteran of the profession, journalists are concerned that the HAM was subject to political pressures. In 2005, JED twice challenged HAM decisions: the suspension of RAGA broadcasters in June; and the September suspension, without a hearing, of three newspapers. JED called the latter action "totalitarian" and "lacking in independence." Despite these incidents, JED leader M'baya believed the HAM's overall record in 2005 was positive. He noted that the HAM had, for example, initiated codes of conduct for media coverage of political parties during the election period, and that it had "brought in some order" on the regulatory front.

ETHIOPIA

The government unleashed a sudden and far-reaching crackdown on the independent press in November following clashes between police and antigovernment protesters that left more than 40 people dead. Authorities detained more than a dozen journalists, issued a wanted list of editors and publishers, and threatened to charge journalists with treason, an offense punishable by death in Ethiopia. Dozens of journalists went into hiding during the crackdown, virtually silencing the local private press.

For nearly a week, security forces in Addis Ababa battled opposition supporters who accused Prime Minister Meles Zenawi of rigging polls in May that returned him to power. In June, security forces fired on demonstrators in similar protests.

The government accused members of the private press of acting as "mouthpieces" for the opposition Coalition for Unity and Democracy (CUD), which had refused to participate in the government after the disputed elections. It published a list of those it planned to prosecute for trying to "violently undermine the constitutional order in the country." The list identified 17 editors and publishers from eight private newspapers, as well as Kifle Mulat, president of the Ethiopian Free Press Journalists' Association (EFJA).

Security forces arrested scores of opposition leaders, along with thousands of their followers, human rights activists, lawyers, academics, and other prominent figures who had commented on the elections. At least 13 journalists whose names were on the government's list were held and denied bail. One was sentenced in December to eight months in prison on defamation charges dating to 2003. Medical personnel who gave casualty information to reporters working for international outlets were arrested, along with some local journalists' family members. Only a handful of mostly pro-government private newspapers were able to publish; more than a dozen others were blocked from publishing by security forces stationed at the state-owned printing press. On November 9, the prime minister said that treason charges would be brought against opposition leaders and journalists arrested in connection with the clashes. In a telephone interview with CPJ, Information Minister Berhan Hailu declined to give examples of evidence that would warrant a treason charge against a journalist.

State-owned media, which include Ethiopia's sole radio and television station, carried propaganda smearing private and foreign media. State broadcasters showed photographs of many of the journalists on the government's "wanted list," and called on the public to inform police of their whereabouts. An Information Ministry statement broadcast on state-owned media accused EFJA leaders of "playing a key role in implementing the plan for violence."

The minister said that the U.S. government-funded Voice of America (VOA) and the German Deutsche Welle radio were opposition mouthpieces "bent on destabilizing the peace and stability of the country," the state-owned *Ethiopian Herald* reported. Both stations are popular news sources in Ethiopia, which has no local independent radio stations. Local journalists told CPJ that the minister's remarks, which came on the heels of a violent attack on a VOA stringer by unidentified assailants, could endanger the safety of VOA and Deutsche Welle reporters in Ethiopia. In June, the Information Ministry had revoked the accreditation of three local correspondents working for VOA and two working for Deutsche Welle, accusing the journalists, all Ethiopian citizens, of filing "unbalanced reports" on the elections. Several fled the country, fearing further persecution by authorities.

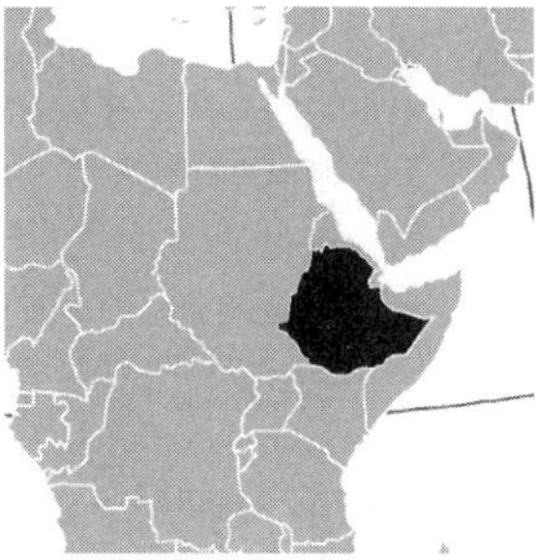

The November crackdown followed lesser attempts to curtail press freedom in the wake of the May 15 elections, which were marred by violence, allegations of fraud, and pointed criticism by European Union monitors. While the vote was initially marked by a peaceful, high turnout, demonstrations erupted a month later as opposition supporters protested delays and irregularities in announcing the results. On June 8, security forces fired on protesters in the capital, Addis Ababa, killing more than 30 people, while thousands of opposition supporters were arrested without charge. Official results eventually pronounced Zenawi's ruling Ethiopian People's Revolutionary Democratic Front the winner, with significant gains for the CUD. The CUD claimed that the election had been stolen.

CPJ documented a surge in court cases against journalists who reported on the election aftermath; other journalists resorted to self-censorship. After the June protests, the Justice Ministry warned that any journalist found to be "disseminating fictitious reports that could not be substantiated" would be prosecuted. Between June and September, at least 17 editors of private Amharic-language weeklies were arrested because of their post-election coverage. At least seven were accused of criminal offenses such as defaming the Defense Ministry and the military. Several editors were arrested more than once.

Under Ethiopia's press law, criminal charges can be brought against journalists for defamation, incitement to violence, and the publication of false news, among other offenses. Court cases can drag on for years, and journalists are regularly jailed for not being able to pay bail or for missing court hearings. Editors, who are held legally responsible for the content of their newspapers, routinely have multiple charges pending against them.

In August, two newspaper editors were found guilty of contempt of court for refusing to reveal the sources of anonymous quotes criticizing a controversial Supreme Court verdict in a case involving the National Electoral Board. The verdict had rejected the opposition CUD party's claim that the election board improperly announced provisional results before the final count was determined. *Satanaw* editor Tamrat Serbesa was sentenced to a month in jail for contempt, while *Ethiop* editor Andualem Ayle was fined.

Authorities arrested Fikre Gudu, a prominent newspaper distributor in the capital, on June 8 and jailed him for a month without charge. In August, police rearrested Gudu and held him for four days in connection with an interview he gave to the private weekly *Asqual* about his previous imprisonment. In the interview, Gudu described poor prison conditions and said that his arrest was part of the crackdown on independent media following the elections. According to local sources, police accused Gudu of using the interview to spread false information and defame the prison system.

Journalists based outside Ethiopia were also targeted. In August, Zenawi and other high-ranking officials pressed charges in a U.S. court against four Ethiopians accused of broadcasting defamatory reports on Tensae Ethiopia Voice of Unity radio, a station run by expatriate Ethiopians in Europe and the United States. Tensae broadcasts on shortwave and on the Internet to Ethiopia. The charges were dropped in September, perhaps as the result of international pressure.

In October, federal police summoned and questioned four leaders of the EFJA about the organization's activities while it was officially banned from late 2003 to the end of 2004. The Federal High Court later ruled the ban illegal. In the interrogations, police accused the EFJA leadership of illegally carrying out EFJA activities, including issuing press releases and speaking with reporters on press freedom issues, during the ban. Some local sources thought that the police action against EFJA president Mulat, vice president Taye Belachew, accountant Habetamu Assefa, and treasurer Sisay Agena came in retaliation for the organization's reporting on the legal harassment of journalists following the elections.

Fighting between government forces and secession movements, particularly the Oromo Liberation Front (OLF), remained sensitive topics for Ethiopian journalists. The OLF wants a separate state for Oromos, one of the country's largest ethnic groups, in southern Ethiopia. In 2004, violent protests by Oromo students led to a government crackdown on ethnic Oromos, including state-employed journalists—many of whom fled the country. In May 2004, two Oromo journalists at Ethiopian Television (ETV) were arrested and accused of aiding the OLF. Shiferaw Insermu, an ETV entertainment reporter, and Dhabasa Wakjira, news director of ETV's Oromo-language service, remained in jail at year's end. It was not clear whether their imprisonment stemmed from their journalism.

THE GAMBIA

The tightening of repressive media laws and the failure to solve the December 2004 murder of veteran journalist Deyda Hydara added to the climate of violence and intimidation faced by private media in 2005. President Yahya Jammeh said that the Gambia allowed "too much freedom of expression," and local journalists feared that government repression could worsen in the run-up to presidential elections in 2006.

In March, news emerged that Jammeh had secretly signed into law two pieces of repressive media legislation, which both the Gambia Press Union (GPU) and Hydara, managing editor and co-owner of the independent newspaper *The Point*, had opposed.

One measure, an amendment to the Newspaper Act, raised the bond that print media owners must post to register with the government, from 100,000 dalasis (US$3,480) to 500,000 dalasis (US$17,400). It extended this requirement to broadcast media owners and instructed all media owners to reregister. Local journalists called the sum prohibitive, and said it would hinder media development.

The other measure amended the criminal code, replacing fines with mandatory prison sentences of at least six months for media owners or journalists convicted of publishing defamatory, "seditious," or false information. It also allowed the state to confiscate without judicial oversight any publication deemed "seditious."

Under local and international pressure, the government later revised the criminal code a second time. It removed the mandatory prison provision and brought back the option of a fine. But at the same time, it doubled the minimum jail sentence to one year. The GPU slammed the amendment as a step backward and expressed concern over a provision allowing courts to impound presses used to print offending materials.

At the start of the year, it looked as if the country's small independent press—notably, the leading newspapers *The Point* and *The Independent*—might not survive the fallout from Hydara's murder. *The Point* had lost its editor and leading light. *The Independent*'s then-editor, Abdoulie Sey, fled the country, while Managing Editor Alagi Yorro Jallow decided to remain abroad. Both men had been threatened and feared for their safety.

Despite the loss of senior staff, both *The Point* and *The Independent* managed to publish with editorial help from Demba Jawo, who was then the GPU secretary-general. Remarkably, journalists at *The Independent* also overcame the loss of their newspaper's printing capability.

In May, *The Independent* was forced to stop publishing after the pro-government, private *Daily Observer* abruptly terminated an informal printing arrangement. *Independent* Editor Musa Saidykhan told CPJ that other Gambian printing and publishing houses refused the paper's requests for a contract. He said they had been threatened not to print *The Independent* and feared that their presses could be attacked.

The Independent remained closed for more than a month while it sought to solve the printing problem. Finally, it switched to a different format that relied on photocopying rather than a printing press. Independent journalists suspect the *Daily Observer* had political motives for terminating its agreement with *The Independent*. Momodou Sanyang, the *Daily Observer*'s managing editor at the time, told CPJ that he made the decision after learning of problems with his paper's printing facilities, including the need for spare parts and extra printing capacity.

During a mission to the Gambia in April 2005, CPJ observed the deep mistrust between the government and the independent media. CPJ called on Jammeh and his government to take a number of steps to improve the environment, including affirming a commitment to press freedom and journalists' safety.

Jammeh did the opposite. In July, he said he had provided "too much freedom of expression and media rights," according to the Media Foundation for West Africa, an independent organization based in Ghana. In an interview with the state broadcaster to mark the 11th anniversary of the July 22 coup that brought him to power, Jammeh said that he had introduced the new press laws because "journalists are only bent on character assassination of people."

The official investigation into Hydara's killing stagnated. In June, the government released to the press a "confidential" report compiled by the National Intelligence Agency, which was supposed to investigate the crime. The report failed to detail any forensic evidence or to explore possible links between Hydara's murder and other unsolved attacks on the independent media. Instead, it alleged that he was a "serial womanizer" who had "recklessly provoked" a large number of people. The report was widely condemned as unprofessional and viewed as a government effort to smear Hydara's reputation.

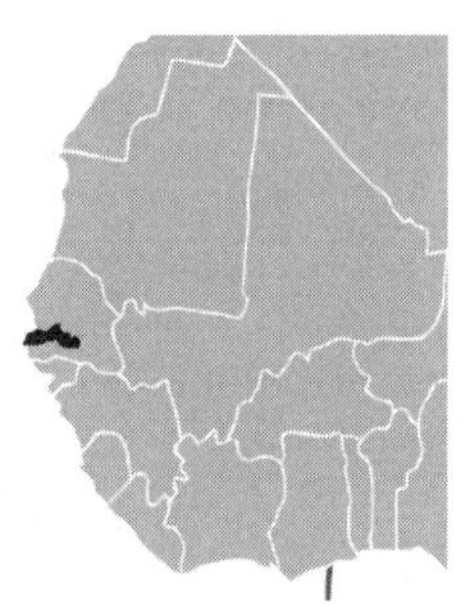

Hydara, who also worked as a correspondent for Agence France-Presse and Reporters Without Borders (RSF), was shot in the head and chest by unidentified assailants while he drove home from his office in the capital, Banjul, late on December 16, 2004. Two other staff members of *The Point* were wounded. Hydara was a frequent critic of the government and a leading campaigner for press freedom. He wrote a column called "Good Morning Mr. President," in which he criticized Jammeh. Many local journalists suspect that his attackers may have been linked to government security forces.

Journalists said they were also deeply concerned by the government's failure to solve a series of arson attacks, including a 2000 attack on private broadcaster Radio 1 FM; an August 2004 attack on the home of BBC correspondent Ebrima Sillah; and an October 2003 attack on the offices of *The Independent*. A second attack on *The Independent* in April 2004 destroyed the newspaper's new printing press. Several employees who were in the building at the time barely escaped.

IVORY COAST

In a climate of violence and political tension, journalists were frequently threatened, assaulted, and censored. The country has been divided since a 2002 uprising into a rebel-held north and government-held south. Some 10,000 French and United Nations peacekeepers oversee a fragile cease-fire. The rebels kept the press in their areas on a tight leash, but pro-government forces carried out the majority of the attacks on the media reported in 2005.

The "Young Patriots," one of several militia groups that support President Laurent Gbagbo, attacked and harassed journalists in Abidjan, the country's main commercial and administrative city, and home to most of its media outlets.

On July 24, the Young Patriots forced their way into the offices of state broadcaster Radiodiffusion Télévision Ivoirienne (RTI) after an unidentified armed group attacked and briefly held the town of Agboville, 45 miles (72 kilometers) from Abidjan. The Young Patriots demanded that RTI broadcast in full a speech by their leader, Charles Blé-Goudé, who blamed the rebels for the capture of the town. The rebels denied involvement. In his speech, Blé-Goudé called for a ban on pro-opposition newspapers. RTI management condemned the Young Patriots and requested government protection.

The next day, the Young Patriots disrupted the distribution of eight independent and pro-opposition daily newspapers around Abidjan and issued threats that forced some to evacuate their premises, according to local sources. The Young Patriots entered the distribution company Edipresse, where they destroyed hundreds of newspaper copies. A number of the targeted dailies received threats that their headquarters would be burned down and their staffs killed, according to CPJ sources. In November 2004, during a wave of anti-rebel and anti-French violence in the south, the Young Patriots had attacked some of the same dailies, torching their offices, looting, and destroying equipment as the staff fled for their lives.

On July 26, the Young Patriots savagely beat a journalist from one of the private papers as he prepared to cover an opposition press conference in Abidjan. Militia members disrupted the meeting and attacked opposition supporters, according to local news reports. Political reporter José Stéphane Koudou was beaten with iron bars and seriously injured, colleagues said. His assailants confiscated his press card, which showed he worked for the private daily *Le Jour Plus*. At the end of October, *Le Jour Plus* announced it was suspending publication to protest ongoing threats to its staff.

Not only has the government failed to curb the Young Patriots, but high-level officials have openly intimidated the press. At a meeting with local journalists in August, Gen. Philippe Mangou, the head of Ivory Coast's armed forces, threatened to ban newspapers that failed to work "in the interests of the nation." According to local and international news reports, Mangou warned journalists to be patriotic. "Otherwise," he said, "we will have to assume our responsibilities and close those newspapers that continue to be apologists for violence and for the rebellion."

Mangou also demanded a press blackout of statements by dissident army officers Mathias Doué and Jules Yao Yao, who had recently called for the removal of Gbagbo. At the same meeting, Republican Guard commander Dogbo Blé Brunot told journalists, "Ivory Coast is at war, and when a country is at war, even in so-called developed democracies, there is no freedom of the press."

Government forces have also tried to set the agenda of the national broadcaster, RTI. At the end of July, a group of armed, uniformed soldiers stormed RTI's Abidjan offices and instructed its directors not to broadcast footage of opposition members. In response, RTI's general manager, Kébé Yacouba, announced that RTI would suspend coverage of all political parties, including the ruling Front Populaire Ivoirien (FPI). RTI's board lifted the suspension the following month, saying that the political climate had improved.

Under an April 2005 accord, the parties to Ivory Coast's conflict agreed that RTI "must be used in favor of unity and national reconciliation." This followed international condemnation of the role played by RTI in November 2004, when pro-government forces ousted Yacouba, took over the RTI broadcasting facility, and used radio and television to incite hostility toward foreigners and Ivoirian ethnic groups deemed sympathetic to the rebels.

A particular target was France, the former colonial power, which had destroyed much of the Ivoirian air force in retaliation for the bombing of French forces during government air raids on the northern rebel stronghold of Bouaké in early November. Following the broadcasts, deadly clashes erupted between demonstrators and French peacekeepers in Abidjan. The United Nations condemned the broadcasts, and the government subsequently reinstalled Yacouba and his management team.

Independent observers said that, under Yacouba, RTI's programming was generally professional. However, international concern about xenophobia in the Ivoirian media continued.

In a report to the U.N. Security Council in September, Secretary-General Kofi Annan said that "incitements to violence, exclusion and intolerance, and calls for a resumption of the armed conflict continued uninterrupted by the Ivorian media, in particular those associated with the ruling party." The report added that, following massacres in the west of the country in June and the violent incidents in July, some media had also been targeting members of the U.N. mission in Ivory Coast.

Some pro-government politicians and media, such as the FPI daily *Notre Voie*, have also waged a campaign against France, which they accuse of supporting the rebels. France mediated the first peace agreement following the rebel uprising in 2002. It also sent troops to the country to help oversee the accord.

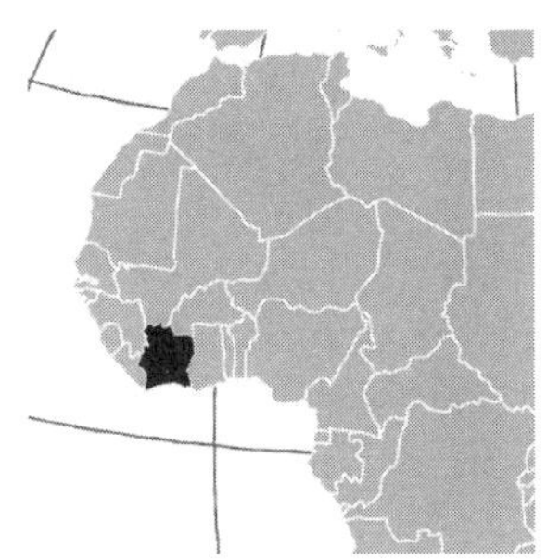

In mid-July, Ivoirian authorities shut down the FM broadcasts of Radio France Internationale (RFI). The National Council on Communication, an official regulatory body known by its French acronym, CNCA, accused RFI of biased reporting and of citing a U.N. report on civilian massacres that a U.N. mission spokesman later said did not exist. The CNCA ordered RFI to pay a fine of nine million CFA francs (US$16,577) and to broadcast a retraction of its reports "at least five times" once back on the air. RFI stood by its reporting.

RFI's FM broadcasts had been cut off several times before during politically sensitive periods, according to CPJ research. For example, in November 2004, unidentified assailants crippled FM transmissions of international radio stations, including RFI, just before the government conducted air raids on rebel positions in the north.

The murder of RFI correspondent Jean Hélène by an Ivoirian police officer in October 2003 continued to cast a deep pall over journalists working in the country. In a rare instance of justice in an attack on a journalist, the officer was convicted and sentenced to 17 years in jail in early 2004, although no motive for the murder was given. The military court that tried the officer did not make public any finding on whether he acted alone or on the orders of others. Local and international human rights activists continued to protest the court's finding of "mitigating circumstances" for Hélène's killer.

The government also came under fire for its failure to solve the case of missing journalist Guy-André Kieffer. Kieffer, a freelance reporter of French and Canadian descent, disappeared from Abidjan in April 2004. At the end of October, Michel Legré, the only named suspect, was released provisionally. Legré, a businessman and brother-in-law of first lady Simone Gbagbo, was the last person known to have seen Kieffer alive. He was charged in 2004 by Ivoirian authorities as an accessory to kidnapping and murder. Kieffer's body has never been found. A French judge investigating the case also charged Legré with complicity in the journalist's abduction and confinement.

RWANDA

The arrival of private radio stations did little to improve the climate for media in Rwanda, where repression by the government of President Paul Kagame and self-censorship by journalists all but stifled critical coverage. Local media and human rights groups often failed to speak out against intimidation and attacks on the press. Previous acts of violence against journalists remained unpunished.

At least nine commercial, community, and religious radio stations were on the air by year's end, as were new provincial stations belonging to state-owned Radio Rwanda; however, CPJ sources said that the new stations broadcast few critical political programs or investigative reports. Television broadcasting remained a state monopoly.

After several years' delay, "gacaca" courts finally began trying suspects in the 1994 genocide, in which some 800,000 ethnic Tutsis and moderate Hutus were killed in little more than three months. The courts, adapted from a form of Rwandan traditional justice, were set up to try tens of thousands of suspects who have been held in overcrowded jails for more than 11 years.

International human rights groups and independent observers expressed concern that genocide allegations were being used in some cases to settle personal scores and to punish government critics, including journalists. In the gacaca system, the accused is judged by peers and has no recourse to a defense lawyer. The courts can hand down prison sentences and, for lesser crimes such as looting, order civil reparations. Prison sentences can be partially converted into community service in cases where suspects confess their crimes.

In a move that made international headlines, Rwandan authorities arrested Belgian Catholic priest and journalist Guy Theunis as he passed through the capital, Kigali, in early September. They accused him of publishing material that had incited people to participate in the 1994 genocide; a few days later, Theunis became the first foreigner to appear before a gacaca court. The charges against Theunis related to publication of material from the newspaper *Kangura*, whose editor was sentenced by the United Nations International Criminal Tribunal for Rwanda (ICTR) in 2003 to life imprisonment for genocide.

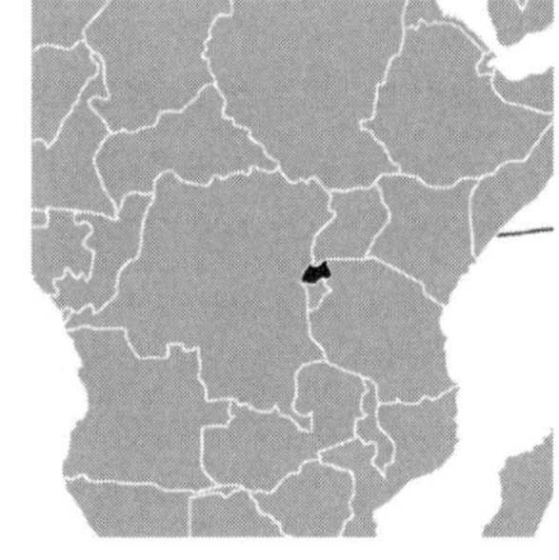

Theunis worked as a missionary in Rwanda from 1970 to 1994, and edited the French-language review *Dialogue*, which covered social and political issues. Theunis told the gacaca court that he was astonished by the accusations and that he had merely translated excerpts from *Kangura* as part of a press review in *Dialogue*. CPJ sources also expressed shock at the allegations, saying they were probably motivated either by politics or by personal animosities. Theunis was a critic of the rebel Rwandan Patriotic Front (RPF), which is now in power. Following strong diplomatic pressure from Belgium, the former colonial power, Rwanda agreed to transfer Theunis to Belgium for trial.

In September, journalist Jean-Léonard Rugambage was jailed on the orders of gacaca authorities and accused of participating in a genocide-related murder, although several local sources told CPJ they believe he was jailed for his journalistic work. Rugambage, a reporter for the twice-monthly newspaper *Umuco*, was held in the central town of Gitarama. His arrest came shortly after he wrote an article for the August 25 edition of *Umuco* that accused gacaca officials in the Gitarama region of corruption, mismanagement, and witness tampering.

CPJ sources said the evidence against Rugambage appeared to be flimsy. In November, Rugambage was found in contempt of a gacaca court and sentenced to a year in prison after he protested that the presiding judge was biased. Rugambage said the judge refused to consider defense evidence or testimony, according to CPJ sources. The underlying charge remained pending.

Umuco, which is based in Kigali and publishes mainly in the local language Kinyarwanda, has been targeted for its criticism of the authorities. In August, its editor, Bonaventure Bizumuremyi, was twice held by police for questioning following publication of an article on police corruption and a story that called for the release of jailed opposition leader and former president Pasteur Bizimungu. In mid-September, police seized copies of *Umuco* and summoned Bizumuremyi several times for questioning. He said he had also received anonymous telephone threats. One article in the seized edition likened Kagame to his predecessors and called him a dictator.

At the beginning of the year, Rwango Kadafi and Didas Gasana became the latest in a series of journalists from the critical weekly *Umuseso* to flee the country in fear for their safety. Gasana had been detained and threatened by unidentified armed men at the Ugandan border in December 2004, while Kadafi and another *Umuseso* journalist were victims of a vicious knife assault the same month. The attackers were subsequently identified as two government soldiers and a civilian, according to CPJ sources. All three attackers were arrested and held for a week, but they were then released. No further action has been taken against them.

In March, a Rwandan appeals court stiffened a previous sentence against *Umuseso* Editor Charles Kabonero, who was convicted of defaming the deputy speaker of parliament, Denis Polisi, in a 2004 article. The court imposed a one-year suspended prison sentence and ordered Kabonero to pay the equivalent of US$2,000 in damages. The trial court had earlier imposed only a symbolic fine and acquitted him on the more serious criminal charge of "divisionism."

A media law introduced in 2002 imposes criminal sanctions on the media for a wide range of ill-defined offenses such as "divisionism," which is punishable by one to five years in prison. Accusations of divisionism as well as "genocide ideology" have been used to intimidate journalists. In 2004, they were used to purge the Rwandan League for the Promotion and Defense of Human Rights, LIPRODHOR, of government critics, forcing several of its leaders into exile and closing its two specialized publications on human rights and justice. *Le Verdict*, LIPRODHOR's well-established monthly journal on justice issues, stopped publishing in July 2004. CPJ sources said its absence has left a marked gap in coverage.

SOMALIA

A Transitional Federal Government (TFG) was mandated by a peace conference of warlords and political leaders to restore order to Somalia, which has been without an effective central government since 1991. But the TFG split and political rivalries sparked violence, especially in the capital, Mogadishu.

Amid ongoing lawlessness, impunity, and increased political tension, journalists faced threats, censorship, arbitrary detentions, and murder. Two journalists were killed and one narrowly escaped assassination. Attacks came from "warlords, regional administrations, independent militias, clan-built Islamic courts, armed business groups, and bands of soldiers," according to the National Union of Somali Journalists (NUSOJ).

Somalia was carved into rival, clan-based fiefdoms following the overthrow of dictator Siad Barre in 1991. The south remained subject to violence and insecurity in 2005. The self-declared republic of Somaliland in the northwest, and the self-declared autonomous region of Puntland in the northeast were relatively stable.

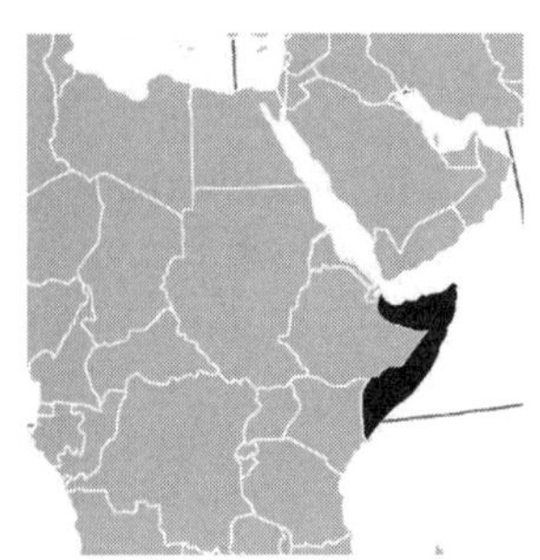

Private radio stations have proliferated in Mogadishu and elsewhere, but many continue to struggle to cover Somali issues across regional and clan divides, and to shake off accusations of clan bias. Attacks on the press increased as the TFG split. TFG President Abdullahi Yusuf, a Puntlander, refused to move to Mogadishu for security reasons, and Mogadishu-based TFG leaders remained in the capital.

Kate Peyton of the BBC, one of several foreign reporters who entered the country to cover the peace process in early 2005, was killed in Mogadishu in January, shocking the journalist community. Peyton was shot from a passing car outside the well-guarded Sahafi Hotel, where other foreign journalists were also staying. Local sources said Peyton, a Briton who had lived in Africa for 10 years, may have been targeted to discourage foreigners and to maintain a climate of insecurity.

In June, radio journalist Duniya Muhyadin Nur was shot dead while covering a protest in Afgoye, 19 miles (30 kilometers) from Mogadishu. She was a reporter for the Mogadishu-based radio station Capital Voice, owned by the HornAfrik media company.

In May, veteran journalist Abdallah Nurdin Ahmad, who also works for HornAfrik, was wounded when an unidentified gunman opened fire at close range outside the snack bar Nurdin operated in Mogadishu. The same month, at least two journalists were injured in a huge blast at a Mogadishu stadium, where they were covering a rally by TFG Prime Minister Ali Mohamed Gedi. At least 15 people were killed in the blast and dozens were injured, according to news reports.

Executives of NUSOJ (formerly the Somali Journalists Network) complained of death threats via anonymous phone calls during the run-up to a NUSOJ General Assembly in Mogadishu in August. They said unidentified, heavily armed militia members were cruising around the organization's premises.

In August, HornAfrik reporter Abdullahi Kulmiye Adow was imprisoned in Jowhar, 56 miles (90 kilometers) north of Mogadishu, for five days by a militia loyal to local faction leader Mohamed Dhere. Dhere is a supporter of TFG President Yusuf, who had recently established a temporary headquarters in Jowhar. Yusuf was appointed interim president in 2004 following two years of peace talks.

Adow was released without charge but was expelled from the town. Speaking through an interpreter, Adow told CPJ that he was transported out of Jowhar under armed guard and told not to return. Adow's arrest came after he reported that TFG officials had taken over Jowhar school buildings for their operations, displacing some 1,500 students. HornAfrik told CPJ that the station considered it too dangerous to send a reporter back to Jowhar to cover the TFG leadership's activities there. TFG institutions are supposed to oversee disarmament, demobilization, and a reunification of the country under a loose federal arrangement.

In Puntland, journalists who dared criticize the regional authorities or the TFG were frequently intimidated, imprisoned, and censored. TFG President Yusuf continued to wield considerable influence in Puntland, according to local sources.

Puntland authorities harassed the critical weekly newspaper *Shacab* (Voice of the People). In April, *Shacab* editor Abdi Farah Nur and reporter Abdirashid Qoransey were detained, tried, and acquitted on charges of incitement and insulting the president. Those charges were based on a mid-April article suggesting that citizens with complaints about the Puntland government contact their representatives in Parliament, and on a reader's letter criticizing authorities, according to Farah.

In May, authorities issued a decree ordering *Shacab* "temporarily suspended" for publishing unspecified articles that they claimed could lead to unrest. In June, police arrested Farah after *Shacab* tried to resume publication in defiance of the ban. Farah was released without charge after two and a half weeks but then fled the country, fearing for his life.

Puntland officials exerted pressure on radio stations in the region to avoid coverage of controversial political issues such as whether neighboring states should be allowed to send peacekeeping troops to Somalia, according to NUSOJ and other local sources. They said members of the public had criticized the government's stance on such issues during radio talk shows. Sources told CPJ that, at a press conference in Bossasso in April, Deputy Information Minister Ibrahim Artan Ismail threatened to ban call-in shows. These sources said that the talk shows were continuing but tended to focus on social rather than political issues.

In Somaliland, which declared independence from the rest of Somalia in 1991 but has not won international recognition, the government kept the media on a tight leash. Private radio stations were banned. In March, two reporters for government-owned Radio Hargeisa were fired after they were accused of working for Horyaal Radio, a pro-opposition station based in London. Horyaal had begun broadcasting into Somaliland via shortwave and the Internet only days earlier, according to CPJ sources.

TOGO

The death of President Gnassingbé Eyadema on February 5 gave local journalists hope that a new era of press freedom would follow years of repression. Instead, Eyadéma's Rassemblement du Peuple Togolais (RPT) held on to power, resorting to censorship, harassment, and intimidation of the media as the army suspended the constitution and named the president's son, Faure Gnassingbé, head of state.

Local FM broadcasts of Radio France Internationale (RFI), an influential news source in Togo, were cut for several days after Communications Minister Pitang Tchalla criticized foreign media coverage of the succession and accused RFI of conducting "a campaign of disinformation and destabilization." Officials also denied a visa to a France-based RFI reporter who tried to enter the country from neighboring Benin.

Amid pro-opposition protests and growing unrest in the capital, Lomé, authorities censored radio stations that aired critical debates and interviews about the turmoil. On February 10, a Togolese Armed Forces spokesman told media owners at a meeting convened by the official High Audiovisual and Communications Authority (known by its French acronym, HAAC) that private broadcasters were "playing a very dangerous game." He warned them that the army was "following all the stations very closely." The spokesman singled out the popular Lomé-based independent stations Nana FM, Radio Nostalgie, and Kanal FM, along with the Catholic station Radio Maria.

From February 11 to 14, security forces visited the offices of seven private broadcasters in Lomé, including Nana FM, Kanal FM, and Radio Nostalgie, and ordered them off the air, citing unpaid broadcasting fees. A Lomé court later issued a one-month suspension of several of the same stations after the HAAC accused them of inciting "civil disobedience" and "racial hatred." Riot police clashed with demonstrators trying to prevent the stations' closure, according to the Panafrican News Agency.

All of the stations were allowed back on the air by late February, as Togolese authorities bowed to international pressure and scheduled presidential elections for April

24. However, repression of the press resumed amid pre-election violence. In mid-April, the HAAC banned private broadcasters from "organizing special programs or debates featuring the candidates or their representatives," and from "carrying out any media coverage" of the campaigns. Only days before the vote, the HAAC suspended Kanal FM again, calling a broadcast editorial "tendentious, defamatory and insulting." The piece had accused members of the ruling party of widespread human rights abuses, called the HAAC a tool of the ruling party, and denounced the ban on campaign coverage.

The day after the election, the HAAC suspended Radio Maria and Radio Nostalgie for one month for mistakenly reporting that the government had imposed a curfew in the capital, as opposition supporters refused to accept official results declaring Faure Gnassingbé the winner. Rioting spread throughout the country. Nana FM shut down temporarily for fear of being attacked. Mobs attacked radio stations, both pro-government and pro-opposition, in several small towns. Local journalists told CPJ that many phone lines were cut, making it difficult to report events to the outside world.

Several government ministers and state-owned media blamed foreign journalists for the post-election violence. "It is you who have ignited the fire," Foreign Minister Kokou Tozoun told international correspondents at a press conference, according to The Associated Press. "It is you who are at the origin of the massacre." Some of these journalists, who included seasoned war correspondents, told CPJ that the comments had endangered their safety. Some said they scaled back their activity.

Shortly after the election, RFI's FM broadcasts were again cut, this time to "preserve national cohesion," according to the communications minister. RFI protested the censorship and introduced new shortwave frequencies. The FM broadcasts remained off the air until November, when they were restored on the first day of an international media summit organized by the International Union of the Francophone Press. Hervé Bourges, the union's president and a former president of RFI, raised the issue with Togolese authorities before the summit opened, he told the United Nations' IRIN news service.

A U.N. report in September noted that during the election HAAC and RPT officials threatened journalists and ordered some broadcast media owners to suspend program hosts judged overly critical of the government. The report criticized the HAAC for acting as a government censor instead of in its official role as a media regulator.

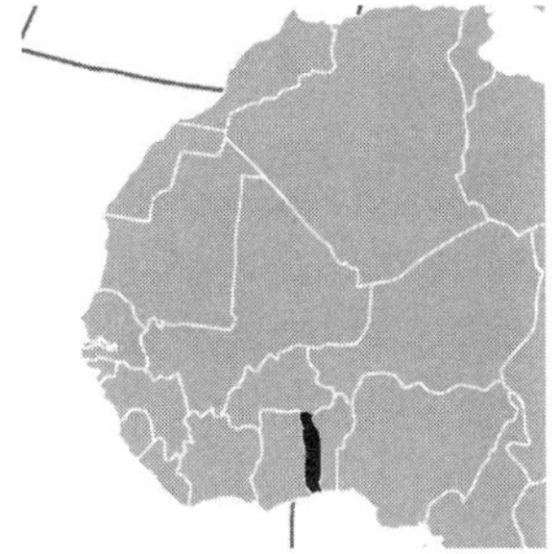

Relations between the government and the private press eased after July as the violence tapered off, although local journalists continued to censor themselves, according to CPJ sources. In August, newly appointed Communications Minister Kokou Tozoun, who was previously foreign minister, made a conciliatory tour of private broadcasters around the country. The minister also agreed to introduce financial aid for the private press in the

2006 budget, including tax relief on media supplies and lower communications costs, following proposals by local journalists' associations. Some local journalists expressed fears, however, that authorities would use aid as a tool to influence coverage.

In September, the government approved a new set of HAAC members, and created a position for a representative of the private press in an attempt to fulfill the previous government's 2004 promise to guarantee the agency's independence. This pledge was part of an extensive democratization plan aimed at regaining European Union aid, which was suspended in 1993 in response to Eyadéma's dismal human rights record. The EU announced some limited financial assistance for development and elections-related projects in 2005.

Some local media organizations never recovered from the year's turmoil. Privately owned Radio Lumière in the coastal town of Aného was shuttered by police in February after it broadcast critical debates as well as opposition statements calling for protests. It re-opened only to be raided and torched by security forces following the election.

ZIMBABWE

In the run-up to parliamentary elections in March, the government of President Robert Mugabe further tightened repressive legislation that has been used to drastically reduce the independent media and its freedom to operate. Independent journalists continued to face police harassment, official intimidation, and the constant threat of arrest under the draconian laws. Several more journalists went into exile, joining a growing diaspora and underscoring Zimbabwe's reputation as one of Africa's worst abusers of press freedom and human rights. The country's economy foundered amid skyrocketing inflation, further impeding the few remaining independent news outlets.

Officials with the ruling ZANU-PF party disdain even the concept of a free press. The party's mouthpiece, *The Herald*, argued in March that "it does not take a rocket scientist to foresee that the media is irrelevant and ineffectual, particularly in Africa," and proclaimed in July that "one of the biggest problems Zimbabwe [has] faced over the past five years is the problem of media terrorism." In February, the ZANU-PF's Department of Information and Publicity released a booklet listing Zimbabwean "traitors"—including veteran journalists Basildon Peta and Geoffrey Nyarota, both of whom are living in exile, and Trevor Ncube, an exiled journalist and media entrepreneur who is now CEO of neighboring South Africa's independent *Mail and Guardian*.

In a special report, "Zimbabwe's Exiled Press," CPJ's Elisabeth Witchel found that at least 90 Zimbabwean journalists, including many of the nation's most prominent reporters, now live in exile in South Africa, other African nations, the United Kingdom, and the United States, making it one of the largest groups of exiled journalists in the world. The report, published in October, was based on interviews with 34 exiled Zimbabwean journalists, analysts, and human rights advocates. Some of these exiled journalists left as a direct result of political persecution, others because the government's crackdown virtually erased opportunities in the independent press, according to CPJ's analysis.

In January, Mugabe signed into law an amendment establishing a two-year prison penalty for violation of the Access to Information and Protection of Privacy Act, known as AIPPA. The law makes it a crime to work as a journalist or to run a media outlet without a license from the government-controlled Media and Information Commission (MIC). Since its introduction in 2002, AIPPA has been used to harass dozens of journalists and to shutter newspapers, including the *Daily News*, which was Zimbabwe's only independent daily newspaper. Mugabe also signed into law in 2005 the Criminal Law (Codification and Reform) Act, which introduces penalties of up to 20 years in prison and heavy fines for publishing or communicating "false" information deemed prejudicial to the state. This penalty is significantly heavier than any contained in AIPPA or the Public Order and Security Act, which has also been used to detain and harass journalists since 2002.

Government control of the media is near complete. Zimbabwe today has no independent daily newspapers, no private radio or television news coverage, and only a handful of independent weeklies. Authorities made full use of their dominance in the weeks before the March 31 parliamentary election, restricting opposition access to state media and orchestrating effusive coverage of the ruling party. They shuttered a newly launched private weekly, harassed several well-respected journalists into leaving the country, and hand-picked foreign correspondents for accreditation.

The ZANU-PF party was pronounced the overwhelming winner of the March vote, gaining a two-thirds parliamentary majority that allowed it to push through changes to the constitution. The party lost no time in doing so, enacting amendments almost immediately to further entrench Mugabe's power and to create a new upper legislative chamber, the Senate, whose members were elected in November. The Senate elections triggered a split within the opposition Movement for Democratic Change (MDC) over whether to participate, further weakening that party.

Violence was much less evident during the March campaign than in the national elections of 2000 and 2002, when hundreds of MDC supporters were attacked and scores were killed. Independent observers such as the Zimbabwe Election Support Network said that the March vote was seriously flawed, and monitors from the United States and United Kingdom were barred from observing the elections. Nonetheless, a team of monitors sent by the Southern African Development Community, a 14-member group of mostly friendly neighbor states, gave it a clean bill of health. South Africa's President Thabo Mbeki has been heavily criticized, including by journalists in his own country, for failing to speak out publicly on press freedom and human rights abuses in Zimbabwe.

A month and a half before the March election, three freelance journalists working for foreign media fled the country, fearing arrest by security forces after police repeatedly visited their shared offices. Officials variously accused Angus Shaw of The Associated Press, Jan Raath of *The Times* of London, and Brian Latham of Bloomberg News, all Zimbabwean citizens, of participating in espionage; lacking proper accreditation; transmitting information prejudicial to the state; and using an unlicensed satellite phone. Cornelius Nduna, another freelance journalist, briefly went into exile in February after police raided his office looking for "sensitive tapes" depicting youth training camps reportedly used to train pro-government militia.

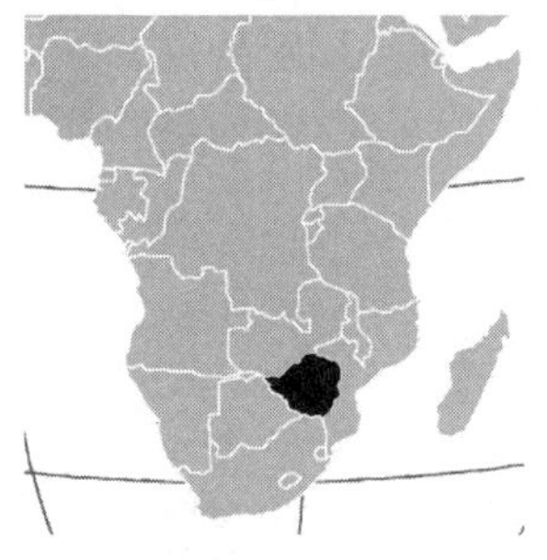

In February, the MIC suspended for one year the publishing license of the newly founded *Weekly Times*, saying it violated AIPPA by misrepresenting information on its application. MIC Chairman Tafataona Mahoso said the *Weekly Times* had promised to make social issues a priority but had focused instead on political advocacy. Based in the northern city of Bulawayo, the *Weekly Times* had covered economic and political problems and provided a platform for the airing of regional grievances.

While no foreign journalists have been allowed to reside full-time in Zimbabwe since 2003, the government allowed foreigners to apply for accreditation to cover the elections, and authorities claimed to have granted hundreds of passes. Yet many journalists were explicitly denied permission to enter the country, including all staff of the BBC and the Australian Broadcasting Corporation. And the limited accreditation was not enough to protect journalists from harassment once they arrived in Zimbabwe; authorities arrested and deported Swedish television journalist Fredrik Sperling the day after the election, despite his accreditation. According to Sperling, he drew authorities' attention while filming a large farm expropriated by the Zimbabwean government and later occupied by a relative of Mugabe.

Security officials arrested and detained two British staff members of *The Sunday Telegraph* at a polling station on election day and charged them with violating AIPPA by working without accreditation, leaving them open to two-year jail terms. During their trial, *Sunday Telegraph* reporter Toby Harnden and photographer Julian Simmonds argued that they had traveled to the country as tourists. They were denied bail and spent two weeks in jail. Represented by media and human rights lawyer Beatrice Mtetwa, who took up their case, both were acquitted on April 14 and swiftly deported.

Mtetwa, who has defended many journalists under government attack, was a recipient of CPJ's 2005 International Press Freedom Award for her courage and integrity.

The growing Zimbabwean diaspora boasts a number of media outlets founded by exiled journalists, which the government frequently accused of being fronts for hostile foreign interests. Authorities particularly targeted the British-based independent newspaper *The Zimbabwean*, which is distributed both inside and outside Zimbabwe and is run by *Daily News* founder Wilf Mbanga, and the shortwave broadcaster SW Radio

Africa, also based in Britain. Before the election, SW Radio's signal within Zimbabwe was scrambled, a problem that continued throughout the year. The scrambling threatened the broadcaster's financial survival and raised fears that Zimbabwe was using sophisticated censorship technology from China, an important ally.

On May 18, freelance journalist Frank Chikowore was arrested as he filmed police clearing Harare's business district of street vendors, and was detained overnight without charge despite holding press accreditation. Chikowore had stumbled across the start of the government's Operation Murambatsvina, or "Clean Up the Trash," a brutal, nationwide sweep by security forces to destroy informal housing and commercial structures. The operation left hundreds of thousands homeless and millions facing starvation, according to a U.N. report. Done under the guise of urban renewal, the demolitions were aimed at breaking traditional opposition strongholds, critics said.

A handful of nominally private but pro-ZANU-PF papers continued to publish, in addition to the independent weeklies *The Standard* and *Zimbabwe Independent*. In September, the *Independent* reported that the Central Intelligence Organization (CIO) had covertly sought to take over private newspapers and had succeeded in controlling the pro-government *Daily Mirror* and *Sunday Mirror* by buying majority shares with taxpayer funds, starting in 2002. The article added to Zimbabwean journalists' fears that the government used secret tactics to control the media in addition to its well-known, overt techniques. The story quickly became a scandal dubbed "Mediagate."

The *Daily News*, which was shut down in September 2003, continued its ongoing legal battle for registration throughout 2005. Although the Supreme Court ordered the MIC in March to re-examine the *Daily News'* application, the newspaper remained closed. In a blow to local journalists' organizations, the same ruling upheld AIPPA as constitutional for the second time, reinforcing fears that purges and government intimidation had successfully eroded the court's independence.

Although AIPPA has been used to harass and detain dozens of journalists, no successful prosecutions were brought under the law. In August, a lower court in the capital, Harare, acquitted former *Daily News* journalist Kelvin Jakachira of working for the paper without accreditation from the MIC. The judge ruled that, since the reporter had applied for accreditation, he was entitled to work while awaiting the outcome of his application. The verdict could represent an important precedent for other journalists facing the same charges, including most of the former staff of the *Daily News*. Jakachira was successfully defended by Mtetwa, the lawyer whose defense of journalists was responsible for most of the rare good news for the Zimbabwean press in 2005.

SNAPSHOTS: **AFRICA**

Attacks & developments throughout the region

BOTSWANA

- In August, Rodrick Mukumbira, a Zimbabwean who had been working in Botswana for the *Ngami Times*, Agence France-Presse, and IRIN, was forced to leave the country after the government withdrew his work permits. Local press freedom organizations expressed fears that this may have been related to his reporting.

BURUNDI

- Radio and online journalist Etienne Ndikuriyo was jailed for nine days in June over a report that said the transitional president, Domitien Ndayizeye, was "depressed" by his party's election defeat. He was accused of "violating the honor and the privacy of the head of state" and released on bail.
- In July, the National Communications Council (CNC), an official media regulatory body, ordered Radio Publique Africaine (RPA) off the air indefinitely, alleging that RPA's recent election coverage was biased and that it had insulted the council. RPA Director Alexis Sinduhije called the suspension unjust and said the station intended to stay on the air despite the order.
- A week later, police shut down RPA, despite a compromise agreement with the CNC mediated by journalists' organizations. The station was allowed to reopen five days later. After the CNC chairman resigned, former president Domitien Ndayizeye replaced the council and included RPA's deputy director among its new members. The reopening of the station and the shakeup at the CNC followed a public outcry over the censorship attempt.

CENTRAL AFRICAN REPUBLIC

- In May, three well-known journalists received death threats following critical coverage of the second round of national elections. CPJ sources said the threats were linked to reports carried by the independent radio station Radio Ndeke Luka and the independent daily newspaper *Le Citoyen* that armed forces had intimidated voters at polling stations. The journalists targeted were Zéphirin Kaya and Patrick Akibata of Radio Ndeke Luka; and Maka Gbossokotto, managing editor of *Le Citoyen*.
- President François Bozizé promulgated a law that decriminalized most press offenses, including defamation and "insult." But the law, which was welcomed by local journalists' groups, maintained criminal sanctions for offenses such as inciting criminal activities and provoking ethnic or religious hatred.

COMOROS

- In January, authorities on the semi-autonomous island of Anjouan ordered the suspension of all news broadcasts on Radio Dzialandzé Mutsamudu (RDM), a popular, privately owned station that is a rare independent source of local and international news for the island's residents. The order stemmed from a recent RDM interview with a doctor who defended a strike by the island's medical personnel; government officials had previously criticized the strike. The suspension was lifted two weeks later.

DJIBOUTI

- Officials cut off Radio France Internationale's FM broadcasts in January. RFI and French media said this was because of its reporting of an ongoing French legal inquiry into the 1995 death in Djibouti of Bernard Borrel, a French judge.

EQUATORIAL GUINEA

- In June, police at the airport in the mainland city of Bata seized 200 copies of *La Verdad*, a publication run by the tiny opposition Convergence for Social Democracy party. The seizure was linked to the newspaper's often critical political coverage, according to a CPJ source. State-owned and government-friendly outlets dominate Equatorial Guinea's media; while a handful of private papers are licensed, they rarely publish and are subject to strict censorship by authorities. Although the constitution guarantees press freedom, criticism of the government in the local press is not tolerated.

ERITREA

- According to CPJ's annual census of imprisoned journalists, 15 journalists remained in prison or otherwise deprived of their liberty, the victims of a ruthless crackdown on dissent in September 2001. The journalists had worked for local independent publications, all of which were shut down by the government at the same time. Journalists were jailed without charge and held largely incommunicado. There are no local private media in Eritrea.

GABON

- In August, the National Communications Council (CNC), a government-controlled media regulatory body, suspended the independent bimonthly newspaper *Nku'u Le Messager* over an editorial it said insulted the council. The paper was allowed to reopen three weeks later, after it bowed to the CNC's instructions and reshuffled its editorial team.

GHANA

- Frank Boahene, editor of the private weekly *Free Press*, was jailed for 15 days in July for contempt of court. The ruling stemmed from failure to appear in court over the paper's alleged refusal to comply with a November 2004 civil libel ruling.

GUINEA

- In February, security forces arrested *La Lance* journalist Mohamed Lamine Diallo—known by his pen name, Benn Pépito—searched his home, and detained him for three days without charge. Pépito's arrest coincided with the publication of a critical editorial by the journalist in which he compared the situation in Guinea, where President Lansana Conté has ruled since 1984, to that of Togo, where the army moved to install longtime ruler Gnassingbé Eyadema's son as president following Eyadema's death.
- Conté signed a decree allowing private broadcasting in Guinea, one of the last countries in Africa, along with Zimbabwe and Eritrea, to have banned it. The law, signed in August, enables private citizens and organizations to broadcast but excludes political parties and religious movements. Local journalists welcomed the new law, but remained concerned that the government could delay its implementation or use red tape to block license applications.

KENYA

- In January, journalist Kamau Ngotho of the independent daily *The East African Standard* was charged with criminal libel in a Nairobi court in connection with a story detailing alleged links between the government and big business. The government dropped the charges six days later, after Ngotho was granted a request to challenge them in the High Court on constitutional grounds.
- In April, Managing Editor David Makali of the Nairobi-based *East African Standard's* Sunday edition was acquitted of criminal charges stemming from a 2003 investigative article about the murder of a key player in Kenya's constitutional reform process. The article was based on leaked excerpts of confessions made by suspects in the murder, believed by some to have been a political assassination. In addition to ruling that the prosecution had not established its case against Makali, the judge said that to convict the editor would contravene constitutional guarantees.
- On the night of May 2, the eve of World Press Freedom Day, first lady Lucy Kibaki stormed into the offices of the independent daily *The Nation* with six bodyguards and the Nairobi police chief, to protest what she called unfair coverage of her family. She stayed for about five hours, insulting and threatening journalists and slapping a cameraman who filmed her, according to local and international news reports.
- In October, Anderson Ojwang', a correspondent for *The East African Standard*, was beaten by youths bearing whips and sticks. Ojwang' was trying to cover a government meeting in the western town of Kakamega that was called to raise support for a new draft constitution. The attack came after a government minister had asked the press to leave and accused journalists of giving negative coverage to those backing

the draft constitution. The draft was rejected in a November referendum.

LIBERIA

- A Monrovia court ordered the offices of the privately owned weekly *Forum* shuttered for "contempt of court" in March. The action came after the paper's managing editor allegedly missed several summonses in connection with an ongoing civil libel case. The paper reopened two weeks later, after paying a fine.
- In November, journalists complained of attacks and death threats made by supporters of failed presidential candidate George Weah. His party, the Congress for Democratic Change (CDC), claimed fraud in the presidential runoff won by Ellen Johnson Sirleaf. The Press Union of Liberia advised journalists not to cover functions at CDC headquarters in the capital, Monrovia, until the party could guarantee their safety. The union said it had documented five cases of CDC supporters beating journalists at the headquarters. It later lifted its advisory, saying CDC leadership had apologized and offered assurances about journalist security.

MADAGASCAR

- In March and April, Lola Rasoamaharo, the publication director of the private daily *La Gazette de la Grande Ile*, was sentenced to four jail terms ranging from one to two months in connection with four separate criminal defamation charges. *Gazette* Editor James Ramarosaona was also given a one-month jail sentence in one of the cases. Both remained free pending an appeal.
- French journalist Olivier Péguy was forced to leave the country in May after the government refused to renew his work permit. The reasons for the nonrenewal were unclear, and some CPJ sources said it might have been linked to Péguy's reporting. Péguy had reported from Madagascar for four years for Radio France Internationale and other international news organizations.

MALAWI

- In March, police arrested BBC reporter Raphael Tenthani and Mabvuto Banda of the independent daily *The Nation* after the journalists reported that President Bingu wa Mutharika had moved out of the presidential palace because of fears it was haunted. The journalists were detained overnight and charged with "publishing a false story likely to cause public fear." A charge of "causing ridicule to the high office of the President" was later added, AFP reported.

MALI

- In July, unidentified assailants kidnapped and brutally beat Hamidou Diarra, a commentator for independent Radio Kledu. Local journalists said they believed the assault was linked to Diarra's radio program, in which he frequently criticizes abuses of power by local politicians and others.

MOZAMBIQUE

- A fugitive in the 2000 murder of investigative reporter Carlos Cardoso was returned to Mozambique in January. Anibal Antonio dos Santos Junior, better known as Anibalzinho, had fled custody in May 2004 after he was convicted of murder, along with five co-defendants, and sentenced to 28 years in prison. He was later captured in Canada, where authorities eventually agreed to return him to Mozambique. Anibalzinho was granted a retrial, which opened in December.
- In January, two men commandeered the car of Jeremias Langa, news director at the private television station STV, held guns to his head, and threatened to kill him. Before ejecting the journalist from the car, the assailants told Langa, "You're going to die like Carlos Cardoso," referring to the crusading investigative journalist who was murdered in 2000 for his aggressive coverage of a corruption scandal involving the state-controlled Commercial Bank of Mozambique.

NIGER

- In March, authorities harassed journalists and sought to suppress media coverage of strikes and protests organized by a coalition of civil society organizations against a new tax on basic commodities in this impoverished country. The country's interior minister appeared on state television to warn journalists against covering the coalition's activities.
- By the end of March, five leaders of the Coalition Against Costly Living were behind bars, facing accusations of threatening state security after giving interviews on local radio stations criticizing the new tax. Police shuttered the offices of privately owned Radio Alternative for more than a week, possibly in connection with the detention of Moussa Tchangari, a leading member of the coalition who directs the station's parent company.
- Starting in late April, authorities sought to repress local coverage of a developing nationwide famine for fear that the news would tarnish the country's image, according to the Media Foundation for West Africa. In early August, President Mamadou Tandja publicly denied the existence of famine in Niger, despite widespread media reports and a vast international aid campaign.
- In September, a court in the northern town of Agadez convicted Abdoulaye Harouna, managing editor of the monthly *Echos Express*, of defaming the local governor, Yahaya Yendaka. He was sentenced to four months in jail and fined 520,000 CFA

francs (US$950), but no arrest warrant was immediately issued to take him into custody. Harouna told CPJ that Yendaka filed a defamation suit against him after an article accused the governor of corruption in the distribution of food aid in the Agadez region during a nationwide food shortage.

- The director of a private weekly was arrested in November and placed in preventive detention after State Treasurer Siddo Elhadj filed a criminal defamation suit against him. Salifou Soumaila Abdoulkarim of *Le Visionnaire* was convicted in December and sentenced to two months in jail. Elhadj brought the lawsuit over an article in *Le Visionnaire* that accused him of embezzling 17 billion CFA francs (US$30 million) in government funds.

NIGERIA

- In January, police at an executive meeting of the ruling People's Democratic Party in the capital, Abuja, assaulted at least 10 journalists covering the meeting. One reporter was hospitalized after being beaten unconscious. According to local news reports, police attacked the journalists with batons and gun butts when they moved forward to photograph Chris Ngige, the embattled governor of southern Anambra state.
- Also in January, State Security Service (SSS) agents in the southeastern city of Enugu raided newsstands selling the local tabloid *Eastern Pilot*, harassed vendors, and detained the local chairman of the Newspapers Vendors' Association. Local sources linked the SSS actions to reports in the *Eastern Pilot* about the separatist, ethnic Igbo Movement for the Actualization of the Sovereign State of Biafra(MASSOB).
- On May 2, Omo-Ojo Orobosa, publisher of the weekly *Midwest Herald*, was imprisoned for more than two weeks after his paper accused first lady Stella Obasanjo of corruption. He was freed without charge.
- Police in central Kogi State occupied the local chapter of the Nigerian Union of Journalists in June, demanding to see two reporters who had written stories alleging that armed bandits had humiliated the local police commissioner. The officers harassed the local journalists and detained the local union chairman.
- Also in June, SSS agents arrested Haruna Acheneje, a correspondent for the independent daily *The Punch* in southern Akwa Ibom state, and held him for eight hours before releasing him without charge. Acheneje was pressured to reveal his sources for an article about the recently impeached deputy governor of Akwa Ibom, Chris Ekpeyong.
- In August, armed SSS agents raided the offices of the Lagos-based weekly *The Exclusive*, detained and harassed vendors, and seized copies of the newspaper following articles on Igbo secession movements, including MASSOB.

- In October, SSS agents arrested Owei Kobina Sikpi, publisher of the tabloid *Weekly Star* in the southern city of Port Harcourt, and jailed him for more than a month over an article that accused a local official of money laundering. The agents also confiscated the entire print run of the paper. Sikpi was eventually charged with several counts of publishing false information.
- The National Broadcasting Commission (NBC), an official regulatory body, ordered the country's leading independent broadcast network off the air over its coverage of an October airplane crash in which all 117 passengers died. It accused Daar Communications group's African Independent Television and its radio network, Ray-Power FM, of violating journalistic ethics by reporting, among other things, that the crash left no survivors, before the government had officially confirmed the toll. The two media outlets complied with the order but were back on the air the same day following negotiations with the government. President Olusegun Obasanjo said he was shocked by the NBC's order, and that the media outlets should have been commended, rather than closed.
- In late November, security forces under the authority of the federal government stormed a radio station owned by the local government of southern Bayelsa state. The station was closed as federal authorities intensified their efforts to unseat the state governor, Diepreye Alamieyeseigha. Alamieyeseigha embarrassed Nigerian authorities after he jumped bail in London, where he was due to stand trial for alleged money laundering, and returned in disguise to his home district.

SENEGAL

- A trial began in July for Madiambal Diagne, publication director of the independent daily *Le Quotidien*, on charges of threatening national security, publishing false news, and publishing secret government documents. The government has yet to repeal the controversial Article 80 of Senegal's penal code, under which Diagne was placed in "preventive detention" for two weeks in 2004, despite repeated promises to do so. The trial was ongoing at year's end.
- The same month, government officials warned journalists not to broadcast recordings of former Prime Minister Idrissa Seck, after Seck was imprisoned on national security and corruption charges. The police later summoned and questioned several local journalists with alleged ties to Seck, including veteran political commentator Abdou Latif Coulibaly. Jailing Seck, who was considered to be a political rival of President Abdoulaye Wade, called into question Wade's democratic credentials, according to local journalists and political analysts.
- In September, chief caliph Serigne Saliou Mbacké ordered three FM radio stations based in the Muslim holy city of Touba to leave the city within three days, saying

he intended to "preserve the holy city from occult practices contrary to Islam." The commercial station Disso, the local branch of state-owned Radio Télévision Sénégalaise, and community radio station Hizbut Tarqiyah went off the air immediately. Local sources told CPJ that the expulsion could be linked to news and discussion programs broadcast by Disso, including a recent phone-in program in which several callers criticized Touba's elected governing council. Disso's director, Ibrahima Benjamin Diagne, told CPJ that local politicians influenced the caliph, who is a spiritual leader. While not legally binding, a ruling by the caliph carries great practical weight.

- In October, authorities closed the private radio station Sud FM and detained dozens of its staff following the broadcast of an interview with Salif Sadio, a radical member of the rebel movement in southern Casamance. Authorities also banned distribution of the October 17 edition of *Sud-Quotidien*, a newspaper from the same media group as the radio station, which published the text of the interview. Following a public outcry, the station was authorized to resume broadcasting late the same day and the staff members were released. Authorities maintained a ban on "the broadcast, rebroadcast, or publication of the incriminating interview by any media outlet." Local sources said some of the journalists who had been questioned could be criminally charged.

SIERRA LEONE

- Olu Gordon, editor of the satirical newspaper *The Peep*, was detained for three days and threatened with criminal prosecution in February over an article criticizing President Ahmad Tejan Kabbah. Gordon was released without charge.
- In May, managing editor Sydney Pratt and reporter Dennis Jones of the private weekly *The Trumpet* were jailed for three days and charged with "seditious libel" over an article on high-level corruption. Both journalists were acquitted in June.
- In July, Harry Yansaneh, acting editor of the private newspaper *For Di People*, died following a May attack he had blamed on a ruling party MP, Fatmata Hassan. Under domestic and international pressure, the government ordered an inquest. In August, the inquest found that Yansaneh's death was accelerated by the attack, and it ordered the arrest of six people, including Hassan, for suspected manslaughter.
- Paul Kamara, editor and publisher of *For Di People*, was freed from prison in November after spending more than a year behind bars. An appellate court in the capital, Freetown, overturned his conviction on seditious libel charges, ruling that Kamara's actions did not constitute sedition. Kamara had been charged under the draconian 1965 Public Order Act after publishing articles critical of Kabbah. Local journalists have long struggled to have the Public Order Act repealed.

SOUTH AFRICA

- In May, the Johannesburg High Court barred the independent weekly *Mail and Guardian* from publishing a follow-up story on alleged illegal diversion of public funds through the private South African oil company Imvume to the ruling African National Congress party. In June, the gag order was lifted when the paper and lawyers for Imvume chief Sandi Majali decided to settle out of court. The settlement was reached after the revelations were aired in Parliament and reported in the press. The original article later ran in the *Mail and Guardian*.

TANZANIA

- In June, authorities on the semi-autonomous Tanzanian island of Zanzibar banned critical political columnist Jabir Idrissa from writing, accusing him of working without permission from the island authorities. Idrissa disputed the charges, citing his press accreditation from the mainland government. The ban was lifted later the same month, after the journalist applied for and was granted local accreditation.

- In September, a group of prison wardens and prisoners acting on their orders assaulted Mpoki Bukuku, chief photographer for the privately owned *Sunday Citizen*, as he attempted to cover the eviction of families from houses that were being repossessed by the Tanzanian Prisons Department. Christopher Kidanka, information officer for a local human rights organization, was also assaulted. After Home Affairs Minister Omar Ramadhan Mapuri defended the assault, saying that Prisons Department officers had used "reasonable" force in the evictions, local media organizations announced a ban on all coverage of the minister. He later apologized for his statements.

- Also in September, Tanzanian authorities banned HakiElimu, a local nongovernmental organization, from compiling or publishing reports on Tanzania's education system. The Ministry of Education and Culture accused the organization of "disparaging the image of our education system and the teaching profession of our country through [the] media," according to news reports and the local chapter of the Media Institute for Southern Africa. The ministry's action stemmed from a HakiElimu report issued in August that criticized government efforts to reform primary education, press reports stated.

- Amid preparations for delayed national elections, the government ordered two local newspapers to temporarily cease publishing, accusing both of violating the 1976 Newspaper Act. The Swahili-language daily *Tanzania Daima* was suspended for three days for publishing a picture and caption deemed offensive to President Benjamin Mkapa. The newspaper is published by a media company associated with opposition presidential candidate Freeman Mbowe, according to news reports. The weekly tabloid *Amani* was suspended for 28 days for alleged ethical violations. According to the Media Institute of Southern Africa, the Newspaper Act gives the minister of information wide discretionary powers to suspend or close newspapers.

UGANDA

- In June, a local official in the town of Soroti ordered David Enyaku, a journalist working for the government-owned *New Vision*, arrested when Enyaku tried to interview him about land allocation. Enyaku was detained for two nights and charged with "criminal trespassing."
- Authorities shut the independent radio station KFM for a week in August. The action came after the station aired a talk show hosted by veteran journalist Andrew Mwenda, focusing on the July helicopter crash that killed southern Sudanese leader John Garang. President Yoweri Museveni said the government would shut down any news outlet that "plays around with regional security."
- The day after authorities shuttered KFM, police arrested Mwenda and charged him with sedition. The charge stemmed from a KFM program in which Mwenda criticized Museveni and suggested that Ugandan government incompetence was responsible for the helicopter crash that killed Garang. Mwenda was released on bail after three days in detention, but he faces five years in jail and a fine if convicted. In November, the government brought 13 additional charges against him, including sedition and "promoting sectarianism."
- In November, the government threatened to close *The Monitor*, Uganda's leading independent daily, over a story about President Yoweri Museveni's choice for army chief. The newspaper's managing director, Conrad Nkutu, told CPJ that authorities also pressured the paper's management to fire Mwenda, who wrote the article.
- Also in November, the government ordered local journalists not to discuss or comment on the scheduled trial of jailed opposition leader Kizza Besigye on charges of treason, terrorism, and rape. Troops barred journalists from attending a court hearing in the case.
- The same month, police entered *The Monitor* as the paper was printing an issue that carried a paid advertisement soliciting contributions for "The Kizza Besigye Human Rights Fund." They harassed staff, saying the advertisement was illegal. Police also stopped the newspaper's delivery vans at several roadblocks and confiscated the paper in at least two towns.

ZAMBIA

- In June, supporters of the ruling party, armed with machetes, attacked newspaper vendors selling the independent daily *The Post*. Local sources reported that the attacks were carried out in retribution for *The Post*'s criticism of President Levy Mwanawasa for allegedly shielding a Health Ministry official from prosecution for corruption.

- Police threatened to charge radio commentator Anthony Mukwita with sedition after a June 10 broadcast on the privately owned Radio Phoenix in which he read an anonymous fax criticizing Mwanawasa's administration for allegedly failing to crack down on corruption. Following the broadcast, Radio Phoenix management terminated Mukwita's contract, an action Mukwita believes was prompted by threats from Zambian authorities.

- In late June, police questioned Fred M'membe, editor-in-chief of *The Post* and a former CPJ International Press Freedom Award recipient, and threatened to charge him with defaming the president. *The Post* had published a series of editorials accusing Mwanawasa of being a "liar" for allegedly failing to tackle official corruption.

- *The Post*'s M'membe was charged with criminal defamation in November. The charge stemmed from a commentary he wrote in which he accused Mwanawasa of hypocrisy, stupidity, and a "lack of humility." The commentary followed a bitter attack by Mwanawasa on former president Kenneth Kaunda, who had advocated wider consultation on a controversial draft constitution.

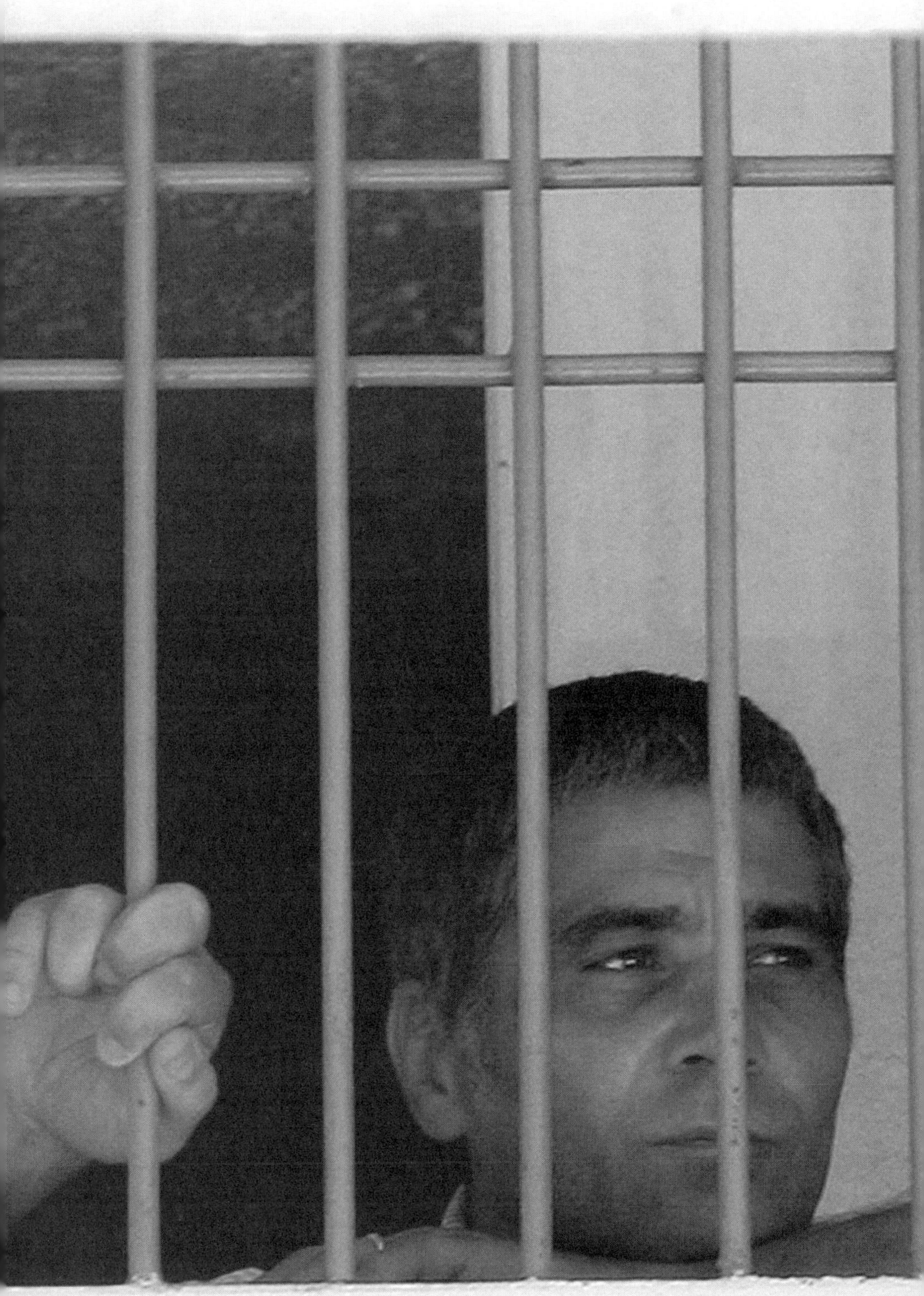

AMERICAS

ANALYSIS

PHOTOS

Section break: Reuters/Eduardo Munoz – *U.S. journalist Kevin Pina looks out from a prison cell in Port-au-Prince, Haiti. He was jailed for three days for filming a police operation.* Analysis (next): Danilo Sarmiento – *Crouching for cover, Colombian journalists Hernán Morales, Rodrigo Avila, and Carlos Pérez try to report on the deactivation of explosives in downtown Arauca.*

AMERICAS

SUMMARIES

ALL THE NEWS THAT CAN'T BE PRINTED

by Carlos Lauría

GOOD INVESTIGATIVE REPORTERS KNOW MORE THAN THEY CAN WRITE. The problem in some Latin American countries is that good reporters are barely writing anything. From Brazil to the U.S.-Mexico border, journalists are looking over their shoulders before sitting down at their computers or going on the air. Most reporters in the region's big cities can still take on corruption and criticize the authorities without fearing for their lives. But in isolated rural areas where the power of the central government is either weak or nonexistent, journalists are at the mercy of anyone with a gun.

Self-censorship is not new in Latin America. It has long been the scourge of journalism in a region where military dictatorships could crush media outlets that did not rein themselves in. The problem today is the extent of self-censorship as lawlessness, drug trafficking, smuggling, and organized crime continue to spread. Editors in countries such as Colombia, Mexico, and Brazil have largely abandoned investigative reporting in areas where they know state institutions such as the police and judiciary cannot or will not guarantee journalists' safety.

The media in Colombia, caught between rebels, the army, and pro-government

> "In Colombia, human rights abuses, armed conflict, corruption, and drugs go uncovered."

paramilitaries, are muzzling themselves for fear of retaliation if they publish anything that could offend any side. In Mexico, drug traffickers and gangland bosses have cowed reporters along the crime-plagued border with the United States into virtual silence. Those journalists who speak out sometimes pay with their lives. Even in Venezuela and Brazil, where the threat is less widespread, editors are ignoring stories for reasons of self-preservation. One victim of this self-imposed silence is democracy. Burning issues such as the pillaging of natural resources, trafficking in drugs and people, and corruption are deprived the oxygen of public debate.

Some reporters have begun to bridle at the restrictions, and are now more willing to talk about self-censorship and their fears than in the past.

Reporters and editors in Colombia's lawless interior openly admit that they censor themselves in fear of physical attack from all sides in the civil war, a 2005 CPJ investigation found. CPJ's Bogotá correspondent, Chip Mitchell, traveled to three of the most troubled areas—Arauca, Córdoba, and Caquetá—and interviewed 36 media professionals for a report titled "Untold Stories," which was published in October.

Mitchell found that editors are pressured by those who are the targets of media investigations to censor news before publication. Probing journalists who ignore warnings are murdered, or forced to leave the country. Frequently, the police do not even investigate crimes committed against members of the press. The issues that do not get covered as a result are human rights violations, armed conflicts, political and corporate corruption, drug trafficking, and links between officials and illegal armed groups. Sometimes officials encourage self-censorship by accusing journalists of having guerrilla ties. In Saravena, Arauca province, the town's only full-time journalist, Emiro Goyeneche, was charged with "rebellion" and accused of being a guerrilla. Goyeneche languished in prison for more than 20 months. Local journalists commend his work and believe the accusation against him is baseless.

High-ranking officials, including President Álvaro Uribe, also try to link journalists to guerrillas. At a conference of news executives, the Colombian president urged media outlets to exercise "self-control," and to consider barring the publication of interviews with members of illegal armed groups. Colombia's overburdened justice system has been incapable of solving the nearly 30 cases of journalists murdered during the last decade, perpetuating a climate of impunity. In a number of extreme cases, journalists have been forced to leave their homes.

Almost every reporter in Arauca fled the province in early 2003 after two radio journalists were murdered within a nine-month period. Death threats from both rebels and paramilitaries, along with the appearance of a mysterious list naming 16 journalists as murder targets, prompted the exodus. Simple economics are also behind some self-censorship. Many media outlets are poor and understaffed. They expect their reporters to sell advertisements. Journalists are therefore less likely to produce hard-hitting stories about the businessmen and politicians whose advertising helps pay their wages.

The only bright spot in this picture is that fewer journalists are now being killed. But one of the reasons for the fall in numbers is self-censorship. As noted in a report released in September by the Organization of American States, Colombian journalists are simply not reporting on issues that could get them killed. The report, titled "Impunity, Self-censorship and Armed Internal Conflict: An Analysis of the State of Freedom of Expression in Colombia," states that "the drop in the statistics on violence against journalists stems in part from self-censorship by journalists themselves." The report was prepared by Eduardo Bertoni, the OAS special rapporteur for freedom of expression.

> "Self-censorship is rampant in northern Mexico, where drug trafficking endangers the press."

Self-censorship is also rampant in northern Mexico, where drug trafficking and organized crime have turned the region into one of the most hazardous places for journalists in Latin America. Since the war between powerful drug cartels intensified two years ago, scores of reporters working along the U.S.-Mexico border have fallen silent because authorities are unable to provide even minimal protection.

In Nuevo Laredo, on the border with Texas, the daily *El Mañana* has stopped in-depth coverage of crime and drug trafficking. "We can't do investigative journalism on these topics, as the state does not guarantee the security of our reporters," explains Editorial Director Heriberto Cantú.

El Mañana, founded in 1932, has been censoring its news coverage since its editor, Roberto Javier Mora García, was stabbed to death in March 2004. CPJ is investigating whether the murder was related to his journalism. According to Cantú, violence along the border with the United States has soared in the past few years, making it impossible for Mexican journalists to report freely without fear of reprisal. "There is no freedom of expression without guarantees to exercise journalism," says Cantú.

Reporters trying to cover crime encounter government and law enforcement officials who are openly corrupt, along with criminals who operate without constraint. As a result, reporters from *El Mañana* and several other Nuevo Laredo–based publications cover only official news, omitting any context or analysis that might offend. *El Imparcial*, a daily in Hermosillo, in the northwestern state of Sonora, has shied away from investigating drug traffickers since the disappearance in April of crime reporter Alfredo Jiménez Mota.

"After Alfredo vanished, we were shocked," says a top editor, Jorge Morales. "I met with reporters and came to the conclusion that we will not do any kind of investigative reporting on organized crime until Alfredo's situation is resolved."

> "Venezuelan television stations pulled opinion programs to comply with a social responsibility law."

Self-censorship is less rampant outside Colombia and Mexico but is still practiced in countries such as Brazil and Venezuela.

Brazil remains a dangerous place for journalists, who are often targeted by corrupt politicians, criminals, and drug traffickers. Four journalists have been killed for their work in the last five years, CPJ research shows. Reporters in cities such as Brasília, São Paulo, and Rio de Janeiro enjoy more protection than their colleagues in isolated regions of the Amazon or in the northeast. In April, editor Maurício Melato Barth, who had spoken out against political corruption, went into hiding with his family two weeks after being attacked by gunmen. Barth, owner and editor of the bimonthly newspaper *Info-Bairros* in the southern city of Itapema, was attacked after publishing articles denouncing government corruption. Police believe the gunmen's intention was not to kill, but to scare Barth into silence.

In Venezuela, the situation is more complicated because self-censorship results from legal restrictions rather than violence against the press. Private television stations have altered programming to comply with the Law of Social Responsibility in Radio and Television, which was approved by the National

Assembly and signed into law by President Hugo Chávez in December 2004. Elsy Barroeta, news director of Globovisión, told CPJ that the station had not restricted its coverage, but acknowledged that some colleagues were concerned about self-censorship. Barroeta said that, under the new guidelines, images of violence during street protests could be aired live but not repeated throughout the day.

The Instituto Prensa y Sociedad (IPYS), a regional press organization, found that three of the most important television stations—Venevisión, Televén, and Radio Caracas Televisión—had dropped 50 percent of their opinion programs since late 2004. María Alejandra Díaz, director of social responsibility with Venezuela's Ministry of Information and Communication, told CPJ that the law restricted only "yellow journalism." She dismissed claims of self-censorship, saying that no one had been fined or sanctioned. Díaz said that proceedings launched by the ministry against more than 20 radio stations were strictly administrative—for not broadcasting the required percentage of Venezuelan music.

Yet overt government action is not the primary threat. Self-censorship is undermining the press in Latin America, especially in those lawless areas that most need investigative reporting and the free flow of information. Drug trafficking, crime, corruption and other issues that affect the daily lives of ordinary people are not being covered fully. This all comes at a crucial moment as voters in Mexico and Colombia prepare for elections in 2006.

Self-censorship is now so pervasive that journalists have begun to talk about it publicly. That may be a glimmer of hope not only for journalism, but also for democratic government.

• • • • • • • • • • •

Carlos Lauría is CPJ's Americas program coordinator.

ARGENTINA

The Argentine press continued to work freely and largely without fear of physical attacks. But several provincial administrations and the national government have manipulated the allocation of state advertising to punish critical reporting and reward supportive media. Two new studies determined that the politically based distribution of government advertising undermines the free press in Argentina.

Poder Ciudadano, a nongovernmental organization that promotes civic participation, found that the distribution of state advertising is governed by "no objective rule," enabling officials to favor "friendly" media outlets. The group's analysis showed that *Clarín*, the largest daily, with a 420,000 weekday circulation, received the most government advertising, a total of 7.1 million pesos (US$2.3 million).

But the study uncovered anomalies elsewhere. *La Nación*, the second-largest daily with a weekday circulation of 160,000, received 17 percent less in government advertising revenue than *Página 12*—even though it reached more than twice the number of readers on weekdays.

"This distortion contrasts with the circulation of both dailies," the report said. The national newsweekly *Noticias*, which criticized the government vigorously, did not receive any government advertising at all.

Poder Ciudadano, which released its report in September, noted that the national government's advertising budget was 88 million pesos (US$29 million). Regional agencies buy advertising as well; the ads publicize such things as hospital services and school programs, and they inform citizens of obligations and rights. The report concluded that "freedom of the press is affected as those outlets that benefit from official advertising could restrict coverage on sensitive issues or provide information influenced by the flow of state money."

A report released in December by the Open Society Justice Initiative, a New York–based group that promotes law reform worldwide, and the Argentine nongovernmental group Asociación por los Derechos Civiles also examined the distribution of government advertising.

The report, titled "Buying the News," found "an entrenched culture of pervasive abuse by provincial government officials who manipulate distribution of advertising for political and personal purposes," and indicated that such decisions are particularly "insidious" in provinces where official advertising is critical for the survival of many media outlets.

• • • • • • • • • • •

Summaries in this chapter were reported and written by Americas Program Coordinator **Carlos Lauría** and Senior Research Associate **Sauro González Rodríguez**. CPJ Washington, D.C., representative **Frank Smyth** reported and wrote the United States summary. The Robert R. McCormick Tribune Foundation provided substantial support toward CPJ's work in the Americas in 2005.

In one of the four provinces studied, Tierra del Fuego, the media derived 75 percent of its advertising revenue from government agencies, the report found.

While national media outlets depend less on government advertising, the report said, "this does not stop the federal government from allocating advertising in ways that can only be described as political favoritism."

In a national survey of reporters, 53 percent of respondents identified the media's dependence on state advertising as the most pressing problem facing the profession. The results, released in November, were based on data provided by 282 respondents to a nationwide questionnaire from the press group Foro de Periodismo Argentino (FOPEA).

The press continued to have a contentious relationship with President Néstor Kirchner and his administration. In July, Kirchner accused the media of being "hysterical" when press reports said increases in retiree payments were politically motivated. Mabel Moralejo, FOPEA's executive director, said the government often sought to discredit journalists who questioned its policies. Kirchner and other officials said the government was expressing its right to disagree with its critics.

Journalists said the government has not been forthcoming or open, citing the lack of even one presidential press conference since Kirchner took office in 2003 and the mere handful of interviews he has given in that time. "The best journalists are the photographers, because they don't ask questions," Kirchner told cabinet members during a July photo-taking session.

Access to public information remains limited, prompting reporters to rely on leaked information and confidential sources. A freedom of information bill, which had been seen by press groups and nongovernmental organizations as an important step toward eliminating government secrecy, died in Congress in 2005. As originally drafted, the measure would have allowed citizens to request, among other things, information about government contracts and the use of public funds. But changes introduced by the Senate would have required those requesting information to explain their reasons, to file an application similar to an affidavit, and, in some cases, to pay a fee. Supporters said the Senate revisions contradicted the goal of the legislation, and the measure languished in the Chamber of Deputies.

A 2003 executive decree from Kirchner was billed as a way to improve public access to government information, although a study by Buenos Aires University questioned its effectiveness. The study found that the executive branch fulfilled just 18 of 71 requests made in a three-month period between April and July. The government claimed a far higher rate, saying that it had fulfilled 96 percent of 386 requests made between April 2004 and July 2005, *La Nación* reported.

BRAZIL

Brazil's constitution guarantees free expression and prohibits censorship. But in practice, the news media are impeded by defamation lawsuits so common they're known as the "industry of compensation" and by lower court judges who routinely interpret Brazilian law in ways that restrict press freedom.

Authorities won important convictions in the recent murders of two journalists, although Brazil remains a dangerous country for the press. Four journalists have been killed for their work in five years. As in much of Latin America, journalists who work in large government and business centers such as Brasília, São Paulo, and Rio de Janeiro often enjoy more protection than their colleagues in impoverished, isolated regions of the Amazon and the northeast. In the country's vast interior—where the influence of government is weak and that of drug trafficking and corruption, strong—journalists censor themselves for fear of retaliation.

In recognition of outstanding journalism in such dangerous conditions, CPJ honored Lúcio Flávio Pinto with one of its International Press Freedom Awards in 2005. An award-winning journalist based in the city of Belém, in the Amazonian state of Pará, Pinto has faced dozens of criminal defamation lawsuits and received numerous threats for his critical reporting on a variety of subjects, including drug trafficking, environmental devastation, and political and corporate corruption. Owner of the small semimonthly *Jornal Pessoal*, Pinto has also criticized the local media for its superficial coverage of the Amazon region.

CPJ has documented a pattern of judicial censorship over several years. In the name of protecting privacy and personal honor, judges banned media outlets from covering corruption allegations involving public officials. Lower court judges used Article 20 of the civil code, in particular, to grant injunctions against the press. In September, for example, a payroll administrator accused of embezzling public funds persuaded a judge to ban the daily *A Tribuna*, based in the port city of Santos, from covering administrative hearings into the charges. The judge also set a daily fine of 50,000 Brazilian reals (US$22,000) should the newspaper fail to comply with his order. The São Paulo State Court of Justice, an appellate court, temporarily set aside the ban while it examined the judge's decision.

Criminal and civil defamation lawsuits against the media have numbered in the thousands over the last five years, according to local news reports. Businessmen, politicians, and public officials often file multiple lawsuits against news outlets and journalists as a form of pressure, straining their financial resources and forcing them to halt their criticisms. As part of the "industry of compensation," plaintiffs seek disproportionately high amounts of money for "moral and material damages."

According to surveys done by legal publications and media associations, judges often admit such lawsuits into court, eventually ruling against the press. Both the penal code and the infamous 1967 Press Law—the latter approved under a military regime—

criminalize defamation and slander. The Press Law sets prison terms of six months to three years for slander, while the penal code calls for three months' to a year's imprisonment for defamation.

In an encouraging sign, one high-ranking judge has been vocal in questioning the press law. Edson Vidigal, president of the Superior Tribunal of Justice, Brazil's second-highest court, has said in several widely covered speeches and interviews that the law was "implicitly revoked by the 1988 Constitution." Vidigal, himself a former journalist, has also declared that Article 20 of the civil code is incompatible with constitutional guarantees of free expression, and that journalists' ability to cover the news will be severely restricted as long as both laws remain in effect.

In August, Magistrate José Celso de Mello Filho of the Supreme Federal Tribunal—Brazil's highest court—issued a ruling that was widely hailed as an important precedent for press freedom. Dismissing allegations of subversion against three journalists of the newsweekly *Veja*—which had published several articles critical of the government—Mello Filho wrote: "It should be noted...when criminal repression of journalistic criticism is sought, as it is in this case, that the state does not have any power over the words, ideas, and convictions voiced by communications media professionals."

The concentration of media ownership remained a concern, particularly in a broadcasting sector dominated by the Organizações Globo group, one of the world's largest telecommunications companies and the national leader in advertising revenue. In some of the largest domestic markets, the same media group controls newspapers, network and cable TV channels, radio stations, and Internet portals. A number of regional politicians own broadcast media outlets, particularly in the northeastern states of Alagoas, Maranhão, and Ceará.

During 2005, community media organizations complained that ANATEL, the telecommunications regulatory agency, closed dozens of community radio stations operating without broadcasting licenses and confiscated their equipment. Several thousand community stations currently on the air have formally requested licenses, but the approval process takes several years. In February, the government established a group of officials from several ministries to find ways to expedite licensing and supervise the operations of community radio stations.

In a positive development, several men charged with murdering journalists in two separate cases were brought to justice. Six men accused in the 2002 murder of TV Globo reporter Tim Lopes were tried, convicted, and sentenced to more than 20 years in prison. The seventh and final defendant, whose testimony helped convict the other six men, was sentenced in October to nine years and four months in prison. Lopes was beaten by members of an organized crime gang and brutally murdered by the group's leader while working on an investigative story about drug traffickers allegedly involved in the sexual exploitation of minors in a Rio de Janeiro slum.

The mastermind was convicted in the Lopes case and received a 28-year sentence. That was doubly encouraging because masterminds are convicted in fewer than 15 percent of journalist murders worldwide, CPJ research shows.

In June, two men charged with involvement in the 2002 murder of journalist Domingos Sávio Brandão Lima Júnior were convicted and sentenced to 15 and 17 years in prison. In September 2002, hired gunmen killed Brandão, the owner and publisher of the Cuiabá-based daily *Folha do Estado* in the state of Mato Grosso. João Arcanjo Ribeiro, identified by federal and state prosecutors as the head of the Mato Grosso mafia, has been charged with killing Brandão in retaliation for his newspaper's criticism of organized crime and illegal gambling. Arcanjo Ribeiro, in prison in Uruguay, was awaiting extradition.

COLOMBIA

In May, CPJ identified Colombia as one the world's five most murderous countries for journalists, a notoriety earned by 12 work-connected slayings in the country since 2000. Over the past decade, 28 journalists in Colombia have been killed for their work.

Still, deadly violence tapered off for the second consecutive year, with only one journalist slain in 2005. The government claimed credit for the decline, but many journalists assert that pervasive self-censorship has now replaced widespread murder. An October investigative report by CPJ found that threats, assaults, and intimidation continue from all sides in the ongoing civil war, causing the press to severely limit its coverage of armed conflict, human rights abuses, organized crime, drug trafficking, and corruption.

For CPJ's report, "Untold Stories," Bogotá-based journalist Chip Mitchell interviewed three dozen journalists during reporting trips to strife-ridden provinces such as Arauca, Córdoba, and Caquetá. Editors, reporters, and other media professionals said they routinely muzzle themselves because they fear physical retribution from leftist guerrillas and right-wing paramilitaries, along with harassment from government troops and officials. News is sometimes censored before broadcast or publication. In other cases, probing journalists are forced to abandon stories because of intimidation. Most frequently, investigations never even get started because the threat of violence is so pervasive. Self-censorship is most extreme among regional media in provincial areas, where the government's presence is weak and state protection minimal.

Although the government exerts little formal control over news content, Colombian authorities, including high-ranking officials in President Álvaro Uribe's administration, often persuade media outlets to withhold reporting. Economic factors also contribute to self-censorship. Journalists at short-staffed news outlets must often sell advertising, putting themselves in the difficult position of reporting on the very people who help them make a living. Most full-time Colombian journalists earn less than 800,000 pesos (US$350) a month.

"Untold Stories" was released on October 29 at a CPJ conference in Bogotá. CPJ Deputy Director Joel Simon moderated a panel discussion that was co-sponsored by the Colombian Fundación para la Libertad de Prensa (FLIP). Carlos Cortés, FLIP's executive director, and María Teresa Ronderos, the group's president, participated in the panel. Four journalists quoted in the report gave detailed presentations on the dangers and implications of reporting in Colombia. One panelist, Angel María León, from the conflict-ridden province of Arauca, said death threats had forced the local press corps to travel in armed caravans simply to get to press conferences.

During CPJ's mission to Bogotá, Simon met with Vice President Francisco Santos and other government officials to discuss how the government can better enable local journalists to work without fear. Government officials acknowledged that armed groups continued to menace the press but pointed to their efforts to provide bodyguards to journalists in conflict zones. They also said that the government's peace and counterinsurgency efforts are creating a safer environment for all Colombians, including journalists.

But issues vital to Colombian voters, including crime and corruption, are going uncovered as the 2006 parliamentary and presidential elections approach. In a report released in September, Eduardo Bertoni, special rapporteur for freedom of expression for the Organization of American States (OAS), concluded that "many journalists have been forced to resort to self-censorship on certain topics in certain regions." Based on interviews with journalists, human rights activists, and community leaders in April, the OAS report—titled "Impunity, Self-censorship, and Armed Internal Conflict: An Analysis of the State of Freedom of Expression in Colombia"—linked the recent drop in journalist killings to the rise of self-censorship in the local media.

Frank Smyth, CPJ's Washington, D.C., representative and a security expert, visited the southwestern province of Valle del Cauca in June to assess press conditions. Smyth, who traveled with a delegation of press freedom organizations, found a prevailing climate of fear among provincial journalists.

At times, the administration of President Álvaro Uribe has contributed to that climate by accusing journalists of having ties to the guerrillas. During a radio interview in June, Uribe falsely suggested that reporter Hollman Morris had advance word of a guerrilla attack on government troops in the southern province of Putumayo. Uribe later retracted the claim, but Morris, who was working on a documentary for the BBC, had to cut short his visit to Putumayo in fear of retaliation.

Impunity continues to be the norm in Colombia. An overburdened justice system has been incapable of solving the 28 cases of journalists slain over the last decade. CPJ reported in May that murder is the leading cause of job-related deaths among journalists worldwide and that murder with impunity is the most urgent threat to all journalists.

A veteran radio news host was killed in the northeastern city of Cúcuta on January 11. Julio Hernando Palacios Sánchez, whose Radio Lemas program focused heavily on local corruption, was gunned down by two unidentified men aboard a motorcycle. Palacios had survived an attack nine years earlier, when assailants hurled a grenade into his office that failed to explode, The Associated Press reported. No one has been charged in his murder.

That sort of impunity weighs heavily on the news media, especially in the country's interior. Local reporters told CPJ that there are many topics they dare not touch.

If not for fear of reprisal, "I would be investigating the links from politicians to the paramilitaries and guerrillas, and the money laundering by certain individuals and these same groups," said Jorge Eliécer Quintero Cuéllar, a journalist with *Diario de Huila* in Caquetá. Added Alfredo Martín Rodríguez of La Jota Estéreo in Valle del Cauca: "One thing you don't want to touch is drug trafficking. Even more risky is corruption."

Minimal state presence in vast areas of the country continues to leave journalists at the mercy of illegal armed groups. In October, a nearly monthlong armed blockade by leftist guerrillas in the northwestern province of Arauca left journalists confined to the capital city. The media were not able to report about serious events during the blockade, such as rebels torching vehicles and blowing up bridges and electricity towers.

Journalists in Bogotá and other large urban centers work more freely than their colleagues in the country's interior, but they, too, face pressure and intimidation. Funeral wreaths were delivered in May to the offices of three nationally known journalists. The wreaths came with cards inviting the journalists to their own burials. One of the three, Daniel Coronell, also received e-mail messages threatening the life of his 6-year-old daughter.

Coronell, who directs a news show on the TV network Canal Uno and writes a column for the weekly magazine *Semana*, tracked the messages to a computer in the Bogotá mansion of former congressman Carlos Náder Simmonds, a close friend of Uribe. Náder later admitted sending one e-mail but claimed it was misinterpreted. An investigation by the attorney general's office shed little light.

Fearing for the life of his daughter, Coronell accepted a one-year fellowship at Stanford University in the United States and left Colombia with his family in August. He took a leave from his TV show but continued to write his column for *Semana*. He told CPJ's Mitchell: "The possibilities for investigation have deteriorated. But the safety of my daughter comes first."

CUBA

Cuba remained one of the world's leading jailers of journalists, second only to China. Two journalists were imprisoned during the year, joining 22 others who have been jailed since a massive crackdown on the independent press in March 2003. On the second anniversary of that notorious sweep, more than 100 prominent Latin American writers—including Tomás Eloy Martínez, Sergio Ramírez, Carlos Fuentes, Elena Poniatowska, Daniel Santoro, and Antonio Caballero—joined CPJ in signing a letter to President Fidel Castro Ruz calling for the immediate, unconditional release of the imprisoned journalists.

Castro's government had paroled six journalists in 2004 to help win renewed diplomatic ties to the European Union. But without a political incentive in 2005, his government paroled only one journalist, Mario Enrique Mayo Hernández, subjected many others to harassment, and hardened its rhetorical line once again. In an ominous speech in July, Castro likened opposition activities to "barefaced acts of treason."

Most of the jailed journalists remained far from their homes, adding to the heavy burden on their families. They denounced unsanitary prison conditions and inadequate medical care, and they complained of being fed rotten food. Many of them were allowed family visits only once every three months and marital visits only once every four months—a schedule of visits far less frequent than those allowed most inmates. Relatives were harassed for talking to the foreign press, protesting the journalists' incarceration, and gathering signatures calling for their release.

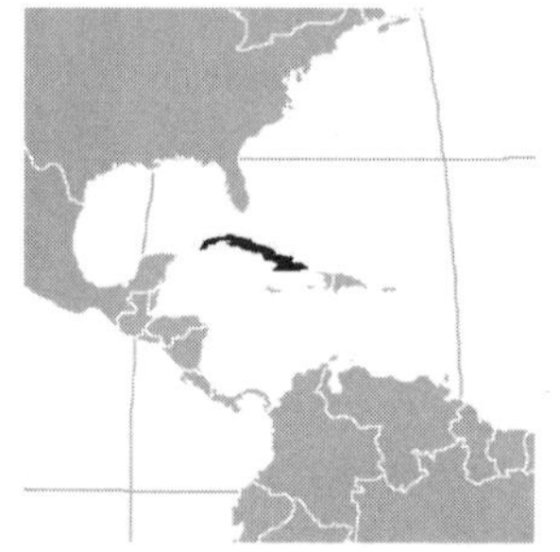

Journalists who were ill before being jailed saw their health worsen in prison; some were transferred to the hospital at Combinado del Este Prison in Havana or to prison infirmaries. Others, such as Víctor Rolando Arroyo and Adolfo Fernández Saínz, went on hunger strikes to protest the poor conditions. Because prison authorities limited outside contact and refused to disclose information, families were unable to monitor the journalists' health.

But punishing journalists for exercising their right to free expression had some unintended consequences for the Cuban government: An increasing number of imprisoned journalists smuggled reports out of jail for publication abroad, on Miami-based Web sites such as *CubaNet* and *Nueva Prensa Cubana*. And relatives of imprisoned journalists and dissidents joined Cuba's growing independent press movement, reporting details about prison conditions and disclosing cases of mistreatment.

Two journalists released on medical parole in 2004—Raúl Rivero and Manuel Vázquez Portal—were allowed to leave the island in 2005. Rivero settled in Madrid, Spain, where he wrote for the online *Encuentro en la Red*, which is run by Cuban exiles, and began a column in the daily *El Mundo*. Vázquez Portal settled in Miami, where he became an editor for *CubaNet* and started a column in the Spanish-language edition of *The Miami Herald*. Two other journalists paroled in 2004, Oscar Espinosa Chepe and Jorge Olivera Castillo, continued to work as independent journalists in Havana, despite warnings they could be sent back to prison if they didn't maintain "good behavior."

In May, authorities detained and expelled at least five foreign journalists—two Italians and three Poles—who traveled to Cuba to cover an unprecedented gathering of opposition activists. The two-day meeting, the first such event held by the opposition, was organized by the Assembly to Promote Civil Society (APSC), an umbrella group of civil-society and dissident groups. The government said that the journalists were expelled for violating Cuban immigration law because they traveled on tourist visas, not work visas. But CPJ's analysis shows that it is unlikely journalists could have obtained work visas to report on opposition activities. Under Cuban immigration regulations, foreign reporters must apply for journalist visas through Cuban embassies abroad. According to CPJ research, Cuban officials grant visas to foreign journalists selectively, and they routinely exclude media outlets deemed unfriendly.

Repression intensified midyear after Castro delivered a speech in July warning that the government wouldn't tolerate dissent. Referring to an opposition protest that was met with a police crackdown, Castro said, "This time the people, angrier than before over such barefaced acts of treason, intervened with patriotic fervor and didn't allow a single mercenary to move. And this is what will happen whenever traitors and mercenaries go a millimeter beyond the point that our revolutionary people...are willing to accept."

Oscar Mario González, a journalist who covered the APSC congress, was one of the first victims of this renewed crackdown. González, a journalist with the independent news agency Grupo de Trabajo Decoro, was arrested on July 22 and held without trial. According to Ana Leonor Díaz, director of Grupo de Trabajo Decoro, a police investigator told González's relatives that he would be prosecuted under Law 88 for the Protection of Cuba's National Independence and Economy. The law provides for up to 20 years in prison for anyone who commits "acts that in agreement with imperialist interests are aimed at subverting the internal order of the nation and destroy its political, economic, and social system."

A second journalist who covered the APSC meeting, Albert Santiago Du Bouchet Hernández, was imprisoned the next month. Du Bouchet Hernández, director of the independent news agency Havana Press, was arrested on August 6, tried three days later, and handed a one-year jail term—all without the knowledge of his family, who learned of his detention only after the journalist smuggled a note out of prison. He was detained while on a reporting trip to the town of Artemisa, 38 miles (60 kilometers) from Havana, and charged with "disrespecting" the local chief of police and resisting arrest. His wife, Bárbara Pérez Araya, said that the charges were fabricated and the journalist did not have access to a lawyer before or during the trial.

Starting in July and continuing throughout the year, the government organized demonstrations known as "repudiation acts." Government supporters congregated outside the homes of opposition members and independent journalists, intimidated the occupants, and prevented them from leaving their homes or receiving visitors. On October 10 and for the next three days, dozens of government supporters harassed a group of independent journalists who had launched an online magazine, *Consenso*, in December 2004. According to a statement from *Consenso*, the crowd kept journalists from entering a building in Havana for a weekly meeting, hurled insults, and accused the journalists of being "anti-Cuban and counter-revolutionary." Two journalists were pushed around and another was detained by police for two hours.

In addition to outright confrontation, authorities kept up a low-intensity intimidation campaign. In February, for example, state security officials summoned journalist Iván García Quintero to a Havana police station, where they interrogated him for two hours and threatened to imprison him for subversion. García continued to write despite the risk.

HAITI

Amid civil unrest, political turmoil, and spiraling violence, the poorest country in the Western hemisphere remained a very dangerous place for journalists. The fall of former President Jean-Bertrand Aristide in 2004 created a political vacuum; street gangs, drug traffickers, corrupt police, ex-soldiers from the disbanded military, and the ousted leader's supporters sought violently to fill it. Journalists found themselves targeted from several directions.

Rising insecurity was the most notable sign that the transitional government led by Prime Minister Gérard Latortue had failed to gain a strong grip on authority. Like the country's interim leaders, the United Nations Stabilization Mission in Haiti (MINUSTAH), with 7,500 troops, drew sharp criticism for doing too little to curb frequent kidnappings and killings.

The absence of effective state control endangered journalists covering the turmoil. Robenson Laraque, a reporter with the private radio station Tele Contact in the city of Petit-Goâve, was critically injured during a March 20 clash between U.N. peacekeepers and ex-soldiers. Laraque was covering the gun battle from the balcony of Tele Contact's offices when he was struck by two shots, to the head and neck. Transferred to a hospital in Cuba, he died two weeks later.

Several witnesses reported that the shots appeared to have been fired by U.N. peacekeepers, Wilner Saint-Preux, a Tele Contact journalist, told CPJ. Witnesses also reported that Laraque was holding a microphone when he was shot, Tele Contact editor Fritz Ariel Nelson said. David Beer, the U.N. Civilian Police Commissioner at the time of the skirmish, said U.N. officials were investigating the shooting and would make public their findings. Col. El Ouafi Boulbars, spokesman for the U.N. forces in Haiti, told CPJ in late October that the inquiry was continuing.

Journalists in the capital, Port-au-Prince, severely limited their movements in response to a wave of murders, kidnappings, rapes, and gang-related crimes. People were abducted in broad daylight, and shootings emptied downtown streets. Human rights groups and news organizations reported in the fall that more than 1,000 people had been killed in unrest in Port-au-Prince over the previous 12 months. More than a dozen journalists in Port-au-Prince went into exile.

This blight was reflected in the July 2005 slaying of Jacques Roche, a well-known poet and cultural editor of the Port-au-Prince-based daily *Le Matin*. Roche was kidnapped and killed; his handcuffed, bullet-ridden body was found in a Port-au-Prince slum. The *St. Petersburg Times* reported that the kidnappers who seized Roche sold the journalist to a gang that wanted him dead for sympathizing with an anti-Aristide group.

According to Franck Séguy, a colleague at *Le Matin*, there is wide speculation that Roche may have been killed because he hosted a television show for the 184 Group, a coalition of civil-society organizations that opposed Aristide.

Judge Jean Peres Paul, who is in charge of the investigation, told CPJ that three suspects had been identified and preliminary charges filed. He said he couldn't comment on the possible motive. CPJ is continuing its own inquiries.

Insecurity and corruption further rotted the country's judicial system. Virtually no progress was reported in the government's troubled investigation into the 2000 murder of Jean-Léopold Dominique, owner and director of Radio Haïti Inter and one of the country's most renowned journalists. In March, Minister of Justice Bernard Gousse named a new examining judge to conduct the government's third investigation into the murder. The appointment of Judge Peres Paul came nine months after an appeals court ruled that proceedings had to resume after being stalled for nearly a year.

The Dominique case has been fraught with problems. The first examining judge, Claudy Gassant, fled Haiti in 2002 after being threatened. The next judge, Bernard Saint-Vil, sent a 33-page indictment to prosecutors accusing purported gang members Dymsley Millien, Jeudi-Jean Daniel, Philippe Markington, Ralph Léger, Ralph Joseph, and Freud Junior Desmarattes of the killing. Yet charges were dropped against three of the defendants, and the others escaped from custody. Dominique's wife, Michèle Montas, has called the investigation flawed and said that authorities "failed to charge the masterminds behind the murder." News reports in March said that documents in the Dominique case were missing, but Gousse denied those reports and said the files were intact.

The Haitian press is deeply polarized, and many journalists are seen as having close ties to political factions. Journalists sympathetic to Aristide and the Lavalas political party harshly criticized Haitian authorities for failing to crack down on alleged corruption and human rights violations by police, accusing the interim government of launching a campaign aimed at intimidating the independent media.

Government officials, in turn, criticized several private radio stations for giving airtime to pro-Aristide gangs, called *chimères*, which dominate Port-au-Prince slums such as Cité Soleil and Bel Air. And Aristide supporters have accused the interim government of jailing hundreds of Lavalas militants without formal charges.

On July 20, Haiti's Council of Ministers directed the ministers of justice, culture, public works, transportation, and communications to "take appropriate measures" against journalists and news outlets providing a forum to slum residents to spread "hate speech," the local media reported. On August 5, more than 10 Port-au-Prince-based radio stations suspended news broadcasting in protest.

Guyler Delva, secretary-general of the Haitian Journalists Association, called the directive "arbitrary" and said that it was an attempt to stifle the press. The interim government did not ultimately impose any sanctions against news outlets.

Haitian journalists have voiced concern that the presidential and legislative elections, planned for 2006, would do little to bring stability to the country. They say that truly free elections cannot take place in a climate of fear.

In September, journalists and media executives representing several private outlets created a new press group called the Association of Independent Media of Haiti. The group included journalists from Radio Mélodie FM, Radio/Teleginen, Radio Solidarité, Télémax, Tropic FM, Chaine 11, Chaine 46, Megastar, Haïti en Marche, and Agence Haïtienne de Presse. The group is expected to monitor press freedom and other journalism issues. A second organization, called SOS Journalistes, was formed to protect and defend the Haitian press. Its leaders include Delva, a Reuters reporter and longtime press advocate.

MEXICO

Journalists working along the U.S.-Mexico border were under siege from organized criminals targeting them for coverage of drug trafficking. One reporter was killed for her work and another went missing, making northern Mexico one of the most dangerous spots for journalists in Latin America. Facing intimidation and attack, journalists in the northern states reported greater self-censorship.

Guadalupe García Escamilla, a crime reporter with Stereo 91 XHNOE in Nuevo Laredo, died on April 16 from injuries she suffered in an April 5 shooting in front of her radio station. Alfredo Jiménez Mota, a crime reporter for the Hermosillo-based daily *El Imparcial*, has been missing since April 2 and is feared dead. CPJ is also investigating the

April murder of Raúl Gibb Guerrero, owner and director of *La Opinión*, a daily newspaper in the eastern state of Veracruz, to determine whether it was directly related to his journalism.

In the wake of these deadly attacks, Mexican President Vicente Fox met with a CPJ delegation at the organization's Manhattan headquarters on September 15. In response to the violence, Fox announced he would ask Mexico's attorney general to appoint a special prosecutor to investigate crimes against free expression. Fox also promised to consider the creation of a panel of national experts to evaluate how federal authorities can fight crimes against the press.

Before meeting with Fox, CPJ sent the president's office a proposal urging greater and more permanent involvement by federal authorities in the investigation of crimes against free expression. Protection of free expression was particularly urgent, CPJ representatives said, in light of presidential elections in July 2006. Fox, whose term ends in 2006, said he recognized the problem of violence against border reporters and pledged his government's commitment to protecting journalists.

The meeting with the Mexican president culminated months of intensive advocacy and investigation by CPJ. Four Mexican journalists have been killed in direct reprisal for their work during the last five years, and CPJ is investigating the slayings of five other journalists during that same period to determine whether those killings were work-related. State and local authorities, those normally responsible for investigating murders, have failed time and again to solve crimes against the press, CPJ found.

CPJ research shows that state and local authorities are more prone to corruption, have fewer resources, and are subject to less accountability. Their investigative failures, in turn, have created a climate of impunity that leave the media open to continuing attack.

Concerned about the sluggish pace of the investigations, CPJ representatives traveled to Mexico City in June to meet with José Luis Vasconcelos, the top prosecutor in the organized crime division of the federal attorney general's office. Federal authorities had recently stepped in to take over three of the murder investigations, among them the 2004 slaying of Tijuana editor Francisco Ortiz Franco.

Vasconcelos told CPJ that the Arellano Félix drug cartel was behind the slaying of Ortiz Franco, an editor with the muckraking weekly *Zeta*. Federal authorities, he said, rounded up more than 100 people as part of a broad crackdown against the gang. Vasconcelos noted that one of the suspected gunmen, Jorge Eduardo Ronquillo Delgado (known as "El Niño"), was executed by fellow members of the Arellano Félix cartel in October 2004.

At large, Vasconcelos said, were the two alleged masterminds: Arturo Villarreal Albarrán (known as "El Nalgón") and Jorge Briceño (known as "El Cholo"). Authorities had warrants seeking their arrest on drug trafficking charges, he said.

The federal government took other steps in response to the violence. In July, the attorney general's office launched a telephone hotline for journalists who have been threatened or intimidated. The hotline, which received dozens of calls in its initial weeks, solicited tips and offered advice on responding to threats.

Beginning in August, the attorney general's office appointed its own representatives in several states—including Baja California, Chihuahua, Durango, Michoacán, Sinaloa, Tabasco, Yucatán, and Oaxaca—to investigate aggression and threats against journalists.

Journalists in Mexico City continued to report freely on crime and political corruption. But as the war between Mexico's powerful drug cartels intensified in the north, some local newspapers stopped their investigations into organized crime as a way to avoid danger. One northern newspaper, the Nuevo Laredo–based *El Mañana,* decided to limit its coverage after editor Roberto Javier Mora García was stabbed to death in March 2004. Heriberto Cantú, the editorial director, said the paper's reporting now excludes context for and analysis of sensitive issues.

After the disappearance of reporter Jiménez in the northern state of Sonora, *El Imparcial* announced it would no longer investigate drug trafficking and organized crime. Jorge Morales, a top editor of *El Imparcial,* said the decision came after a meeting with the paper's reporters. "There are no guarantees for journalists who cover crime and drug-related issues," Morales told CPJ. "We decided to stop doing our own investigations after Alfredo disappeared. It's a very dangerous business."

PANAMA

Panama took steps to improve press freedom, lifting broad deterrents against criticism of public officials and repealing laws that gave authorities vast censorship powers. The National Assembly approved a bill with wide-ranging reforms in May, and it was signed by President Martín Torrijos two months later.

Panamanian journalists said the changes were encouraging given the country's history of institutionalized harassment of the press. But they also noted that some of the changes were cosmetic, eliminating provisions that had already fallen into disuse. Criminal defamation statutes remain on the books, they said, and pose a serious, ongoing threat to journalists.

The 2005 measure did repeal many of the country's infamous "gag laws," the set of restrictive statutes and decrees enacted under military rule in the late 1960s and commonly used by Panamanian authorities to quash dissenting views and prosecute those who reported critically.

The new law explicitly bars public officials from imposing monetary or penal sanctions against journalists and others who allegedly "disrespect" them. These *desacato* (disrespect) provisions had been scattered throughout Panama's criminal and administrative codes, protecting the president, legislators, judges, prosecutors, governors, mayors, and clerics.

The new measure repealed Law 11, adopted in 1978 under the military rule of Gen. Omar Torrijos. Law 11 empowered a government censorship board to block publication of what it considered to be "false" news or "false" facts. The archaic Decree 251, a remnant of military rule enacted in 1969, was also scrapped. Under Decree 251, a censorship board could block materials "that make the moral texture of the media weaker, deforming the concept of human, moral, and family values." Laws granting the government the authority to license journalists were also struck from the books.

While lifting many onerous provisions, the 2005 measure imposed a restrictive new requirement on the press. The law states: "All individuals who feel offended by a publication or broadcast in the media have the right to publish or broadcast in those media the clarifications or replies they deem necessary." The "clarifications or replies" must be published or broadcast within a day and with the same prominence, according to the measure. The law does not explicitly say that the clarifications must be based in fact.

The new law does not shield journalists from criminal penalties, either. Panama's penal code still includes criminal defamation provisions that allow for penalties of up to two years in prison. Any journalist who "spreads false, exaggerated, or misleading news or propagates rumors" that endanger the national economy can be imprisoned for up to three years; the sentence can be doubled if the news leads to the devaluation of the national currency. Some journalists and press freedom advocates also expressed concern that Articles 307 and 308 of the penal code still contain language similar to the former *desacato* provisions.

An egregious reminder of the consequences faced by journalists came in July, when Supreme Court Judge Winston Spadafora filed a criminal defamation complaint against Jean Marcel Chéry, a reporter with the Panama City-based daily *La Prensa*. Chéry wrote that month that a Supreme Court decision effectively canceled Spadafora's US$2 million debt to a government canal agency known as the Interoceanic Regional Authority.

In a separate case, Spadafora filed a civil lawsuit that sought US$2 million in damages from EPASA, publisher of the Panama City daily *El Panamá America*, for a 2001 report that allegedly "insulted" him when he was minister of government and justice. The suit also named the story's authors—Gustavo Aparicio and Chéry, who was reporting for *El Panamá América* at the time. In addition, Spadafora sought confiscation of Chéry's salary in the amount of US$18,753.

The article said that public money was used to build a road leading to private property owned by Spadafora and Comptroller Alvin Weeden. Aparicio and Chéry were initially sentenced to a year in prison in 2004, but in August of that year outgoing president Mireya Moscoso pardoned them, along with 85 other Panamanian journalists then facing criminal defamation charges.

PERU

Attacks and threats against the press, particularly in Peru's interior, continued a disturbing upward trend that began in 2004. After lessening in frequency and severity after President Alberto Fujimori fled office in 2000, assaults on journalists were reported regularly in 2005. The Lima-based press freedom organization Instituto Prensa y Sociedad, considered the authoritative local source, documented 19 attacks in the first nine months of 2005 alone. CPJ's analysis found that most of these were carried out by peasant and worker groups, protesters, security guards, businessmen, and relatives of government officials whose actions were scrutinized by the press. The threat was fundamentally different from the government-sponsored attacks that marked the Fujimori era.

Authorities in two different regions moved to prosecute local mayors on charges of plotting the murders of journalists in 2004. In December, Yungay Mayor Amaro León and two accomplices were convicted in the 2004 slaying of Antonio de la Torre Echeandía, a radio host who had criticized the mayor for alleged corruption. A judge in the northern region of Ancash sentenced the defendants to 17 years in prison.

Also in November, an appellate court found sufficient evidence to try Pucallpa Mayor Luis Valdez Villacorta on charges of ordering the April 2004 murder of radio host Alberto Rivera Fernández. A political activist and president of the local journalists association in the city in the eastern Ucayali region, Rivera had accused the mayor of involvement in drug trafficking. Six other men were being held pending trial; two of the defendants were said to have implicated Valdez as the mastermind.

Although journalists in Peru are free to work without government restrictions, a number were targeted with criminal defamation lawsuits designed to punish and silence them. Over the last several years, CPJ has documented a pattern of government officials and business people filing such cases. They include a prominent businessman who filed at least three criminal defamation complaints; a ruling party congressman who lodged a similar criminal lawsuit; and an influential government official who responded to published reports of government corruption by threatening to file lawsuits and launch investigations of journalists.

In May 2005, Judge Alfredo Catacora Acevedo found British freelance journalist Sally Bowen guilty of criminal defamation and ordered her and her publisher to pay 10,000 Peruvian soles (US$3,000) to businessman Fernando Zevallos. Catacora also sentenced Bowen to one year of probation and restricted her movements both within and outside of the country. International and local press freedom organizations, including CPJ, protested Bowen's conviction and denounced the chilling message it sent to all Peruvian journalists.

In June, after finding numerous irregularities in Catacora's handling of the trial, an appellate court overturned Bowen's conviction and ordered a retrial before a new judge.

In his criminal complaint, Zevallos said that Bowen, who is based in the capital, Lima, where she has lived for the last 16 years, and co-author Jane Holligan had irreparably harmed his image in their book, "The Imperfect Spy: The Many Lives of Vladimiro Montesinos." Proceedings were pending against Holligan, who lives in Scotland.

Zevallos' lawsuit revolved around a single sentence in the 493-page book, which details the activities of now-imprisoned former intelligence chief Vladimiro Montesinos. The book quotes an imprisoned U.S. Drug Enforcement Administration informant as saying Zevallos was a drug trafficker with close ties to Montesinos.

Catacora, in reaching his now-defunct verdict, said Zevallos had never been convicted of a crime. Zevallos, founder of the former AeroContinente airline, has denied drug trafficking allegations, although official accusations have dogged him for years. Drug trafficking charges against him were pending in Peru in late 2005; the U.S. government has labeled him a "significant foreign narcotics trafficker" and barred U.S. businesses and individuals from doing business with him.

In May, U.S. Sen. Bill Nelson of Florida asked Peruvian President Alejandro Toledo to open a new investigation into the 1989 murder of *Tampa Tribune* reporter Todd Carper Smith. Nelson's request was prompted by information that emerged in late 2004, including a December 2004 report by The Associated Press that cited a transcript from the secret trial of a Shining Path Maoist guerrilla member convicted of the murder in 1993. The AP, citing the transcript, reported that a police intelligence report had identified Zevallos as an alleged mastermind in the killing.

According to local reports, drug traffickers mistook Smith for a U.S. drug enforcement agent and recruited the Shining Path to abduct and execute him. Smith was in Peru on a working vacation to write about the Maoist guerrillas. Despite Nelson's request, no new investigation was immediately opened.

UNITED STATES

An investigation into the leak of a CIA officer's identity erupted, with one reporter compelled to testify about his confidential source, another jailed for 85 days before she testified, and a high-level White House aide indicted on federal charges of perjury, false statements, and obstruction of justice. Confidentiality of sources was under attack in a number of other U.S. cases as well. In New Orleans, authorities restricted media access and harassed journalists in several incidents in the aftermath of Hurricane Katrina. And in Washington, D.C., federal auditors concluded that the Bush administration had broken the law by disseminating "covert propaganda."

New York Times reporter Judith Miller was jailed in July for refusing to disclose information about a confidential source before a federal grand jury investigating the 2003 leak of the identity of CIA operative Valerie Wilson. (Wilson was first identified by her maiden name of Valerie Plame in a July 2003 column by syndicated writer Robert Novak.) *Time* magazine's Matthew Cooper, who was under subpoena and on the verge of imprisonment, testified in July after he said he received a personal waiver from his source, Vice Presidential Chief of Staff I. Lewis "Scooter" Libby.

Miller agreed in September to testify under limited conditions after receiving what she described as a voluntary and personal waiver from the same source. The grand jury indicted Libby a month later for allegedly lying about his role in the leak. He was not charged directly with identifying the CIA officer; instead, the government alleged that Libby lied to investigators and the grand jury about what he told reporters and how he learned the CIA officer's identity. Karl Rove, the White House deputy chief of staff, remained under investigation. Special prosecutor Patrick Fitzgerald convened a new grand jury in November, shortly after *Washington Post* reporter Bob Woodward acknowledged to investigators in a sworn deposition that he had received information about Wilson's wife in June 2003.

Miller, Cooper, and other journalists could be called as witnesses if the case against Libby or any other defendant goes to trial.

CPJ denounced Miller's jailing, saying it sent the wrong message to the world. Regimes in Venezuela, Cameroon, Nepal, and Egypt cited the imprisonment to justify repressive measures in their own nations. Lawmakers in the U.S. House and Senate introduced bills to establish a federal "shield" law to protect journalists from revealing confidential sources. But the measures, which echo laws already on the books in more than 30 states, did not advance toward passage during the year. Miller herself became the focus of controversy as other journalists and her own colleagues questioned how much she had disclosed to her editors as the case proceeded. Miller defended her actions but resigned from *The Times* in November.

Miller was not the only U.S. journalist confined in 2005. Jim Taricani, an investigative reporter with the NBC-owned WJAR-TV in Providence, R.I., was released in April after serving four months of home confinement for refusing to identify the person who gave him an FBI surveillance tape. A federal judge imposed home confinement rather than jail because of Taricani's heart condition.

The year ended with two major stories built on confidential government sources. In November, *The Post* reported that the CIA operated secret prisons in foreign countries. The next month, *The Times* exposed a secret government program to eavesdrop without warrants on certain phone and e-mail conversations. The prison revelation prompted an international uproar, and the eavesdropping disclosure prompted Congressional outcry.

At the same time, the confidential sources themselves came under government scrutiny, raising the possibility of new confrontations over free press issues. The Justice Department launched a criminal investigation into the sources for the eavesdropping story; the CIA asked the department to probe the prison story as well.

In a high-profile civil case, judges continued to demand that reporters disclose their confidential sources. In November, a federal judge held *Washington Post* reporter Walter Pincus in contempt for refusing to name his sources in a lawsuit filed against the government by Wen Ho Lee. The former U.S. nuclear scientist, who was suspected but cleared of espionage charges, alleges in his lawsuit that government officials illegally leaked his personnel files to the press. The same month, an appellate court refused to consider an appeal from four other reporters previously held in contempt in the case.

After Hurricane Katrina struck New Orleans and the Gulf states on August 29, the Federal Emergency Management Agency urged news organizations not to photograph dead bodies. Numerous bodies were left in public areas for days after the hurricane amid a government recovery effort that was widely criticized for being slow and ineffective. *The Washington Post* reported that in at least one instance state authorities echoed the demand not to photograph the dead.

New Orleans police adopted an aggressive stance in several reported cases. On September 1, city police ripped a camera from the neck of Lucas Oleniuk of the *Toronto Star* and removed the camera's memory cards, robbing the photographer of more than 350 images. The seized images included "officers delivering a fierce beating to two suspects," the *Toronto Star* reported. The same day, Gordon Russell of the New Orleans–based *Times-Picayune* wrote that he and another photographer were slammed against a wall and had their gear thrown to the ground by police. On September 7, NBC News anchor Brian Williams reported that he and his crew were ordered to stop filming a National Guard unit securing a downtown store. "I have searched my mind for some justification for why I can't be reporting in a calm and heavily defended American city and cannot find one," Williams told *The Washington Post*.

On October 18, a New Orleans police officer was caught on film harassing an Associated Press Television News producer whose crew was filming two other officers beating a man suspected of public intoxication. Two of the officers were fired and one was suspended.

In Washington, federal auditors concluded that President George W. Bush's administration disseminated "covert propaganda," in violation of U.S. law, by purchasing favorable domestic news coverage of national education policies. A report from the Government Accountability Office (GAO) found that the administration made undisclosed payments to commentator Armstrong Williams to promote the administration's education agenda. The administration also used public funds to hire a public relations firm to analyze media perceptions of the Republican Party, the GAO reported. The case was referred to federal prosecutors for further review.

In late November, the *Los Angeles Times* reported that the U.S. military secretly paid Iraqi newspapers to run stories that favorably depicted conditions in Iraq without disclosing that the articles were written by military "information operations" officers. The articles were placed in Baghdad newspapers through a private, Washington, D.C.-based firm. Senate leaders sought explanations from the Pentagon.

Another investigation centered on political influence on the news media. The former chairman of the Corporation for Public Broadcasting (CPB), Kenneth Y. Tomlinson, resigned from the board in October after an inquiry by the agency's inspector general. Investigators found that Tomlinson had steered a conservative-oriented talk show onto public television and used "political tests" to hire a former Republican national chairman as the agency's new president. CPB, a federally funded nonprofit, provides $400 million annually to public television and radio; by law, it is to be free of political influence. Tomlinson contested the findings, saying he sought to instill balance in public broadcasting.

The Guardian of London reported in September that U.S. military interrogators allegedly tried to recruit a detained journalist as a spy. Interrogators allegedly told a journalist for Qatar-based Al-Jazeera that he would be released if he agreed to inform U.S. intelligence authorities about the satellite news network's activities.

CPJ interviewed military officials and the journalist's lawyer, and reviewed letters said to have come from the journalist. The journalist, Sami Muhyideen al-Haj, an assistant cameraman for Al-Jazeera, was arrested by Pakistani authorities along the Afghan-Pakistani border while on assignment in December 2001. He was later transferred to the U.S. military facility at Guantánamo Bay, where he was held as an accused "enemy combatant," according to his lawyer, Clive Stafford Smith.

U.S. Navy Lt. Cmdr. Chris Loundermon declined to respond to the allegation or to confirm al-Haj's detainment. Loundermon, a spokesman for the U.S. Southern Command, which administers the Guantánamo military facility, said the topic involved confidential intelligence information.

In Iraq, CPJ documented seven cases in which local reporters, photographers, and camera operators were detained by U.S. forces for prolonged periods without charge or the disclosure of any supporting evidence. At least three documented detentions exceeded 100 days, while the others spanned many weeks. The detentions involved journalists working for CBS News, Reuters, The Associated Press, and Agence France-Presse, among other news agencies.

Four of those Iraqi journalists were still in custody on December 1, when CPJ conducted its annual worldwide census of imprisoned journalists. U.S. military spokesmen said the detainees were deemed security threats but would not disclose any specific supporting evidence. CPJ and other news and advocacy organizations continue to seek information about the imprisoned journalists.

VENEZUELA

CPJ traced a decline in physical attacks against journalists in 2005, as five years of violent political upheaval finally subsided. President Hugo Chávez Frías further consolidated his control following a tumultuous recall vote the previous year that saw journalists assaulted and harassed by government supporters, opposition activists, and security forces. In 2005, the frequency of physical assaults declined by half, and the severity of the assaults diminished as well, CPJ data show. But one type of threat was replaced by another, as the Chávez administration moved toward institutionalized repression and new legal restraints against the press.

Two restrictive new legal measures—one expanding *desacato* (disrespect) provisions, the other setting "social responsibility" constraints on radio and television—went into effect during the year. These new measures could be used to silence government opponents and create a climate of self-censorship, according to CPJ's analysis.

Pro-government legislators gave final approval in January to a bill overhauling the penal code. The changes expanded the categories of government officials protected by *desacato* provisions, which criminalize expressions deemed offensive to public officials and state institutions, and drastically increased criminal penalties for defamation and slander. The maximum prison term for defamation, for example, went from 30 months to 48 months under the measure. Chávez signed the provisions affecting the press, and they went into effect on March 16. CPJ's analysis shows that the changes were approved hastily, with the intention of quelling dissent and criticism.

Also taking effect were parts of the Law of Social Responsibility in Radio and Television, which was approved by the National Assembly and signed into law by Chávez in December 2004. The measure, backed by pro-government legislators, contains vaguely worded restrictions that severely limit freedom of expression.

Under Article 29, for instance, television and radio stations that disseminate messages that "promote, defend, or incite breaches of public order" or "are contrary to the security of the nation" may be forced to suspend broadcasts for up to 72 hours. If a media outlet repeats the infractions within the next five years, its broadcasting concession may be suspended for up to five years. Article 7 of the law forbids "graphic descriptions or images of real violence" on the air from 5 a.m. to 11 p.m., except when the broadcast is live and the content is either "indispensable" or emerges unexpectedly.

Private television stations have altered programming to comply with the "social responsibility" law. Elsy Barroeta, news director of the 24-hour news channel Globovisión, told CPJ that the station had not restricted coverage, but she acknowledged that some colleagues were concerned about self-censorship. Barroeta said that images of violence during street protests could be aired live but could not be repeated throughout the day, according to the new guidelines. The Instituto Prensa y Sociedad (IPYS), a regional press freedom organization, found that three prominent television stations—Venevisión, Televén, and Radio Caracas Televisión—dropped half of their opinion programs since late 2004.

Venezuelan government officials continued to be intolerant of critical news coverage in the foreign and local press. At a February press conference, then–Minister of Information and Communication Andrés Izarra accused the U.S. government of mounting a propaganda campaign via several U.S. and Venezuelan media outlets to isolate Venezuela and destabilize it in preparation for a U.S. invasion. Izarra alleged that more than 45 news articles were Bush administration propaganda, including stories in the Caracas-based dailies *El Universal* and *El Nacional* and articles written by British journalist Phil Gunson in *The Miami Herald*. The government was particularly upset when Gunson wrote that Venezuela was acquiring new weapons and developing a defense doctrine centered on resisting a possible U.S. invasion.

Without offering any supporting evidence, Izarra said, "Don't be surprised if in the future...we discover that Mr. Gunson and *El Nacional* are receiving funds from the U.S. government." Gunson and *El Nacional* said the comment had no basis in fact, and Izarra later termed his accusation a "presumption." His comment followed weeks of heightened tensions between the U.S. and Venezuelan governments, including statements by Chávez saying the U.S. government would be to blame for any assassination attempts against him.

Gunson told CPJ that "in a context in which journalists have been physically attacked for their supposed alignment with one political faction or the other, to be called a paid agent of imperialism represents an obvious security risk." CPJ condemned Izarra's statement and said that it endangered the safety of journalists. Izarra responded that journalists in Venezuela had no reason to fear physical retaliation for their work, but he continued to suggest that some journalists were spreading U.S. government propaganda.

In July, the attorney general's office invoked *desacato* provisions to investigate a local newspaper. Attorney General Isaías Rodríguez Díaz ordered a criminal investigation of *El Universal* after it published an editorial on July 25 criticizing his office and the judiciary. The front-page editorial, headlined "Justicia arrodillada" (Justice on Its Knees), said that the criminal justice system had become politicized, had lost its autonomy, and had grown ineffective. As a result, the editorial argued, the attorney general's office and Venezuelan courts were losing their legitimacy. By August, the attorney general's office said it planned to drop the investigation because, as an institution, it was not covered by the *desacato* provisions.

Provincial journalists faced retaliation by drug traffickers, death squads, and corrupt members of the security forces. In states bordering Colombia, journalists also encountered illegal armed groups and hired assassins.

The repercussions of a 2004 slaying were felt throughout the year. Mauro Marcano, a radio host and columnist, was killed in September 2004 by unidentified gunmen in the city of Maturín, in the eastern state of Monagas. Marcano, who was also a municipal councilman, had aggressively denounced drug trafficking and police corruption.

Marcano's relatives told CPJ they had received threats after a March 2005 press conference in which they denounced the lack of progress made in the murder investigation. A special legislative committee looking into the murder issued a report three months later, recommending the replacement of several police investigators and prosecutors assigned to the murder probe, and urging police protection for Marcano's family.

In the fall, prosecutors told CPJ that they had concluded the investigation and were ready to file preliminary charges against several suspects in the Marcano murder. They declined to comment on the motive. CPJ continues to monitor the case to determine whether Marcano was killed for his journalistic work.

Government officials and pro-government politicians filed criminal defamation lawsuits against at least four journalists during the year. And at least two journalists received citations from prosecutors that demanded they answer questions about leaks in high-profile criminal investigations.

BOLIVIA

- Giovanna Rodríguez Castro and David Zagardia Muños, members of a news team from the private television channel Bolivisión, were harassed and threatened while covering antigovernment protests in Santa Cruz on January 11. Protesters blocked their vehicle and punctured its tires, Rodríguez Castro told CPJ. Rodríguez Castro, who was four months pregnant, said that one man threatened to beat her.

CHILE

- Paola Briceño Verdina, a reporter for Radio Bío-Bío, was detained and beaten by police after covering a student protest in Santiago on May 4. A police agent approached Briceño Verdina shortly after she aired a report on the demonstration, which included clashes between students and police. Although Briceño Verdina identified herself as a reporter and showed her press credential, she was taken to a police vehicle and beaten with a baton on the arms and legs. She was jailed briefly before a commanding officer intervened and ordered her release.

- After three years of delay, Congress and President Ricardo Lagos enacted a measure in August that eliminated *desacato* (disrespect) provisions in the penal code and the code of military justice. Articles 263, 265, and 268 of the penal code were repealed. Article 264 of the penal code redefined attacks on public officials to exclude insulting language. Article 276 of the code of military justice, which defined the offense of "improper sedition" in broad terms, was recast to prohibit any action that "induces or incites military personnel to disorder, indiscipline, or nonfulfillment of military duties."

COSTA RICA

- In a bid to limit the grounds and liability in defamation cases, and to broaden access to information, local journalists and press freedom advocates created an independent organization called Instituto de Prensa y Libertad de Expresión (IPLEX) on June 8. The group was established to provide training for journalists, encourage independent and diverse media, and defend local journalists in their work. Eduardo Ulibarri, former editor of the leading daily *La Nación*, was named the group's president.

ECUADOR

- Julio Augusto García Romero, a photographer, died on April 19 while covering a demonstration in Quito against then-President Lucio Gutiérrez. Protesters were moving toward the Palacio de Carondelet, the seat of the executive branch, when police fired tear gas grenades into the crowd. García Romero, who worked for the Chilean news agency La Bocina and the weekly *Punto de Vista*, collapsed and went into cardiorespiratory arrest. Protests were frequent after Supreme Court magistrates—appointed by Gutiérrez and his allies in Congress—dismissed corruption charges against two former presidents. Gutiérrez was later forced from office and faced prosecution himself.

GUATEMALA

- The Constitutionality Court, the nation's highest court, suspended enforcement of *desacato* provisions in the penal code on June 14. The court said it would review the constitutionality of Articles 411, 412, and 413, which criminalize expressions deemed offensive to public officials and state institutions. The move followed a number of recent rulings in Latin America striking down *desacato* laws.

HONDURAS

- The Supreme Court struck down the *desacato* provision in the penal code. In its May 19 ruling, the court found that Article 345 was unconstitutional because it provided special protection to public officials and restricted freedom of expression. The article set penalties of two to four years in prison for insulting a public official, and three to six years for insulting senior officials, legislators, or Supreme Court justices.

NICARAGUA

- A judge found a local politician guilty in the November 2004 murder of journalist María José Bravo. Eugenio Hernández González, convicted on January 26, was later sentenced to 25 years in prison. Bravo, a correspondent for the Managua daily *La Prensa*, was covering an electoral dispute in the city of Juigalpa. She had just left a local vote-counting center and was talking to several people when she was shot once at close range. Police arrested Hernández González, ex-mayor of the town of El Ayote, later that night.

PARAGUAY

- On August 3, unidentified attackers set fire to the studios of Catholic radio station Quebracho Poty, based in the town of Puerto Casado on the Brazilian border. The attackers set the station's broadcasting equipment ablaze and cut the antenna's cables, according to local journalist Charles Saldívar. Radio Quebracho Poty had supported the national government's expropriation of land surrounding the town. The land was owned by the sect of Sun Myung Moon, head of the Unification Church.

URUGUAY

- Marcelo Borrat, a former television reporter for media company Multimedio Plural, was abducted, beaten, and threatened with death by unidentified assailants on October 17, the journalist's lawyer, Edison Lanza, told CPJ. While driving home, Borrat was intercepted by three hooded assailants who forced him to get into their car, Lanza said. Borrat was taken to a nearby beach and assaulted, suffering facial injuries. His attackers demanded he destroy unspecified cell phone recordings, then left Borrat in the water, the lawyer said. Borrat had received death threats earlier in the year after investigating irregularities in the public health system. He also aired a controversial report in September about workers fired from one of Multimedio's outlets, TV Libre. Multimedio canceled Borrat's show soon afterward but said it had nothing to do with the fired-worker report.

GAG
US NO
AS JEANS CO.

ANALYSIS

As Radio Grows Powerful, Challenges Emerge 92

At home, in the car, even in the fields, more Asians are getting their news on the radio than ever before. An explosion of community stations and an infusion of international financing have made radio a powerful force.

by Abi Wright

PHOTOS

Section break: AP/Pat Roque – *A Philippine journalist marks World Press Freedom Day on May 3.* Analysis (next): AP/Darko Bandic – *An Afghan man has his ear to Kabul Radio.*

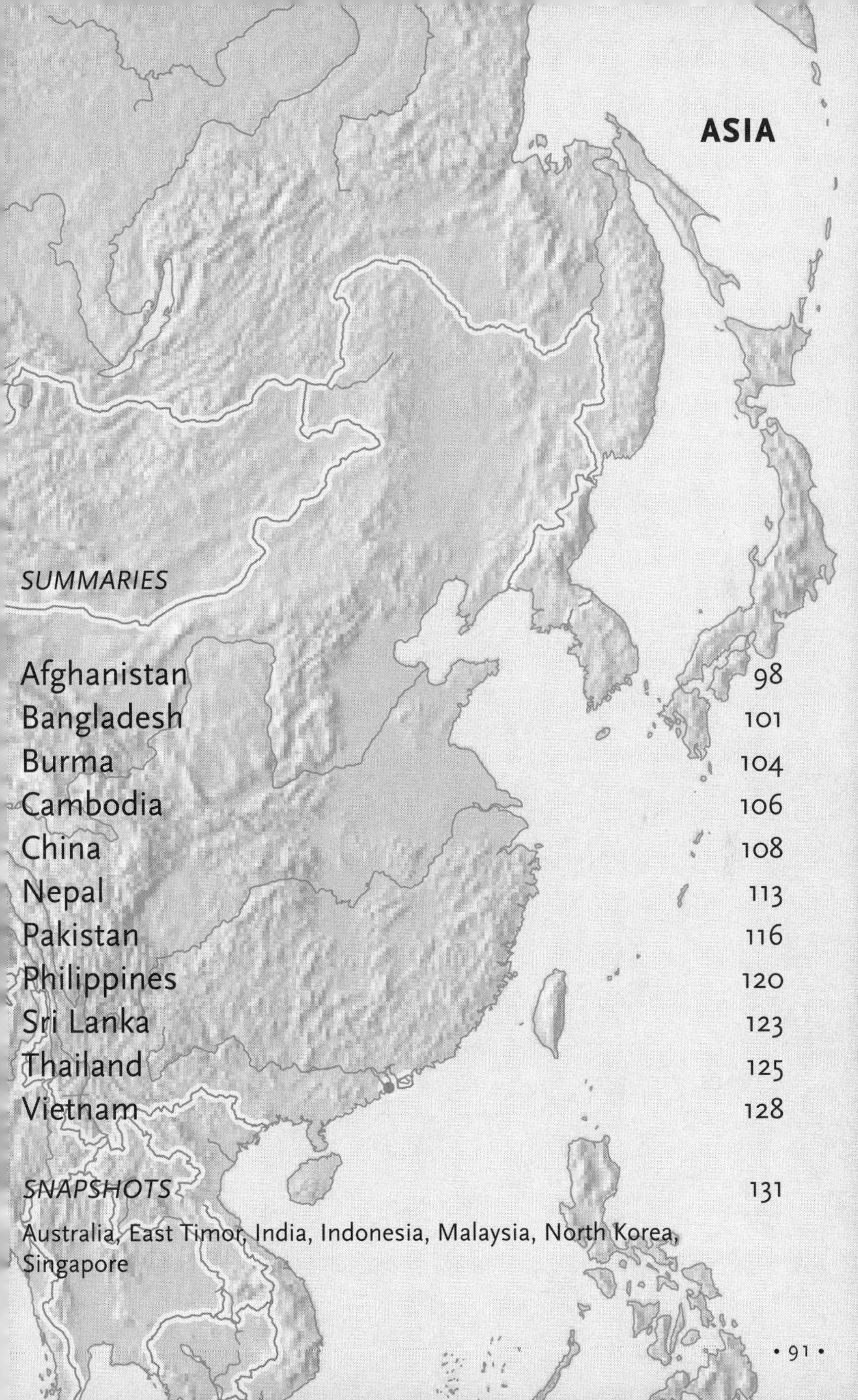

ASIA

SUMMARIES

AS RADIO GROWS POWERFUL, CHALLENGES EMERGE

by Abi Wright

AT HOME, IN THE CAR, AND EVEN IN THE FIELDS, MORE PEOPLE across Asia are getting their news on the radio than ever before. Increasingly, this accessible and affordable medium is bringing real-time information to remote areas of Indonesia, Nepal, the Philippines, Afghanistan, and Thailand, parts of which were previously days or even weeks behind the news cycle. In Afghanistan, 83 percent of the population say they tune in to radio news, the Afghan consulting firm Altai found in 2005. In the Philippines, the audience is even larger, with 87 percent reporting that they listen to news on the radio, according to a poll by the national broadcast regulator KBP.

The region-wide flowering of community radio stations and a shift from shortwave relay to local FM transmission of international news broadcasts has made the medium more accessible than ever. Funding from Western governments and international media training organizations such as Internews has enabled new stations to start and existing stations to increase their range in countries from Afghanistan to Indonesia.

International broadcasters such as the BBC and the U.S. government-funded Voice of America remain popular in many countries, but they must now compete with local stations and no longer dominate the dissemination of news and information.

"International broadcasters no longer dominate and must now compete with local stations."

Radio has also become an instrument of reform in countries plagued by corruption. One Afghan listener told a BBC survey in 2004, "We want to be kept aware of the government's activities, and some corrupt people in the government should be exposed." In the Philippines, provincial listeners believe that outspoken commentators give voice to their concerns. "The level of trust in the government is low, police don't work, and people are poor," said Weng Carranza-Paraan, a member of the journalists' union. "Radio makes people feel empowered."

This scrutiny of both local and national governments, however, has not always been welcome. In Nepal and Thailand, leaders retaliated in 2005 with crackdowns on radio stations, while radio journalists in Afghanistan and the Philippines frequently faced threats and violence from officials because of their reporting.

A look at the state of radio news across the region reveals both the power of news and the growing number of obstacles local radio journalists face.

PHILIPPINES: The Philippine press is one of the freest and least regulated in Asia. It also operates in one of the world's most murderous countries for journalists, particularly radio commentators, according to CPJ research. Over the last five years, 22 journalists have been murdered in retaliation for their work. At least 17 were broadcasters on radio stations in rural areas.

A CPJ mission in June found that violence against broadcasters fits into a larger pattern of crime, corruption, and impunity. Government officials have been implicated in as many as half of the killings, according to the local Center for Media Freedom and Responsibility.

The high death toll for radio journalists also reveals a crisis in the media. Many journalists complained to CPJ about an absence of professional standards and ethics among some broadcast journalists, particularly "block-timers" who lease airtime from station owners. "Commentators are vulnerable because they are free to criticize anybody—and the people who are criticized don't have access to the KBP [broadcast regulator]," said Nandy Vitalicio, news director of the

Manila Broadcasting Company, the largest radio network in the Philippines. Vitalicio said journalists must work to reform themselves in order to stop the killings.

"In the name of fighting an insurgency, Nepal's government halted FM news programs."

NEPAL: Governments pose another threat to the news radio boom. On February 1, Nepal's King Gyanendra declared a state of emergency, sacked his government, and shut down the free press, including what had been the pride of Nepal's media, its independent news radio operations. Some 46 independent FM stations across Nepal, 14 in Kathmandu alone, were ordered in the name of fighting the country's Maoist insurgency to replace all news programs with music and entertainment.

FM radio stations broadcast to an estimated 70 percent of the population, according to the BBC. A 2003 Supreme Court decision allowed the broadcast of news bulletins on private radio, a groundbreaking step for the region. Even India, the world's largest democracy and Nepal's influential neighbor, permits radio news broadcasting only on the state-run All India Radio network.

That era ended on February 1, when soldiers descended on studios at stations such as Radio Sagarmatha. With an estimated 1.5 million listeners, Radio Sagarmatha is one of the largest stations in the Kathmandu Valley. The troops ordered station staff at gunpoint to stop broadcasting news. "I think we had been marked, and they felt threatened by us. The current thinking is that FM radio stations are dangerous because they're capable of inciting people to revolt," station chief Ghama Raj Luitel told Inter Press Service in April.

The king sought to justify the media crackdown by saying that Maoist rebels, who have been fighting to depose the government since 1996, were using the press to advance their cause. In fact, the *Nepali Times* reported in August that the Maoists took advantage of the radio news blackout to broadcast news and propaganda on Radio People's Republic, using a dozen reporters with mobile radio units. Further attempts to muzzle the media followed.

Journalists fought back with court challenges and street protests until October, when permanent amendments to the press law were announced, codifying onerous prohibitions on the media that include a permanent ban on broadcasting news on the radio. Journalists who broadcast criticism of the king now face up to two years in prison.

AFGHANISTAN: The number of news media outlets available to Afghans has grown dramatically since the collapse of the Taliban regime in December 2001. During their five-year rule, the Taliban outlawed the independent press, music programming, and female news readers on the airwaves. Radio broadcasts were confined to religious programs and government announcements on the officially sanctioned Voice of Sharia.

Today, news vendors sell hundreds of different newspapers and magazines in major cities, and more than 50 FM radio stations beam news and information throughout the mountainous country. Small radio stations airing local news programming are particularly popular, according to Internews, a media training organization that has helped set up a network of dozens of stations.

International aid has helped bolster independent women's community stations, whose listeners are largely illiterate. Their operations are low-tech. One station staffed by young women in the northern city of Mazar-i-Sharif, Radio Rabia Balkhi, broadcasts from a one-room studio lit by a lantern and powered by a car battery, *The Washington Post* reported. The broadcasters say they are able to help inform many Afghan women about issues relating to their lives and the world. Isolated by tradition, many women do not have access to any other sources of news.

Radio journalists played a key role in educating listeners about candidates and issues during the landmark presidential elections in 2004 and the parliamentary elections in 2005. As their audience grows, so does the number of threats radio journalists say they face from warlords, corrupt officials, and insurgents. A survey for the Afghan media training group Nai reported that 54 percent of Afghan radio journalists say they were "intimidated" while covering the presidential elections. The prevalence of threats and harassment from warlords and conservative figures causes self-censorship, local journalists told CPJ.

International broadcasters still play an important role on the airwaves in Afghanistan. A December 2004 survey by Radio Free Asia/Radio Liberty's Afghan service, called Radio Free Afghanistan or Radio Azadi, found that nearly two-thirds of the country's listeners tuned in to their programming weekly. RFE/RL, the BBC, and Voice of America all compete with the growing output of local stations on the FM dial.

Even the Taliban, who continue to fight coalition

"The number of outlets available to Afghans has grown dramatically since the collapse of the Taliban."

forces in the south, are back in the radio game. Spokesman Abdul Latif Hakimi announced the relaunch of the Taliban's Voice of Sharia radio station in April. It now broadcasts antigovernment commentaries and religious hymns twice a day from a mobile transmitter.

INDONESIA: Radio stations devastated in the December 2004 tsunami have been resurrected in the provincial capital, Banda Aceh. With support from international donors and domestic broadcasters like the Jakarta-based radio network 68-H, which provided temporary transmitters and equipment to seven of its Aceh-based member stations, they are now playing a part in the region's recovery. The founder of 68-H, Santosa (who, like many Indonesians, goes by only one name), told CPJ that he hopes to set up another 20 stations across the battered region by the end of 2006. "We see an opportunity from the tsunami to open access to information in more remote areas," he said.

Internews received funding from the Knight Foundation to help train radio and television journalists in Aceh, helping to ensure the future of broadcasting.

Another local station, Radio Prima, lost 22 of its reporters in the tsunami. It was broadcasting again one month later from its owner's back yard. According to news director Uzair, government restrictions previously in place in this war-ravaged province have been eased since the disaster. He told CPJ that the station now airs news programs and call-in shows on more controversial subjects, such as the debate over whether the influx of Western aid workers is increasing the risk of HIV/AIDS in the region. "We are testing new waters," Uzair said.

THAILAND: In the five years since community radio became legal in Thailand, an estimated 2,000 low-frequency FM stations have surfaced throughout the country. Reaching growing audiences, some of these independent broadcasters have even dared criticize Prime Minister Thaksin Shinawatra's government, which dominates much of the country's media.

"In tsunami-ravaged Aceh, radio stations are playing a vital part in the recovery."

Thaksin tried to fight back through a new National Broadcast Commission. The nominally independent body was charged with redistributing the country's radio and television frequencies from the state to the private sector as required by the 1997 constitution. But media reformers immediately argued that the new body represented the same vested interests—including the mili-

"Despite new dangers, radio news gives Asians a voice in their communities."

tary—that already control the country's electronic media. The reformers won a victory in November when a court voided the commission's formation.

At the same time, the government brought criminal charges against a former rice farmer, Satien Chanthorn, who had established the community station FM 106.75 MHz in Ang Thong province in July 2002. Satien's coverage of the local government's handling of flood relief budgets brought him into direct conflict with authorities. Police confiscated his broadcasting equipment and charged him with illegally possessing a radio transmitter and operating a radio station without a license. Many community stations operate without licenses, and press freedom advocates say that Satien was targeted because of his critical broadcasts.

In August, police also raided and shut down FM 92.25, a Bangkok community radio station known for its critical reporting of the prime minister, and threatened to arrest its journalists if they continued to broadcast news.

REGIONAL CHALLENGES: Despite new dangers confronting radio broadcasters—from hostile governments, criminal groups, and militant elements—radio news is giving listeners in Asia a voice in their communities and on a national level. Support from international organizations has helped resurrect and expand media structures in the wake of wars and natural disasters throughout Asia.

Competition between stations is growing along with the number of radio outlets, producing higher-quality programming in some countries and pressure for higher ratings in others. Journalists in Afghanistan, Indonesia, and the Philippines have told CPJ about their desire for more training in ethics and journalistic standards and practices.

As the number of stations grows across the region, enemies of the media will have a harder time controlling what is broadcast. Keeping these stations on the air and maintaining the free flow of information will be critical to Asia's emerging democracies.

• • • • • • • • • • •

Abi Wright is CPJ's Asia program coordinator.

AFGHANISTAN

The number of news outlets grew yet again, continuing an expansion of the media that began with the fall of the Taliban regime in December 2001. With journalism's higher profile, however, came increases in threats, attacks, and detentions targeting the press. These cases had a chilling effect on the news media, leading to greater self-censorship and creating a more complex press freedom landscape.

Conservative religious elements clashed with liberal factions over journalists' rights, and the country's recently ratified media laws ensnared journalists in a volatile cultural debate. Afghanistan retains deeply traditional societal mores that have been tested by the rapid emergence of electronic media and print publications that push boundaries on sensitive topics such as religion, women's rights, and the regional warlords who continue to control much of the country. Those who broached these subjects faced threats, harassment, arrest, and jail time as part of an emerging pattern of press freedom abuse that targets such reporting as "anti-Islamic."

The editor of a magazine on women's rights, Ali Mohaqiq Nasab, received a two-year prison sentence after he was convicted on blasphemy charges in a Kabul court in October, stunning the local journalism community and international press freedom groups. According to international news accounts, religious leaders complained after Nasab published an article questioning the use of harsh punishments under traditional Islamic law, such as amputating the hands of thieves as punishment for stealing, and publicly stoning or whipping those found guilty of adultery.

Writings considered anti-Islamic are prohibited under a revised media law signed in March 2004, but the law is vaguely worded, and local journalists have been uncertain about what constitutes a violation. The media law also stipulates that journalists be detained only with the approval of a 17-member commission of government officials and journalists. Police did not have such consent when they arrested Nasab on October 1, yet he was convicted three weeks later.

Judge Ansarullah Malawizada said that his ruling in Nasab's case was based on recommendations from the conservative Ulama Council, a group of the country's leading clerics. "The Ulama Council sent us a letter saying that he should be punished, so I sentenced him to two years' jail," Malawizada told The Associated Press. Although an appeals court in December reduced Nasab's sentence and ordered him released, local journalists said the case had a damaging effect on the press.

Another target for religious groups was the progressive and controversial Tolo TV,

• • • • • • • • • • •

Summaries in this chapter were reported and written by **Abi Wright**, Asia program coordinator; **Kristin Jones**, Asia research associate; and **Shawn W. Crispin**, Asia program consultant.

which can be seen throughout much of the country. The channel draws younger audiences with hard-hitting investigative news programs and a groundbreaking music video program called "Hop," which tested traditions by showing male and female presenters in the same shot. Some religious leaders believed Tolo went too far. In March, the Ulama Council condemned Tolo for broadcasting programs "against Islam and other national values of Afghanistan."

A female music video presenter, Shaima Rezayee, was fired soon afterward and was found murdered in her home in May. Police blamed members of her family for her murder but were unable to substantiate those accusations, and no arrests were reported. Women still present videos on "Hop," and Tolo employed a large number of women by local standards—almost one-third of its 200 employees, according to a report by the Institute for War & Peace Reporting (IWPR).

Another popular presenter, Shakeb Isaar, a member of the Hazara ethnic minority, was threatened and forced to flee the country in the summer. A senior journalist with the channel was forced off the air for several months. Sayed Sulaiman Ashna, host of the evening news program "Tawdi Kharabari" (Hot Talk), began receiving threatening phone calls after an interview with ex-Taliban Foreign Minister Wakil Ahmad Mutawakil. He told CPJ that unidentified callers threatened to kill him and his family. He left Kabul for several months before returning to the show in late September.

Even in the face of controversy, the demand for television programming continued to grow. Tolo broadcast 24 hours a day. The Ariyana Television Network was launched in five cities in August, becoming the nation's fourth private channel. The channels broadcast local and international news and informational programming in both of the country's languages, Dari and Pashto, as well as Indian films and other foreign-made programs popular with young audiences.

Radio remained the most popular news medium because of the country's low literacy rates and mountainous terrain, which makes transporting newspapers and magazines difficult. International broadcasters such as the BBC and two U.S. government–funded stations, Radio Free Europe/Radio Liberty and Voice of America, continue to draw wide audiences and respect. However, they now compete with the 29 local community radio stations established since 2003 by the international media development organization Internews, along with roughly 20 other commercial stations. The new generation of radio reporters says it faces growing risks. A study by the Afghan media organization Nai found that 54 percent of radio reporters reported being intimidated, primarily by warlords and local government officials.

In June, after two years of debate within the media community, journalists finally formed two organizations dedicated to protecting press freedom, publicizing attacks against local journalists, and pressuring authorities to defend their rights. The Afghan

Independent Journalists Association and the Committee to Protect Afghan Journalists monitored and documented press freedom abuses, met with officials to lobby for their colleagues, and alerted the international community when egregious attacks on the press occurred, such as the jailing of editor Nasab.

Afghanistan's media helped monitor the country's first free parliamentary elections in September, when almost 6,000 candidates ran for the lower house, or Wolesi Jirga, and for provincial assemblies. Covering the campaign brought risks. Unknown assailants kidnapped Mohammed Taqi Siraj, editor of the weekly *Bayam*, and cameraman Baseer Seerat on September 14 as they returned from Nuristan province, where they had filmed the campaign of a female parliamentary candidate, Hawa Alam Nuristani. They escaped from their kidnappers one week later.

Self-censorship affected election coverage, Western observers alleged. The press was seen as overly cautious in its coverage of the candidates out of fear of reprisal; there were few probing questions about candidates who had been military commanders, warlords, or drug traffickers, or who had acted as their surrogates. More than half of those elected to the parliament were regional warlords, according to the government-sponsored Afghanistan Independent Human Rights Commission. Local journalists worried that the new body could be openly hostile to the press and might try to amend the freedoms guaranteed to journalists in the country's constitution and media law.

Coming one year after the country's groundbreaking presidential elections, the parliamentary elections were supposed to be another significant step toward establishing democratic institutions in Afghanistan. Reports of irregularities at the polls and lingering questions about many of the candidates, however, raised questions of legitimacy, according to international news reports. *The Christian Science Monitor* reported protests in Kabul and across the country in October against mujahedeen, warlords, and former Taliban commanders accused of paying off voters, stuffing ballot boxes, and using intimidation tactics. Election officials threw out 680 ballot boxes because of suspicions of irregularities, the *Monitor* reported.

Among the winners was Abdul Rasul Sayyaf, a powerful warlord whom human rights groups accused of committing atrocities during the country's civil war.

In October, a court sentenced two brothers to death for their role in the November 2001 murders of four journalists from Western news organizations who were traveling from Pakistan into Afghanistan during the fall of the Taliban. The victims were Reuters cameraman Harry Burton, Reuters photographer Azizullah Haidari, *El Mundo* reporter Julio Fuentes, and *Corriere della Sera* reporter Maria Grazia Cutuli, who was raped before being murdered. Zar Jan and Abdul Wahid, brothers, confessed to involvement in the killings, which took place on a highway 50 miles (80 kilometers) east of Kabul. Another suspect in the brutal slaying, Reza Khan, was found guilty of the murder last year and sentenced to death. Khan claimed that the group had acted on the orders of a Taliban commander.

Despite many obstacles, journalists continued to start independent newspapers, radio stations, and television channels. In addition to the 60 publications circulating in the northern regions, the first independent daily, *Baztab*, was launched in the northern city of Mazhar-i-Sharif in April, according to the IWPR. Samay Hamed, an Afghan writer, publisher, and press freedom advocate honored by CPJ in 2003 with its International Press Freedom Award, published the newspaper.

Editor Shafiq Payam said his daily intended to spread free expression to the region so that warlords could no longer monopolize information. The launch could have an impact. One of Payam's colleagues, editor Qayoum Babak, told the IWPR: "The publication of this daily is the beginning, and it will encourage journalists and other media outlets to publish the facts. If this type of publication spreads, the warlords' hold on the north will collapse."

BANGLADESH

Bangladesh was mired in a political crisis heightened by the wide-scale August 17 attacks by Islamic militants involving hundreds of small, near-simultaneous bombings throughout the nation. Journalists covering the bombings and their aftermath said they were more vulnerable than ever to violent reprisals.

Bangladesh was already one of the most dangerous countries for the press in Asia, according to CPJ research. Even by that poor standard, death threats and physical attacks against journalists spiked in 2005. Traditional enemies of the press such as criminal gangs, underground leftist groups, police, politicians, and student activists continued to lash out at journalists. The newer and potentially graver threat from radical Islamist groups exacerbated the treacherous landscape.

In May, CPJ named Bangladesh one of the world's five most murderous countries for journalists. Nine journalists were killed over five years, eight of them in the lawless southwestern Khulna district, which is rife with criminal gangs, outlawed political groups, and drug traffickers. Seven of the victims received death threats beforehand. Investigations into the murders have yielded no convictions.

Journalists in rural provinces faced threats from the growing number of illegal groups. In February, the Janajuddha faction of the outlawed Purbo Banglar Communist Party sent death threats to eight journalists in the southwestern city of Satkhira. The Janajuddha called the journalists "class enemies" and threatened them with execution because of their reporting on the faction's leader.

In September, five of the same journalists and four others received pieces of white cloth, symbolizing funeral shrouds, accompanied by letters co-signed by the outlawed Islamic militant Bangla Bhai and the radical movement Ahle Hadith. These letters warned journalists not to write about their groups' activities and threatened to kill ethnic Hindu reporters.

The Bangladeshi press operates largely without direct government interference, and it routinely exposes government corruption. But retaliatory physical attacks and threats occur frequently and with impunity. Despite promises from officials to track down those responsible for the attacks, little is done to punish offenders—even in high-profile murder cases.

The February murder of Sheikh Belaluddin illustrates the seemingly intractable pattern of impunity. A journalist with the conservative national daily *Sangbad*, Belaluddin died after a homemade bomb detonated outside the Khulna Press Club. A breakthrough in the case was reported in July, when a former leader of the Islami Chhatra Shibir, the student wing of the Islamic fundamentalist political party Jamaat-e-Islami, confessed to taking part in the deadly bombing. Yet three weeks later, the suspect was freed on bail, and his whereabouts were unknown, according to local press reports.

Belaluddin's murder shocked the nation's press, prompting protests and briefly uniting the country's polarized journalists. Editors from across the political spectrum came together to form a new group, the Forum to Protect Journalists, which rallied in the capital, Dhaka, soon after Belaluddin's killing. The protesters marched to the National Press Club and called for justice in all of the murdered journalists' cases. But longstanding divisions kept the forum from following up with more action, local journalists said.

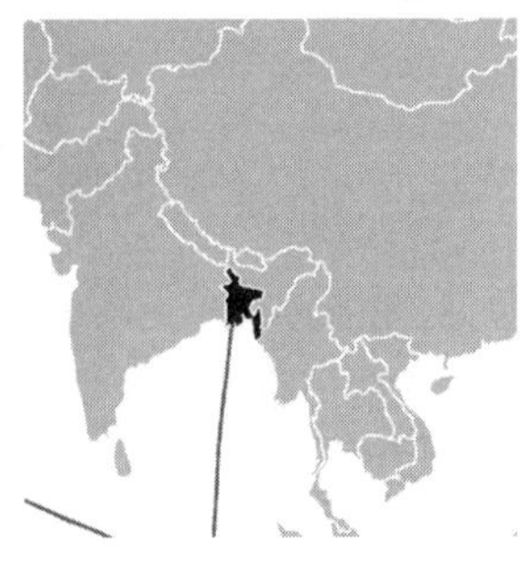

The government has professed a commitment to solving the 2004 murders in Khulna of veteran reporter Manik Saha and editor Humayun Kabir Balu. Arrests have been made in both cases, but family members are skeptical about the proceedings and don't believe that the masterminds have been apprehended, according to *The Daily Star* of Dhaka and CPJ sources.

Police brutality was a continuing problem, particularly for photographers covering the country's growing political tensions. In May, baton-wielding riot police on the Dhaka University campus beat seven photographers and camera operators who were covering protests. When journalists staged their own demonstration in July to protest the mistreatment, intelligence officers assaulted nine photojournalists in full view of police.

Islamic militant activity in Bangladesh is on the increase, according to local and international news accounts. Prime Minister Khaleda Zia's Bangladesh Nationalist Party rose to power in 2001 through an alliance with conservative Islamic parties. Her government had flatly denied the existence of militant groups, saying that journalists reporting on the trend were engaged in "informational terrorism."

Covering this emerging story in the face of official denials carried risks for journalists. Government leaders harshly criticized a January *New York Times Magazine* article that described the rise of militant Islamism. Intelligence officers questioned and harassed people interviewed for the article and journalists who cooperated in its reporting. The family of *Time* reporter Saleem Samad was among those targeted. In June, four men identified as cadres of Jagrata Muslim Janata Bangladesh (JMJB), an outlawed militant group headed by Bangla Bhai, attacked *Janakantha* reporter Shafiqul Islam in the northwestern town of Rajshahi because he had helped other journalists report on the JMJB's activities, according to *The Daily Star*.

The government was finally forced to confront the rise in radical groups' activities after the nationwide attacks on August 17. In a well-coordinated, half-hour-long series of strikes, hundreds of small bombs exploded across the country, killing at least two, injuring hundreds, and dealing a heavy psychological blow to the nation. The Supreme Court, the Foreign Ministry, airports, and at least seven press clubs were targeted in the bombings, which went off in 63 of the country's 64 districts. Leaflets said the bombs were a message from the banned Islamic militant group Jamaat-ul-Mujahideen Bangladesh (JMB) to Western leaders to leave Islamic countries. The leaflets also called for the establishment of Islamic sharia law.

Militant groups made use of the media to publicize their ideas, according to local news reports. The popular daily *Prothom Alo* reported in late 2004 that radical groups were increasingly using the media to recruit and spread propaganda about jihad. "Books, magazines, and cassettes are on sale in the capital urging people to join in a jihad," according to *Prothom Alo*. Books with titles such as "Why Should We Participate in Jihad" were selling briskly.

An imprisoned journalist was released in April. Authorities freed Salah Uddin Shoaib Choudhury, editor and publisher of the weekly tabloid *Blitz*, after he spent 17 months in jail awaiting trial on sedition charges stemming from his attempt to travel to Israel in November 2003 to participate in a conference with the Hebrew Writers Association. Bangladesh has no formal relations with Israel, and it is illegal for Bangladeshi citizens to travel there. The initial charge of violating passport restrictions was later dropped in favor of the more serious sedition charge.

Choudhury told CPJ that, because the sedition charges were pending, he was forced to appear in court once a month. He said that his passport was not returned, and that he was still at risk; after the August bombings, he received threatening letters from radicals. Choudhury relaunched the weekly *Blitz* in October.

Joynal Hazari, the member of parliament accused of ordering the savage beating of reporter Tipu Sultan in 2001, continued to elude justice as legal proceedings against him stalled. Despite the many delays, Sultan focused instead on journalism, covering the news for Bangladesh's most popular daily, *Prothom Alo*.

Sultan told CPJ that four years after thugs smashed the bones in his right hand in retaliation for his reporting on local corruption, he was excelling professionally and investigating many of the paper's lead stories. CPJ honored Sultan for his courage with an International Press Freedom Award in 2002.

BURMA

International pressure goaded Burma's ruling military junta into releasing several journalists and hundreds of political prisoners in 2005. But five journalists were among the more than 1,300 remaining detainees, and Nobel Peace Prize–winner Aung San Suu Kyi was still under house arrest.

On January 3, the junta released journalists Thein Tan and Ohn Kyaing, who had both served long terms in atrocious prison conditions, and editor Zaw Thet Htway, who had been sentenced to death. Thein Tan, a freelance writer with ties to the opposition National League for Democracy, served more than 14 years. Ohn Kyaing served more than 15 years on charges of "writing and distributing seditious pamphlets" and "threatening state security." Zaw Thet Htway, editor of the popular sports magazine *First Eleven*, had been jailed since 2003 for "high treason."

On July 6, the junta released freelance journalist Sein Hla Oo and documentary filmmaker Aung Pwint. Sein Hla Oo was jailed in 1994 for "fabricating and sending anti-government reports" to foreign embassies and news outlets. Aung Pwint and his partner Nyein Thit were arrested in October 1999 for making documentary films about poverty in Burma. CPJ honored the two with International Press Freedom Awards in November 2004. Aung Pwint returned home to Rangoon, but Nyein Thit was still in jail when CPJ conducted its worldwide census of imprisoned journalists on December 1.

Also still imprisoned was prominent 75-year-old journalist U Win Tin, who was arrested and sentenced in 1989 on the bizarre charge of arranging a forced abortion for a member of the opposition party. U Win Tin helped to establish many pro-democracy publications in the run-up to the 1988 street uprisings. The senior journalist's health has sharply deteriorated in recent years.

Burma is one of Asia's most repressive countries for media. The government controls all print, radio, and television outlets, and a draconian 1996 decree prohibits all speeches or statements that might "undermine national stability." The State Development and Peace Council (SPDC) has since tightened those restrictions.

The army-led junta strengthened its grip with an October 2004 purge of the once-powerful military intelligence apparatus MIS. Apart from jailing hundreds of former MIS operatives, news publications affiliated with MIS were closed, harassed, or brought under SPDC control.

In April, the SPDC established the Press Scrutiny and Registration Division (PSRD) under the Ministry of Information, which took over censorship duties from the MIS-run Press Scrutiny Board. All publications were required to reregister with the new PSRD, a process that entailed providing detailed information about publications' ownership, finances, and staff journalists.

Maj. Tint Swe, the PSRD's top-ranking censor, promised in July to allow news outlets greater editorial independence. The Ministry of Information, meanwhile, instituted a new press conference format, including unprecedented question-and-answer sessions with Minister of Information Brig. Gen. Kyaw Hsan, Minister of Home Affairs Maj. Gen. Maung Oo, and Director General of the Military Police Force Brig. Gen. Khin Yi. Still, journalists were expected to report government statements without critical analysis.

At the same time, the PSRD tightened existing censorship guidelines and expanded its control over the press. In July, Tint Swe announced a ban on publishing op-ed pieces and forbade any critical reporting on regional allies China, India, and the Association of Southeast Asian Nations (ASEAN). He also announced that natural disasters could be reported only if the news did not affect "national dignity" and that critical reports about government policies would be judged on a journalist's "reasons and aims."

The PSRD routinely censored news and advertisements, particularly items that might affect the hard-line regime's public image. Most periodicals publish as weeklies because of the amount of time required to obtain censors' approval. The SPDC famously blacked out all news about the December 2004 tsunami's impact on Burma. Publications are still barred from reporting on HIV-AIDS in Burma, which international health experts say has reached epidemic proportions.

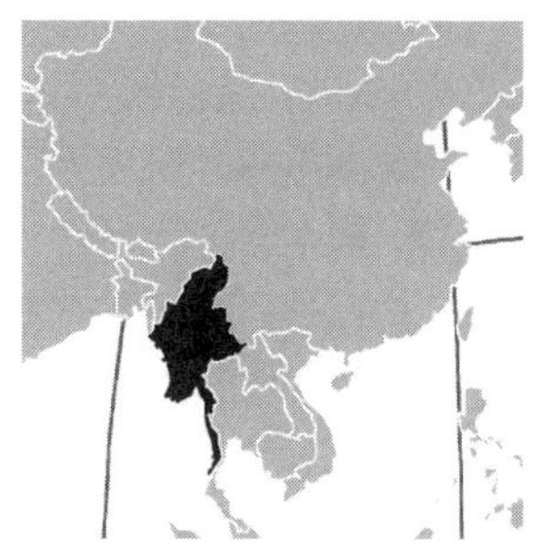

On May 7, 2005, the PSRD censored reporting on a coordinated bomb attack on two shopping malls and a trade center in the capital, Rangoon. Two hours after the blast, the Ministry of Information issued a press release claiming that 11 people had been killed. Hospital workers were ordered not to speak with reporters. Independent sources put the death toll above 11, with some reports in the Thai press estimating casualties at more than 40. The sources said that the sophistication of the attacks pointed to the possible involvement of former MIS officials.

Less sensitive news also fell victim to the censors. Two monthly publications, *Nwe Ni* and *Myanma Dana,* were banned from publishing in February because they had failed to submit their cover pages for PSRD approval. Another privately owned magazine, *Han Thit,* was banned for two months after running an advertisement for a Valentine's Day celebration—on the reasoning it promoted "negative" Western influences.

The Voice, a Rangoon-based weekly, was barred from distributing in May as punishment for a front-page story it ran in late March about Vietnam's withdrawal from Burma's New Year water festival celebrations, a story that the PSRD contended used "falsified sources and was written with a negative sense." *The Voice* was also banned from distributing in February after the Ministry of Hotels and Tourism questioned the accuracy of a report it published on the construction of a hotel in remote Chin state.

Through August, the SPDC granted licenses for the establishment of 32 new publications, on the condition that editors notify authorities about the identity, past history, and political views of its staff members. New publications were also required to publish government statements, announcements, and articles when requested, according to the SPDC's new guidelines. When the *Myanmar Times* attempted to report on the new requirements, the paper's August 16 Burmese-language edition was banned from distribution.

The junta also attempted to rein in the Internet by taking control of Bagan Cybertech, Burma's main Internet service and satellite-feed provider. Ye Naing Win, the son of former MIS chief Khin Nyunt and the communication company's chief executive, was sentenced to 40 years in prison for unspecified "economic crimes." The junta has since deactivated many e-mail accounts run by Bagan, and blocked access to exile-run Web-based news sites, including *Irrawaddy* and *Mizzima News*.

Another exile-run news group, the Democratic Voice of Burma (DVB), based in Oslo, Norway, began transmission in May of a television news program dedicated to Burmese issues, including political reports that typically would be censored inside Burma. Many Burmese were able to receive the programming through satellite dishes. By July, however, the SPDC had banned new satellite dish licenses and ordered local authorities to inform the public that viewing the DVB-produced program was illegal and punishable by seven years in prison.

CAMBODIA

The jailing of a prominent radio journalist in Phnom Penh and assaults on journalists in remote, lawless regions raised concerns about Cambodia's commitment to press freedom guarantees enshrined in its 1993 Constitution and 1994 Press Law.

On October 11, police arrested Mam Sonando for an interview he conducted on Radio Sambok Khmum (Beehive Radio) FM 105 about territorial concessions that the government of Prime Minister Hun Sen planned to make to Vietnam to secure a border demarcation treaty. Journalists Sok Pov Khemara of Voice of America and Ath Bunny of Radio Free Asia fled to Thailand later in the month, fearing that they might be arrested for related reports that were rebroadcast over Beehive Radio. Both the European Union and the United Nations condemned Sonando's detention. Several trade union activists were also imprisoned for discussing the concessions.

Sonando, a former opposition politician, was charged with criminal defamation. He was refused bail while the government conducted an investigation, which his family was told could take up to six months. Sonando, 64, was being held with 11 other prisoners in a poorly ventilated cell slightly larger than 6 by 20 feet (2 by 6 meters). The government later filed an additional charge of "disseminating false information," which increased the potential prison term to two years.

It was the second time that the government had imprisoned Sonando for his broadcast journalism. He was jailed for 11 days in February 2003 for broadcasting inflammatory comments during riots that led to the destruction of the Thai embassy in Phnom Penh.

The government detained another journalist, Hang Sakhorn, on criminal defamation charges on December 2. The charges stemmed from an article in the Khmer-language *Ponleu Samaki* alleging a state prosecutor had accepted a bribe.

Concerns about further restrictions on the media stemmed from an October 21 order that banned journalists from entering and reporting from law courts in Phnom Penh. Journalists protested the order, arguing that the ban breached press freedom guarantees. Chev Keng, the court's director, repealed the order on October 31, but new restrictions on using cameras and tape recorders in the courtroom were maintained.

Phnom Penh–based journalists told CPJ that the government's crackdown had led to increased self-censorship by the print media. Pen Samitthy, editor-in-chief of *Rasmei Kampuchea*, the country's largest Khmer-language daily, said the arrests represented a "backward step" for press freedom and that his newspaper was more reluctant to publish criticism of the government. He noted that only one of the country's 15 or so Khmer-language publications ran critical commentary about Sonando's arrest.

After Hun Sen's Cambodia's People Party seized power in a 1997 political purge in which scores of opposition supporters were murdered, six publications critical of the government were closed down. Since then, only one Khmer-language newspaper, *Monea Sicha*, has regularly presented the opposition's views.

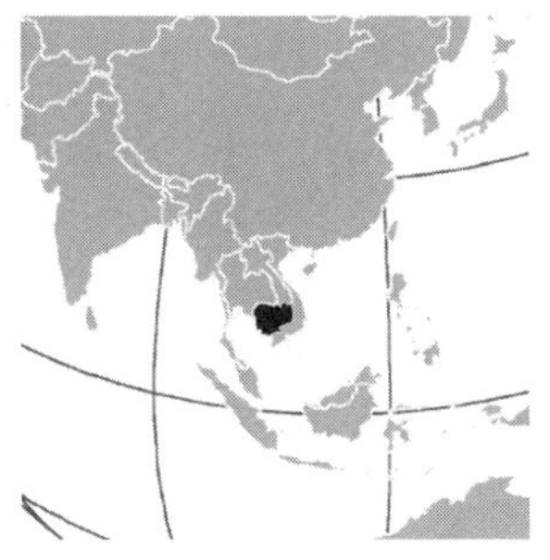

Michael Hayes, editor-in-chief of the English-language daily *Phnom Penh Post*, one of the country's few independent newspapers, told CPJ that "government thugs" frequently harassed him and accused him of siding with the Khmer Rouge, a radical Maoist group that killed as many as 1.7 million people when it controlled Cambodia in the 1970s. Hayes said that the *Phnom Penh Post* sometimes ran stories and pictures about former members of the Khmer Rouge now in government. Hayes said that he was once assaulted by unidentified assailants while walking home from work, and he believes the attack could have been related to his newspaper's reporting on the Khmer Rouge.

The situation for journalists in Cambodia's lawless provinces remained precarious. Nhen Sokha, a journalist with the Khmer daily *Kampuchea Thmei*, was assaulted on September 12 by a military intelligence officer in Pusat province after reporting on illegal logging. The journalist later filed a lawsuit against the officer. The case was pending in Pusat's provincial court.

Ratha Visal, a reporter with Radio Free Asia, was hit and injured by a military vehicle while taking photographs of alleged illegal logging presided over by military officials in remote Ratanakiri province on September 30. Visal said a military official fired three shots into the air before running him over, according to reports compiled by the Cambodian Association to Protect Journalists (CAPJ), a press freedom advocacy group.

The Club of Cambodian Journalists (CCJ), the country's largest press association, urged the government to open independent investigations into the mysterious traffic accidents that resulted in the deaths of two provincial journalists, one of whom had reported about alleged official complicity in illegal logging in Kampong Cham province, and the other about police corruption in Koh Kong province. As of November, the CCJ said, the government had not taken up their request. The journalists' names were withheld by the CCJ for security reasons.

The Cambodian government maintained tight control over the electronic media, dominating the news agenda for all seven television stations and all but two radio frequencies. In November, the government barred state-owned television and radio stations from reading or commenting on newspaper stories on the air. Widespread poverty and illiteracy have stunted the development of any self-sustaining, provincially oriented print media. To promote more regional news reporting, the U.S. aid organization Care International volunteered in June to help establish the country's first community radio station. The Ministry of Information rejected the proposal and delayed drafting legislation for the licensing of such stations.

CHINA

President Hu Jintao consolidated his leadership in March during a legislative session that formalized the transition of power from Jiang Zemin. Hu's administration distinguished itself by its hard-line stance against dissidents, intellectuals, and activists, intensifying a far-reaching and severe crackdown on the media. Central authorities arrested and prosecuted journalists under broad national security legislation, while simultaneously ramping up the regulations that undermine the right to express opinions and transmit information in China.

The government's ambitious project of media control is unique in the world's history. Never have so many lines of communication in the hands of so many people been met with such obsessive resistance from a central authority. The Chinese government has merged its participation in the world market and political affairs with a throwback attachment to Mao-era principles of propaganda. By fostering technological and commercial growth, it has placed the media in the hands of ordinary citizens—and then used these same capabilities to ensure that its citizens cannot blog the word "democracy," publish an independent analysis of cross-straits relations, send a text message about a gathering protest, or report on the workings of the Propaganda Department.

More people use cell phones in China than anywhere else in the world, even as authorities continue to monitor and censor text messages. The nation's Internet users surpass 100 million by most estimates, although they face a massive and sophisticated government firewall restricting news and information.

This is repression of a different order. As in the former Soviet Union, regimes in North Korea and Burma have exerted more direct and absolute control over a few, limited paths of communication. China, by contrast, is encouraging greater commercialization of the mass news media; broadcast and print news outlets have broadened their roles, and the press corps has grown to hundreds of thousands of government-accredited journalists. But as the Chinese government promotes market-based mass media, it still censors to great effect. The government-run *People's Daily* reported in February that censorship agencies permanently shut down 338 publications in 2004 for printing "internal" information, closed 202 branch offices of newspapers, and punished 73 organizations for illegally "engaging in news activities."

The death of Zhao Ziyang in January offered international observers an opportunity to witness the kind of top-down censorship that marks events involving Communist Party leadership, past and present. Zhao, a former party chief, was ousted from his position and placed under lifelong house arrest after appealing to students to leave Tiananmen Square before the military crackdown of June 4, 1989. After his death, propaganda authorities permitted newspapers in China to carry just a few state-produced sentences about his life and death. The official government obituary issued by the Xinhua News Agency and read on Chinese TV after his unpublicized memorial service cited Zhao's "serious mistakes" during the "political disturbance" of 1989. Internet bulletin boards hummed with eulogies that vanished like the sound of voices a moment after they appeared. Only statements in code or oblique metaphor survived online in China, while overseas Chinese-language Web sites were flooded with memory and protest.

The blackout of Zhao's death seemed to spring from the government's fear that the event could generate protests or calls for reforms, as other reformists' deaths have done previously. Three months later, China saw the kind of mass, unauthorized urban protests it feared—albeit in an unexpected form. Japan's approval of a textbook that glossed over World War II atrocities sparked large demonstrations in China's major cities over a period of weeks. Protesters initially found some support in the strongly nationalist rhetoric of editorials and news articles from newspapers under direct government control. Authorities acted to stop the protests only after groups and individuals had circulated a petition signed by millions to keep Japan out of the United Nations Security Council and organized spontaneous nationwide demonstrations through Internet chat rooms and cell phone text messages. Censorship agencies suppressed coverage of the protests, and references to the demonstrations on Web sites were excised.

News reports said that several people were arrested for inciting protests online. Local media reported that Shanghai resident Tang Ye was sentenced to five years in prison for "disturbing public order" for distributing a guide to an April 16 protest via text message and the Internet. Writer Yang Maodong, commonly known by his pen name Guo Feixiong, was held for 16 days after applying for a permit to hold a protest; he later told reporters he believed he was detained because he was an Internet writer. Guo was arrested again in September for his online writing and advocacy of villagers' campaign to recall an elected chief in the Guangdong village of Taishi. This time, Guo was held for three months before being released in late December. Prosecutors told him he would not be indicted.

In September, the government announced a fresh set of restrictions on Internet news content that seemed to reflect its concerns over the anti-Japan demonstrations and increasingly frequent rural protests. The rules added two new areas of forbidden content to a list that already included news that "divulges state secrets," "jeopardizes the integrity of the nation's unity," "harms the honor or interests of the nation," or "propagates evil cults" (an apparent reference to the banned Falun Gong religious sect). The new regulations also banned content that incites "illegal" gatherings or demonstrations, or is distributed in the name of "illegal civil organizations." Web sites posting restricted news content would be fined or shut down, according to the regulations.

The new Internet restrictions also aimed to stem independent reporting and commentary by requiring bulletin board systems, Web sites associated with search engines, and online text messaging services to register as news organizations. The rules stated that Web sites that had not been established by an official news outlet ("news work unit") were forbidden from gathering or editing their own news or commentary. The regulations outlawed the kind of self-generated news and commentary that had become a fixture of search portals like *Sina* and *Sohu* and popular bulletin board systems such as *Xici Hutong*. Administrators of these sites had long censored their own news content and monitored public discussions to avoid being shut down by authorities, but the new restrictions added a layer of direct government involvement in their practices while circumscribing their legitimate scope.

Less than a week after these regulations were issued, the popular bulletin board system *Yannan* posted a notice that it would be closed for "cleanup and rectification" until further notice. The Web site's administrators had earlier deleted all entries related to the turbulent recall campaign in the village of Taishi, which pitted hundreds of protesting villagers against local officials and police. The Taishi protests captivated observers around the country, who saw it as a test of the government's commitment to experiments in "grassroots" democracy. *Yannan* was pivotal in providing updated information and commentary that went further in scope and diversity of opinion than the restricted coverage allowed in mainland print and broadcast news. Guo was arrested after writing extensively on Taishi for *Yannan*.

Later, two foreign journalists who traveled to the area were beaten, while others were harassed and interrogated. The attacks on foreign correspondents highlighted the problem of violence against the media in China, which much more often targets local journalists.

According to CPJ research, China was the world's leading jailer of journalists for the seventh consecutive year in 2005, with 32 behind bars on December 1. Yet, imprisoning journalists is not the government's principal means of keeping a rein on the press. Instead, a program of self-censorship and direct censorship is achieved through administrative mechanisms that guarantee a hierarchy of control extending from the central government to news editors. Editors are much more often fired, demoted, or otherwise penalized by the Propaganda Department than criminally prosecuted, local journalists told CPJ. Loopholes in this system of control are quickly identified, first by reporters, and then by authorities who seek to close them. Hong Kong and international newspapers reported that propaganda officials worked to close one such loophole in 2005 by cracking down on "extra-territorial reporting" (*yidi baodao*), a common practice of conducting investigative reporting outside the jurisdiction of local officials in a newspaper's home area.

Criminal prosecution is devastating for the individuals involved and sends a strong warning to other journalists. The detention in April of Hong Kong journalist Ching Cheong, a veteran reporter for the Singapore daily *The Straits Times*, set off shock waves among his many supporters worldwide. It sent a disturbing signal particularly to Hong Kong journalists accustomed to protection from repressive mainland laws. Ching's wife told CPJ and international reporters that Ching was detained while seeking transcripts of interviews with Zhao Ziyang. After international media reported the news a month after his arrest, a spokesman for the Chinese Foreign Ministry released a statement accusing Ching of spying for an overseas organization. Ching was unable to give his side of the story; authorities used the national security accusation to deny him access to a lawyer.

A small bomb explosion at the offices of the independent Hong Kong newspaper *Ming Pao* gave journalists there another shock in November. It was unclear what motivated the attack. One staffer was injured.

The espionage charges leveled against Ching, a Hong Kong citizen, were uncommon, and extraordinarily serious. But authorities frequently imprison mainland Chinese journalists on national security–related charges, especially those of "inciting subversion" and "divulging state secrets." In November, CPJ honored imprisoned journalist Shi Tao with its 2005 International Press Freedom Award. Shi, an editor of the Changsha-based *Dangdai Shang Bao*, was arrested in late 2004 and convicted of divulging state secrets abroad for posting online his notes summarizing Propaganda Department instructions to his newspaper. The information contained in the notes outlined only the broad areas of concern brought up in the meeting, including the government's warning about the possible destabilizing effect of dissidents' returning to mark the 15th anniversary of the crackdown at Tiananmen Square, and instructions to news editors to gather relevant information. For that, Shi was sentenced to 10 years in prison in April.

The Chinese law on state secrets is toxic to the development of a free press. The government counts several categories of official data on land use, labor protests, unemployment, public health issues, environmental pollution, war casualties, and ongoing investigations of party leaders among its "state secrets," according to a widely cited list compiled by a Chinese blogger and considered to be authoritative. In September, Xinhua reported that the death toll in natural disasters would no longer be labeled a state secret. But the classification can also be applied after the fact by the State Secrecy Bureau, as it was in Shi's case. The law is vague enough to be used against any journalist who reports on politically inconvenient news, including information that is widely known or has been previously published. Once applied, it allows detention for renewable periods of months without access to a lawyer and without charge or trial. *New York Times* researcher Zhao Yan, arrested under this law on suspicion of leaking advance information about Jiang Zemin's retirement, remained in jail without trial more than a year after he was initially detained in September 2004. Zhao was finally indicted in December on charges of leaking state secrets.

An outbreak of the avian flu, including a handful of human cases, was not officially treated as a state secret in the manner of SARS, and the government pledged full transparency. But an editorial in the pioneering Beijing-based *Caijing* magazine accused officials of withholding information and criticized the local media for being slow to report the story. In November, officials covered up news of a toxic slick from a chemical plant explosion, initially attributing a disruption in the water service in the northeastern city of Harbin to pipe repairs. When authorities later admitted that 100 tons of poisonous chemicals had spilled into the Songhua River, the national news media condemned the actions of officials responsible for withholding information and called for accountability. The official cover-up, coming on top of the avian flu problems, further undermined the government's credibility.

Writers working outside of China's regulatory framework remained at huge risk in 2005. Two freelance journalists, both contributors to banned overseas news Web sites, were charged and sentenced to long prison terms for "inciting subversion," and another was indicted on the same charge. Zhang Lin, a longtime dissident, was sentenced to five years in prison in July for essays criticizing the Communist Party. His wife believes that he was also punished for his reporting on labor protests and official scandals. On September 1, he launched a hunger strike that he sustained for nearly a month. Another Internet essayist, Zheng Yichun, was sentenced to seven years in prison on the same charge. Freelance journalist Li Jianping was detained on suspicion of defamation in May, apparently for his online writings criticizing party leaders. Authorities brought subversion charges against him in August.

Prosecution of journalists, though not widely reported, was not lost on their colleagues. In June, more than 2,000 Chinese journalists signed an open letter to a Guangdong court urging the release of imprisoned *Nanfang Dushi Bao* employees Yu Huafeng and Li Minying.

Amid the increasingly visible media crackdown of 2005, foreign players in the information sector came under pressure from the Chinese government and scrutiny from CPJ and other international observers. Throughout the year, the government announced a series of regulations restricting foreign influence and investment in news, film, and other cultural products. Backing off a liberalization of foreign investment rules in 2004, which appeared to be promulgated in preparation for Beijing's hosting of the Olympics in 2008, the government made it more difficult for foreign companies to participate in joint media ventures. At the same time, the intensity of the crackdown raised inevitable questions of international companies' complicity in China's censorship and prosecution of journalists.

In July, the news Web site *Boxun News*, which is banned in China, reported that American Internet giant Yahoo had provided account information used to prosecute journalist Shi. When international newspapers picked up the story, Yahoo responded by stating that, as a global company, it had to follow the laws, regulations, and customs of the countries in which it was operating. In August, Yahoo beat its rivals to win a large stake in the Chinese e-commerce company Alibaba.com.

NEPAL

King Gyanendra Bir Bikram Shah Dev seized direct power on February 1, dealing an unprecedented blow to press freedom. He cut all telephone lines, blocked Internet service, and sent the army to major media outlets to censor the news line by line. Hundreds of political leaders, civil activists, and journalists were detained. The king dismissed his multiparty government and declared a state of emergency, which lasted three months.

Negative reporting or commentary about the king and his royal coup were banned. The Ministry of Information and Communication (MOIC) ordered journalists to vet with security forces all reporting on the conflict between the government and Maoist rebels, who have been fighting since 1996 to overthrow the monarchy. Most devastating of all was a ban on news on the country's more than 40 private FM radio stations, a primary source of information for many Nepalese who are illiterate or do not have access to print or TV news. Up to 2,000 radio journalists faced unemployment, and only radio stations run by the state or by Maoist rebels continued broadcasting news.

While some of these restrictions were temporary, others were not. A draconian media ordinance issued in October codified much of the king's censorship as law, making a return to democracy under the monarch appear increasingly unlikely.

Journalists outside the Kathmandu Valley were hardest hit. Long before Gyanendra assumed absolute control in February, reporting had been dangerous for rural journalists, especially those in the districts affected by fighting between rebels and security forces. Both sides routinely targeted journalists with threats, physical attack, and prolonged, often brutal detention. After the state of emergency was declared, local officials took liberties in interpreting the bans on reporting, and rural journalists often faced the greatest restrictions. Some newspapers stopped publishing entirely. Reporters paid by the story were not compensated when their work was censored. Journalists arrested far from the capital did not have immediate access to local and international media or to human rights organizations that could advocate for their release.

Some rural journalists accused rebels of imposing their views on coverage in the same way as the king. Maoists continued to abduct journalists in retaliation for negative reporting. In May, rebels abducted Som Sharma, a reporter for the weekly newspaper *Aankha*, from his home in the eastern district of Ilam. He was held for nearly two months. Journalist Bikram Giri was kidnapped by Maoists in far western Darchula district and held for roughly a week. Rebels also bombed rural telecommunications and television towers.

A frightening development in 2005 was the emergence of anti-rebel militias trained by the army. In March, a reporter for the Kathmandu-based Nepali-language magazine *Himal Khabarpatrika* disappeared while reporting on anti-rebel violence in the district of Kapilbastu. Encouraged by the government, mobs there had displaced thousands by razing houses and killing suspected Maoists. Reporter J.B. Pun Magar called his editor to say that he had been abducted by rebels. But when he was released three days later, he told colleagues that he suspected his kidnappers were pro-government vigilantes.

As violence in rural Nepal continued unabated, it was journalists in Kathmandu who were best positioned to challenge the king's curtailment of press freedom. Protest, muted at first, grew as reporters and editors around the country were summoned and interrogated by civil and military personnel for violations of the reporting bans. In the capital, journalists soon found ways to circumvent restrictions. The Internet was a vital way of transmitting information abroad, and sales of shortwave radios soared as citizens tuned in to the BBC Nepali service. During the first days of the state of emergency, editorials obliquely protested the king's move. Newspaper copy cut by military censors appeared as blank spaces until these spaces, too, were banned. The king allowed English-language and online media greater freedom to criticize the government, perhaps to give the impression to the international community that reports of a crackdown were exaggerated. But within weeks, Nepali-language publications, including Kantipur Group newspapers and some weeklies, had begun resisting the government's efforts at censorship.

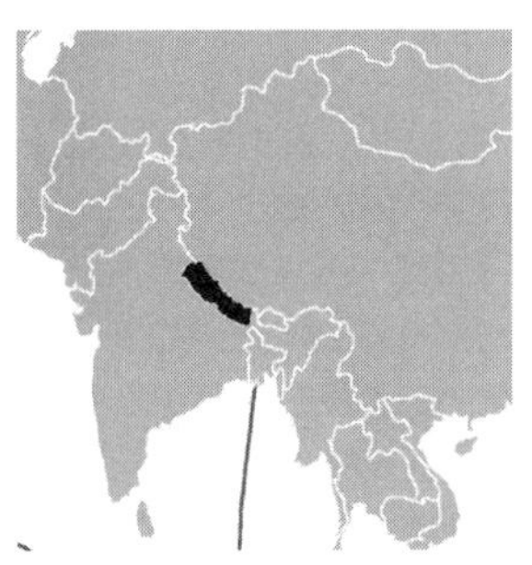

International censure of the king's dismissal of the multiparty government was swift and strong. Gyanendra responded to the criticism by assuring foreign allies and donors that the state of emergency would be lifted within 100 days. Technically, he kept his promise, and rescinded the order that had given security forces sweeping authority. But the king was silent on the status of the press restrictions, creating an environment of uncertainty that kept journalists on guard. In June, reports that he planned to pass a new ordinance amending the media law heightened fears that emergency restrictions would become permanent.

Journalists stepped up demonstrations demanding the restoration of a free press and the release of imprisoned colleagues. In Kathmandu, marches spearheaded by the Federation of Nepalese Journalists and the Save Independent Radio Movement entered areas of the capital where protests were restricted, and many of the marchers were arrested.

Supporters of the Nepalese press, including CPJ, kept a steady spotlight on the conditions confronting journalists. CPJ representatives made three research and advocacy missions to Nepal in 2005. In April, CPJ Executive Director Ann Cooper and BBC reporter Daniel Lak met with journalists in Kathmandu and the city of Nepalgunj in midwestern Nepal to report on threats and harassment, the sharp restrictions placed on print publications, and the elimination of radio news. In July, CPJ Asia consultant Shawn Crispin traveled to Nepal with delegates from nine international organizations to meet with representatives of the government, army, civil society, and media to discuss ongoing censorship. And in late October, Lak returned to Nepal as a CPJ representative to meet with an imprisoned journalist and report on a Supreme Court battle that had taken center stage in the fight for press freedom.

Gyanendra left the press with few options for challenging his edicts. The ousted political parties were powerless, the cabinet did the king's bidding, and the army remained loyal. Journalists appealed to the Supreme Court to uphold the shreds of a constitution that had enshrined democracy in Nepal just 15 years earlier.

Several legal challenges to the injunction against FM radio news had some positive effect. In May, the director of a banned radio production company, Communication Corner, filed a challenge with the Supreme Court. The court ruled in favor of the company, which continued producing programs. In a separate case in August, the Supreme Court stayed a government order to shut down Nepal FM 91.8 after the station defied the prohibition against broadcasting news. Independent news radio stations read the decision as confirmation that the ban was illegal. After more than six months of silence, dozens of independent FM radio stations across the country resumed broadcasting news.

The victory was short-lived. In October, the ax fell again on Nepal's press when the king promulgated the media ordinance that journalists had been protesting, reinstating the ban on FM radio news broadcasts. It placed limits on ownership that seemed specifically to target Kantipur, the nation's largest and most independent media group; codified restrictions on criticizing the king and the royal family; and increased the maximum penalty for defamation to two years in prison.

Media groups again filed petitions with the Supreme Court in hopes that the judiciary would overturn the law. At the same time, the financial effects of the king's clampdown proved durable. The government withdrew advertising from independent news outlets, depriving them of a major source of revenue. Most newspapers significantly reduced the number of pages published.

Scores, perhaps hundreds, of journalists were arrested after February 1. Most were detained only briefly, but others were held for weeks or even months under harsh antiterrorism legislation that allows lengthy detention without trial. By December 1, when CPJ conducted its annual census of imprisoned journalists worldwide, only one Nepalese journalist, Tel Narayan Sapkota, remained in confinement. The former editor of the weekly *Yojana* has been held since November 2003, when police arrested him at a printing facility. Sapkota told CPJ that he was kept blindfolded for five months before his transfer out of police barracks. He has never been convicted of a crime.

Torture by Nepal's security forces is commonplace. In July, journalist Chandra Giri, formerly chief reporter of the Kathmandu weekly *Shram*, told CPJ that he had been blindfolded and tortured with electric shocks, beatings, and cold water following his detention on December 31, 2004. Security forces interrogated him about his alleged Maoist connections and news sources. Giri was released from prison in June after a habeas corpus petition was filed with the Supreme Court on his behalf. He later sought damages from the army.

In October, imprisoned journalist Maheshwar Pahari died in custody after multiple illnesses he endured in custody. Local doctors had recommended transferring Pahari to Kathmandu for treatment, but authorities refused, citing security concerns. Pahari, a reporter for the weekly *Rastriya Swabhiman*, was detained in January 2004 and rearrested multiple times under antiterrorism laws. Local journalists told CPJ that security forces might have held him to gather information about his contacts within the Maoist movement. He was never charged or tried.

While the king defended his moves as a necessary component of his fight against the Maoist insurgency, the rebels were no weaker at year's end than before. They continued to control much of the country, and ousted opposition leaders agreed to meet with Maoist negotiators in India after the rebels called a cease-fire in the fall.

PAKISTAN

Striking contradictions emerged during the sixth year of Gen. Pervez Musharraf's rule. Baton-wielding police attacked journalists in several high-profile incidents, including two on World Press Freedom Day in May, even as the administration publicly proclaimed its commitment to press freedom. Journalists faced new threats of imprisonment for defamation and programming deemed "vulgar," while the broadcast sector blossomed with the launch of numerous commercial television and radio stations.

When a massive 7.6-magnitude earthquake struck in the mountainous northern region of Kashmir in October, journalists faced their greatest professional challenge. The death toll climbed above 87,000 after the October 8 earthquake, and the journalistic community was not spared. At least 11 journalists died and others were unaccounted for, while dozens of others lost relatives and homes, according to the Pakistan Federal Union of Journalists (PFUJ). The PFUJ worked with other press organizations to raise money to help deliver supplies to journalists in the devastated areas. Local and international journalists traveled amid the destruction and widespread hardship to transmit reports from the remote region.

Throughout the year, local journalists described disturbing patterns of economic pressure, threats, and attacks against individual reporters, newspapers, and publishing groups. The brutal February murders of two journalists in Pakistan's tribal areas marked a low point for reporters covering the military's effort to flush out members of al-Qaeda and the Taliban from the semi-autonomous region. Unknown gunmen opened fire on a bus carrying 10 journalists in Wana, capital of South Waziristan, killing Mir Nawab, a freelance cameraman with Associated Press Television News, and Allah Noor, a reporter with *The Nation* and Khyber TV. Two others were injured: Anwar Shakir, a stringer for Agence France-Presse, and Dilawar Khan, who was working for Al-Jazeera.

Returning from the town of Sararogha, where they covered the surrender of suspected tribal militant Baitullah Mehsud, the journalists had just entered government-controlled territory when the attackers sprayed their bus with gunfire. In a letter faxed to newspapers, an unknown group calling itself "Sipah-e-Islam" (Soldiers of Islam) took responsibility for the killings and accused journalists of "working for Christians" and of "being used as tools in negative propaganda...against the Muslim mujahedeen." Local journalists who witnessed the attack complained that no attempt was made to stop the gunmen's vehicle and that no real investigation has taken place since.

Hayatullah Khan, a reporter for the Urdu-language daily *Ausaf* was kidnapped on December 5 by unidentified gunmen in the North Waziristan tribal region bordering Afghanistan. Five men with AK-47 assault rifles forced Khan's car off the road, said his brother, Mohammad Ehsan, who was in the vehicle. Four days earlier, Khan had covered an explosion in the town of Haisori. His reports contradicted Pakistani authorities' claim that Abu Hamza Rabia, a senior al-Qaeda commander, died when munitions exploded inside a house. Khan quoted local tribesmen as saying the house was hit by a missile fired from an aircraft. U.S. networks ABC and NBC both reported that the blast appeared to have been caused by a U.S. missile fired from an unmanned, remote-controlled Predator aircraft.

Journalists in tribal areas said they were increasingly at the mercy of militants, some of them alleged Taliban members, making conditions too dangerous to report the news. Mujeebur Rehman, a correspondent for the Lahore-based national *Daily Times* and a stringer for Reuters, narrowly escaped assassination in Wana in May when masked gunmen fired repeatedly in a drive-by shooting. Security forces systematically restricted access to conflict zones in tribal areas, effectively prohibiting even local journalists from covering their activities.

In larger cities, journalists suffered an increasing number of violent attacks, often at the hands of police and local political parties. On April 14, brass-knuckled men from the regional Jamhoori Watan Party stormed the office of Kamran Mumtaz, editor of the *Daily Mashraq* in the western city of Quetta, and punched the journalist in the face. The men claimed that articles in the newspaper were biased against their party. When other journalists protested the attack in a demonstration in Quetta days later, police tore down their banners and forcibly dispersed the group, according to the state-run Pakistan Newswire.

Police obstructed coverage of opposition leader Asif Ali Zardari's visit to Lahore on April 16, when 50 journalists traveling with him were detained at the airport for three hours. Police commandos confiscated their gear and beat them. Police warned other journalists that they were given instructions from "the top" to take the equipment, the *South Asia Tribune* reported.

The gap between government rhetoric and police harassment was never more apparent than on May 3, World Press Freedom Day. Journalists rallying in the capital, Islamabad, were harassed and as many as 30 were detained for several hours, according to local journalists and news reports. Journalists marching for press freedom in Lahore were attacked by baton-swinging police. The same day, Federal Information Minister Sheikh Rashid Ahmed told the audience at a "Free Press for Free Pakistan" conference that the "government believes in the freedom of press and welcomes positive criticism," the Pakistan Newswire reported.

Another example of official disconnect occurred in August, when Prime Minister Shaukat Aziz told a delegation of journalists from Sindh province that there was complete press freedom in Pakistan. Just weeks later, political activists beat senior journalist Tajammul Hussain and stole a bag containing his notebooks in full view of police at a polling station in the Sindh capital, Karachi, according to the Pakistan Press Foundation.

After revelations that two suicide bombers involved in the July 7 attack on the London transit system had traveled to the cities of Karachi and Lahore in November 2004, the Sindh government launched a crackdown on conservative newspapers. It raided the offices of several Karachi-based publications in July and banned three weekly newspapers in August for creating "sectarian extremism and hatred." Several editors were arrested, including Mohammad Tahir, editor and publisher of the conservative weekly *Wajood*. Tahir was held for almost two months on charges of publishing "hate material" before being granted bail. Tahir told the BBC in a jailhouse interview that police cited his criticism of the government as the reason for his arrest. "They never mentioned anything about hate material," he said. The Sindh High Court lifted the ban on the weeklies in late August, but the charges against Tahir stood.

The government continued to use its advertising expenditures to pressure news outlets. It discontinued ads in two papers from the conservative Nawa-i-Waqt publishing group from May through August in retaliation for critical articles in the publications, according to local journalists' groups. Newspapers are highly dependent on government ads; agencies responsible for railroads, telecommunications, and highway construction can provide as much as 50 percent of many newspapers' ad sales. Private companies frequently follow the government's example and withdraw their own ads, according to local sources. In 2004, the government cut advertising in the group's papers for 10 months.

The provincial government of Sindh stood out on this front, too. Beginning in May, it withheld advertising revenue from the national daily *Dawn* as punishment for critical reporting, media sources told CPJ.

Foreign journalists were restricted in their movement and required to apply for visas for travel outside of the capital, Islamabad. In August, three European documentary filmmakers were held incommunicado for 16 days in Peshawar, capital of the Northwest Frontier province, after taking video of what turned out to be a military compound.

Local journalist and fixer Khawar Mehdi Rizvi was vindicated in April, when a Quetta antiterrorism court acquitted him of sedition charges. The charges stemmed from his work in December 2003 with two journalists from the French newsweekly *L'Express*. Rizvi traveled with them to Quetta, in southwestern Pakistan, where they reported on Taliban activity in the Afghanistan-Pakistan border area. Rizvi had been held incommunicado for five weeks after his initial arrest. He left the country in late 2004.

A positive trend came in the broadcasting sector. A dozen new radio stations were launched, including several dedicated to news; the government also awarded licenses to 20 cable television channels, although all must broadcast from outside the country. State Minister for Information Anisa Zeb Tahirkheli announced in June that the government was installing transmitters nationwide to help radio station development. Eighty-four FM stations were broadcasting by the government's account, but the transmission of radio news was still restricted. In April, authorities canceled the license of FM 103 in Lahore after it aired hourly Urdu-language bulletins from the BBC World Service, the BBC reported. The station's license, they said, did not allow news broadcasts.

In November, officers from the Pakistan Electronic Media Regulatory Authority (PEMRA) raided another FM 103 station, this one in Karachi, seizing transmission equipment and halting broadcasts after the station allegedly violated the ban on rebroadcast of foreign news. The station had aired an Urdu-language BBC program about the October earthquake.

A bill strengthening PEMRA passed in the lower house of the National Assembly in May, alarming press freedom advocates. It would allow PEMRA to ban news outlets in the name of "national interest," "national security," or "vulgarity," and violations could be punishable by three years imprisonment and fines of 10 million rupees (US$160,000). The bill lapsed before being brought in front of the upper house of parliament, the Senate, and was referred to a parliamentary mediation committee at the end of the year. The bill's future remained uncertain.

ASIA

The investigation into the 2002 kidnapping and murder of *Wall Street Journal* reporter Daniel Pearl continued, with two notable arrests. Police detained Mohammed Sohail in March in Karachi and said that Sohail had confessed to involvement in the murder. He was suspected of filming Pearl's murder. Another suspect, Hashim Qadeer, was arrested in the eastern city of Gujranwala in July. Qadeer was accused of setting up the first meeting between Pearl and his kidnappers. The four men who were convicted in Pearl's murder in 2002 were again denied appeal hearings.

PHILIPPINES

The epidemic of murderous attacks on the Philippine press corps finally forced the government to reverse its longtime denial of the problem and to step up efforts to combat the violence. Some limited progress in law enforcement, a landmark conviction in one murder case, and growing support for broadcast reforms could signal a change for the better for the Philippine press.

Four journalists were killed in retaliation for their work in 2005, down from a record high of eight in 2004—and bringing to 22 the number of Philippine journalists murdered since 2000, according to CPJ research. The death toll drew international attention when CPJ named the country the most murderous in the world for journalists in a May report.

The brazen March murder of a crusading female columnist sparked outrage among press freedom groups and the public. A gunman walked into the home of Marlene Garcia-Esperat on Easter weekend and shot her in the head in front of her two children. Garcia-Esperat had made many enemies while investigating corruption for her weekly column in the *Midland Review* on the southern island of Mindanao. Task Force Newsmen, a Philippines National Police unit launched by President Gloria Macapagal Arroyo in 2004 to track down journalists' killers, arrested four suspects two weeks later. The suspects accused two Mindanao agriculture officials of plotting the murder.

Tensions between the press and the government came to a head in May when two more journalists were murdered in less than a week. The killings came just as CPJ released "Marked for Death," a worldwide analysis of press attacks that found the Philippines to be the most murderous country. The designation startled many Filipinos, who had grown numb to the ongoing violence. Efforts by CPJ and other domestic and international press freedom organizations to raise awareness of the deadly trend had been rebuffed by government officials time and again. Presidential spokesman Ignacio Bunye discounted a 2004 CPJ assessment as "misplaced and misleading," and he initially dismissed the "most murderous" label as "unfair and exaggerated."

But two days after CPJ released "Marked for Death," the death toll grew higher still. Radio broadcaster Klein Cantoneros died on May 4 after being shot several times by motorcycle-riding gunmen in Dipolog City on Mindanao. Cantoneros, who leased airtime through a controversial practice known as "block-timing," was known for hard-hitting commentary in which he accused local officials of corruption and illegal gambling. He fired back at his assailants with a .45-caliber pistol but succumbed to his injuries later that day. In September, police arrested a suspect after a witness identified him as one of three gunmen.

On May 10, publisher Philip Agustin was shot in the head through an open window in his daughter's home, about 70 miles (113 kilometers) northeast of Manila. Agustin was about to release a special edition of his paper, the *Starline Times Recorder*, dedicated to corruption and illegal logging in the nearby town of Dingalan. He was also a critic of the mayor of Dingalan, Jaime Ylarde. The gunman, arrested four days later, accused the mayor of plotting the murder, according to news reports. Ylarde has repeatedly denied any involvement and has not been charged.

Outraged at the growing death toll, reporters in Manila started a group called ARMED—the Association of Responsible Media—to train journalists in firearms and security issues. Images of gun-toting journalists on firing ranges received widespread international coverage, but local Philippine groups like the National Union of Journalists questioned the wisdom of adding more firepower to an already deadly situation.

Facing a new wave of violence and international attention, the government finally modified its public response to the killings. Arroyo called the murders of journalists "acts of violence against the nation itself." She launched a five million peso (US$92,500) Press Freedom Fund to offer rewards for information on the killings, instituted witness-protection programs, and assured the country that "the whole criminal justice system has been alerted and put in motion."

A CPJ delegation visited the Philippines in June to investigate the reasons behind the killings, traveling to the capital, Manila, and provinces in Luzon, the Visayas, and Mindanao. The delegation consisted of Abi Wright, CPJ's Asia program coordinator; Roby Alampay, executive director of the Southeast Asian Press Alliance; and A. Linn Neumann, executive editor of the Hong Kong-based daily *The Standard*. In a subsequent special report, "On the Radio, Under the Gun," CPJ's Wright found that a deeply entrenched culture of impunity, rampant corruption, gun violence, and a rising overall crime rate conspired to create deadly conditions for the press. Government officials have been linked to half of the journalist murder cases, and police officers are frequently named as suspected gunmen.

Journalists also told CPJ that professional reforms were needed to raise ethical standards. Block-timing, in which radio commentators lease airtime and solicit their own commercial sponsors, drew particular concern. Critics said block-timers are more likely to abuse their power and engage in questionable practices. One such practice is called "AC/DC journalism: Attack, collect. Defend, collect." These broadcasters attack and defend reputations based on who is paying them off.

CPJ found that 17 of the 22 journalists murdered in the Philippines over the last five years were radio broadcasters. At least seven were block-timers, according to the Center for Media Freedom and Responsibility, a local press freedom organization.

Another outspoken block-timer was gunned down in July on Mindanao. Rolando "Dodong" Morales was ambushed and shot at least 15 times by a gang of assailants on motorcycles while he was on his way home from work. Police cited his anti-drug commentaries as a possible motive in the attack. In August, police in General Santos City arrested and filed murder charges against two suspects in Morales' murder, including the alleged mastermind.

The government claimed that it had solved half of the journalist murders committed since 1986, but CPJ and others found the claim to be misleading. The government defines a case as "solved" at the mere identification of a suspect. While more criminal cases were filed against suspects since Task Force Newsmen was formed, convictions in these cases remained extremely rare.

The 2005 murder cases showed law enforcement acting more quickly than in the past, but the record is far from complete. The murder charges brought against the purported masterminds in the Garcia-Esperat murder were dropped in September because of conflicting evidence. Although the gunman in the Agustin murder alleged that the local mayor had hired him, no legal action was immediately taken against the politician. Suspects have been arrested in the Cantoneros and Morales cases, but they have yet to go to trial.

Journalists were encouraged by a guilty verdict in one closely watched murder trial. Former police officer Guillermo Wapile was convicted on November 29 of gunning down Edgar Damalerio, an award-winning editor and radio commentator, in Pagadian City in 2002. Damalerio's widow, Gemma, had successfully lobbied to move the trial to Cebu City—away from local violence and corruption—in hopes of getting a fair proceeding.

Two witnesses to the Damalerio murder were slain while the case was pending. In February, unidentified gunmen killed witness Edgar Amoro as he left the high school where he taught. The other, Jury Lavitano, was murdered in 2002. The sole remaining witness, Edgar Ongue, testified despite threats to his life.

Judge Ramon Codilla sentenced Wapile to life imprisonment. A courtroom filled with the journalist's family, friends, and supporters erupted in applause as the judge's verdict was read aloud. Damalerio's widow told CPJ she was "very happy" with the verdict, and she thanked press groups for their efforts to secure justice for her husband.

Press freedom advocates were hopeful that the verdict would sustain the momentum in the campaign for safer and more just conditions. Yet considerable challenges remain. Three more journalists were gunned down in less than two weeks in late 2005. CPJ is investigating to determine whether the slayings were connected to the victims' work.

SRI LANKA

The slow unraveling of a cease-fire between the government and the separatist Liberation Tigers of Tamil Eelam (LTTE) complicated Sri Lanka's efforts to recover from the December 2004 tsunami and hindered the media's ability to cover the disaster and other important stories. Two Tamil journalists were murdered in 2005 and others were threatened. Independent journalists were not only caught in the feuding between the government and the rebels, known as the Tamil Tigers, but also in the conflict between Tamil factions.

Any sense of national solidarity that arose following the tsunami, which killed 30,000 people on the island, was short-lived. The LTTE accused the government of failing to help the Tiger-controlled areas of the ravaged east coast. Under international pressure, President Chandrika Kumaratunga agreed to share international relief aid with the Tigers. The deal stalled, however, after intense opposition by the hard-line Sinhalese nationalist party, the People's Liberation Front (JVP).

The east, which bore the brunt of the tsunami, was also hit by violence between the Tigers and a splinter group led by a rebel commander known as Colonel Karuna. The government denied an LTTE allegation that the Karuna faction, which emerged in March 2004, was backed by the Sri Lankan army. But many international observers believe that the government is involved in the inter-Tamil conflict, making that fighting a breach of the cease-fire. The killings ebbed following the tsunami but soon resumed, with both sides targeting each other's supporters, including journalists.

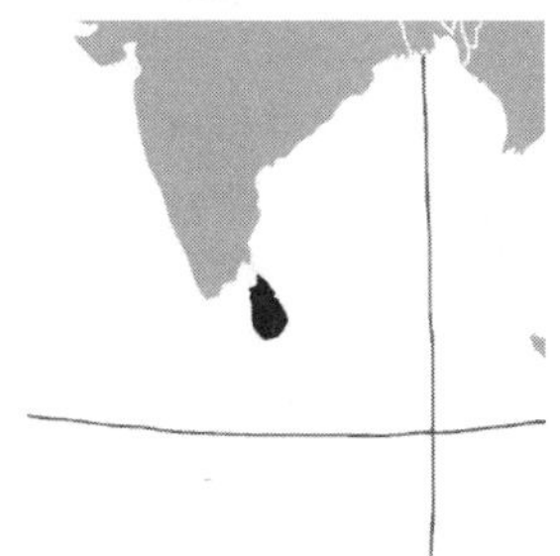

In April, veteran Tamil journalist Dharmeratnam Sivaram was seized outside a police station in the capital, Colombo, and shot dead. Sivaram was a founding member and contributor to the *TamilNet* news Web site and a military and political columnist for the English-language *Daily Mirror*. He had written sympathetically about Tamil nationalism and the Tigers, putting him at odds with the government and, more recently, with the Karuna faction. Accused by state media in 2001 of being a spy for the LTTE, Sivaram had been under threat for years. In 2004, police twice searched his house looking for weapons. His last article in a Tamil-language newspaper had criticized Karuna.

Police launched an investigation into Sivaram's death that yielded one arrest—a member of the formerly militant and now mainstream People's Liberation Organization of Tamil Eelam (PLOTE), which opposes the LTTE. Another man was arrested but later released for lack of evidence. These developments did not, however, ease the doubts of many Sivaram supporters, who saw the government as unable or unwilling to investigate and prosecute the journalist's killers. Police had yet to make any arrests in connection with the murders of two Tamil journalists in 2004.

After condemning Sivaram's killing, members of the Free Media Movement, an advocacy organization based in Colombo, received death threats in May from a group calling itself "Theraputtabhaya Force" that claimed responsibility for Sivaram's murder. The group is named for a Buddhist monk who fought Tamils in the second century B.C. The editor of the English-language *Sunday Leader*, Lasantha Wickramatunga, requested police protection after a government official called him a terrorist. Other journalists feared that they would be targeted in retaliation for Sivaram's murder because they had written critically about the Tamil Tigers.

Tamil journalists abroad also reported threats from rival groups that escalated in the wake of Sivaram's murder. In May, burglars broke into the London offices of the exiled Tamil radio station Tamil Broadcasting Corporation (TBC) and stole equipment, temporarily forcing the station off the air. The station's program director, V. Ramaraj, blamed the LTTE for the attack.

On August 12 in Colombo, unidentified gunmen killed popular Tamil broadcaster Relangi Selvarajah and her husband. Selvarajah was a radio and television host for the state-run Sri Lanka Broadcasting Corporation (SLBC) and for the Sri Lanka Rupavahini Corporation. Local newspapers reported that Selvarajah also produced an SLBC program that was known for criticizing the LTTE. Her husband was affiliated with PLOTE, raising the possibility that their killings might be related to Sivaram's murder. Political leaders blamed the Tigers, who denied the charges. No arrests had been reported by year's end.

On the same day, assassins killed Sri Lankan Foreign Minister Lakshman Kadirgamar. The Tamil Tigers were widely blamed for the assassination, but they denied responsibility. The killing was seen as a major blow to the peace process, which has been stalled since the LTTE walked out of negotiations in 2003. In November, Prime Minister Mahinda Rajapakse was elected president in a tight race against the more moderate opposition candidate, Ranil Wickremesinghe. LTTE leaders had denounced both candidates, and turnout was low in Tamil areas. Rajapakse's win raised more questions about the possibilities for peace; the new president's supporters opposed concessions to the Tigers, including the prospect of power sharing.

Independent reporting on the conflict in the rebel-held north and east is rare, and journalists in Sri Lanka have recognized the need for media that are free of political influence to meet the challenge. For Tamil journalists and media workers in particular, the tight link between some newspapers and political actors is a dangerous one; media workers are often targeted for their perceived association with militant factions. In June, Kannamuthu Arasakumar, a distributor of the pro-LTTE newspaper *Eelanathan*, was killed while traveling between Batticaloa and Ampara in the eastern region.

But even the most independent reporters put themselves at risk when covering military issues. In July, Kumaratunga accused defense correspondent Iqbal Athas of publishing information harmful to Sri Lanka's national security and threatened legal action against him. Athas, a reporter for the English-language *Sunday Times*, was honored with CPJ's International Press Freedom Award in 1994. No charges were brought against him, but the president's remarks, delivered in front of military personnel, were perceived as a threat to his security.

As the mid-November presidential election approached, fears increased in anticipation of the same violence that had accompanied previous elections. In late August, the Colombo-based Tamil-language newspaper *Sudar Oli*, which had been targeted previously by both LTTE and anti-LTTE forces, was again hit by a spate of attacks. On August 29, grenades lobbed into its printing works killed a guard and injured two staff members. Also in August, three *Sudar Oli* reporters were assaulted; in one case, JVP activists protesting LTTE killings mobbed a photographer and turned him over to the police as a member of the LTTE. Police released him the next day.

In October, two attacks targeted *Thinamurasu*, a Tamil-language newspaper associated with the Eelam People's Democratic Party, which opposes the LTTE. Kingsley Weeratana, a distributor for *Thinamurasu*, was shot and killed while handing out the newspaper in Colombo. Fifteen minutes later, a van parked outside the newspaper's office exploded. No one was injured in that attack.

Later that month, a group of armed men entered a building south of Colombo that housed the printing press for the English-language weeklies *Sunday Leader* and *Midweek Leader*, and the Sinhala-language weekly *Irudina*. The men set fire to bundles of newspaper and warned the factory manager to stop publishing the papers, the *Sunday Leader*'s Wickramatunga told CPJ. The attack came shortly after the *Sunday Leader* published allegations that the prime minister had misappropriated funds intended for tsunami relief.

THAILAND

Press conditions worsened markedly, reflecting the fourth year of deterioration since Prime Minister Thaksin Shinawatra took office in 2001. Most worrisome was the frequent use of litigation that sought criminal penalties and disproportionate monetary damages. The cases echo the repressive practices of neighboring Malaysia and Singapore, where authoritarian governments have long used overwhelming legal threats to intimidate journalists and stifle critical reporting.

The number of criminal and civil defamation suits filed by politicians and their affiliated business interests against journalists and editors rose considerably. Cases in which the Thai Press Council provided bail money for accused journalists had more than doubled, to 55, through September. At the same time, monetary damages sought in civil cases soared and included some of the largest figures ever requested for libel anywhere in the world.

Hearings began in July in the highly anticipated criminal defamation case filed by

the Shin Corp. against media activist Supinya Klangnarong and three senior editors of the Thai-language daily *Thai Post*. Shin, a communications conglomerate founded by Thaksin and majority-owned by his family, charged that the activist damaged the company's reputation in published remarks that hinted at a conflict of interest between Thaksin's public office and his family's private businesses. The four defendants faced the possibility of two years' imprisonment in the case; a verdict was expected in early 2006. In an accompanying civil complaint, Shin sought 400 million baht (US$10 million) in financial damages. The civil suit was scheduled to begin in 2006.

Politically connected corporations and state agencies followed Shin's example, filing punitive legal actions to curb media scrutiny of their activities. Picnic Corp., a cooking-gas company majority-owned and managed by family members of then–Cabinet minister Suriya Lapwisuthisin, filed criminal and civil defamation charges in July against the Thai-language newspaper *Matichon* and its sister publication *Prachachart Tooragit* for reports on alleged accounting fraud at the company. Thailand's Securities and Exchange Commission later suspended trading in Picnic's publicly listed shares due to concerns about the quality of the company's financial disclosure.

Picnic nonetheless sought a stunning 10 billion baht (US$240 million) in damages from *Matichon*, and an additional 5 billion baht (US$120 million) from *Prachachart Tooragit* in the civil suits. The company also sought a punitive court injunction against *Matichon* editors that would bar them from working in journalism for a five-year period.

Two state agencies, the Airports Authority of Thailand and the New Bangkok International Airport, filed criminal defamation charges in August against the English-language daily *Bangkok Post* for a story it published and later retracted about cracks in the runways at the new Bangkok airport.

Bangkok Post managers fired two veteran editors who worked on the story after the government filed its charges, which also included a demand that the newspaper publish and broadcast public apologies in a number of local and foreign news outlets, including CNN and the BBC. The two agencies have also threatened to file a 1 billion baht (US$25 million) civil suit.

Thaksin filed criminal and civil defamation charges against veteran journalist Sondhi Limthongkul and Sarocha Porn-udomsak in September for remarks they made on a television talk show. The journalists alleged that Thaksin had been disloyal to the country's monarch, Bhumibol Adulyadej, by usurping functions traditionally administered by the king, such as the appointment of the Buddhist Sangha supreme patriarch. The government abruptly canceled the popular program, "Muang Thai Rai Sapda," which was carried on state-owned Channel 9 through a concession agreement, on grounds that the show had "promoted misunderstanding among the public."

Thaksin later filed 500 million baht (US$12.5 million) defamation charges against the daily *Manager* for publishing critical comments made by a respected Buddhist monk, Luangta Maha Bua Yannasampanno, who said in a sermon that Thaksin's government was "destroying" the country. The prime minister refrained from filing charges against the monk, even after the outspoken ascetic publicly dared him to do so.

By December, Thaksin said he was withdrawing his several complaints against Sondhi, Sarocha, and Manager Media, according to news reports. His announcement came two days after King Bhumibol Adulyadej publicly invited press scrutiny of the highest levels of Thai government. In a speech given on his 78th birthday, the king said that he was not infallible and that he could be criticized.

Faced with legal and financial uncertainties, Thai publications were targeted for hostile financial takeovers by close associates of the prime minister. In September, GMM Grammy, founded and managed by Paiboon Damrongchaitham, a political ally of the prime minister, took controlling stakes in both *Matichon* and Post Publishing Co., which publishes the *Bangkok Post*.

After public protests by staff and press freedom advocates, GMM Grammy sold down its stake in *Matichon* from 32 percent to 20 percent, allowing *Matichon*'s co-founder, Kanchai Boonpan, to keep control of the company. But GMM Grammy retained its controlling stake in Post Publishing, raising concerns that the *Bangkok Post* may come under managerial pressure to soften its coverage of Thaksin's government.

Family members of Suriya Jungrungreangkit, secretary-general of Thaksin's Thai Rak Thai political party, gradually increased their collective stake in the Nation Group from around 20 percent to more than 22 percent, making them the largest collective shareholder in the staunchly independent media company. Senior Nation Group editors told CPJ they feared that, if the Jungrungreangkit family increased its stake to more than 25 percent, it would have the voting rights to change management.

Krungthep Tooragit, the Nation Group's aggressive Thai-language business daily, broke a story in May revealing irregularities and alleged corruption in Suriya's oversight of the procurement of scanners for Bangkok's new international airport.

Amid spiraling violence in Thailand's southern border regions, Thaksin issued an executive decree in July that empowered the government to censor news for reasons of national security. The government did not use its new censorship powers in the initial months, but democracy advocates said the decree had undermined many of the civil liberties protected under the 1997 constitution, including legal guarantees for freedom of expression and press freedom.

The National Broadcast Commission (NBC), an independent body charged with redistributing the country's radio and television frequencies from the state to the private sector as required by the 1997 constitution, was finally formed in October after a controversial selection process that took more than seven years. Media reform advocates alleged the new body disproportionately represented the same vested interests, including the

Thai military, that already monopolize the country's electronic media.

The NBC was short-lived. In November, the Central Administrative Court nullified its formation due to irregularities in the selection process.

The NBC had aimed to rein in the recent proliferation of community radio stations, many of which provide alternative views to those aired over state- and military-controlled radio stations. More than 2,000 new community stations have established operations since 2000, spurring the prime minister's office to issue new regulations aimed at curbing their wattage and coverage areas.

The government's Public Relations Department and police in August closed FM 92.25, a popular Bangkok-based community radio station that had broadcast many critical reports about the government, claiming that the station's transmission signal interfered with air-traffic signals. The station defiantly streamed its critical reports over the Internet instead.

VIETNAM

Press conditions in Vietnam largely stagnated in 2005, despite efforts by the country's leaders to project an image of greater openness. Three writers remained imprisoned on antistate charges for material distributed online; print and broadcast media continued to work under the supervision of the government; and attacks on journalists were common.

Prime Minister Phan Van Khai traveled to the United States in June, marking the first such trip by a high-level leader since the end of the war in 1975. It was an opportunity for the prime minister to showcase the economic progress that his country had made, to seek foreign investment from a top trading partner and former enemy, and to promote Vietnam's bid for accession to the World Trade Organization.

Coming just two months after the country celebrated the 30th anniversary of the end of U.S. military involvement, the visit was given glowing coverage by Vietnam's state-controlled press, despite demonstrations over the government's human rights record.

Before meeting with Microsoft Chairman Bill Gates during the first leg of his trip, Khai said that demonstrators, especially Vietnamese émigrés, failed to understand the progress of recent years. "If they come back to the homeland and have returned, in reality, they will have different views," Khai said, according to The Associated Press. But human rights and press freedom organizations, including CPJ, noted that repression of religious leaders, dissidents, and independent journalists belied the government's representation of reform.

Vietnam released the journalist and physician Nguyen Dan Que in February in one of several recent amnesties of high-profile political prisoners. Que remained under tight surveillance after he was released, however, and faced continuing restrictions on communication and travel outside his home. In March, he gave an interview to the U.S. government-funded Voice of America in which he called for democracy and decried Internet restrictions, censorship of the media, and Vietnam's lack of a private press. Following the interview, police surveillance of Que's house intensified, visitors were harassed, and the writer faced ongoing restrictions on his travel and communication, according to his brother.

In April, in advance of celebrations of the 30th anniversary of the end of the war, articles in state media denounced dissident writer Tran Khue as a reactionary. State media also published a letter, purportedly from a veterans group, that called for writer Nguyen Thanh Giang to be "rid from public life." Meanwhile, independent writers Nguyen Khac Toan, Nguyen Vu Binh, and Pham Hong Son remained imprisoned on sentences of 12, seven, and five years, respectively, for news and commentary distributed via the Internet.

A growing newspaper market has engendered competition for stories that attract readers, but the Ministry of Culture and Information conducts meetings and issues orders to manage coverage and ensure that the media remain accountable to central authorities. Reiterating the common government line on the press, President Tran Duc Luong in June praised state news agencies for helping the public "understand the party and government's policies and the revolutionary cause in general," according to the Vietnam News Agency. He called on all media to join in the government's fight against corruption, bureaucracy, and waste.

Criticism of the Communist Party and national leaders remained off-limits to the press. But the government's qualified encouragement of investigative reporting on topics such as corruption and health issues has led to some results. Investigative journalists for the daily *Thanh Nien* in August revealed potentially hazardous lapses in the nation's efforts to control the avian flu. While local agriculture officials were incensed, the report generated vows of reform from the nation's top legislative body, according to *The Washington Post*.

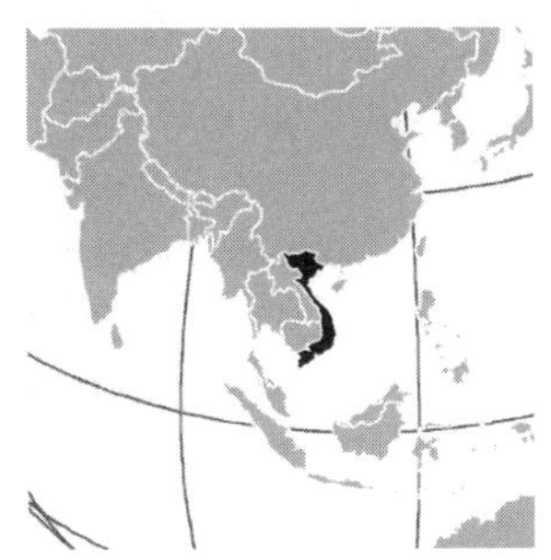

The mixed role of the media as both an arm of the government and a narrow kind of watchdog was reflected in the unusually public investigation of journalist Nguyen Thi Lan Anh. In January, Lan Anh was indicted and placed under house arrest for "appropriating state secrets" in her reporting for the popular state-owned daily *Tuoi Tre*. In a May 2004 article, she cited a leaked Health Ministry document that recommended a comprehensive investigation of a pharmaceutical company accused of price gouging. After authorities began an inquiry into how the reporter got the evidence, *Tuoi Tre* and other newspapers came to her defense. In April, criminal charges against Lan Anh and the official who leaked the document were dropped, according to local media.

Attacks on journalists have increased in recent years, as competition forced them to become more aggressive. In October, Phuong Thao, a reporter for the *Khuyen Hoc* and *Dan Tri* newspapers, was briefly handcuffed by a police officer outside the French embassy. *Dan Tri* responded to the incident by publishing other journalists' complaints of harassment and assaults. *An Ninh The Gioi* (Global Security) reporter Trang Dung, whose story was accompanied by a photograph of his bloodied face, recalled an incident in which security guards beat him and destroyed his camera even after he showed his media credentials. Reporter Do Van Khanh, of the newspaper *Lao Dong*, wrote that he had been attacked for his work and called on authorities to take journalists' complaints seriously. "To me, journalism is the foundation of a democratic society, and an attack on a journalist becomes an attack on democracy itself," he wrote.

Another reporter, Mai Xuan Cuong, said that whether assailants did not understand the role of journalists, or were purposely aiming to inhibit journalists from fulfilling their duties, "it seems to be a systemic problem." Cuong urged the government to bring the perpetrators of the attacks to justice.

The officer who harassed Phuong Thao was later dismissed for "violating work procedures while doing duty, causing negative consequences," The Associated Press reported, quoting state media. Observers pointed out that it cost authorities little to penalize the officer, and that the decision to allow newspapers to publicize this relatively minor incident might have been intended as a warning to low-level officials who act outside their authority.

Use of the Internet has skyrocketed in just a few years. State media reported in 2005 that Vietnam had more than seven million Internet users, nearly double the year before. Along with this huge increase in use have come regular attempts by the government to monitor and block online content. In July, government agencies issued a joint circular requiring additional certification for the owners of Internet cafés and demanding that anyone seeking Internet access at these cafés' provide identification before going online.

The government does not consider writers who use the Internet to distribute uncensored news and commentary to be journalists, and it targets them as dissidents. All three of the journalists who have been held in Vietnamese prisons since 2002 were jailed for their online work. Toan, convicted of disseminating information about farmers' protests, will remain imprisoned until 2014 if he serves his full sentence for espionage. Son, a medical doctor, was arrested on "antistate" charges after he translated and posted online an essay titled "What Is Democracy?" that had first appeared on the U.S. State Department Web site. Binh, formerly a journalist at the official *Tap Chi Cong San* (Journal of Communism), was sentenced on charges of writing and exchanging "information and materials that distorted the party and state policies" in articles that called for reform and criticized Vietnam's border agreements with China.

SNAPSHOTS: **ASIA**

Attacks & developments throughout the region

AUSTRALIA

- The chief judge of the County Court in the state of Victoria filed contempt charges in October against two reporters for the Melbourne-based *Herald Sun* who refused to divulge the source for a story on government plans to cut veterans' benefits. Gerard McManus and Michael Harvey could face jail if found in contempt.

EAST TIMOR

- The government repeatedly harassed the daily *Suara Timor Lorosae* in February, apparently in retaliation for its reporting on famine-related deaths. The Land and Property Department ordered the newspaper's management to vacate its premises. Prime Minister Mari Alkatiri imposed an indefinite boycott of the paper, banning its journalists from attending official press conferences.

INDIA

- Eight journalists were injured in Srinagar on July 25 after a grenade attack by Islamic militants triggered fighting with security forces. Journalists reporting on the initial explosion were caught in the crossfire of the ensuing gun battle. Cameraman Muzaffar Ahmad Bhat was seriously wounded.

INDONESIA

- After the tsunami of late December 2004, Indonesian authorities allowed local and foreign media unprecedented access to the hard-hit province of Aceh. Some restrictions on foreign journalists traveling outside of Banda Aceh and on reporters covering military affairs remained in effect. Local and foreign journalists were harassed and threatened by intelligence officers after trying to report on the conflict between the government and the rebel Free Aceh Movement (GAM), which signed a peace accord in August.
- Using antiquated criminal laws dating back to Indonesia's colonial era, a district court in the city of Lampung found two journalists guilty of defamation in May and sentenced them to nine months in prison. Darwin Ruslinur, chief editor of the weekly tabloid *Koridor*, and Budiono Saputro, the paper's managing editor, were freed pending appeal.
- Elyuddin Telaumbanua, a reporter based on the island of Nias, was reported missing five days after leaving his house on an assignment for the Medan-based *Berita Sore* in August. An editor at the newspaper told local media that Telaumbanua may have disappeared while investigating a murder in the island's southern district. He had also recently reported on criminal gangs, local corruption, and irregularities in

local elections. Colleagues feared the journalist had been murdered.

MALAYSIA

- In February, police questioned Malaysian blogger Jeff Ooi for two hours in connection with a contributor's September 2004 posting to his Web log. The contributor made a disparaging remark about Prime Minister Abdullah Badawi's view of Islam. Ooi promptly deleted the message and issued an apology, but police filed their own complaint against him. Sources reported that Ooi was investigated under a section of the nation's penal code that prohibits acts fostering "religious disunity," a charge that carries a penalty of two to five years in prison.
- The National Security Bureau of Malaysia confiscated the June 2 edition of the *Epoch Times*, a Chinese-language newspaper associated with the Falun Gong, and banned subsequent editions of the publication. In July, the government sent an official letter accusing the paper of presenting a negative image of China.

NORTH KOREA

- In November, the government-controlled news agency denounced CNN as a "reptile broadcasting service" and "a political waiting maid for the U.S. administration" after the U.S. news channel aired footage of a public execution said to have been smuggled from the country by a defector. The Korean Central News Agency said that while the government had allowed CNN rare foreign access to the country in the past, the network had "dug its own grave" by broadcasting "lies" about the judicial process in North Korea.

SINGAPORE

- A government agency threatened to file a defamation suit against blogger Jiahao Chen, prompting him to shut down his Web site on April 26 and post an apology. Officials frequently use civil libel suits in Singapore to silence dissent in the traditional media, but this was the first reported threat of legal action against a blogger.
- Police began an investigation in May of independent documentary filmmaker Martyn See under the country's Films Act. The act bans "party political" films; violation of the ban carries a penalty of up to 100,000 Singapore dollars (about US$60,000) in fines or two years in jail. See was forced to withdraw "Singapore Rebel"—which chronicles the civil disobedience of an opposition activist—from the Singapore International Film Festival in March. Police later questioned See and confiscated his camera and existing copies of the film.

EUROPE AND CENTRAL ASIA

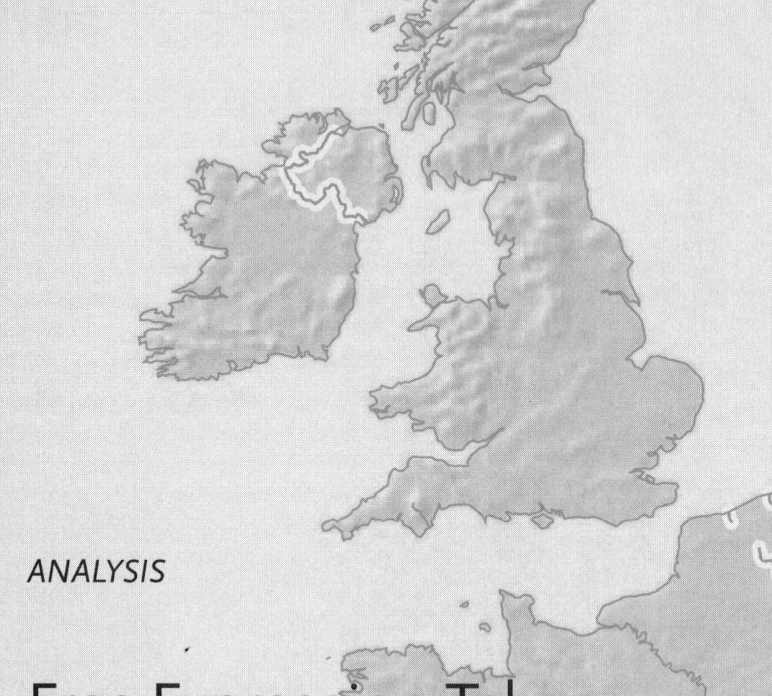

ANALYSIS

Free Expression Takes a Back Seat 136

The Bush administration says that cooperation with the region's authoritarian leaders strengthens U.S. leverage to promote press and democratic reforms. But its advocacy for free expression has been selective—coming in the absence of competing security concerns.

by Alex Lupis

PHOTOS

Section break: Reuters/Eduard Kornienko – *The Russian business newspaper* Kommersant *left blank spaces in its January 31 edition to protest a defamation verdict.* Analysis (next): Reuters/Joe Raedle – *U.S. Defense Secretary Donald Rumsfeld arrives in Dushanbe, Tajikistan, in July to discuss cooperation between the two countries.*

EUROPE AND CENTRAL ASIA

SUMMARIES

FREE EXPRESSION TAKES A BACK SEAT

by Alex Lupis

TO GAIN MILITARY FOOTING AND ACCESS TO ENERGY RESOURCES in the former Soviet empire, the United States has diverted its attention from human rights and press freedom issues in Eurasia. The U.S. policy of close cooperation with the region's authoritarian leaders has undermined free and independent reporting in several Eurasian nations—from Russia, where coverage of the Chechen rebels is itself likened to terrorism, to Kazakhstan, where the government has waged a vast campaign to censor critical news reporting.

Nowhere are the inherent conflicts between U.S. security policies and free expression more evident than in Uzbekistan, where government forces, including members of a U.S.-trained counterterrorism unit known as Bars, opened fire on antigovernment protesters in the eastern city of Andijan in May. Hundreds of unarmed civilians were killed, according to independent accounts.

After the massacre—which the government denied and obscured—Uzbek forces imposed an information blockade, intensified legal persecution of independent journalists, and waged a smear campaign linking reporters to Islamic terrorists. CPJ and other press organizations documented dozens of cases of government-sponsored threats, detentions, searches, and assaults against journalists from several news organizations.

The Andijan killings raised some of the most troubling questions yet about U.S. policies in Eurasia. In a bid to promote stability and reform in the region, President George W. Bush's administration provided expanded U.S. training of Uzbek security forces, while gaining permission for a U.S. military presence in the southern Karshi region. The Bush administration appeared to gamble that expanded U.S.-Uzbek diplomatic relations could moderate the policies of the country's dictator, President Islam Karimov.

In the aftermath of Andijan, the United States responded less assertively in public than did the European Union. Within a week of the massacre, the EU called for an independent, international inquiry. In October, it imposed an arms embargo on Uzbekistan and visa restrictions on officials implicated in the killings. By contrast, the Bush administration initially called for a "credible" and "transparent" domestic inquiry. U.S. diplomats did work to prevent the forced repatriation of refugees from Andijan, but it wasn't until mid-June that the White House called for an international inquiry into the Andijan slaughter. All the while, U.S. officials were reticent about addressing the Uzbek government's campaign of intimidation and repression of the independent media.

Despite the moderated U.S. response, Karimov moved in late July to evict U.S. forces from the Karshi-Khanabad air base.

The U.S. government's efforts to improve ties in the region were understandable. Following the terrorist attacks on New York and Washington, D.C., on September 11, 2001, Deputy Assistant Secretary of State Lynn Pascoe declared that "it is critical to the interests of the United States that we greatly enhance our relations" with the former Soviet republics. To help overthrow the Taliban regime in Afghanistan, which had provided safe haven to al-Qaeda terrorists, the Pentagon negotiated landing rights at airports throughout the region and established bases in Uzbekistan and Kyrgyzstan to support operations in Afghanistan. It also expanded training of local security forces. The State Department expanded diplomatic relations, pushed for greater U.S. access to oil and natural gas reserves, and pressed local authorities to secure nuclear material left over from the former Soviet Union.

The White House argued that closer cooperation would strengthen U.S. leverage to promote

"The White House argues that cooperation strengthens leverage to promote reforms."

democratic reforms in the region. "Any deepening or broadening of our cooperation will depend on continued progress in respecting human rights and democracy," Lorne Craner, then assistant secretary of state for Eurasian affairs, said in June 2002. The State Department, in fact, can point to a number of specific efforts on behalf of press freedom in Eurasia. Diplomats repeatedly called for accountability in the 2004 slaying of Paul Klebnikov, an American editor killed in Moscow; they assisted journalists covering the conflict in the Russian republic of Chechnya; and they publicly backed the Azerbaijani television station ANS when it was harassed by the government. Craner's successor, Daniel Fried, told reporters in October that while the administration was realistic about what could be done, "we are very clear about what we want."

Yet the greatest U.S. leverage has not materialized at critical moments in strategically important countries. In May 2003, then-Secretary of State Colin Powell sidestepped Congressional restrictions on U.S. aid to Uzbekistan by claiming that Uzbek authorities were making democratic reforms, despite continued censorship of the media and imprisonment of journalists, among other abuses. When the State Department withheld $18 million in aid because of human rights abuses the following year, Air Force Gen. Richard Myers, then chairman of the Joint Chiefs of Staff, described the step as "shortsighted" and boosted military aid by $24 million.

> "The Bush administration is largely silent in response to Kremlin press harassment."

Karimov and his subordinates were eager to use antiterror language as political cover to suppress independent news reporting—and the Bush administration was reluctant to challenge them. In September, Uzbek Deputy Prosecutor General Anvar Nabiyev accused local journalists and foreign correspondents working for the BBC, Deutsche Welle, Radio Free Europe/Radio Liberty, *Ferghana.ru*, and the London-based Institute for War & Peace Reporting (IWPR) of "providing informational support to terrorism" with their reporting on Andijan. At least four journalists working for the IWPR—including 2005 CPJ International Press Freedom Award recipient Galima Burkharbeava—fled the country after being threatened with criminal prosecution.

Journalists have also been accused of helping terrorists in neighboring Russia, where cooperation between the Bush administration and the Kremlin on combating terrorism and securing nuclear facilities has sidelined U.S. efforts to

"The United States tempers its message on press freedom in relation to strategic concerns."

promote democracy and press freedom. The Kremlin's control over vast oil and gas reserves, powerful security services, and political influence in the Caucasus and Central Asia made Russia a key strategic ally in the "war on terror."

The Bush administration has remained largely silent in response to the Kremlin's growing harassment of the media, its takeover of national television, and its indifference to the unsolved murders of 12 journalists since 2000. Despite these troubling developments, Bush warmly welcomed Russian President Vladimir Putin to the White House in September, calling him "a strong ally in Russia in fighting the war on terror" and saying that "we'll work to advance freedom and democracy in our respective countries and around the world."

Since Putin came to power in 2000, reporting on the war in Chechnya has become acutely sensitive because each new attack or public statement by Chechen rebels undermines the president's claim that Russia is winning the war against the separatists. CPJ has documented more than 70 serious cases of harassment, threats, obstruction, detention, and assaults against journalists since the second Chechen war began six years ago.

Russian authorities have increasingly accused journalists reporting on Chechnya of supporting terrorists, and they have relied more frequently on antiterror and antiextremist laws to suppress coverage of statements made by Chechen rebel leaders. In September, for example, prosecutors in the Volga River city of Nizhny Novgorod charged Stanislav Dmitiyevsky, editor-in-chief of the monthly human rights newspaper *Pravo-Zashchita*, with inciting ethnic and religious hatred for publishing statements by Chechen rebel leaders calling for a peaceful resolution to the conflict.

The Kremlin also intensified pressure on foreign media reporting on Chechnya. When the ABC News program "Nightline" broadcast an interview with Chechen rebel leader Shamil Basayev in July, the Foreign Ministry said the interview supported "the propaganda of terrorism," barred ABC reporters from speaking with government officials, and said the journalists' accreditation would not be renewed.

The U.S. government carefully sought to distance itself from the program while affirming ABC's right to broadcast the interview. "The U.S. government has had no involvement in ABC's decision to air the interview," State Department spokesman Sean McCormack said. "The U.S. government has no authority to prevent ABC from exercising its constitutional right to broadcast the interview."

Throughout the region, the United States has tempered its message on press and human rights issues in relation to its strategic concerns. Two oil-rich countries on the Caspian Sea—Azerbaijan and Kazakhstan—have poor media freedom records but have benefited from growing cooperation with the U.S. military and U.S. energy companies.

In Azerbaijan, the Bush administration welcomed Ilham Aliyev when he came to power in October 2003 elections, despite widespread voting irregularities and police violence against protesters and the media. While Azerbaijani authorities imprisoned an opposition editor and used security forces and politicized courts to silence critical media, the United States worked to expand cooperation with Aliyev's government. In the summer, U.S. officials struggled to balance praise for the government's opening of a strategic oil pipeline and its decision to allow the United States to upgrade Soviet-era radar facilities, with calls for fair parliamentary elections and a proper investigation into the murder of a journalist who had strongly criticized Aliyev.

In Kazakhstan, the Bush administration broadened ties with authoritarian President Nursultan Nazarbayev, who ignored mild U.S. criticism for consolidating control over local independent and opposition media. In 2005, Nazarbayev's government prevented the printing of several independent and opposition newspapers, seized entire press runs of critical publications, closed an opposition weekly, and repeatedly blocked an opposition Web site.

Nazarbayev has shrewdly balanced U.S. and Russian competition for regional influence to attract oil and gas investments and military cooperation. Kazakhstan, a member of the Russia-dominated Collective Security Treaty Organization, also provided logistical support for U.S. forces operating nearby in Afghanistan and sent troops to participate in U.S.-led operations in Iraq.

> "The greatest inconsistency is in U.S. treatment of the region's two worst dictators."

U.S. policies have not been uniformly passive in regard to free expression. Kyrgyzstan hosted U.S. military forces at the Manas air base outside Bishkek, but U.S.-backed democracy programs nonetheless helped fuel the popular March uprising that ousted authoritarian President Askar Akayev. U.S. programs not only trained political parties and election monitors, they helped establish the country's first independent printing press, ensuring critical coverage even as the government tried to crack down on the media. When Kyrgyz authorities cut off power to the printing facility in February, the U.S. embassy stepped in with generators that enabled the printer to continue functioning.

> "Belarus, with few energy resources and little strategic role, faces intense U.S. criticism."

The United States invested more in democracy assistance in Kyrgyzstan than in any other former Soviet republic, but there were fewer hard choices to be made there between its own security concerns and Kyrgyzstani rights of free expression. Kyrgyzstan had few energy resources and little Islamic militancy. Akayev had allowed some journalists, human rights activists, and opposition parties to question government policies, and his government did not force the United States into choosing military needs over civil liberties.

But the greatest inconsistency in the Bush administration's promotion of human rights and media freedom was apparent in its treatment of the region's two worst dictators: Turkmenistan's self-proclaimed "president for life," Saparmurat Niyazov, and Belarusian President Aleksandr Lukashenko.

Niyazov has imposed a brutal Stalinist dictatorship in Turkmenistan that controls all local media and bars access to foreign news. Even journalists living in exile in Moscow are placed under surveillance and assaulted by Turkmen security agents for not promoting Niyazov's agenda, CPJ research shows. But the Bush administration has developed cordial relations with Niyazov because Turkmenistan has large natural gas reserves in the Caspian Sea and has granted the U.S. military permission to station troops in Turkmenistan to service cargo planes en route to Afghanistan.

Senior U.S. officials regularly praise Niyazov for security-related cooperation and raise human rights and press freedom issues infrequently and politely. U.S. Deputy Secretary of State Laura Kennedy visited the capital, Ashgabad, in February and said she "appreciated the opportunity to discuss some areas of particular concern to the U.S. government, including religious freedom, the development of civil society, access to prisoners, resumption of [Russian] Radio Mayak broadcasting, and some other issues."

Yet Belarus, which has few energy resources and little strategic role in the antiterrorism fight, has faced intense U.S. criticism for its human rights and press freedom abuses. Indeed, under Lukashenko, the secretive and powerful Belarusian bureaucracy has created a climate of fear for journalists and has nearly erased the independent press.

> "Leaders in Uzbekistan and Russia have draped censorship in antiterror clothing."

"It is time for change to come to Belarus... the last true dictatorship in the center of Europe," U.S. Secretary of State Condoleezza Rice said in April after meeting with a group of Belarusian opposition activists in neighboring Lithuania. Rice warned the Belarusian government that its behavior was being watched by the international community. "This is not a dark corner in which things can go unobserved, uncommented on," she told reporters.

The Bush administration's forceful call for change in Belarus was more than justified. But its advocacy for free expression in Eurasia has been selective, coming mainly in the absence of competing security and energy concerns. At the same time, the administration's antiterrorism agenda has made it easier for the region's resourceful authoritarian leaders to justify repressive media policies in the name of security. Leaders in Uzbekistan and Russia have draped censorship in antiterror clothing, moves largely unchallenged by the United States.

By using selective standards, the Bush administration lost valuable leverage in its efforts to promote free expression, independent media, and the broader process of democratization in some former Soviet republics.

• • • • • • • • • • •

Alex Lupis is senior program coordinator for Europe and Central Asia.

AZERBAIJAN

The murder of a prominent editor, detentions of other journalists, police abuses, and bureaucratic obstruction curtailed independent reporting in the run-up to a November 6 parliamentary election that saw President Ilham Aliyev's ruling Yeni Azerbaijan Party and its allies sweep to victory. International observers said the vote was neither fair nor free, citing improper vote counting and unfair campaign restrictions, but Aliyev and his backers nonetheless maintained their grip on the country's enormous oil wealth. The completion in May of an oil pipeline linking the Caspian Sea to the Mediterranean Sea opened billions of dollars in new oil revenue for Aliyev's secretive and highly centralized government.

Authorities considered independent and opposition journalists to be traitors, and pressured private companies not to advertise in media that did not support Aliyev. The government used tactics large and small. It controlled the two main press distribution agencies—Qasid and Azermetbuatyayimi—and obstructed the work of other private distributors, such as Gaya, that were not seen as loyal to the state. In August, police arrested a subway vendor for selling the opposition daily *Azadlyg* and confiscated copies of the newspaper, according to local press reports.

The Justice Ministry blocked a group of prominent media and political figures from launching the independent Yeni TV and Radio, which would have challenged the dominance of state-run AZTV1 during election season. The ministry denied Yeni a broadcasting license in April, forcing the channel to broadcast to a limited audience by satellite starting in October.

Journalists faced a number of politicized civil libel cases brought in retaliation for criticizing politicians and questioning government policies. The country's largest opposition newspaper, *Yeni Musavat,* stopped publication for several months in early 2005 after a court in the capital, Baku, ordered it to pay 800 million manats (US$160,000) in libel damages to several government officials. The court froze the paper's assets and bank account as part of the order. *Yeni Musavat* and other opposition newspapers resorted to self-censorship in the face of harsh laws that allow authorities to imprison journalists for up to seven years in defamation and insult cases.

Some journalists faced reprisals from police for reporting on government abuses. In February, Akrep Hasanov, an Azerbaijani journalist with the independent weekly *Monitor,* was abducted by military officers and held in detention for five hours in retaliation for writing an article about military mismanagement. *Monitor* has long angered officials with its hard-hitting news and commentary.

• • • • • • • • • • •

Summaries in the chapter were written by **Alex Lupis**, senior program coordinator for Europe and Central Asia, and Research Associate **Nina Ognianova**.

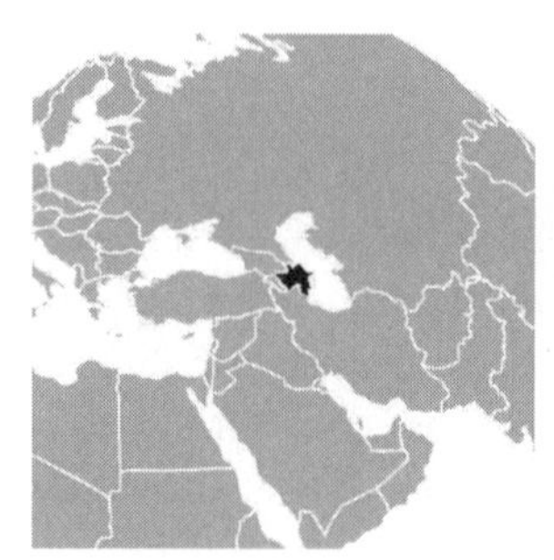

The decade-long Armenian occupation of the western province of Nagorno-Karabakh remained a politically explosive issue in both Azerbaijan and neighboring Armenia. Eynulla Fatullayev, an investigative reporter with *Monitor*, traveled to Nagorno-Karabakh in February to interview leaders of the region's unrecognized "government." He received threats from Azerbaijani nationalists who opposed his trip.

Fear and self-censorship escalated dramatically when Elmar Huseynov, founder and editor of *Monitor*, was gunned down on the evening of March 2 in his apartment building in Baku. The attack appeared to be well-planned; a streetlight at the entrance of the apartment building and several telephones in the area were disconnected at the time of the shooting. Huseynov's family said the editor had received several work-related threats and had been concerned for his safety.

The murder sparked antigovernment protests in Baku; journalists and opposition politicians believed that Huseynov was murdered in retaliation for his work. In April, the National Security Ministry identified several ethnic Azerbaijanis in neighboring Georgia as suspects in the case, but the ministry did not describe any motive or evidence linking them to the crime. Georgian authorities refused to extradite the suspects due to the lack of evidence, and no other developments were reported. Huseynov's family and colleagues criticized authorities for not looking into work-related motives for the murder.

On the defensive about the Huseynov murder, Aliyev issued a March 20 presidential decree releasing 115 political prisoners. Among them was Rauf Arifoglu, editor-in-chief of *Yeni Musavat*. Arifoglu, who is primarily a journalist, is also deputy director of the Musavat opposition party. He was arrested in October 2003 and eventually sentenced to five years in prison on charges of organizing antigovernment riots.

The release of Arifoglu and six other opposition activists failed to meet Western demands that they be exonerated of the criminal charges, which were widely seen as politically motivated. Many journalists told CPJ that Arifoglu was prosecuted for *Yeni Musavat*'s strong criticism of Aliyev and his cabinet. Arifoglu filed an appeal with the Supreme Court seeking to have the conviction overturned, but the court rejected the bid.

International organizations and Western governments, fearing a repeat of the fraud-marred 2003 presidential election, called on Aliyev to institute reforms that would make the November parliamentary election more transparent. Facing international pressure, the parliament approved last-minute election reforms in October that allowed foreign-funded organizations to monitor voting. But the measure did not address another key change sought by international observers, namely, ensuring that election commissions were not stacked with pro-government appointees.

The state-run television channel AZTV1 and a handful of private, pro-government television stations dominated the country's airwaves, remaining the prime source of news for most citizens. The government failed to make good on its commitment to the Council of Europe, a pan-European human rights monitoring organization, to transform AZTV1 into a publicly funded, independent broadcasting service. Instead, authorities changed the state-run AZTV2, a regional channel with a fraction of the staff, into a public broadcaster named ITV. ITV went on the air in August, but it continued the pro-government editorial line of the former AZTV2.

Azerbaijan's broadcasting regulator, the National Broadcasting Council, remained under strict government control, with its nine members appointed by the president. Politicized regulation of the broadcast media meant that local television news coverage faced growing government scrutiny as the elections approached. The New York–based *Eurasianet* news Web site reported that officers from the National Security Ministry in the southern city of Lankaran threatened Baloglan Mirzoyev, director of the local independent Lankaran TV, in August after the channel aired a report on the activities of opposition parties.

Police violence against opposition supporters and journalists reporting on opposition rallies escalated steadily as parliamentary elections approached. On October 9, police severely beat 10 journalists covering an unsanctioned opposition rally, including Idrak Abbasov of the Russian-language daily *Zerkalo*, according to local press reports. Abbasov was beaten unconscious by a plainclothes police officer and hospitalized in Baku; police posted guards at the door to his hospital room and prevented journalists from visiting him. Local press freedom groups such as the Media Rights Institute, Yeni Nesil, and RUH regularly documented, publicized, and protested these and other abuses against journalists.

Authorities prohibited foreign television crews from broadcasting live during the election campaign, according to local and international press reports. "The National Television and Radio Council cannot authorize live TV broadcasts...[because] there are no appropriate legislative norms for this," the Turan news agency quoted council Director Nusiravan Maharramli as saying.

In mid-October, Azerbaijani authorities expelled from the country a truck with satellite broadcasting equipment owned by the Turkish news agency Ilhas, according to press reports. Shortly afterward, on November 4, guards on the Russian-Azerbaijani border confiscated satellite dishes from the Russian state television channels RTR and NTV, those reports said.

The Organization for Security and Cooperation in Europe, an election and security monitoring organization based in Vienna, announced on November 7 that the parliamentary vote was not free or fair because of police abuses, campaign restrictions, voting irregularities, improper ballot counting, and a pro-government bias on state television channels AZTV1 and ITV. Azerbaijani authorities threatened to shutter ANS, the only independent television station to feature more balanced campaign reporting.

Regional journalists continued to face harassment from local authorities, particularly in the repressive southwestern enclave of Nakhichevan. Malahat Nasibova, a reporter for the Turan news agency and Radio Free Europe/Radio Liberty, was repeatedly harassed and detained by Nakhichevan authorities angered by her reporting on politically sensitive topics such as drug addiction. Elman Abbasov, a journalist for the opposition newspaper *Bizim Yol*, received threats from anonymous callers and a National Security Ministry officer in October after he complained to the government in Baku that local authorities were obstructing his journalistic work, Turan reported.

BELARUS

Belarusian dictator Aleksandr Lukashenko continued a systematic crackdown on independent media and nongovernmental organizations, further tightening control over domestic news ahead of the 2006 presidential election. Lukashenko consolidated internal power after a rigged October 2004 parliamentary election and accompanying referendum that eliminated presidential term limits, but he was still left looking nervously over his shoulder at political change happening elsewhere in the region.

Worried about potential spillover from the late 2004 pro-democracy revolt in neighboring Ukraine, Lukashenko strengthened control over the KGB and denounced the changes in neighboring Kyiv as "sheer banditry under the guise of democracy," according to the U.S. government-funded Radio Free Europe/Radio Liberty (RFE/RL). Projecting a Soviet-style siege mentality, he lashed out at the United States and Russia in February for allegedly using the international media to foment dissent and exert "information pressure on Belarus," according to local press reports.

Opposition parties were excluded from the new parliament, and increasingly took their grievances to the streets. But police brutality against protesters, imprisonment of opposition politicians, the imposition of new media restrictions, and ongoing abuses against the independent press squelched most dissent.

The government relied on security forces, prosecutors, judges, media regulators, pro-government businesses, and a secretive and powerful bureaucracy to create a climate of fear for independent journalists. Officials filed lawsuits, imposed fines, revoked accreditations, blocked access to printers, confiscated equipment, and detained and harassed journalists.

Nominally independent radio and television stations avoided politically sensitive subjects for fear of losing broadcasting licenses. The small number of independent newspapers available in the capital, Minsk, and other urban areas dwindled even further. The independent press retrenched but tried to circumvent the crackdown. Limited-circulation underground newspapers were distributed informally and free of charge, the U.S. media training organization IREX reported. Some newsstands secreted independent newspapers behind their counters and sold them in defiance of government regulations.

But going underground was risky, too. The independent newspaper *Zgoda,* which had moved its operations into a Minsk apartment, was raided by the KGB in March for working illegally in a residential location, according to local press reports.

The main opposition daily *Narodnaya Volya* and business daily *Belorusskaya Delovaya Gazeta* were nearly bankrupted by politicized libel convictions that led to the equivalent of tens of thousands of dollars in fines, sizeable amounts in a country where the average monthly salary is roughly equal to US$200.

The obedient state media, closely managed by the administration, continued to flood cities and the countryside with pro-Lukashenko propaganda, vilifying opposition leaders and urging voters to support the president or face Western domination. In May, state-run Belarusian Television sought to link a rise in drug and weapons trafficking to street protests organized by the political opposition, RFE/RL reported.

The state propaganda machine penetrated deeper into society, with students and government workers attending mandatory "ideology classes" promoting Lukashenko's policies and demonizing the West. Even entertainment radio was politicized. The Information Ministry issued official warnings to three FM stations in January—Unistar Radio BDU, Novoe Radio, and Hit FM—for not playing enough Belarusian music during prime time.

The government used politicized courts and a maze of legal regulations to cripple the few remaining pro-democracy organizations operating in the country. Western media training organizations, which had been ousted from the country in 2003, and the Belarusian Association of Journalists struggled to assist independent journalists, despite severe government restrictions on foreign funding for local organizations. In April, the Supreme Court shuttered the Independent Institute for Socio-Economic and Political Research after it published polling data contradicting the official results of an October 2004 referendum, according to local press reports.

A steady flow of new regulations and informal orders put a stranglehold on the media's ability to operate freely. Lukashenko signed a presidential decree on May 31 that banned independent media and non-government organizations from using the words "Belarus" or "national" in their titles and required them to reregister with new names in three months, according to local and international press reports. In June, the president signed a law increasing taxes on newspaper distributors, the Belapan independent news agency reported. That same month, the KGB was authorized to search local and international non-governmental organizations without a warrant, RFE/RL reported.

Police and prosecutors did not report any progress in solving the October 2004 murder of Veronika Cherkasova, a reporter for the Minsk opposition newspaper *Solidarnost* who was stabbed to death in her apartment at a time when she was investigating illegal Belarusian arms shipments to Iraq. Police claimed the murder was related to

Cherkasova's personal life and focused on her 15-year-old son as the suspect. Although family and colleagues believe the murder could be work-related, authorities have refused to consider Cherkasova's journalism as a motive for the crime.

Authorities continued to obstruct an investigation into the July 2000 disappearance of Dmitry Zavadsky, a cameraman for the Russian public television network ORT. In July, police in Minsk violently dispersed a rally in which several dozen of Zavadsky's relatives, friends, and colleagues met to commemorate the fifth anniversary of his disappearance. The journalist's widow, Svetlana Zavadskaya, was hospitalized with a concussion after a police officer punched her in the face and destroyed a portrait of the journalist. Zavadskaya later filed a complaint, but the prosecutor's office refused to open an investigation, Belapan reported.

The KGB reacted aggressively to government criticism on the Web. New government regulations require Internet cafés to register users and to block access to foreign-based news Web sites such as those run by RFE/RL and the Charter 97 human rights organization, IREX reported.

In August, KGB agents raided apartments in Minsk and the western city of Grodno occupied by members of an informal group of computer programmers calling themselves Trety Put (The Third Way). The programmers had produced and posted on the Web a short cartoon clip mocking Lukashenko's authoritarian rule. The KGB questioned several programmers, confiscated 12 computers, and shut down the group's Web site, *mult.3dway*. Prosecutors opened a criminal investigation against three of the programmers on charges of defaming the head of state, a crime punishable by up to five years in jail.

In December, the president signed a measure that effectively criminalized media criticism of the government and set penalties of up to five years in prison. Western governments voiced growing concern over Lukashenko's authoritarian policies, with the Polish government taking a particularly active role in supporting Belarusian journalists, human rights activists, and opposition parties. (Ethnic Poles make up about 4 percent of the Belarusian population.) Authorities in Minsk responded by expelling visiting Polish journalists, seizing control of Polish community organizations, and increasing harassment of local Polish-language media. In May, state printers refused to publish the Grodno-based Polish-language weekly *Glos Zna Niemna*; fake, pro-government copies of the weekly were distributed in June. In July, *Glos Znad Niemna* Editor-in-Chief Andrzej Pisalnik and several other ethnic Polish journalists protesting government abuses were fined or briefly imprisoned.

Authorities were especially harsh with correspondents from the Russian media, a product of ongoing bickering between Belarusian and Russian authorities. Aleksei Ametyov, a correspondent for the Russian edition of *Newsweek* magazine, and Mikhail Romanov, a reporter for the Russian daily *Moskovsky Komsomolets*, were detained and imprisoned for more than a week in April in retaliation for reporting on an opposition rally in Minsk.

GEORGIA

Two years after the Rose Revolution toppled the corrupt regime of Eduard Shevardnadze and ushered in the promise of media reform, independent journalists feared the emergence of a new, subtler wave of repression. Several media owners have close ties to political leaders, journalists said, enabling authorities to exert behind-the-scenes pressure on front-line reporters and editors. President Mikhail Saakashvili and his cabinet directly targeted one critical news outlet, claiming they were fighting media corruption.

Government officials sought to dismiss fears of repression. "Look at our television channels," Deputy Parliament Speaker Mikhail Machavariani said on the independent television channel 202. "Every significant event is discussed in detail, opposition [views] are omnipresent, nobody hides anything. How can there be talk of pressure on the media in this situation?"

Indeed, channel 202's late-night political talk show, "Debatebi" (Debates), became a prominent source for opposition views by midyear. But the station then suffered two serious blows in as many months.

Two executives were arrested in August on extortion charges, and a prominent station journalist was beaten the following month. Journalists feared the incidents came in retaliation for channel 202's critical coverage.

Shalva Ramishvili, channel 202's co-owner and anchor, and David Kokheridze, the station's general director, were accused of extorting 54,000 laris (US$30,000) from Member of Parliament Koba Bekauri in exchange for scrapping an investigative report on his business dealings. Interior Minister Vano Merabishvili stood by the arrests, saying that they were the start of a crackdown on corruption in the Georgian media. Critics called it a selective and politically convenient action against an independent news outlet, the news Web site *Eurasianet* reported.

Irakli Kakabadze, who replaced Ramishvili as anchor of channel 202's political show, was beaten on his way home from work on a Tbilisi street on September 7. Saakashvili and other politicians condemned the attack and pledged a thorough investigation, but the pronouncements were met with skepticism by friends and colleagues, the U.S.-government-funded Radio Free Europe/Radio Liberty said.

Channel 202 had emerged as a leading venue after political and news programming on other Georgian channels went off the air. The independent station Mze canceled the talk show "Archevanis Zgvarze" (On the Verge of Choice), shortly after commentators criticized authorities for forcibly dispersing a July 1 protest in Tbilisi. Host Irakli Imnaishvili told *Eurasianet*: "It is a fact that directly after [the street protests] when members of the ruling party announced on air that they were not satisfied with the coverage, I was told that my program would be taken off the air after July 8." The management of Mze, which is owned by two members of the parliament, said the show was not popular enough to retain.

Mze journalists angered authorities earlier in the year by airing speculation that the February 3 death of Prime Minister Zurab Zhvania might not have been accidental. Zhvania was found dead in a Tbilisi apartment from what the government said was carbon monoxide poisoning caused by a malfunctioning heater.

The once-independent Rustavi-2 station, whose reporting fueled the mass protests that brought new leadership to power during the Rose Revolution, became owned largely by Kibar Khalvashi, a powerful businessman with close ties to Defense Minister Irakli Okruashvili, according to the London-based Institute for War & Peace Reporting.

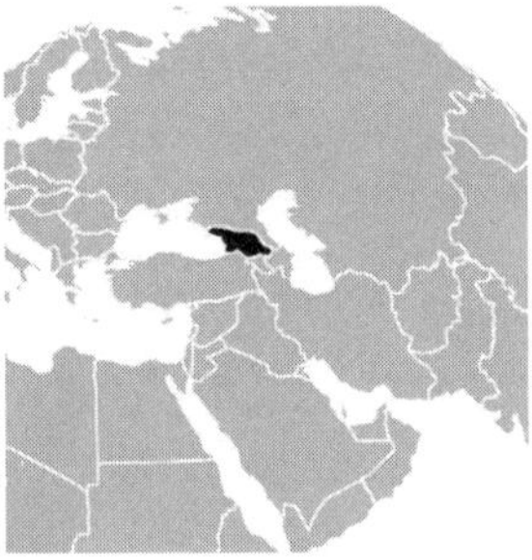

The channel, which once devoted much of its airtime to news, broadcast mainly movies and soap operas. Several of its investigative journalists left the channel to form their own freelance production crew, which produced investigative programs for channel 202.

Most Georgians rely on broadcast media for news. But the Independent Association of Georgian Journalists (IAGJ), a monitoring media group, said watered-down broadcast news has led some people to seek out the print media, which still work in relative independence. The IAGJ said the circulation of the daily *Rezonansi* grew 25 percent in the past two years, while the Georgian-language version of *The Georgian Times* saw its readership climb nearly 60 percent during the same period. Still, print circulation is limited. The six leading Tbilisi-based weeklies have a total combined circulation of 200,000, according to a report by the U.S.-based media training organization IREX.

Assaults against Georgian journalists appeared to decline in 2005, said Zviad Pochkhua, president of IAGJ, but he attributed the trend to greater self-censorship among journalists.

Georgian authorities have not reported progress in their investigation into the attack on Vakhtang Komakhidze, a former Rustavi-2 reporter. Komakhidze was stopped by transit police in the Ajarian city of Batumi in March 2004 and forced out of his car by uniformed men who beat him and stole his camera, tapes, and documents. He had just spent two weeks in Ajaria, an enclave on the Black Sea, investigating alleged corruption involving then-leader Aslan Abashidze.

Saakashvili and his Cabinet continued their efforts to bring the Russia-influenced breakaway republics of South Ossetia and Abkhazia under Tbilisi's control. Rebel leaders in these northern breakaway regions maintained tight control over all local media and often prevented Georgian journalists from traveling within their territory to report on local developments.

KAZAKHSTAN

President Nursultan Nazarbayev took few chances with his political fortunes as December presidential elections approached, using state-controlled media to burnish his image and employing the many levers of his authoritarian government to crack down on opposition and independent news media. His government blocked the printing of several independent and opposition newspapers, seized entire press runs of publications that carried critical articles, shuttered a leading opposition weekly, and repeatedly blocked an opposition Web site. Nazarbayev, who has ruled Kazakhstan for 16 years, gained a third term in the December 4 vote. The national election commission said Nazarbayev took 91 percent of the vote; international observers said the election was marred by media and vote manipulation.

Nazarbayev said repeatedly that he did not fear uprisings similar to the Tulip Revolution in neighboring Kyrgyzstan, the Orange Revolution in Ukraine, or the antigovernment protests in nearby Uzbekistan. Those countries, after all, did not enjoy the economic prosperity of Kazakhstan, he said. An oil-rich nation whose economy was further lifted in 2005 by rising world oil prices, Kazakhstan has boasted one of the highest rates of economic growth among the former Soviet republics, the news Web site *Eurasianet* reported. But the government's actions betray a leadership determined to quell dissent and limit international influence.

Parliament, which is dominated by Nazarbayev's party, Otan, moved up the presidential election a year from its originally scheduled date—a decision made just three months in advance of the rescheduled date. Analysts said the move was designed to catch opposition candidates off-guard and unable to put together viable campaigns.

State-controlled media provided no coverage of the four other presidential candidates but dutifully reported every visit Nazarbayev made to a hospital or factory and every speech he gave about improvements in health care or job creation, according to press reports. State dominance of the news media is nearly total. Every broadcast news outlet and most print outlets are owned and controlled by government allies or by the president's daughter, Dariga Nazarbayeva.

The few newspapers that did cover opposition candidates were subjected to harassment. Six opposition newspapers that had covered the presidential campaign of Zharmakhan Tuyakbai, the candidate of the opposition alliance For a Fair Kazakhstan, were blocked from publishing in late September. The private printing company Vremya-Print did not explain why it refused its services to *Epokha, Svoboda Slova, Zhuma-Taims, Apta.kz, Azat,* and *Soz*. The newspapers resumed publishing later in the fall, although authorities routinely confiscated copies.

CPJ research shows that Nazarbayev and his allies have long

EUROPE AND CENTRAL ASIA

pressured printers not to publish independent and opposition titles, using politicized lawsuits, tax inspections, and criminal investigations as leverage. One week in October offered a particularly disturbing window onto press censorship in Kazakhstan.

On October 19, police in Almaty raided the offices of the Dauir printing house and seized the entire 50,000-copy print run of the weekly *Svoboda Slova* (Freedom of Speech), which carried an article headlined "A Regular Dictator." The story recounted an exchange with CNN journalists in which the president was asked if he was a dictator. Prosecutors said the article damaged Nazarbayev's honor and dignity, local reports said. On October 22, an administrative court in Almaty fined *Svoboda Slova* Editor-in-Chief Gulzhan Yergaliyeva 48,000 tenge (US$360) for printing falsehoods and defaming Nazarbayev, the press freedom group Adil Soz reported.

Almaty police raided Dauir again the next day, seizing the entire print run of the weekly *Zhuma-Taims*, local reports said. The move came without explanation but appeared to be retaliatory. In its previous edition, *Zhuma-Taims* had published an article on what came to be called "Kazakhgate," an investigation into allegations that Nazarbayev and allies accepted bribes from U.S. oil companies in 2000. Since the first reports on the U.S. investigation appeared in opposition newspapers in July 2000, the Kazakh government has used tax inspections and regulatory lawsuits to harass and censor publications that have covered the story, CPJ research has shown.

On October 26, Almaty police confiscated the subsequent edition of *Svoboda Slova* without explanation, the paper reported. Editor-in-Chief Gulzhan Yergaliyeva said the issue carried an article on allegedly aggressive business dealings by Aliya Nazarbayeva, the president's youngest daughter. She heads the major construction company Elitstroi.

Adil Soz, an Almaty-based organization, reported five separate instances in late October in the capital, Astana, and in the northern city of Kostanai in which police confiscated copies of opposition newspapers from vendors and other private citizens.

The same month, according to local and Russian press reports, Kazakh Internet providers moved several times to block the Almaty-based opposition news Web site *Navigator*, which had covered Tuyakbai's presidential campaign. On October 13, the government-controlled Internet carrier KazNIK, owner of the "kz" domain, banned *Navigator* from using the Web address *navi.kz* and forced the site to move to another domain. *Navigator* took a new address in the "net" domain, but an Almaty district court ruled that *Navigator* could not use any combination of "Navi" or "Navigator," on the Internet. When *Navigator* changed its address to *mizinov.net* to comply with the court decision, authorities pressured local Internet providers to block access to the site, according to the Moscow-based news Web site *Ferghana.ru*. The site was operational in late 2005.

Electronic harassment was in keeping with the government's other censorship efforts. In May, the Kazakh Culture, Information, and Sports Ministry closed the leading opposition weekly *Respublika Delovoye Obozreniye*. The May 4 closure order arose from a civil lawsuit filed by a private citizen against the weekly's parent company, Bastau. The plaintiff was reportedly angered by *Respublika Delovoye Obozreniye*'s January publication of a transcript of an interview with Russian ultranationalist Vladimir Zhrinovsky in which he questioned the border delineation between Kazakhstan and Russia. The newspaper resumed publishing under the name *Set.kz*, but it was harassed for alleged registration violations, according to press reports.

Not two weeks earlier, on April 23, police in the Russian city of Volokolamsk detained *Respublika Delovoye Obozreniye*'s exiled editor Irina Petrushova at the behest of Kazakh authorities who wanted to extradite her on tax-violation charges. The prosecutor general's office in Moscow ruled that Petrushova, a 2002 recipient of CPJ's International Press Freedom Award, had been held improperly on an expired Kazakh warrant and ordered her release after two days in detention.

Kazakh authorities have harassed Petrushova repeatedly. Although she has continued to edit the newspaper, Petrushova was forced to leave Kazakhstan in 2002 after enduring threats in retaliation for her reporting on high-level corruption. The paper has had to change its name several times—previous incarnations have been *Delovoye Obozreniye Respubilka, Assandi Times*, and *Respublika*—and has had to switch printers numerous times after government officials intimidated their printing houses.

Nazarbayev's government moved on other fronts to silence dissent. In April, authorities enacted a law banning election-related street rallies. Opposition activists said the law was aimed at preventing the sort of popular uprisings that struck Georgia, Ukraine, and Kyrgyzstan, the U.S. government-funded Voice of America reported.

But a measure adopted by Parliament in June to restrict the activities of international nongovernmental organizations, or NGOs, was found unconstitutional by the Kazakh Constitutional Council, the Interfax-Kazakhstan news agency reported. The council determines whether proposed regulations comply with the country's constitution. The law would have subjected the financing and spending of international NGOs to government screening and approval. Tax inspectors would have had the authority to review bank statements, leaving NGOs vulnerable to state control.

The prosecutor general's office investigated more than 30 NGOs in the aftermath of Kyrgyzstan's Tulip Revolution in March, according to the London-based Institute for War & Peace Reporting. NGOs protested the government's actions as restrictive. The pro-democracy organization Freedom House called the legislative effort "a campaign against political opponents" that would worsen political and civil rights, Interfax said.

KYRGYZSTAN

In a dramatic turnaround, public outrage over fraudulent parliamentary elections forced President Askar Akayev out of office after 14 years of authoritarian rule in this Central Asian nation.

The Akayev administration's aggressively repressive media policies gave way in midyear to a more tolerant press freedom climate under Kurmanbek Bakiyev and his new government. A former prime minister, Bakiyev promised to transform the state broadcaster into an independent outlet, and he pledged to improve overall press conditions. Still, journalists continued to face ongoing political pressures and sporadic physical attacks. Bakiyev, considered an ally of Akayev, was criticized for not moving forward swiftly with some promised reforms.

But the worst abuses against the media occurred early in the year, in the weeks before and after the troubled elections that brought down Akayev. Authorities excluded opposition candidates from the ballot, obstructed political rallies, tampered with ballots, and harassed the independent media during two rounds of voting, in February and in March.

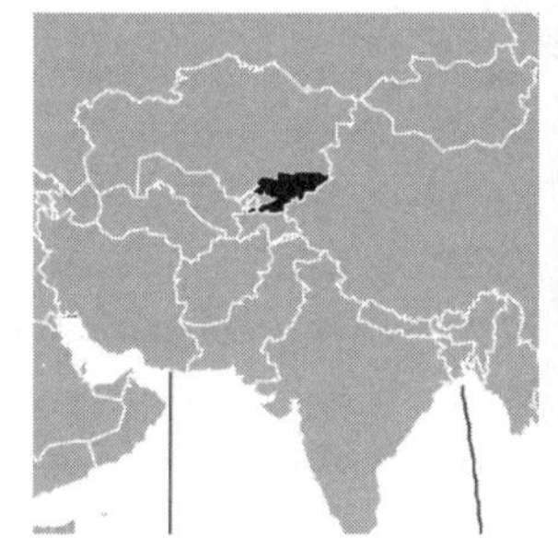

State and private pro-government broadcasters received instructions from the Akayev administration on how to cover the election, and they often engaged in smear campaigns against supposed "extremists" in the political opposition and independent media, according to local press reports. Akayev accused the independent daily *MSN* (formerly *Moya Stolitsa-Novosti*) of waging "systematic information terror" after an article alleging that the president's family was involved in questionable business deals. Akayev threatened legal action, but his many other problems prevented his following through.

In the week before the first round of voting on February 27, authorities scrambled to silence the few sources of independent news by cutting off electricity to the country's only independent printing house and shuttering the influential Kyrgyz service of the U.S. government-funded Radio Free Europe/Radio Liberty (RFE/RL). Independent and opposition news Web sites also experienced technical difficulties, raising suspicions that security agents were blocking reports on growing anti-government sentiment, the Moscow-based radio station Ekho Moskvy reported. The problems continued through the second round of voting on March 13.

Popular frustration at election abuses—added to long-simmering discontent about government corruption and cronyism—finally boiled over in late March, leading to large anti-Akayev rallies in the country's southern provinces and in the capital. The revolt became known as the Tulip Revolution.

Several journalists were injured on March 23, when police and Akayev supporters tried to break up the escalating protests. The head of the country's independent Journalists Trade Union, Azamat Kalman, suffered two broken legs after he was beaten by police officers dispersing protests in the capital, Bishkek, and then pushed off a 10-foot-high ledge by Akayev supporters. Police briefly detained Bolotbek Maripov, a journalist with the newspaper *Obshchestveny Reiting*. Looters seeking to hide their identities roughed up television crews from Moscow-based stations REN-TV and Moskoviya.

At the same time, government officials obstructed or shuttered sources of independent news, according to local reports. Officials at Kyrgyz National University in Bishkek prevented students from getting copies of the opposition newspaper *MSN*, and a state printer refused to publish the independent newspaper *Tribuna*, which reports on human rights abuses, according to the Osh Media Center, a media training organization.

State media were virtually silent on the unrest until it all came to a head on March 24. Senior government officials prevented journalists at the state-run Kyrgyz National Television & Radio Corporation (KTR) from reporting on rallies protesting the conduct of the voting, according to international press reports. Protesters in the country's impoverished south, angered by the state broadcaster's failure to report on the demonstrations, attacked KTR journalists amid the March 24 unrest. "During the demonstrations and disturbances in the south, the [protesters] simply drove away the KTR journalists, breaking their expensive digital cameras," Osh Media Center reported.

While opposition activists stormed government buildings in the capital on March 24, KTR broadcast nature programs. Station management finally fled during the protests, and two KTR journalists appeared on the air to urge calm and to promise that the station would start reporting on the crisis. Its journalists made good on the pledge in large part, although the station was plagued for months by internal disputes over, among other things, its pro-government editorial policy.

Akayev and his family fled the country when angry mobs stormed the presidential building in central Bishkek on March 24. He eventually resurfaced in Moscow and resigned from his post on April 4. This allowed the fractious political opposition that had taken control of Bishkek and parts of the countryside to install Bakiyev as interim leader until a presidential election could be held on July 10. KTR as well as some of the private pro-Akayev media quickly moved to support the interim president.

Amid lingering lawlessness and efforts to track down Akayev's illicit wealth, Bakiyev committed his government to supporting press freedom and transforming KTR into an independent public-service broadcaster. He also appointed one of the country's most famous independent journalists, former *Res Publika* editor Zamira Sydykova, as ambassador to the United States. Nonetheless, some journalists and press freedom activists criticized Bakiyev for stalling the KTR reforms at a time when he was preparing for the presidential election and eager to ensure positive media coverage, according to local reports.

Authorities also imposed some media restrictions in May amid a diplomatic crisis with neighboring Uzbekistan, when several hundred antigovernment protesters fled to Kyrgyzstan to escape persecution by Uzbek security forces. According to the news Web site *monitoring.kg*, local Kyrgyz authorities prevented journalists from interviewing the refugees and in some cases confiscated their equipment, claiming that the news reporting would anger Uzbek authorities, who were insisting on forceful repatriation of the protestors.

In June and early July, acting president Bakiyev received extensive positive media coverage during the presidential election campaign. He easily won the July 10 vote, and appointed as prime minister Feliks Kulov, a charismatic former police chief who had been imprisoned by Akayev.

The new government established media reform commissions in cooperation with media training organizations such as Internews and the Bishkek-based press freedom group Journalists Public Association. These commissions started planning KTR reforms and drafting a new media law and options for privatizing some state media outlets. The prospect of privatization raised concern among state media managers of how they would survive without state subsidies in the impoverished country, according to local and international reports.

In the meantime, though, state media were still plagued by charges of politicized management. KOORT public educational radio and television went off the air in late October when the staff went on strike for a week to protest pressure from managers to praise the Bakiyev government, according to press reports.

Some ongoing lawlessness meant that journalists continued to face occasional threats, harassment, and physical attacks in retaliation for their news reporting. Makhmud Kazakbayev, a journalist for the newspaper *Demos Taimz,* was beaten on the evening of September 14 after having received threats from a politician angered by his articles, according to *monitoring.kg.*

RUSSIA

President Vladimir Putin and his allies continued to expand control over the media, using methods that critics called reminiscent of the Soviet era. Journalists who took on powerful political or business interests sometimes paid with their lives. Two journalists were killed in 2005 for their reporting. In the five years since Putin took power, 12 journalists have been killed in contract-style slayings. None of the killers have been brought to justice.

In the southern republic of Dagestan, Magomedzagid Varisov, a political analyst for the Makhachkala-based *Novoye Delo,* died in a hail of machine-gun bullets in an ambush on June 28. Varisov, who wrote about organized crime and the war in neighboring Chechnya, had received anonymous threats before his murder.

In May, Pavel Makeev, a 21-year-old cameraman for the Puls television station in the southern Rostov region, was killed by a hit-and-run driver while filming illegal drag racing. His body was thrown into a ditch and his camera was tossed into a river in what colleagues believe was an effort to prevent him from reporting on illegal betting in connection with the races.

Authorities appeared to make some progress in solving the June 2004 disappearance of Maksim Maksimov, a reporter for the St. Petersburg weekly magazine *Gorod* who was investigating police corruption. Local prosecutors confirmed on June 27 that three police officers were suspects in Maksimov's abduction and possible murder. Authorities continued to interview witnesses and to search for Maksimov's body.

In July, CPJ addressed the impunity enjoyed by those who attack journalists by organizing an unprecedented conference in Moscow. It brought together relatives and colleagues of the dozen murdered journalists to discuss why police and prosecutors had not made greater progress in solving the cases. Conference participants—who included Russian press freedom advocates and lawyers—issued a statement calling on Putin to publicly acknowledge the killings and demonstrate his commitment to the rule of law. Officials in the prosecutor general's office and the Kremlin refused to meet with a CPJ delegation, and the Kremlin did not respond to the conference statement. But the conference drew wide local and international media attention, and, two months later, the prosecutor general's office provided CPJ with a formal letter outlining the status of the unsolved murder cases. The relatives and colleagues of the slain journalists have continued discussing how they might cooperate to conduct advocacy campaigns and gain additional legal support for their cases.

The prosecutor general reported some progress in the July 2004 slaying of Paul Klebnikov, an American of Russian descent who was an investigative writer and the first editor of *Forbes Russia*. Three suspects were arrested, and court proceedings began in December. The prosecutor general claimed that a Chechen warlord, who was still being sought, had ordered the slaying in retaliation for a book Klebnikov had written about him. Journalists and press freedom advocates noted the lack of evidence linking the warlord to the case and the political convenience of implicating a Kremlin opponent. Despite requests from the U.S. government and the Klebnikov family, Russian officials would not share much information about the case or allow U.S. investigators to participate in the probe. The trial of the three suspects was to be held in secret at the request of prosecutors, who said classified information would be discussed. CPJ protested the move, noting that many courts have successfully protected state secrets by closing portions of testimony and by sealing evidence.

A positive note was sounded when the European Court of Human Rights in Strasbourg, France, agreed to hear more cases related to press freedom. The court has the authority to review the verdicts of domestic courts, issue recommendations, and impose fines. In August, the court agreed to hear charges by Yuri and Zoya Kholodov that Russian authorities had failed to properly investigate and prosecute the murder of their son, Dmitry Kholodov, a reporter for the independent newspaper *Moskovsky Komsomolets* who was killed in 1994 after investigating allegedly corrupt military leaders. Six defendants, four of them military officers, were tried in Russian courts but repeatedly acquitted.

Throughout Russia and the region, politicized criminal investigations have become the favored method of silencing critical media. In September, authorities in the city of Nizhny Novgorod filed two criminal cases against the independent human rights newspaper *Pravo-Zashchita* in retaliation for its publishing statements by Chechen rebels calling for peace talks. Federal Tax Service and local police opened a criminal investigation into the newspaper's publisher on tax-evasion charges. Prosecutors charged Editor-in-Chief Stanislav Dmitriyevsky with having incited ethnic and religious hatred by including the statements in the paper's March and April 2004 editions. His trial began in November; he faces up to five years in prison if convicted. Dmitriyevsky and some of his colleagues also received anonymous death threats during the year.

Foreign correspondents faced growing harassment from regional authorities, particularly when the Kremlin was engaged in diplomatic disputes with neighboring countries. In May, police detained a crew from Latvian public television LTV in a town near the Latvian border and attackers damaged the crew's car while Russian and Latvian authorities were holding sensitive border demarcation negotiations. Later that month, police and Federal Security Service (FSB) agents expelled three journalists from the Polish public television station TVP in the southern republic of Ingushetia after Polish authorities called on the Kremlin to investigate Soviet atrocities during World War II.

Prosecutors increasingly used criminal libel laws to silence criticism of government officials. On June 6, an arbitration court in the central city of Smolensk convicted independent journalist Nikolai Goshko on charges of criminal defamation. Goshko was sentenced to five years in a penal colony for defaming three Smolensk officials in a July 2000 broadcast on the independent station Radio Vesna. He was released in August after an appeals court reduced the charge to criminal insult. On June 22, an arbitration court in the southern city of Saratov convicted Eduard Abrosimov of criminal defamation and sentenced him to seven months in a penal colony for defaming public officials in two articles published in national and local newspapers in 2004, according to local press reports. An appeals court upheld the verdict but released Abrosimov after he had served six and a half months.

The Kremlin restricted the ability of Russian and foreign reporters to cover the war in the southern republic of Chechnya. Foreign broadcasters faced growing government pressure in retaliation for their reporting. The Foreign Ministry criticized London-based independent television broadcaster Channel 4 and Stockholm's independent news agency TT for carrying interviews with Chechen rebel leader Shamil Basayev in February and March, respectively. In August, the ministry barred journalists with the U.S. television network ABC from speaking with government officials and said it would not renew their accreditation after the network broadcast an interview with Basayev. The Foreign Ministry also repeatedly pressed authorities in Sweden to shut down the server of the Chechen news Web site *KavkazCenter*, but the site was still operating in late 2005.

The Foreign Ministry continued to obstruct international news coverage of the war by denying visas to some foreign correspondents and accreditation to local journalists working for foreign news agencies. The ministry refused to issue credentials to journalists from the North Caucasus service of U.S. government-funded Radio Free Europe/Radio Liberty (RFE/RL).

The few journalists in the North Caucasus who continued reporting independently on the war endured harassment by local authorities. Yuri Bagrov, an RFE/RL reporter based in North Ossetia, remained virtually stranded in the city of Vladikavkaz throughout most of the year after FSB agents and prosecutors manufactured a criminal case against him in 2004, stripping him of his Russian citizenship and identity documents. It was impossible for Bagrov to pass through the numerous security checkpoints without those papers. FSB agents and police officers repeatedly threatened Bagrov and prevented him from reporting on local public events. Bagrov believed he was persecuted because of his reporting on politically sensitive issues, such as FSB links to a string of unsolved abductions in the neighboring republic of Ingushetia. Bagrov received a temporary identity document in October that allowed him to leave the city and travel within Russia.

Police reported no progress in the investigation into the July 2003 abduction in Ingushetia of Ali Astamirov, an Agence France-Presse correspondent who had endured months of police and FSB harassment in retaliation for his reporting in Chechnya.

Critical reporting on the Chechen war, Putin's overall performance, corruption, and terrorism has become rare in the past five years. Overt pressure by the FSB, bureaucratic obstruction, politicized lawsuits, and hostile corporate takeovers have enabled the Kremlin to intimidate and silence many of its critics. Authorities in the region denied journalists access to basic information, and used their control of printing, newspaper distribution, and broadcasting facilities to restrict news reporting.

The Kremlin was unnerved by the Orange Revolution that swept reformist Viktor Yushchenko to power in neighboring Ukraine in December 2004. Fearing the challenge by ordinary Ukrainians to a Soviet-style regime could inspire opposition activists, pro-democracy organizations, and the independent media in Russia, Putin intensified restrictions on reformist organizations and formed a pro-Kremlin youth group, Nashi, to crack down on young pro-democracy activists.

The Kremlin expanded its considerable control of the three national television channels to promote Putin's image as a strong leader. In June, it tested a 24-hour satellite-TV news channel broadcasting in English to promote a more positive image of Russia abroad. Called Russia Today, the channel went on the air in December. Domestic audiences also received two new pro-Kremlin television channels. In February, the Defense Ministry launched the television channel Zvezda, which carries military and patriotic films and propaganda. In July, the Russian Orthodox Church launched the religious satellite-TV channel Spas.

Accusations of political censorship of broadcast media escalated in May, when 1,500 Moscow protestors demanded greater freedom on the airwaves, and again in June, when a coalition of liberal, communist, and right-wing parties called on the Kremlin to relax restrictions on broadcast media.

Two potential opposition candidates for the 2008 presidential election faced troubles from state and private pro-Kremlin media. Former Prime Minister Mikhail Kasyanov endured a politicized criminal investigation and media smear campaign during the summer, while world chess champion Gary Kasparov was denied substantive coverage on the powerful state-controlled national channels.

Companies with close ties to the Kremlin bought an influential television station and some of the few remaining newspapers that criticized Putin. The acquisitions were seen as efforts by Kremlin allies to prepare media coverage of what was expected to be a Kremlin-orchestrated handover of the presidency to a chosen successor in 2008.

Two Kremlin allies bought another influential Moscow-based television station, which had provided relatively independent news. The steel and automotive group Severstal and the oil company Surgutneftegaz each purchased a 35 percent stake in Ren-TV during the summer and installed a Kremlin-friendly management in October. In November, Ren-TV managers dismissed outspoken news anchor Olga Romanova after she publicly criticized the station in a radio interview for censoring her news coverage about politically sensitive topics that might anger the Kremlin. One such story was the decision by authorities not to prosecute the son of Defense Minister Sergei Ivanov for a fatal car accident in May.

A booming oil industry and enormous corporate wealth lifted the advertising revenues of large broadcasters, but political controls and widespread self-censorship prevented financial independence from translating into independent editorial policies. Only the Moscow-based radio station Ekho Moskvy, which was taken over by a subsidiary of the state natural-gas monopoly Gazprom in 2001, has retained editorial independence in the national broadcast media. Its journalists own a significant stake in the company.

The Kremlin has allowed a number of independent newspapers and news Web sites to engage in lively debate and government criticism, but these are read by a relatively small, well-educated urban audience. Pressure on print media increased in September 2004 following news reports of official mismanagement during a hostage crisis in the southern city of Beslan. Raf Shakirov, editor-in-chief of the leading Moscow daily *Izvestia*, was forced to resign after government officials angered by the paper's coverage of the Beslan school siege put pressure on the daily's owner, the pro-Kremlin Prof Media. *Izvestia* published graphic photos of the assault to free the hostages in which more than 400 people were killed. It was also one of the first media outlets to criticize the government for claiming that only 350 people had been taken captive when journalists at the scene put the number at more than 1,000.

During the latter part of 2005, companies and businessmen friendly to the Kremlin further restricted the national print media by purchasing three influential newspapers that had remained critical of the government. In June, Gazprom purchased *Izvestia* and five months later appointed a pro-Kremlin editor. In August, Deputy Trade Minister Konstantin Remchukov bought the daily *Nezavisimaya Gazeta*. In October, Moscow-born businessman Arkady Gaidamak purchased the independent Moscow weekly *Moskovskiye Novosti*. Gaidamak said that media should not criticize the government, The *Moscow Times* reported.

TAJIKISTAN

Popular uprisings elsewhere in Central Asia spurred Tajikistan to further crack down on already-limited dissent. Repressive actions flowed from four domestic and regional events: a February 27 parliamentary vote; the Tulip Revolution in neighboring Kyrgyzstan in March; violent unrest in the eastern Uzbek city of Andijan in May; and the prospect of presidential elections in 2006. Timed to each, President Imomali Rakhmonov and his administration censored independent and opposition media, and they harassed and jailed critical journalists.

In January, shortly before the parliamentary election, tax police shut down the printing house that published the popular Tajik-language opposition weekly *Nerui Sokhan*, based in the capital, Dushanbe, for alleged license violations. The move effectively closed *Nerui Sokhan*, which many considered the last prominent independent newspaper on the market. The closure was the latest in a series that began in 2004, when Tajik authorities forced out of print *Ruzi Nav*, *Odamu Olan*, *Adolat*, and other opposition and independent newspapers. The government's most common method: politicized tax inspections followed by charges of tax evasion.

Official results showed that Rakhmonov's ruling People's Democratic Party held its majority in the February election, but opposition parties and international observers questioned the legitimacy of the vote. A 150-member monitoring team from the Organization for Security and Cooperation in Europe reported vote-count manipulations, a refusal to register candidates, government interference in press coverage, and other irregularities.

Rakhmonov and his allies further censored the media after the March revolt in Kyrgyzstan, which resulted in the ouster of President Askar Akayev; and again following the May unrest in Andijan, Uzbekistan, where, according to independent accounts, security troops fired indiscriminately at antigovernment protesters, killing hundreds of civilians.

In April, a media regulatory body known as the Tajik State Licensing Commission ordered the closing of the private television channel Guli Bodom in the northern Tajik city of Kanibadam. Acting on a complaint from the local mayor, the commission alleged that the station broke the law with its election coverage, but it provided no details of the supposed violation, the Tajik news agency Avesta reported. In May, at the commission's behest, tax police shuttered Somonien, the only private television station in Dushanbe, sealing its premises and seizing broadcasting equipment. The commission said the station's license had expired. Somonien and Guli Bodom were among the few television stations that had given airtime to opposition candidates, according to international news reports. Authorities aggressively pursued regulatory efforts throughout the year, independent observers said, to insulate the country from reports of foreign revolt.

Rakhmonov has been in power since 1992. Although a presidential vote is scheduled for 2006, the administration signaled that it has no intention of opening up the press to critical or diverse voices. The London-based Institute for War & Peace Reporting (IWPR), quoting local journalists, reported that the government was effectively blocking new media registrations. Authorities denied the allegations. Journalists who sought to launch an FM radio station told IWPR that justice ministry officials advised them not to bother filing an application because it would be turned down. As of May 2005, IWPR said, about 30 applications for new media outlets were languishing in an administrative limbo. In some cases, applicants were asked time and again to correct supposed paperwork errors.

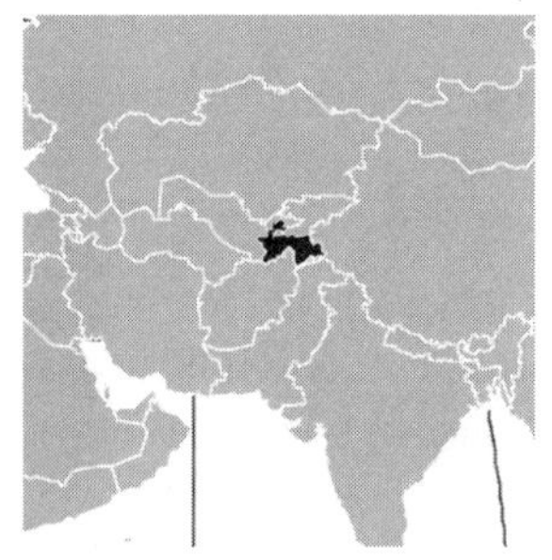

In August, a Dushanbe judge convicted Mukhtor Bokizoda, editor of the shuttered *Nerui Sokhan*, to two years of "corrective labor" and fined him 1,500 Tajik somoni (US$500). Under the "corrective labor" requirement, Bokizoda was to be assigned a job, and then forfeit 20 percent of his monthly salary to the government. The charges dated to February, when tax authorities accused Bokizoda of stealing electricity to power the printing house of his press advocacy group, the Foundation for the Memory and Protection of Journalists—the same facility used to print *Nerui Sokhan*. Bokizoda asked an appellate court to review the verdict.

In a sign of authorities' intolerance of dissent, a judge in northern Tajikistan sentenced independent journalist Jumaboy Tolibov in June to two years in a prison colony on charges that included hooliganism and trespassing. The National Association of Independent Media of Tajikistan, a press freedom group, said the charges were fabricated in retaliation for three commentaries in which Tolibov criticized the local prosecutor. An appeals court overturned most of the verdict in October, but Tolibov was not freed for another two months.

Many disturbing questions about the country's brutal 1992–97 civil war remained unresolved. In 2004, after prodding by CPJ, the prosecutor general created a special investigative unit to probe the unsolved slayings of journalists that occurred during the war, but the unit has not reported any results. At least 17 journalists were killed in direct connection to their work, according to CPJ research, while another 12 were killed under circumstances that remain unclear. The People's Front, a paramilitary group led by Rakhmonov, is believed to have been responsible for many of the killings. A number of People's Front leaders later assumed top positions in the government.

Tajikistan began tilting diplomatically away from the United States and toward Russia in 2004. Rakhmonov and Russian President Vladimir Putin signed an agreement in October of that year, providing Tajikistan with military and economic assistance in exchange for allowing Russia a permanent military base in the country.

Rakhmonov reminded journalists of their obligation to support the state in a March 20 address. "The media, regardless of ownership, are equally responsible for observing the current laws and ensuring the country's information and cultural security," Rakhmonov was quoted as saying on the Web site *Eurasianet*. "This responsibility demands of journalists a developed sense...of patriotism and the protection of Tajikistan's state and national interests."

TURKMENISTAN

Saparmurat Niyazov, the self-proclaimed president for life, steered his nation farther down the path of international isolation, barring foreign publications as well as libraries, and keeping so tight a grip on the news media that vital issues went unreported.

The state owns all domestic news media, and the Niyazov administration controls them closely, appointing editors and censoring content. In power for 15 years, Niyazov calls himself "Turkmenbashi"—the father of all Turkmen—and he uses the thoroughly submissive media to promote his cult of personality. Foreign television news is available to only a small number of urban elites who can afford satellite dishes, while foreign radio broadcasts are available via shortwave only. The lack of independent media forces citizens to rely on rumor for basic information.

State media were silent when a series of murders erupted in Mary, the nation's second largest city, in July. The absence of reliable information fueled widespread fear among residents and sparked the spread of sensational rumors about the case, according to the London-based Institute for War & Peace Reporting (IWPR).

Other major stories were ignored by state media, including the spread of AIDS; rampant drug addiction and dealing; and social woes ranging from unemployment to prostitution. Few heard or read about a May massacre in neighboring Uzbekistan in which government troops killed hundreds of civilians during antigovernment protests.

Reporters who contribute to international media and Web sites use pseudonyms to try to avoid persecution from the ruthless National Security Ministry (MNB). Foreign correspondents have dwindled to a handful, primarily from Russian news outlets. Even they are sometimes denied visas and accreditation, or they are harassed in other ways. MNB agents detained Viktor Panov, Ashgabat correspondent for the Russian state news agency RIA Novosti, on espionage charges in late February, expelling him two weeks later.

Yet Niyazov's most audacious moves came in a one-two punch in April. The president banned without explanation the import and distribution of foreign publications,

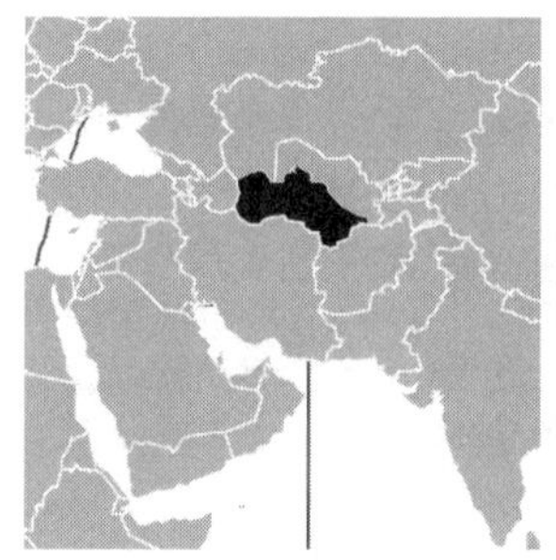

which mainly affected newspapers and magazines published in neighboring countries, RIA Novosti said. Niyazov had already banned subscriptions to foreign publications several years ago. The only remaining Russian-language newspaper in Turkmenistan was the state-controlled *Neitralny Turkmenistan*, according to RIA Novosti.

Niyazov ordered the closing of libraries that same month, robbing citizens of one of the few avenues for obtaining information from the outside world, including foreign literature, magazines, and news periodicals. "No one goes to libraries to read books anyway," Niyazov told his cabinet, according to IWPR. The president was also quoted as saying that the books Turkmen needed were already in their homes, schools, and workplaces. The move followed a series of presidential decrees in recent years that have banned opera, ballet, the circus, and movie theaters.

Bookstores are not an alternative for outside information. Their shelves are filled with Niyazov's own writings, notably *Rukhnama* (Book of the Soul), his 400-page guide for living, according to IWPR. *Rukhnama* is compulsory reading in all schools, public employees are tested on its contents, and houses of worship are directed to display it next to the Koran and the Bible. Critics say the book is full of historical errors. *Rukhnama* denies any influence from other cultures on Turkmenistan's development; it claims that Turkmen invented writing.

Niyazov moved to isolate his country even from the former Soviet republics that constitute the Commonwealth of Independent States (CIS), an economic alliance. He announced in August that Turkmenistan would reduce its membership in the CIS from full to associate status. State television lauded the move as "the latest glorious victory of independent, neutral Turkmenistan," the U.S. government-funded Radio Free Europe/Radio Liberty reported.

UKRAINE

Expectations were high that new President Viktor Yushchenko would sweep away the legacy of repression left by Leonid Kuchma's authoritarian regime. Yushchenko won a December 26, 2004, presidential runoff held after hundreds of thousands of protesters flooded the streets of the capital, Kyiv, to denounce an earlier, rigged vote in which Kuchma protégé Viktor Yanukovych was declared the winner. The uprising, termed the Orange Revolution after Yushchenko's campaign color, was seen as heralding a new era in which democratic reforms would take hold, with the news media as guarantors.

Inaugurated on January 23, Yushchenko pledged his commitment to fostering a free and independent press, and he vowed to prosecute political crimes such as the 2000 slaying of Georgy Gongadze, editor of the opposition news Web site *Ukrainska Pravda*. Allegations of high-level involvement in the Gongadze murder had dogged Kuchma throughout his second term.

As hope met reality in 2005, the press and the public found the new administration moving forward on investigations and reforms but leaving much work incomplete. The government reported arrests in the Gongadze case, but many believed that the masterminds would remain unpunished. Broadcast reform was widely discussed, but action was far more limited.

Yushchenko's platform called for reforming the National Television Company of Ukraine (NTCU), the Soviet-style, state-run television and radio broadcaster. The national television channel UT-1, which is part of NTCU and covers 98 percent of Ukraine's territory, was widely discredited for broadcasting false and misleading reports in the months leading up to the Orange Revolution. But turning it into a publicly funded independent broadcaster proved arduous. Tatyana Lebedeva, chairman of the National Council for Television and Radio Broadcasting (NCTRB), which is charged with developing a reform plan, told journalists and advocates at a May briefing in Washington, D.C., that there is internal opposition to revamping NTCU. In particular, some government officials backed the creation of a new state-controlled broadcaster.

With little progress to show, Yushchenko appointed Vitaly Dokalenko as the new president of the NTCU in late October. Dokalenko said his top priority would be ensuring that UT-1 provides unbiased coverage in the run-up to the March 2006 parliamentary elections.

Throughout the year, the administration was embroiled in a politically charged dispute with NTN television over the private station's bid to expand its broadcasting to 75 Ukrainian cities. NTN broadcasts in Kyiv and is financed by the Donetsk-based oligarch Eduard Prutnyk, an adviser to Yanukovych.

The NCTRB rejected the application, first made in November 2004, and said the station could gain access to the public frequencies only through competitive bidding. NTN took its case to court in Kyiv and won approval of its license expansion. In October, the Supreme Court overturned the expansion, saying the station had to compete for the frequencies. Natalya Katerynchuk, NTN's editor-in-chief, called the government's opposition a politically motivated attempt to settle scores and silence a political foe.

Whether motivated by politics or a desire to foster greater access to the airwaves, Yushchenko made clear his displeasure with the existing distribution of broadcast licenses. In March, he told a Council of Europe conference that the media are "divided between three families." By most accounts, those families include Kuchma's son-in-law, Viktor Pinchuk, who owns more than 280 television broadcast licenses; Kuchma's former chief of staff, Viktor

Medvedchuk, who controls all major radio frequencies; and the so-called Donetsk business group, which includes Prutnyk and two other oligarchs in the industrial east who control more than 180 television licenses. "We see and understand this problem, and we are ready to find ways to resolve it," Yushchenko said, leaving unsaid what his administration specifically intended to do.

The president's own honeymoon with the media came to an end in July, when a reporter from *Ukrainska Pravda* asked at a press conference how the president's 19-year-old son, Andrei, could afford a BMW and an expensive mobile phone. An angry Yushchenko admonished the reporter to be polite and stop acting like a "hired killer," local reports said.

About 200 Ukrainian journalists and media activists called for an apology in an open letter to Yushchenko published online by *Ukrainska Pravda* on July 26. Yushchenko replied, but he did not apologize: "I highly value the role of the Ukrainian journalists in the victory of democratic forces during the Orange Revolution, and respect the point of view which the Ukrainian mass media takes in the processes of the democratization of the country... It is good that we live in a country where no topic or person is taboo for discussion. It is right that the president and his family live under the watchful eye of the press, but it is not a reason to take away my family's right to private life."

Yushchenko's election reignited the long-stalled probe into the September 2000 abduction and murder of *Ukrainska Pravda* editor Gongadze. Investigators detained two police officers on March 1. Former Interior Minister Yuri Kravchenko was found dead three days later—his death termed a suicide—just hours before he was to be interviewed under oath by investigators. On audiotapes made secretly by a former presidential bodyguard, Kuchma is allegedly heard to instruct Kravchenko to "drive out" Gongadze and "give him to the Chechens," according to transcripts obtained by news agencies. Also in March, the Interior Ministry acknowledged that its officers had conducted surveillance of Gongadze shortly before he was abducted.

On August 1, the prosecutor general's office announced that it had completed the first phase of its investigation and had identified four suspects in Gongadze's slaying: police officers Nikolai Protasov, Aleksander Popovych, and Valery Kostenko; and Gen. Aleksandr Pukach, former head of the Interior Ministry's criminal investigation department. The officers faced trial in late year, while Pukach was being sought on an arrest warrant. Prosecutor General Svyatoslav Piskun said authorities would continue to seek others believed to be responsible for ordering the murder.

In September, a parliamentary commission investigating the case accused Kuchma, the late Kravchenko, Parliament Speaker Vladimir Litvin, and former Ukrainian Security Services chief Leonid Derkach of plotting the journalist's murder. The commission recommended that the prosecutor general open criminal cases against Kuchma, Litvin, and Derkach. But the commission, which dissolved after its sensational September 20 announcement, had no judicial authority, and prosecutors were not bound to act upon its findings. Its conclusions were met with virtual silence throughout the rest of the government:

Yushchenko, the Interior Ministry, and law enforcement agencies offered no comment.

Gongadze's widow, Myroslava, who was granted political asylum in the United States after her husband's murder, said that Ukrainian authorities still lack the political will to solve the case. During a trip to Ukraine in April, she pressed Piskun to authenticate the bodyguard's tapes so that they could be admitted as court evidence but did not get a commitment, the U.S. Public Broadcasting System program "Frontline" reported.

Despite arrests and reports of progress, the deep-seated flaws in the investigation led to additional political fallout late in the year.

In November, the European Court of Human Rights (ECHR) in Strasbourg, France, found the Ukrainian government liable for 100,000 euros (US$118,000) in damages in a lawsuit filed by Myroslava Gongadze in 2002. The court ruled that Ukrainian authorities had failed in their duty to protect the life of the 31-year-old editor; had failed to thoroughly investigate his death; and had treated Myroslava Gongadze in a degrading manner by not giving her access to materials in the case and by issuing contradictory statements.

"By filing this lawsuit, I wanted to urge Ukrainian authorities to fully investigate my husband's murder and punish the organizers and perpetrators of this crime who hampered the appropriate investigation with their deliberate actions or criminal inertia," the Itar-Tass news agency quoted Gongadze as saying.

By the time of the ECHR's ruling, top prosecutor Piskun was no longer involved in the case: He was fired by Yushchenko on October 14. The president's office said Piskun had dragged out important investigations for too long. The former prosecutor's deputy, Aleksandr Medvedko, was named to the post the following month.

High-level changes such as this were common during this period. In September, Yushchenko sacked his entire government, headed by his former Orange Revolution ally Yulia Tymoshenko, amid allegations of corruption. Yuri Yekhanurov, governor of the eastern Dnepropetrovsk region and a longtime supporter of Yushchenko, was approved by Parliament as acting prime minister on September 22 and immediately formed a new government. Its main task, he said, was economic reform.

After her dismissal, Tymoshenko said she would lead her political party, the Yulia Tymoshenko Bloc, as an independent candidate in the March 2006 parliamentary elections, thus severing ties with Yushchenko. For his part, the president told reporters in October that his administration would ensure that the press could cover the campaign without fear of repercussions, UT-1 said.

UZBEKISTAN

President Islam Karimov engaged in a full-fledged offensive against the independent press. Unrelenting government persecution drove out more than a dozen foreign correspondents and local reporters working for foreign media; continual harassment forced at least two news agencies and a media training organization to close their offices. Karimov and his allies used trumped-up charges of terrorism and extremism to jail media critics, political opponents, and human rights advocates. At least three journalists were imprisoned, and a number of others were detained for brief periods. Using police intimidation and a state-media smear campaign, the Karimov regime made clear that it would not tolerate any deviation from its official, sanitized version of events.

The year's defining moment came on May 13, "Bloody Friday," when demonstrators in the eastern city of Andijan stormed a local prison and freed 23 businessmen they said were unjustly accused of Islamic extremism. Protests in downtown Bobur Square later grew to include an estimated 10,000 people upset by pervasive poverty and unemployment in the surrounding Ferghana Valley. Although demonstrators called for the resignation of Karimov's government, independent journalists said the protests were peaceful.

Government security forces opened fire on the crowd without warning, according to independent accounts, killing between 500 and 1,000 civilians and drawing comparisons to the Chinese government's brutal 1989 crackdown in Tiananmen Square. Uzbek authorities denied the high number of civilian deaths, putting the death toll at 187 and claiming that security forces had no choice but to shoot at the "armed Islamic terrorists" who had tried to "overthrow the constitutional order of Uzbekistan," state media said.

Authorities blocked foreign television, including CNN, BBC, and the Russian networks REN and NTV, from gaining access to Andijan. The popular Andijan radio station Didor was taken off the air. State television broadcast only brief, official statements without footage, and authorities blocked foreign television transmissions into the country for days. They also barred reader access to popular news Web sites such as *Ferghana.ru*, *Lenta.ru*, and *Gazeta.ru*, effectively preventing the flow of nongovernment information into and out of the region. In the ensuing weeks, authorities maintained a virtual information blockade on the region, making reporting difficult and risky.

The government also moved aggressively to purge Andijan of independent journalists. From May 14 to May 16, police sealed the city and, citing safety concerns, ordered journalists to leave. Shamil Baygin of Reuters and Galima Bukharbaeva, then with the London-based Institute for War & Peace Reporting (IWPR), were detained by Andijan police late on May 13 and released the next day.

Bukharbaeva, one of a handful of journalists who reported from Bobur Square, was named a recipient of CPJ's 2005 International Press Freedom Award. Bukharbaeva reported that government troops shot indiscriminately at protesting civilians, including women and children. The reporter barely escaped herself as a bullet tore through her backpack. Then director of the local IWPR office, Bukharbaeva went into exile in the United States as authorities threatened to prosecute her on charges of operating the news bureau without government accreditation.

Harassment of IWPR reporters continued. On June 4, police in the southern city

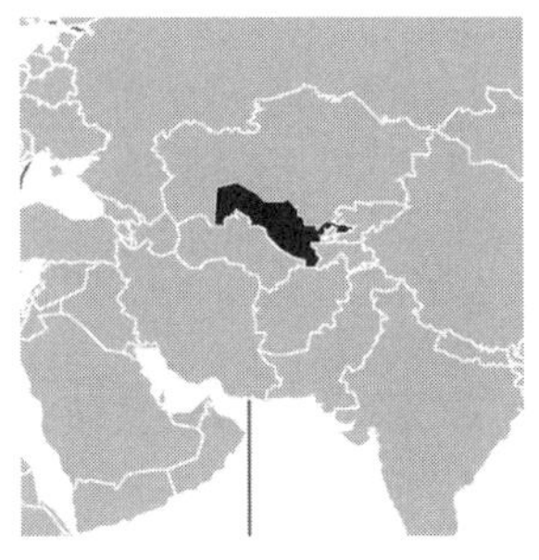

of Karshi arrested correspondent Tulkin Karayev. Karayev said an unidentified woman attacked him on the street without provocation, IWPR reported, but authorities instead charged the journalist with "hooliganism," tried him without legal counsel, and jailed him for 10 days. Just two days after his release, Karayev was detained briefly without charge or explanation and his passport was seized. He told CPJ that Uzbek security agents had also interrogated his family. State media maliciously accused Karayev and other journalists of cooperating with terrorists, carrying out antistate activities, and giving distorted news accounts. A May 25 article in the government newspaper *Pravda Vostoka* called IWPR correspondents "enemies of the state." Karayev and several colleagues fled to neighboring Kyrgyzstan in July, and IWPR closed its office in the capital, Tashkent, in the face of continuing persecution by the government.

The U.S. government-funded Radio Free Europe/Radio Liberty (RFE/RL) documented more than 30 cases of government-sponsored attacks on its local correspondents after Andijan. In a detailed report published in September, RFE/RL recounted threats, detentions, searches, and physical assaults. Staffers were placed under surveillance and their families threatened and harassed, the news service reported. By year's end, the Foreign Ministry had refused to renew accreditation for RFE/RL's Tashkent bureau.

On August 4, a judge in Tashkent convicted two staffers of Internews Network, a U.S.-based media training and advocacy organization, of producing television programming without a license and publishing information illegally. The presiding judge said the organization had "started meddling in the politics of Uzbekistan," Internews said. Internews disputed the charge, saying it had simply trained Uzbek stations to produce their own reports. The staffers avoided a prison term, but on September 9 a civil court ordered the closure of Internews Network based on the convictions. "The judge refused our request to call witnesses, denied all our petitions, and was blatantly biased," Internews Network Director Catherine Eldridge said.

On August 11, Uzbek authorities at the Tashkent airport detained Igor Rotar, a Russian correspondent on assignment for the Norway-based human rights news Web site *Forum18*. He was deported the next day. Furkat Sidikov, a press officer at the Uzbekistan Embassy in Washington, D.C., told CPJ that Rotar was stopped because he did not have the appropriate press accreditation from the Foreign Ministry.

Uzbekistan remained the leading jailer of journalists in Europe and Central Asia, with six behind bars when CPJ conducted its annual census of imprisoned journalists on December 1. Two reporters—Sobirjon Yakubov of the weekly *Hurriyat*, and Nosir Zokirov, a Namagdan correspondent for RFE/RL—were imprisoned during the year in retaliation for critical reporting, according to CPJ research.

Yakubov was detained on April 11 and charged with "undermining the constitutional order," which could bring up to 20 years in prison. The charge was based on allegations of religious extremism, which authorities did not detail. Colleagues said that the charges were politicized and that Yakubov was being punished for advocating democratic reforms in an article published in March.

Zokirov was charged with insulting a security officer after he called a National Security Service (SNB) office in Namagdan on August 6 to protest SNB pressure on an Uzbek poet who had criticized the violent crackdown in Andijan. He was detained, tried without a lawyer or witnesses, and sentenced to six months in prison, all on August 26, RFE/RL said.

Ongoing government harassment prompted the BBC to close its Tashkent bureau on October 26 and withdraw its staff. Seven BBC journalists had to leave Uzbekistan from June to October after enduring threats, intimidation, and a smear campaign in the state media, the BBC said.

Journalists also endured physical attacks. In the eastern city of Jizzakh, independent journalist Ulugbek Haydarov was hospitalized in April with a broken collarbone and multiple bruises after an assailant beat him and shouted, "I will teach you how to write," according to local and international press reports. Haydarov had written articles saying that Jizzakh authorities had appropriated crops and deprived local farmers of the best land. Tensions between farmers and the Jizzakh administration resulted in antigovernment protests in the spring.

Aleksei Volosevich, correspondent for the independent Moscow-based Web site *Ferghana.ru*, was attacked and doused with paint near his apartment in Tashkent on November 9, the journalist told CPJ. Volosevich was one of the very few independent journalists who had witnessed the Andijan massacre and remained in Uzbekistan. Two weeks before the attack, Volosevich wrote a critical article on the trial of 15 civilians charged with terrorism in the Andijan unrest.

The Karimov government resisted calls for an independent investigation into Andijan that were made by the United Nations, the European Union, NATO, the Organization for Security and Cooperation in Europe, and the United States. On August 23, the Uzbek prosecutor general's office accused the U.N. High Commissioner for Refugees of "protecting terrorists" by helping more than 400 Uzbek refugees resettle temporarily in Romania, according to press reports.

Faced with the government's resistance, the EU acted on November 14 to bar 12 top Uzbek officials from visiting its member states and to block member states from selling arms to Uzbekistan, international press reports said. The same day, Karimov signed a mutual defense pact with Russian President Vladimir Putin in Moscow. The pact pledged that Uzbekistan and Russia would work to "build and develop allied relations on a long-term basis" and that "an act of aggression on one side will be considered as aggression against both sides," the news Web site *Eurasianet* said. The pact signaled Tashkent's shift away from the strategic influence of the United States and toward that of Russia.

SNAPSHOTS: **EUROPE AND CENTRAL ASIA**

Attacks & developments throughout the region

ARMENIA

- Despite recommendations from the Council of Europe and other international organizations, the government in February rejected for the 10th time a broadcast license application filed by A1+, the independent television station pulled off the air in 2002. The station continued to operate a popular news Web site, publish a weekly newspaper, and produce programs for regional television stations.
- In February, the Interior Ministry closed its investigation into a 2004 arson attack on a car owned by editor Nikola Pashinian of the independent daily *Haikakan Zhamanak* in the capital, Yerevan. No arrests were made. *Haikakan Zhamanak* reported that police never interviewed a politician whom the newspaper believed to be responsible.
- Arson was used as a means of attack again on April 1, when someone burned the car of Samuel Aleksanian, editor-in-chief of the state weekly *Syunyats Yerkir* in the southern city of Goris, according to local press reports. Aleksanian said the attack followed his criticism of the local governor.
- Armenian politicians cited the "war on terror" as reason for passing legislation restricting press coverage of terrorism. President Robert Kocharian signed the measure on April 19, ignoring concerns over vaguely worded prohibitions on reporting of antiterror tactics, the Yerevan Press Club reported.

CROATIA

- Drago Hedl, editor of the weekly *Feral Tribune*, received an anonymous death threat by mail on December 6, according to press reports. Hedl said the letter, which also threatened a source, cited a July article about the abduction, torture, and murder of ethnic Serb civilians in Osijek in 1991 and 1992. The source implicated the current head of the Osijek municipal council, who denied responsibility. Police said that they were investigating the threat and providing Hedl with protection, the state news agency HINA reported.

CYPRUS

- The European Court for Human Rights ruled in March that Turkish authorities conducted a flawed investigation into the 1996 murder of journalist Kutlu Adali in northern Cyprus. The court ordered the government to pay 20,000 euros (US$26,000) in damages to Adali's wife, Ilkay. Adali, a political columnist with the leftist daily *Yeni Duzen* who opposed the division of Cyprus, was shot outside his home in Nicosia. The court faulted the investigation, saying there was "no real coordination or monitoring of the scene of the incident by the investigating authorities, the ballistic examination carried out by the authorities was insufficient, and the investigating authorities failed to take statements from key witnesses."

FRANCE

- Mihye Kim, a reporter for the South Korean television network KBS, was beaten by a gang while she was reporting on riots in the northern Parisian suburb of Aubervilliers on November 5, Agence France-Presse reported. Four or five young men surrounded Kim and her cameraman and tried to rob them; one man kicked the reporter, rendering her unconscious. Police officers came to the defense of the journalists when they heard their cries.

GERMANY

- Police and prosecutors raided the Berlin home of freelance journalist Bruno Schirra on September 12 and confiscated his entire research archive. The Federal Office of Criminal Investigation (BKA) began investigating Schirra after he profiled al-Qaeda leader Abu Musab al-Zarqawi in the April edition of the Potsdam monthly *Cicero*. Authorities claimed that al-Zarqawi's mobile phone number, included in the story, came from a classified BKA document. Schirra said the telephone number was revealed during a 2003 terrorism trial in Germany. Prosecutors accused Schirra of aiding a BKA official in violating secrecy laws. The journalist faces up to five years in prison if convicted.

ITALY

- In February, President Carlo Azeglio Ciampi pardoned Lino Jannuzzi, the 77-year-old former editor-in-chief of the Naples daily *Il Giornale di Napoli*. Jannuzzi was facing a 29-month prison sentence for criminal libel, stemming from articles published between 1987 and 1993 that criticized judicial authorities investigating organized crime, according to press reports.

- Six police officers searched the Milan headquarters of *Corriere della Sera*, Italy's leading national daily, looking for documents that the paper had used in a report on Iraqi militants' use of Italian-made semiautomatic Beretta pistols. Raffaele Fiengo, an editor at *Corriere della Sera*, told CPJ that the search was conducted after the newspaper refused to disclose its sources to authorities.

MOLDOVA

- President Vladimir Voronin and the ruling Communist Party used politicized media regulators to help ensure his re-election. In the weeks before the March election, the Broadcasting Coordination Council expanded the broadcasting range of pro-government stations such as NIT, and the Justice Ministry refused to register newspapers run by opposition parties such as the Social Democratic Party, according to local reports.

- In February, Moldovan authorities stationed on the de facto border with the Trans-Dniester region prohibited newspaper deliveries going in either direction. The media has been a pawn in political tensions between the central government in the capital, Chisinau, and the separatist Trans-Dniester region.
- In June, financial police officers searched the offices of the Russian-language Chisinau weekly *Kommersant PLUS*, according to local reports. Editor-in-Chief Artyom Varenitsa said police confiscated documents and computer disks. Voronin's government often uses police to harass news outlets that criticize the government.

ROMANIA

- In a notable step forward for press freedom, libel is no longer a crime under criminal code amendments that took effect in June. Slander, while still a felony, is no longer punishable by prison.
- Journalists in the capital, Bucharest, strongly criticized the government in January for the widespread practice of wiretapping journalists' phones. The scandal emerged after security officials confirmed they had sought permission to wiretap the AM Press and Mediafax news agencies to identify a supposed media source in the Interior Ministry. Officials also acknowledged tapping the phones of two Romanian journalists working for foreign media, according to international press reports.
- A government ethics panel confirmed in January that managers for TVR state television and SRR state radio censored news reports and tried to discredit an opposition candidate during the November 2004 presidential and parliamentary elections, according to international news reports. Romania's new president, Traian Basescu, promised greater respect for press freedom, but he was criticized in February for seeking to replace TVR's director, an appointment ordinarily handled by Parliament.
- In May, the government adopted reforms to make its secretive advertising distribution more transparent and less political. The new law is a first step toward preventing bureaucrats from channeling state advertising revenue to politically loyal media outlets.

SERBIA AND MONTENEGRO

- In March, posters and graffiti appeared in downtown Belgrade calling for a boycott of the Belgrade-based radio and television station B92. The posters—which included the B92 logo inside the Star of David and proclaimed "Serbia for Serbs"—criticized the station's "anti-Serb influence," along with its "dangerous influence on Serbian youth" and its alleged support of drug use and "other Western sicknesses."

- Investment Minister Velimir Ilic and his press secretary, Petar Lazarevic, threatened B92 journalist Ana Veljkovic at an August press conference. The reporter had asked why Ilic had taken steps to quash a criminal case against the son of former Serbian President Slobodan Milosevic. Lazarevic said he would "kill" B92's top editor, Veran Matic. Ilic told Veljkovic she was "sick" and "in need of psychiatric help" and he warned her not to get "in our way."
- About 600 journalists and supporters of the political opposition held a rally in the capital, Podgorica, on May 27, marking the first anniversary of the murder of Dusko Jovanovic, owner and editor-in-chief of the opposition daily *Dan*. Jovanovic was killed in a drive-by shooting outside the *Dan* office. One suspect went to trial, and Serbian authorities handed over a second suspect to Montenegrin authorities in May. Jovanovic's colleagues and lawyers have criticized police and prosecutors for the slow pace of the inquiry.
- On June 11, an anonymous death threat was made against Grujica Spasovic, editor-in-chief of the Belgrade daily *Danas*. The day before, *Danas* had reported that the Serbian government had identified the town where indicted war criminal Ratko Mladic was hiding. A man characterizing himself as "personal security of General Ratko Mladic from Republika Srpska" called the *Danas* newsroom and said: "Pass [Spasovic] the message: From today on, he is dead. We will kill him, cut off his head, legs, and arms, for what he wrote [and] published about General Mladic." The police waited a week before meeting with Spasovic to discuss the threat.
- Bardhyl Ajeti, a 28-year-old reporter for the Albanian-language daily *Bota Sot*, died in a Milan hospital on June 25, three weeks after being shot in Kosovo and evacuated to a hospital in Italy, Agence France-Presse reported. Unidentified assailants shot the journalist from a passing car on June 3. Ajeti had written editorials criticizing opposition politicians.

UNITED KINGDOM

- British authorities issued a gag order on November 23, threatening legal action against news outlets if they reported further from a leaked government document alleging U.S. President George W. Bush had considered bombing the Qatar headquarters of the satellite-TV station Al-Jazeera in April 2004. After London's *Daily Mirror* broke the story on November 22, Attorney General Peter Goldsmith warned three newspapers—the *Daily Mirror*, *The Guardian*, and *The Times*—that they would be prosecuted under the Official Secrets Act if they published further details from a classified transcript of a conversation between Bush and British Prime Minister Tony Blair.

THE MIDDLE EAST AND NORTH AFRICA

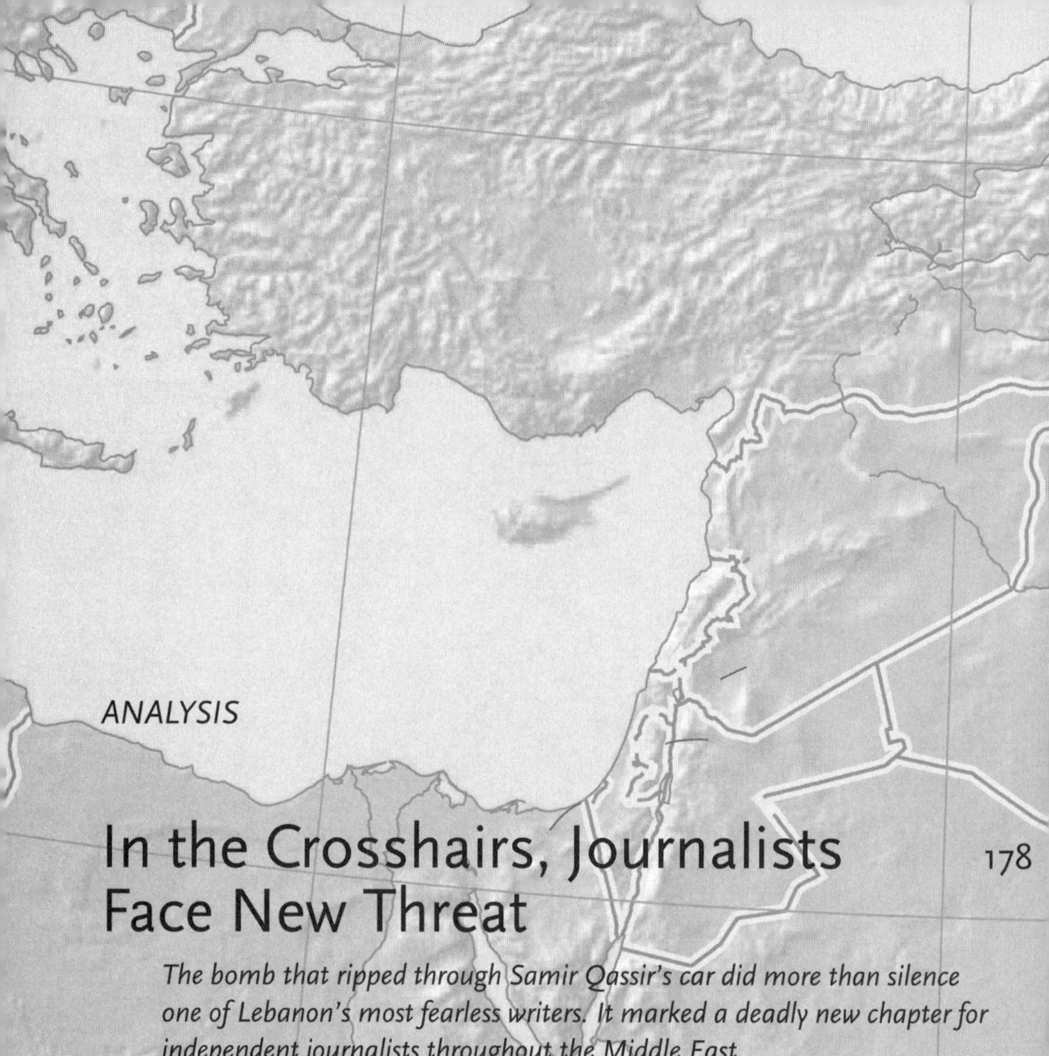

ANALYSIS

In the Crosshairs, Journalists Face New Threat 178

The bomb that ripped through Samir Qassir's car did more than silence one of Lebanon's most fearless writers. It marked a deadly new chapter for independent journalists throughout the Middle East.

by Joel Campagna

PHOTOS

Section break: Reuters/Ali Jasim – *A car bomb explodes in front of a Baghdad school as a photographer springs to action.* Analysis (next): Reuters/Mohamed Azakir – *A Lebanese woman carries a poster of news anchor May Chidiac during a demonstration in Beirut.*

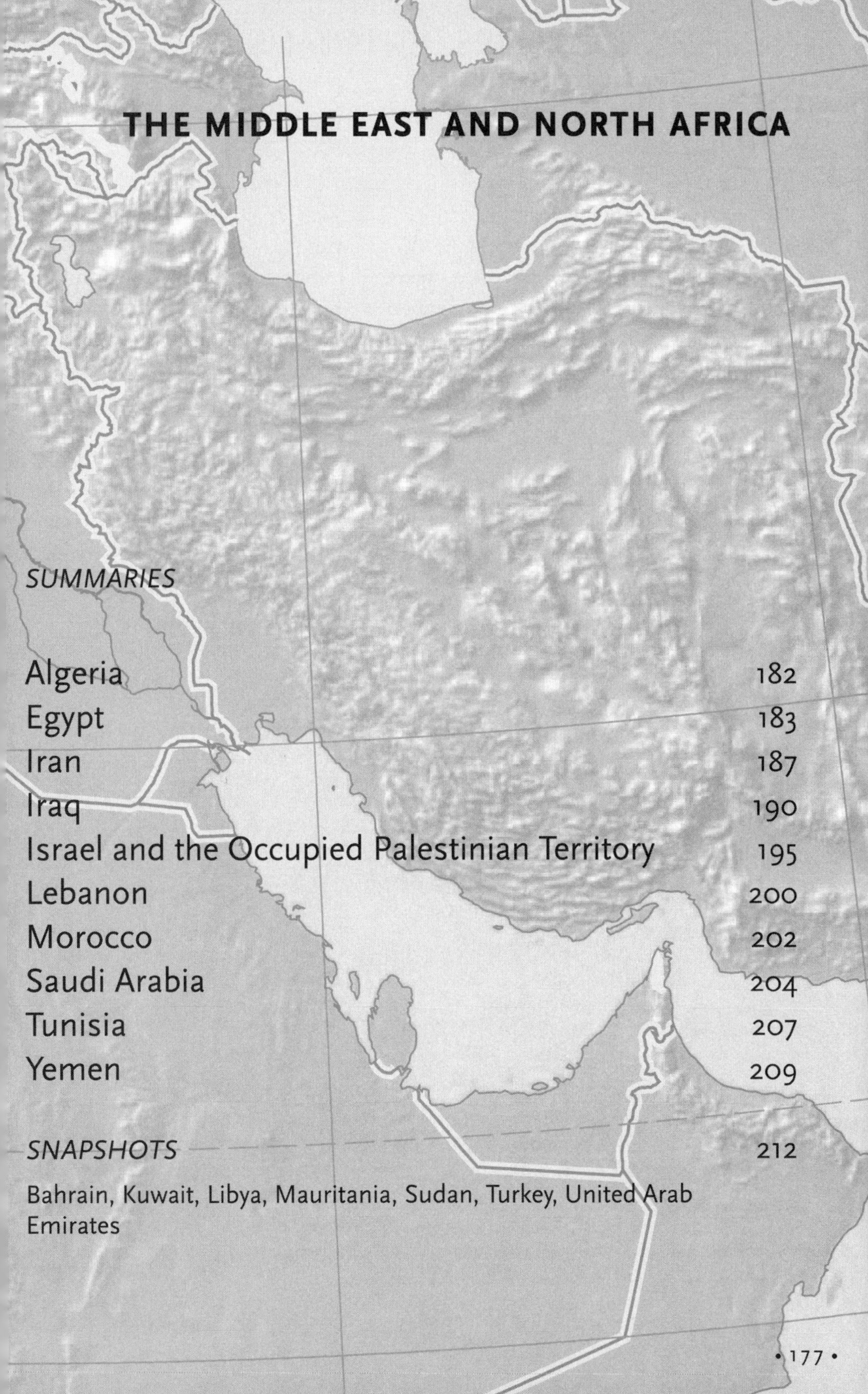

THE MIDDLE EAST AND NORTH AFRICA

SUMMARIES

IN THE CROSSHAIRS, JOURNALISTS FACE NEW THREAT

by Joel Campagna

THE BOMB THAT RIPPED THROUGH SAMIR QASSIR'S WHITE ALFA ROMEO on June 2, 2005, silenced Lebanon's most fearless journalist. For years, Qassir's outspoken columns in the daily *Al-Nahar* took on the Syrian government and its Lebanese allies when few reporters dared do so. The assassination sent shockwaves across the region, and reminded the media of the perils of being an independent journalist in the Middle East.

As friends and colleagues mourned Qassir and fretted over the implications of his murder, reports emerged in Libya that the body of journalist Dayf al-Ghazal al-Shuhaibi had been found on a suburban Benghazi street with a single bullet to the head. Al-Ghazal, who for years worked in Muammar Qaddafi's tightly controlled, state-run press, had gone missing almost two weeks earlier. He had contributed dissenting articles to a number of London-based opposition Web sites and had been interrogated by Libyan agents about his writings.

Qassir and al-Ghazal were hardly the first journalists in the region assassinated for their work, and they would not be the last. *Al-Nahar* Managing Director and columnist Gebran Tueni was murdered in Beirut in December, punctuating a year in which journalists in the Middle East endured violent attacks as never before. Seizing the moment of broader calls for political change, many journalists have sought to expand the debate and challenge the status quo. In some countries journalists have capitalized on small political openings brought about by the deaths of autocrats to boost debate in the local media. They have seized on new technologies often beyond the reach of repressive governments—the Internet and satellite television—to exchange ideas. External forces have also played a role. The September 11, 2001, attacks on the United States and the war in Iraq have prompted discussions on political reform and pushed local democrats, including independent journalists, to clamor for greater rights as well as government accountability.

"Journalists increasingly find themselves the targets of brazen, violent attacks."

Over the years, Arab governments have efficiently discouraged critical, introspective journalism in their domestic media through nonviolent methods: the use of ominous press laws, criminal libel statutes, imprisonment, bureaucratic restrictions, job dismissals, and admonishments from security agents. Governments and political actors such as the various Palestinian factions and Lebanese groups have traditionally controlled the press by buying loyalty, or by co-opting the media through threats or harassment.

But in some countries the rules of the game have changed. Amid citizens' clamor for greater rights, governments and political groups have demonstrated their own insecurity by responding to press criticism with ruthless oppression. Journalists who refuse to play by the new rules have found themselves increasingly in the assassin's crosshairs, or as the targets of other brazen, violent attacks. A growing number of attacks against journalists have been carried out with impunity, forcing independents across the region to ponder the consequences of what they write.

Just three months after the murders of Qassir and al-Ghazal, Lebanese Broadcasting Corporation journalist May Chidiac lost an arm and a leg when a bomb exploded under the driver's seat of her car near the port city of Jounieh. On the day of the attack, Chidiac hosted a political talk show addressing Syria's possible involvement in the killing of former Lebanese Prime Minister Rafiq al-Hariri in February. United Nations investigators eventually implicated Syrian and Lebanese intelligence and concluded that senior Syrian officials likely had knowledge. On December 12, the day that investigators issued an updated report, another car bomb took the life of Tueni, a fierce critic of the Syrian government. The perpetrators in all of the attacks remained at large, and some Lebanese feared more killings of outspoken journalists.

In Yemen, where the government was on its heels amid economic woes and public protests, journalists have witnessed a sharp rise in assaults and threats at the hands of government agents and armed groups. In August, editor Jamal Amer was abducted by gunmen who, during his four hours in captivity, beat him repeatedly, and accused him of defaming unspecified "officials." Amer said the car that spirited him away belonged to the Yemeni Republican Guard. At year's end, Yemeni authorities had provided little indication that those responsible would be apprehended.

Amer's ordeal was eerily reminiscent of an incident that occurred in Egypt 10 months earlier, when four men assaulted and briefly abducted Abdel Halim Kandil, an editor and columnist at the opposition weekly *Al-Arabi* and a staunch critic of President Hosni Mubarak. The attackers took Kandil's mobile telephone and glasses before dumping him in the middle of a desert road, stripped to his underwear, with a warning to stop writing about "important people." That case, too, was unsolved.

"Iran dealt a near death blow to the independent media through systematic arrest and torture."

Even more ominously, the government in Iran has dealt a near death blow to the country's independent media, not only by shutting down pro-reform newspapers, but also by the systematic arrest and torture of press critics. Several writers, bloggers, and dissident journalists have been detained, placed in solitary confinement, and physically abused during their imprisonment. In late 2004 and early 2005, writer Fereshteh Ghazi and bloggers Omid Memarian and Ruzbeh Mir Ebrahimi, among other journalists, discussed their own experiences of abuse in testimony before a presidential commission looking into the treatment of prisoners.

Nowhere is the sense of vulnerability to violence and impunity more pronounced—and its effects so dramatic—than in the region's major conflict areas. In terms of media casualties, the bloody war in Iraq has surpassed the grim toll of Algeria's civil conflict, which claimed the lives of 58 journalists between 1993 and 1996. Already in Iraq, a total of 82 journalists and media support staffers have died since the U.S.-led invasion in March 2003. As in Algeria in the 1990s, many of the journalists killed have been hunted down by armed groups and murdered in retaliation for their work. Insurgents, perhaps

"Once unheard of in the Occupied Territories, journalist kidnappings have become commonplace."

taking a cue from armed Algerian groups, have compiled so-called "hit lists" of journalists in some cities, which they post in public places or in mosques. Their victims have mostly been local Iraqi reporters working for domestic or international media who were targeted because of their perceived support of the U.S. and Iraqi governments, or because of editorial stances viewed as hostile to the insurgents.

The attacks on the media in Iraq are further evidence of just how vulnerable conflict reporters have become. Today, the concept of journalists as neutral noncombatants applies less and less in places like Iraq, making it increasingly difficult for journalists to gather and report the news from the field without mortal threat. Journalists there have been targeted under suspicion that they are "spies," because they are viewed as partisans, or because they work with "foreigners." Armed groups have also attacked or abducted members of the media for political gain, to maximize publicity, to use as bargaining chips, or to squelch unwanted reporting.

A case in point—though without the same lethal results—is the West Bank and Gaza Strip, where armed groups have taken advantage of the power vacuum left by a debilitated Palestinian Authority to prey upon media critics. News organizations routinely endure threats, violent attacks, and have their offices ransacked. Once unheard of in the Occupied Territories, kidnappings of media workers have become commonplace in the last two years.

The rash of deadly attacks inspires appreciation for the bravery of front-line reporters who continue to report the news despite the threat of abduction, assault, or death. They also underscore how much a free and open press hinges on the ability of journalists to carry out their mission without threat to life and limb. That's why it's essential to demand accountability when journalists are attacked or murdered for their work, and to bring to justice those responsible. When impunity thrives, a free press can no longer function. Enterprising journalists, who are its engine, will no longer be willing to take their chances.

• • • • • • • • • • •

Joel Campagna is senior program coordinator for the Middle East and North Africa.

ALGERIA

Authorities continued to use legal harassment as the primary means of intimidating the private press, wielding a penal code that criminalizes defaming the president, the judiciary, Parliament, and the military. Emboldened by his re-election in 2004, President Abdelaziz Bouteflika, together with his political and business allies, registered hundreds of legal complaints against private newspapers critical of the government. Criminal defamation cases against the press were heard routinely in Algiers courtrooms.

In contrast to 2004, when three journalists were imprisoned, no members of the press were jailed during the year. However, Mohamed Benchicou, publisher of the now-defunct Algiers daily *Le Matin*, remained in prison on charges of violating currency laws, which many colleagues believe were brought in retaliation for *Le Matin*'s criticism of Bouteflika and powerful state ministers. Authorities lodged additional defamation charges against Benchicou after his two-year sentence began in 2004, including at least one charge of defaming the president.

Faced with the threat of legal action, journalists continued to censor themselves when writing about the president and powerful security and military personnel. Some also complained that authorities leveraged a huge public-sector economy to exert financial pressure on newspapers. State-owned companies advertise much more prominently in newspapers that support the government, and they generally avoid advertising in critical publications, journalists said.

Authorities occasionally denied newspapers access to printing facilities in 2005, although they did so less frequently than in previous years. Most private newspapers rely on state-owned printing presses, although a few have bought their own presses to circumvent the government's attempt at control.

Algerian journalists had to cope not only with harsh press laws, but also with a judiciary that did not appear to be acting independently in its handling of press-related cases. In April, several journalists associated with the shuttered *Le Matin* were convicted of defamation. According to local journalists, reporters Abla Cherif and Hassan Zerrouki were sentenced to two months in prison for defaming a businessman from the United Arab Emirates, based on a 2003 article in *Le Matin* about his involvement in procuring a license for a company in which he had a stake. The paper's former editor-in-chief, Youssef Rezzouj, and reporter Yasmine Ferroukh were also found guilty of defamation.

• • • • • • • • • • •

Summaries in this chapter were reported and written by **Joel Campagna**, senior program coordinator for the Middle East and North Africa; Research Associate **Ivan Karakashian**; program consultant **Kamel Labidi**; and freelance writers **Hani Sabra** and **Rhonda Roumani**.

They were sentenced to three months in prison on charges arising from a 2003 article that accused Minister of Energy and Mining Chakib Khelil of abusing state funds. All four journalists were freed pending appeal.

In May, a criminal court in Algiers found current and former employees of the French-language daily *Liberté* guilty of defaming the president. Cartoonist Ali Dilem was fined 50,000 Algerian dinars (US$700) for cartoons published in summer 2003 that satirized Bouteflika and his re-election campaign. Former *Liberté* director Farid Alilat was sentenced to one year in prison for having published the cartoons. Alilat, who now lives in France, was sentenced in absentia.

Le Soir d'Algérie journalists Fouad Boughanem and Ridha Belhajouja, who publishes under the name Hakim Laalam, were also found guilty in May of defaming the president. They were sentenced to two months in prison; both were freed pending appeal. The charges against the journalists stemmed from articles published in late 2003 that were critical of Bouteflika's re-election campaign.

In a positive development, Ahmed Benaoum, chief officer of the Errai al-Aam media group, was released in June after an appeals court overturned a 2004 ruling that sentenced him to two years in prison. Benaoum—who, like *Le Matin*'s Benchicou, had several cases lodged against him—had been charged with defamation and financial misappropriation. The New York–based Human Rights Watch attended the appeals court hearing in which his release was ordered.

Television and radio, major sources of news for much of Algeria's population, are state-controlled and support Bouteflika's policies. But many Algerians rely on pan-Arab and European-based news channels for information. Journalists told CPJ that the government appears unlikely to loosen its grip on local television and radio anytime soon.

The foreign media in Algeria remain hampered by the state bureaucracy. The two most popular pan-Arab stations, Al-Jazeera and Al-Arabiya, have yet to acquire Ministry of Information approval to open bureaus in Algiers. Independent journalists blame the government's refusal on a desire to control Algeria's image in the broader Arab world.

EGYPT

Press freedom was dealt a triple blow in 2005—in Parliament, in court, and on the street. President Hosni Mubarak failed to honor promises made in 2004 to introduce legislation that would decriminalize press offenses. A criminal court handed jail terms to three journalists from one of the country's few independent newspapers for defaming a minister. Security forces and thugs believed to have been hired by the ruling party assaulted reporters covering antigovernment protests and parliamentary elections.

In April, a Cairo criminal court sentenced three journalists with the Cairo daily *Al Masry al-Youm* to one year in prison following an article reporting that authorities had searched the housing minister's office and that he had been suspended. The newspaper, founded in 2004, stood by the story and appealed the verdict. The case against Abdel Nasser al-Zuheiry, Alaa al-Ghatrifi, and Youssef al-Oumi for "defamation of a public employee" was pending in late 2005. The sentences were imposed a year after Mubarak's call to eliminate criminal penalties in cases of defamation and other press infractions. But Parliament did not amend the 1996 Press Law, nor other laws—such as the penal code, the 1971 Law on the Protection of National Unity, the 1977 Law on the Security of the Nation and the Citizen, and the Emergency Law, in force since Mubarak assumed power in 1981—under which journalists may be jailed. The 1996 Press Law prescribes prison sentences of up to two years for defamation. The penal code can be used to imprison journalists for "violating public morality" and "damaging national interest."

On May 25, government supporters beat demonstrators and several foreign and local journalists who were covering a protest, organized by the Kifaya (Enough) movement, against the limited nature of a constitutional amendment to allow more than one candidate to run in presidential elections. Protesters called on Mubarak to step down and accused him of paving the way for his son Gamal to succeed him. Journalists interviewed by CPJ said that they were punched, kicked, and slapped by the assailants, and that Egyptian security forces did not intervene. The journalists said they suspected that some of the assailants were actually plainclothes security agents, although they believed the majority were thugs hired by the ruling National Democratic Party. Some female reporters told CPJ that the assailants groped them.

More than a dozen journalists filed complaints with the authorities against the leadership of the National Democratic Party and security officers. Subsequently, at least two female reporters were pressured by security forces to withdraw their complaints. One journalist, Shaymaa Abol Kheir of the weekly independent newspaper *Al-Dustour*, who was beaten and groped by female government supporters, said that security agents had conveyed messages to her through relatives and neighbors. Abol Kheir said that agents told her neighbors that her brothers would be detained and that she would face legal charges unless she dropped her complaint.

Another journalist who lodged a formal complaint, Abeer al-Askary, also from *Al-Dustour*, told local reporters that her family had received a visit from individuals who identified themselves as State Security Intelligence officers, warning her and her family that they would face serious consequences unless she withdrew her complaint. Journalists who spoke to al-Askary told CPJ that she was informed that her siblings would lose their government jobs and that her parents could be detained. Neither journalist dropped her complaint.

No progress was reported in bringing to justice the perpetrators of these assaults and others committed in past years against journalists critical of the government. Nor was any light shed on the disappearance of Reda Helal, deputy editor of the semioffical *Al-Ahram* newspaper, on August 11, 2003. Helal, whose controversial views, particularly his support of the U.S.-led invasion of Iraq, prompted anger among many in Egypt, mysteriously disappeared from his home in the center of Cairo.

When Egyptians went to the polls for November's parliamentary election, police and security forces detained, beat, and obstructed several reporters seeking to cover the vote for local and foreign news outlets. Throughout the year, the ability of TV stations to cover demonstrations and meetings was often restricted. On May 13, security forces arrested nine journalists, cameramen, and technicians with the Arabic satellite-TV channel Al-Jazeera, holding them for eight hours. The arrest came as they were covering a special meeting of a judges' association, in which some 3,000 judges threatened to refuse to supervise the September presidential election unless they were allowed to control the electoral process. In May, Al-Jazeera and other satellite-TV stations were denied access to a hotel in Cairo where Arab human rights defenders were meeting.

Street protests gained momentum in June after Parliament passed amendments to the 1956 Law on Political Rights, which introduced imprisonment and fines for publishing false information on elections or the behavior or morality of candidates.

Various attacks on press freedom, including use of the entire range of laws available to the government to imprison reporters, spurred unprecedented defiance among journalists at a time when the circle of opposition to Mubarak's rule and the Emergency Law was widening. The Emergency Law gives the president extensive powers to suspend basic freedoms, and it includes the right to arrest suspects and detain them for long periods without trial, to refer civilians to military courts, to prohibit strikes and public meetings, and to censor or close down newspapers in the name of "national security."

In June, following in the footsteps of magistrates and university professors who had publicly called on the executive branch to stop meddling in judicial and academic matters, journalists formed a body called "Journalists for Change." It soon became an influential pressure group within the principal media union, the Journalists Syndicate, which in September sent a strong message to the government by re-electing Galal Aref, an opposition figure, as its chairman.

Journalists still face various forms of legal action that could result in imprisonment and heavy fines. A report published in 2005 by the Egyptian Organization for Human Rights said that "journalists in Egypt suffer numerous forms of discrimination including unfairness in legislation, judicial prosecution of journalists for their writing and opinions, assault and death threats, and sexual assault of female journalists."

Repeated calls to free the media and to remove the longstanding editors of the so-called "national papers" apparently did not fall on deaf ears. (Egypt has a number of state-backed "semiofficial" daily newspapers.) One such editor was Ibrahim Nafie, former head of Al-Ahram news group and a Mubarak confidant. He had been in his post more than

25 years and was beyond the legal retirement age of 65 when he was dismissed last year.

In July, the upper house of Parliament, which is responsible for state publications, appointed younger editors to head the "national newspapers." But the criterion of loyalty to Mubarak and his party seemed to have inspired the architects of these appointments. The only editor with a reputation for critical thinking, Hani Shukrallah, of the English-language *Al-Ahram Weekly*, was unexpectedly replaced, even though he had not yet reached retirement age.

The reshuffle coincided with the review by the country's top administrative court of a case filed by journalists from the state-owned *Al-Ahram* and *Al-Akhbar* demanding that their editors be replaced for "exceeding the retirement age."

No sooner had the new editors been appointed than they made multiple expressions of allegiance to Mubarak, particularly in the run-up to Egypt's first multicandidate presidential election, on September 7. They ridiculed Mubarak's challengers and claimed that giving the president a fifth six-year term would secure a better future for Egypt.

Internal pressure for democratic reform, coupled with a U.S. call on Mubarak to gradually open up the political system, seemed to have led authorities to grant licenses to independent weeklies, including *Al-Dustour* and *Al-Fagr*, and opposition papers, among them, *Al-Ghad* and *Al-Karama*. These papers—particularly *Al-Dustour*, which was banned in 1998 and re-emerged in early 2005—covered sensitive subjects such as Mubarak's health and the political influence exerted by his wife, Suzanne, and son Gamal.

Nevertheless, nearly 80 percent of journalists still work for state media, which were nationalized in 1961. Many of them are employed by the Egyptian Radio and Television Union (ERTU), whose TV channels have been losing audiences to Arab satellite-TV channels, particularly Al-Jazeera. ERTU controls nearly 10 percent of the shares of the most popular private Egyptian TV channels, Dream 1 and Dream 2. Like the country's two private radio stations, Nojoom FM and Nile FM, they focus on entertainment and are not allowed to broadcast news bulletins.

Despite Mubarak's promise in September to work with the next People's Assembly to "endorse the needed amendments" to introduce legislation that would decriminalize press offenses, many journalists and human rights defenders agree that the road to press freedom and protection of journalists in Egypt remains long and arduous. "The lack of democracy and transparency, and the prevailing culture of allegiance to the authorities or the state-appointed editors, had a negative impact on the ability of generations of journalists to uphold professional standards and to protect press freedom," said Karem Yahya, coordinator for Journalists for Change and author of a recent book on the plight of the Egyptian press.

"The legacy of legislative and administrative oppression in the media and other walks of life over the past 50 years makes it difficult for journalists to force the state to loosen its grip over the media," said Yahya, who himself was for a time barred from the offices of *Al-Ahram*, where he worked for years.

IRAN

Hard-liners in government and the judiciary continued a crackdown on the independent media in general and on Internet journalists in particular. In the course of the year, authorities jailed Web bloggers, banned four newspapers for publishing a letter by a reformist cleric, and closed the Tehran bureau of the Arabic-language satellite-TV channel Al-Jazeera.

Over the past few years, authorities have eviscerated the reformist print press, prompting many banned newspapers and pro-reform journalists to move to the Web. Bloggers instantly became a popular source of dissident news and opinion, drawing the ire of Iran's powerful judiciary, which launched a wave of arrests. All the bloggers detained in a 2004 crackdown were released except for Mojtaba Saminejad, who was sentenced in June 2005 to two years in prison and denied appeal. He was convicted of "insulting the supreme leader." Many of the released bloggers said they were tortured in jail. Former Iranian president Mohamed Khatami ordered an investigation into the torture claims, but the judiciary threatened those who made the complaints. Since conservative President Mahmoud Ahmadinejad took office in June 2005, little has come of the investigations. Nobel Peace Prize-winner Shirin Ebadi and other human rights activists were still pursuing the allegations.

Arash Sigarchi, a blogger and editor of the daily *Gilan-e-Emrouz* in northern Iran, was released on bail after spending two months in prison. He was convicted by a revolutionary court of espionage, propaganda against the state, and insulting leaders, and sentenced to 14 years in prison. The court revealed the verdict on February 22. Sigarchi was released on bail, and was not expected to serve his 14-year sentence. He was charged in connection with a report on the arrest of writers for a Web log called *Panhjareh Eltehab*, which is banned in Iran. Before his own arrest, Sigarchi had also given interviews to the BBC and U.S. government-funded Radio Farda.

Ailing online journalist and religious student Mojtaba Lotfi was released on August 27 after serving more than six months in jail. He was convicted in 2004 of publishing lies and harming the state, and sentenced to 46 months in prison. He wrote an article titled "Observing Human Rights in Cases Concerning the Clergy" on *Naqshineh*, a news Web site about the holy city of Qom. Lotfi suffers from lung problems that developed after he was exposed to chemicals during the Iran-Iraq war. Prison conditions caused his health to deteriorate.

Officials continued to pressure Internet service providers (ISPs) to install filters to block access to political blogs and online reformist newspapers. On January 9, the judiciary closed down one of Iran's main ISPs, Neda Rayaneh, for violating state filtering restrictions. In September, the government contracted the Iranian company Delta Global to manage a censorship system for the Internet. The head of the company, Rahim Moazemi, told the Iranian Student News Agency that he wanted to centralize the filtering system in Iran. Authorities reportedly blocked hundreds of political and reformist Web sites and blogs classified as "immoral" and sources of "propaganda against the Islamic system."

The old-guard defenders of Iran's Islamic revolution under spiritual leader Ayatollah Ali Khamenei continued to use state institutions such as the judiciary to close pro-reform newspapers, prosecute independent journalists, and imprison critics.

A prominent imprisoned journalist, Akbar Ganji, drew international attention after claiming that he had been tortured in custody. Ganji was first jailed in 2000 for "taking part in an offense against national security" and promoting "propaganda against the Islamic system." In July 2001, he was sentenced to his current term of six years for "collecting confidential state documents to jeopardize state security" and "spreading propaganda."

In May, Iranian newspapers published an account Ganji smuggled from Tehran's notorious Evin prison in which he attacked Khamenei and claimed authorities used "physical and mental torture" to extract confessions from inmates. He had waged a hunger strike a month earlier to protest a lack of medical treatment.

On May 29, judicial authorities granted Ganji a one-week release from jail so he could be treated for asthma and back pain. By June 8, Tehran's hard-line chief prosecutor, Saeed Mortazavi, signed an arrest warrant claiming Ganji was on the run after the journalist failed to return at the expiration of his temporary leave. Ganji returned to Evin prison three days after the warrant was issued, telling reporters that he would resume his hunger strike.

His wife, Massoumeh Shafii, published an open letter on the *Emrouz* news Web site on October 27, claiming Ganji was tortured and mistreated by security officers while being treated in Tehran's Milad hospital. The United States and the European Union sought Ganji's release and criticized Iran for denying him medical treatment, access to his family, and legal representation.

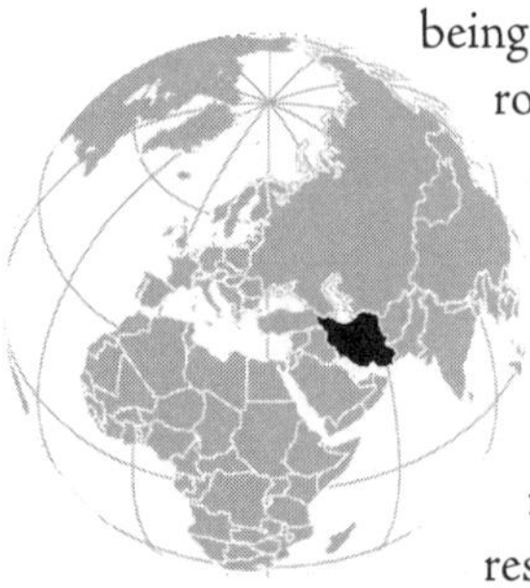

Political unrest increased in Iran's Kurdish region following the election of Ahmadinejad, who is seen by some Kurds as hostile to their demand for greater political autonomy and cultural recognition. Clashes between ethnic Kurds and Iranian authorities resulted in the closing of the Kurdish-language daily *Ashti* and the bilingual Kurdish and Farsi weekly *Asou* by the Ministry of Culture and Islamic Guidance on August 3.

Several prominent Kurdish human rights activists and journalists were detained on August 2, following protests in the city of Sanandaj, capital of Kurdistan province. Among them was Mohammad Sadiq Kabudvand, managing editor of the now-defunct bilingual Kurdish and Farsi *Payam Mardom Kordestan* and co-founder of the Kurdistan Human Rights Organization. A Sanandaj court found Kabudvand guilty of "inciting the population to rebel against the central state" and sentenced him to one year in prison, according to CPJ sources. The court reached its verdict on August 18 but announced it only in mid-October. Kabudvand was not sent to prison and was preparing an appeal. Kabudvand published articles on torture in jails, and he advocated a federal system of government for the Islamic republic.

The judiciary harassed journalists by frequently summoning them for questioning about their writing, a tactic used to spread fear and control news coverage. On August 13, Abolfazl Fateh, managing director of the Iranian Students News Agency, was called in by Investigation Bench 6 of the Government Employees Court to explain why the agency had published remarks by Ganji's wife and a statement by the Iranian Journalists Association, the state news agency IRNA reported. The previous week, Fateh was summoned by Tehran's chief prosecutor to respond to charges of disrupting public order by reporting remarks by Nobel laureate Ebadi, who criticized the judiciary for refusing to allow her to visit Ganji. Fateh was ordered to post bail of 100 million rials (US$11,000) before he could go free. Journalists also suffered bureaucratic harassment. On January 12, the Passport Office banned journalist Shadi Sadr from leaving the country, without providing any explanation.

Since 2000, Iranian courts have closed more than 100 publications, most of which were pro-reform. The repression continued in 2005, as hard-line conservatives dominated all organs of government. On March 10, *Jame-e-No,* a monthly sociopolitical magazine, was ordered closed for failing to publish in accordance with its license, which stipulates that it must be published each month. If it missed an edition, it would be in violation of its license. Fatemeh Kamal, the magazine's license holder, said she believed the real reason for the closure was her marriage to reformist political activist Emadolddin Baghi.

On June 20, Tehran's chief prosecutor banned four daily newspapers—*Eqbal, Aftab, Etemaad,* and *Hayat-e-No*—that had published an open letter from Mehdi Karoubi, a reformist-centrist cleric. Karoubi was defeated in the first round of the presidential elections. He complained of "illegal intervention" in the election by the Revolutionary Guard and the Guardians Council. The council, the most influential body in Iran, has the authority to interpret the constitution and to determine if the laws passed by the parliament are in line with the constitution. It is a criminal offense to criticize the supreme leader in Iran, and numerous publications have been shut down for doing so. *Eqbal,* the newspaper of the main reformist party, the Islamic Iran Participation Front, was suspended indefinitely; the other three dailies were allowed to resume publication the next day.

In April, Iran closed the Tehran bureau of the Arabic-language satellite-TV network Al-Jazeera for reporting that clashes between security forces and ethnic Arab protestors in the provincial capital of Ahwaz had killed three people. Arabs make up approximately three percent of Iran's population of 67 million, and most of them live in the southwest of the country. Yossef Azizi-Banitorouf, a reformist Iranian Arab journalist, was arrested on April 25 immediately after he held a news conference with foreign media on the unrest in Ahwaz and the Iranian Arab revolt against Tehran. He was released from custody on June 28. He had worked for *Hamshahri* for 12 years but was fired when conservatives took over management of the daily.

The authorities have yet to prosecute those responsible for the 2003 death in state custody of Canadian-Iranian photojournalist Zahra Kazemi. In November, an appeals court ordered the case reopened after upholding the 2004 acquittal of Iranian intelligence agent Mohamed Reza Aqdam Ahmadi, who had been charged with "semi-intentional murder." Kazemi's legal team had doubted Ahmadi's guilt all along.

An Iranian government inquiry released in late July 2003 concluded that Kazemi had died as a result of a skull fracture, likely caused by a blow to her head. On March 31, 2005, a former Iranian army doctor, Shahram Azam, alleged that he was the first to examine an unconscious Kazemi, with an armed guard, in Tehran's Baghiatollah hospital four days after her arrest. His allegations were presented at a press conference in Ottawa, Canada, where Azam was granted asylum. Iranian authorities maintained that no doctor of that name ever examined Kazemi and that he had lied to gain asylum. Azam recalled that Kazemi had a fractured skull, several broken bones, missing fingernails, and deep lacerations on her back from flogging.

Canada limited diplomatic contact with Iran because of Tehran's continued refusal to allow an international forensic team to examine Kazemi's body. Kazemi, a contributor to the Montreal-based magazine *Recto Verso* and the London-based photo agency Camera Press, was arrested on June 23, 2003, for taking photographs outside Evin prison. The government has acknowledged that Kazemi was violently beaten in prison, although the judiciary said she died after a fall. Lawyers for Kazemi's relatives believe a prison official beat her to death.

IRAQ

Iraq was an assignment of unending danger for the hundreds of journalists covering the world's biggest news story. Journalist murders, deaths in crossfire, abductions, and detentions continued apace, reinforcing Iraq's distinction as the most dangerous place in the world to work as a journalist and as one of the deadliest conflicts for media in modern history.

Media casualties mounted at an alarming rate, with 22 journalists and three media workers killed in action in 2005. That brought the total to 60 journalists and 22 media support staff killed since the U.S.-led invasion began in March 2003. Continuing a trend that began in 2004, most of the casualties were Iraqis, who have assumed central roles in gathering news for local print and broadcast media as well as major international news organizations. More than 75 percent of all media deaths in Iraq since March 2003 have been local, front-line reporters on assignment in places deemed too dangerous for Westerners, or working local beats for domestic news outlets.

Insurgent attacks remained the leading cause of media deaths. In several cases, armed groups hunted down and murdered journalists. The motives for the murders were not always clear; however, some attacks appeared directed against news outlets perceived as supportive of U.S. and coalition forces. These include the national broadcaster, Al-Iraqiya, part of the Iraq Media Network (IMN), which receives funding from the U.S. government. Several of the station's journalists were murdered or attacked by insurgents during the year, while the station's offices came under constant artillery fire in cities such as Mosul. Other insurgent attacks on the media, such as attacks on Iraqis working for international news organizations, were interpreted by journalists as attempts by insurgents to intimidate local citizens who work with foreigners, or as efforts to single out people they believed worked with the coalition forces, or were "spies." Still other attacks came in retaliation for specific news coverage or the editorial line of a reporter's newspaper.

The case of Al-Iraqiya news anchor Raeda Wazzan underscored the peril. Wazzan was kidnapped in February and found dead five days later on a roadside in Mosul, where the journalist had lived and worked. She had been shot in the head repeatedly. Wazzan's husband said that his wife had received several death threats with demands that she quit her job. Al-Qaeda's affiliate in Iraq claimed responsibility for the attacks in Internet postings, but those claims could not be independently verified. Other journalists narrowly escaped death in attacks by armed groups. Jawad Kadhem, an Iraqi correspondent for the Dubai-based satellite-TV channel Al-Arabiya, was shot and seriously injured at a Baghdad restaurant by men who tried to bundle him into a car. An obscure Sunni group calling itself Jund Al-Sahaba claimed responsibility in an Internet posting that called Kadhem "a malicious Shia." It accused Al-Arabiya of "treason" and of being a "mouthpiece of the Americans." Like other claims, its authenticity could not be confirmed. Iraqi journalists described several other close calls in which they survived threats or attacks from gunmen or insurgent groups.

Insurgent attacks and kidnappings were not limited to local reporters. In the first three months of 2005, armed groups seized at least seven foreign reporters. They included French reporter Florence Aubenas of the daily *Libération*, who was seized in Baghdad along with her interpreter and held for more than five months before her release on June 11. In February, Indonesian reporter Meutya Viada Hafid and cameraman Budiyanto, who work for Indonesia's 24-hour news channel Metro TV, were abducted by gunmen along with their driver and freed after several days. Romanians Marie Jeanne Ion and Sorin Dumitru Miscoci, of the Bucharest-based Prima TV; and Ovidiu Ohanesian, of the daily *Romania Libera*, were taken with their driver in March and released two months later. And Italian reporter Giuliana Sgrena, of the Rome-based daily *Il Manifesto*, was held for a month after being abducted in Baghdad on February 4.

Due to the risk of abduction and attack by insurgent groups, foreign reporters, based mostly in Baghdad, sharply curtailed their movements beyond fortified residential compounds or hotels. Many traveled only with considerable calculation and the assistance of armed guards, staying at a location for short periods only. Few ventured on the dangerous insurgent-controlled roads outside Baghdad. In many instances, the only viable option to report from other parts of the country was to embed with the U.S. military. Journalists complained that the security situation had, in large measure, eroded their ability to cover many aspects of the conflict. The spate of abductions appeared to subside by fall, but in October, reporter Rory Carroll of the London daily *The Guardian* was kidnapped by armed men and released days later unharmed.

In Basra, the southern port city that had witnessed relatively few attacks on journalists, U.S. reporter Steven Vincent was abducted along with his translator and murdered in August. CPJ research found he may have been killed in retaliation for his sensitive reporting on Shiite religious groups in Basra and their infiltration of the local police force, or possibly because of his close relationship with his female Iraqi interpreter, who was gravely wounded in the attack. Fakher Haider, a stringer for *The New York Times*, was killed a month later in the same city.

Underscoring the vulnerability of the foreign press, three car bombs exploded in October outside the Palestine Hotel, which is widely used by foreigners, including journalists. More than a dozen people were killed. Although there were no media deaths, several journalists inside the hotel were injured. In a similar attack in November, suicide bombers detonated explosive-laden vehicles outside Baghdad's Hamra Hotel, which houses journalists and contractors. Several Iraqis were killed in the blast, although there were no media casualties.

The 157,000 U.S. troops stationed in Iraq, along with Iraqi armed forces, were yet another source of danger for the media. U.S. forces' fire remained the second leading cause of journalist fatalities in Iraq. Three journalists were killed by U.S. fire in 2005—13 total since 2003—while several more came under fire. One of the fatalities, Waleed Khaled, a sound technician working for Reuters, was shot several times in the face and chest as he drove with cameraman Haidar Kadhem to investigate a report of clashes between armed men and police in Baghdad's Hay al-Adil district. On September 1, chief military spokesman in Baghdad Maj. Gen. Rick Lynch said soldiers had followed "established rules of engagement" and acted in an "appropriate" manner when they opened fire on Khaled's vehicle, but military officials provided no further details, and it was unclear whether the results of the military's investigation would be released.

The military's record on investigating journalist deaths in Iraq suggested that they might never be made public. A CPJ study published in September showed that the U.S. military repeatedly failed to fully investigate, or properly account for, the killing of journalists by its forces in Iraq, or to implement its own recommendations to improve media safety, particularly at U.S. checkpoints.

Approaching U.S. checkpoints could at times be a hair-raising experience, according to journalists and other civilians. Protocols remained unclear more than two years after hostilities began, despite recommendations from CPJ, human rights groups, and the military itself for improving safety. Several journalists described coming under fire when approaching checkpoints or when operating near U.S. troops.

CPJ and Human Rights Watch wrote to U.S. Secretary of Defense Donald Rumsfeld in June, expressing "ongoing concern about the U.S. military's failure to develop and implement adequate procedures at military checkpoints in Iraq." This followed the release of a military investigation into the checkpoint killing of an Italian agent shot by U.S. troops while spiriting journalist Sgrena to safety.

The two organizations noted, "More than two years after the March 2003 invasion, flawed checkpoint procedures continue to unnecessarily endanger the lives of civilians and U.S. service members." The letter to Rumsfeld also pointed out that in its own report on the Sgrena shooting the U.S. military recommended installing temporary speed bumps and spike strips at checkpoints to slow down vehicles, launching a public awareness campaign to educate the Iraqi population about how to safely approach checkpoints, and using signs in both Arabic and English to warn drivers. However, none of these recommendations appeared to have been implemented by year's end. This became apparent in October when several reporters came under fire without warning from U.S. and Iraqi forces at checkpoints near the International Zone in Baghdad.

Working around U.S. and Iraqi troops carried other risks. Troops routinely detained Iraqi journalists who operated near U.S. and Iraqi forces. Others were detained in neighborhood sweeps by the military. In 2005, CPJ documented seven cases in which reporters, photographers, and cameramen were detained for prolonged periods by U.S. forces without charge or the disclosure of any supporting evidence. The detentions involved journalists working for CBS News, Reuters, The Associated Press, and Agence France-Presse, among others. At least three documented detentions exceeded 100 days; the others spanned many weeks.

In at least five cases documented by CPJ, the detainees were photojournalists who initially drew the military's attention because of what they had filmed or photographed. In several cases, U.S. military officials voiced suspicions that some Iraqi journalists collaborated with Iraqi insurgents and had advance knowledge of attacks on coalition forces. But the military did not provide evidence to substantiate its claims, despite repeated inquiries over many months, and journalists previously detained on such suspicions were released without charge.

When CPJ conducted its annual census of imprisoned journalists on December 1, at least four detainees were in U.S. custody. One of them, Abdul Ameer Younis Hussein, an Iraqi cameraman working for CBS News, was taken into custody after being wounded by U.S. forces' fire on April 5 while he filmed clashes in Mosul, in northern Iraq. CBS News reported at the time that the U.S. military said footage in the journalist's camera led them to suspect he had prior knowledge of attacks on coalition forces. AFP cited

U.S. officials as saying the journalist "tested positive for explosive residue." No charges were made public, and the evidence used to hold him remained classified. *The New York Times* reported that the U.S. military referred Hussein's case to Iraqi justice officials, who reviewed Hussein's file but declined to prosecute him. Nevertheless, Hussein remained in U.S. custody. U.S. military officials issued unspecified accusations that Hussein was "engaged in anti-coalition activity," and that he had been "recruiting and inciting Iraqi nationals to violence against coalition forces and participating in attacks against coalition forces." Military officials did not provide evidence to support those accusations.

Even Iraqi officials took exception to the detentions. In September, Justice Minister Abdul Hussein Shandal criticized prolonged detentions by the U.S. military and expressed concerns that journalists were not being afforded appropriate protection in reporting on Iraq.

In March, the U.S. military said it would not reopen a military investigation that cleared U.S. troops of allegations that they abused three Reuters employees in Fallujah in January 2004. Reuters said military investigators never interviewed the three employees—cameraman Salem Ureibi, journalist Ahmad Mohammad Hussein al-Badrani, and driver Sattar Jabar al-Badrani—but had them fill out a written questionnaire. The three Reuters employees, along with Ali Mohammed Hussein al-Badrani, a cameraman working for NBC, were covering the aftermath of the downing of a U.S. helicopter when they were detained by U.S. troops on January 2, 2004. The four were taken to a U.S. base near Fallujah and released three days later without charge. The Reuters employees alleged that they were beaten and deprived of sleep. They said they were forced to make demeaning gestures as soldiers laughed, taunted them, and took photographs, Reuters reported. Two alleged they were forced to put a shoe in their mouths, and to insert a finger into their anus and then lick it.

Despite the military's indifference, the issue of journalist deaths, checkpoint safety, and journalist detentions at the hands of the U.S. military did get the attention of the U.S. Congress. In October, U.S. Sen. John Warner, chairman of the Senate Armed Services Committee, voiced concerns at a hearing in Washington with Defense Secretary Rumsfeld and senior commanders. "I raised the question of the safety of the press in Iraq and their ability to carry out the very important function of reporting to the American people," Warner told reporters after the hearing. "I've discussed it with the secretary. He's going to take it under immediate consideration." By December, though, there was little indication that the Pentagon had taken steps to address journalists' concerns.

The overall press freedom situation in Iraq wasn't entirely bleak. Iraqi media have flourished since the fall of President Saddam Hussein, who controlled the media with an iron fist, brooking no independent news or opinions. Today, dozens of newspapers and magazines, ranging from political broadsheets to independent dailies, compete for readers and offer a multitude of opinions to citizens. Private radio and television stations also provide local programming, complementing that of the state broadcaster, which is part of the U.S.-backed IMN. A new generation of independent Iraqi journalists serves a growing number of domestic outlets and international news organizations.

Still, Iraqi officials harassed journalists in a number of instances. Ayad Mahmoud al-Tammimi and Ahmed Mutare Abbas of the daily *Sada Wasit* were detained in April after being sentenced to two and four months in prison, respectively, for allegedly defaming former Wasit provincial governor Mohammad Reda al-Jashamy. The newspaper had published articles accusing al-Jashamy of corruption and human rights abuses. Both men were released from jail, but faced new charges of defaming al-Jashamy, the police, and the judiciary in other articles published in the paper. If convicted, they face seven to 10 years in prison.

The government also kept in place its indefinite ban against Al-Jazeera, which has been prohibited from newsgathering in Iraq since former Interim Prime Minister Iyad Allawi announced in July 2004 that the station had been barred for incitement to violence and hatred. Iraqi officials alleged that Al-Jazeera's reporting on kidnappings had encouraged Iraqi militants, and a government statement on the ban accused Al-Jazeera of being a mouthpiece for terrorist groups and contributing to instability in Iraq. Al-Jazeera was still able to cover news from Iraq through local sources, stringers, and a network of contacts.

• ISRAEL AND THE OCCUPIED PALESTINIAN TERRITORY •

In August, Israel facilitated access to hundreds of foreign journalists to witness its withdrawal from the Gaza Strip, even providing shuttle buses to the Jewish settlements that were being dismantled. Such cooperation with the press by the Israel Defense Forces (IDF) was rare the rest of the year. Journalists working in the Occupied Palestinian Territory faced dangerous and unpredictable conditions daily. While no journalists were killed there, the Israeli army and security services continued to commit abuses against journalists, including beatings, arrests, destruction of equipment, and restrictions on freedom of movement. Palestinian journalists bore the brunt of the attacks.

The most serious attack came on January 2, when Palestinian cameraman Majdi al-Arabid, on assignment for Israel's Channel 10 TV, was shot and seriously wounded near Beit Lahia in the northern Gaza Strip. Channel 10 reporter Shlomi Eldar, who witnessed the shooting, told CPJ that IDF troops were responsible. Eldar was standing with al-Arabid about 300 meters (1,000 feet) from a building that was surrounded by Israeli tanks and had three Israeli soldiers on its roof. Al-Arabid waved to the soldiers with his microphone to show them he was a journalist. The area was quiet. Minutes later, Eldar said, a shot rang out from the direction of the rooftop, and al-Arabid fell to the ground. He was hit in the stomach. The IDF said it was investigating the incident.

Fire from Israeli forces has killed several journalists and injured dozens during the years of intense conflict that followed the outbreak of the second Palestinian intifada in 2000. In most cases the Israeli army failed to conduct either a thorough investigation or any investigation at all. On the night of May 2, 2003, an Israeli soldier fatally shot British cameraman James Miller in the town of Rafah. Miller was wearing a flak jacket but was shot in the neck. Witnesses said that he was wearing a helmet marked with the letters "TV," and that he held a white flag illuminated by a flashlight. The soldier, who was not named, was the commanding officer in Rafah.

In March 2005, the military prosecutor general decided against bringing criminal charges but told members of Miller's family that the officer, a lieutenant, would face disciplinary measures for violating the rules of engagement and for changing his account of the incident. An investigation by private British security company Chiron Resources Limited, commissioned by Miller's colleagues and family, found that IDF soldiers had "consciously and deliberately targeted" Miller and his crew.

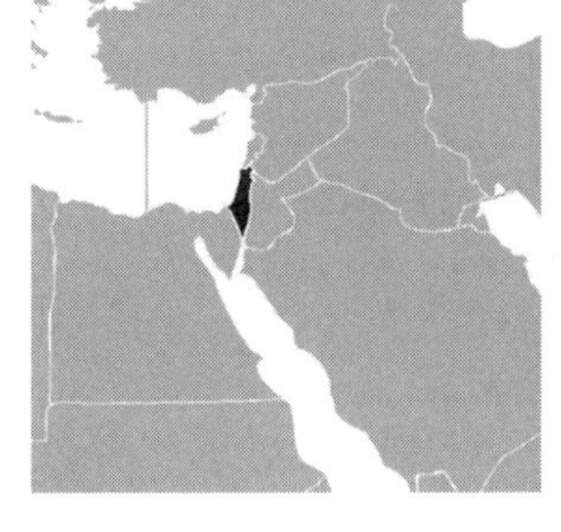

Yet on April 14, 2005, the IDF said that it would not take disciplinary action against the officer. Brig. Gen. Guy Tzur, head of the army's southern command, acquitted the lieutenant of improper use of weapons after a disciplinary hearing, according to international news reports.

Throughout 2005, Palestinian photojournalists and cameramen were often injured covering weekly Friday demonstrations against Israel's security barrier in Bi'lein, west of Ramallah. On March 18, Israeli forces used rubber bullets and tear gas to disperse hundreds of Palestinians peacefully demonstrating in Bi'lein. Several people were injured, including Enric Marti, an Associated Press correspondent and cameraman, who passed out as a result of inhaling tear gas. On May 1, Israeli forces again used excessive force to break up a protest at Bi'lein, injuring several demonstrators and Associated Press cameraman Mohammad Muhaisena, who was hit by two rubber bullets, one shattering his protective head gear, another wounding his shoulder. On September 16, Israeli forces closed the western and northern parts of Bi'lein, surrounding dozens of Palestinian civilians, members of foreign solidarity groups, and Israeli peace activists who were demonstrating peacefully. The soldiers fired rubber bullets and tear gas into the crowd, and beat some of the demonstrators. Euro News cameraman Ala' Badarneh was severely beaten by an Israeli soldier and had his arm broken. On November 4, Nabil al-Mazzawi on assignment for the Qatar-based Al-Jazeera news channel, was covering a demonstration in Bi'lein when several soldiers attacked him, the journalist told CPJ. He said the soldiers punched and kicked him and threw him to the ground.

On several occasions, Israeli forces prevented journalists from carrying out their assignments and resorted to excessive force when the journalists refused to abide by their orders. On February 22, Israeli forces stationed at Tarqomia checkpoint, west of Hebron, chased and threatened a group of journalists covering the release of a number of

Palestinian prisoners, who were being greeted by their families. When Yusri al-Jamal and Ma'moun Wazwaz, a cameraman and a soundman, respectively, for Reuters, and Husam Abu A'lan, a photographer for Agence France-Presse (AFP), tried to resume their work, Israeli soldiers detained them for more than an hour.

On April 24, Israeli forces in Hebron fatally shot a Palestinian. The soldiers then banned journalists from entering the area where the shooting took place. Deutsche Presse Agentur cameraman Abed Al-Hashlamon, who was nearby, was assaulted and severely beaten. He was transferred to Al-Ahli hospital to receive treatment for a head injury. On April 25, Israeli forces at the al-Shaufat checkpoint in east Jerusalem assaulted Awad Awad, an AFP photojournalist and president of the Palestinian Photojournalists Association. The journalist was filming Israeli soldiers preventing hundreds of Palestinians from crossing the checkpoint to attend Friday prayers at Al-Aqsa mosque. The soldiers beat Awad when he refused their orders to stop filming. Awad was detained in a small room at the checkpoint for hours, where he was beaten, then dragged to the police station and held for several hours before being released, Awad told CPJ.

The IDF on several occasions designated certain areas as closed military zones, banning foreign and local journalists from reporting in those areas. On March 31, the Israeli military launched an incursion into the town of Wadi Rahal, northwest of Bethlehem. Soldiers surrounded a number of Palestinian homes, situated to the south of the village, and forcefully evacuated the area, giving the residents merely 25 minutes to collect their personal belongings. The army then began a huge house demolition operation and imposed a strict curfew. Local and foreign journalists were barred from reaching the area and covering the demolitions. On June 30, the army closed the entire Gush Katif area, a bloc of Jewish settlements in the southern Gaza Strip, to all journalists based in Israel. The IDF said the area was unsafe for journalists because of the actions of settlers opposed to the withdrawal.

On September 14, the army prevented Israeli journalists and those with dual Israeli and foreign citizenship from entering the Gaza Strip for 10 days because of what it called security concerns and intelligence that they would be kidnapped. This hindered the coverage of several foreign media outlets, which rely on reporters who are permanent residents of Israel. The Foreign Press Association in Israel complained that this restriction was excessive given that the veteran journalists being barred from entering Gaza were aware of the risks. Israeli and foreign journalists must sign a waiver absolving Israeli authorities of responsibility for their safety before entering the Occupied Territory. Only a handful of Israeli journalists now venture into Palestinian areas, according to Gideon Levy of the Hebrew-language daily *Ha'aretz*, because of declining interest in Palestinian coverage from Israeli editors.

Palestinian journalists faced severe limitations on their freedom of movement in the West Bank and Gaza Strip. Many Palestinian journalists found that they were virtually locked down in a single area. However, on August 21, following Israel's disengagement and removal of all checkpoints within the Gaza Strip, foreign and local journalists no longer faced Israeli restrictions on movements. Gaza had been divided into three separate parts in December 2002. The army blocked the main road, which cuts through Gaza, isolating the southern city of Khan Yunis, the central city of Deir al-Balah, and Gaza City in the north. Palestinian journalists faced particular hardships at the Abu al-Houli checkpoint, which stretches over several hundred meters and divided the Gush Katif settlements from the Green Line, the border that separates Israel from the Gaza Strip.

In January 2002, the Government Press Office, which issued press cards, suspended the accreditation of most Palestinian journalists from the territories, including those who worked with foreign media outlets, citing security concerns. GPO press cards facilitated passage through Israeli checkpoints and gave access to government offices and news events inside Israel. Israel's High Court of Justice ruled in April 2004 that the GPO could not impose a blanket restriction on accreditation for Palestinian journalists. In reality, little has changed since the ruling, and only a small number of Palestinian journalists have received new cards. The Foreign Press Association in Israel proposed that the GPO issue Palestinians cards valid only in the territories. This would have allowed Palestinian journalists to pass through checkpoints but denied them access to press functions in Israel itself, where Israeli officials said they posed a security risk. The GPO, however, rejected the proposal.

Israel continued to bar nuclear whistle-blower Mordechai Vanunu from speaking with the foreign press. It also restricted his movements. In March, a court charged Vanunu with violating these restrictions. While he was not arrested and some of the charges had expired, Vanunu still faced draconian measures that prohibited him from speaking with foreigners, traveling outside Israel, and using the Internet. Israeli officials maintained that the restrictions imposed on Vanunu were necessary for reasons of national security, and they accused Vanunu of passing on sensitive information about the Dimona nuclear facility in recent interviews with the foreign press. Vanunu and his supporters, however, maintained that the former technician revealed everything he knew about Dimona in 1986, and that he did not possess any information that could jeopardize national security since he had not worked at the facility for two decades. Vanunu completed an 18-year prison sentence last April for treason and espionage.

With Israel's withdrawal from Gaza in late August 2005, foreign and Palestinian journalists no longer faced Israeli restrictions on their freedom of movement; however, the power vacuum created by Israel's disengagement made covering the Gaza Strip extremely risky. Journalists were now more vulnerable to attacks by renegade armed groups, whose means of settling internal disputes included kidnappings of foreigners. Moreover, journalists, whether foreign or local, were harassed, threatened, and beaten by Palestinian security forces and the various factions in retaliation for their coverage of Palestinian politics.

The Palestinian National Authority (PNA) was created after the 1993 Oslo peace accords to administer the Gaza Strip and parts of the West Bank. Both areas were captured by Israel in the June 1967 Middle East war. The territories were not considered to be fully autonomous, since Israel still controlled their land and sea borders, as well as their airspace. Israel also reserved the right to carry out military operations there.

On October 12, 2005, Dion Nissenbaum, a U.S. reporter for the Knight Ridder newspaper chain, and British photographer Adam Pletts, a freelancer working for the news organization, were abducted in Gaza by renegade members of the Palestinian Liberation Organization's governing Fatah party, and held for several hours. On August 15, soundman Mohammed Ouathi of France 3 television was kidnapped and held for eight days by unidentified gunmen. In separate incidents during August, gunmen seized five U.N. workers in the Gaza Strip, but released them unharmed the same day. On September 10, Italian journalist Lorenzo Cremonesi, of the newspaper *Corriere della Serra*, was abducted by masked gunmen in the town of Deir el-Balah in the central Gaza Strip. He was released later that day unharmed. All the abductions ended in the safe release of the journalists.

During the Israeli pullout from Khan Younis, the Abu Reish Brigade, an offshoot of Fatah, threatened to kidnap foreign journalists working in the area, forcing them to hide in their hotel. The threat was never carried out. According to AFP Bureau Chief Patrick Anidjar, the Gaza kidnappings and threats may have been efforts to garner media attention. Palestinian factions often kidnapped foreigners to embarrass the PNA or to use as bargaining chips to win the release of imprisoned comrades.

Hospitals were frequent scenes of tension between Palestinian police and the press. Police and security forces regularly prevented Palestinian photojournalists from taking pictures of the wounded in hospitals, several local journalists told CPJ. The photojournalists endured shoving and verbal assaults from police, confrontations that often aroused the crowds against the journalists and made it impossible for them to carry out their assignments.

Infringements of press freedom by Palestinian security forces were often arbitrary. On April 27, journalists were prevented from covering Palestinian President Mahmoud Abbas' visit to the police headquarters in Gaza; when they tried to follow Abbas, police attacked them. Several journalists were beaten, and their equipment was destroyed. In protest, journalists in Gaza refused to cover any police events for a week. Abbas witnessed the incident but did nothing to discipline police.

Foreign and local journalists also faced restrictions on coverage from the PNA. On August 3, the Foreign Press Association in Israel protested a statement by the Palestinian Interior Ministry ordering journalists to inform the ministry in advance whenever they planned to write a story about police or security forces and directing them to fill out a form about the story. Reuters said the directive was issued following the publication of unspecified news reports and photos that the ministry said were "harmful to national security." According to journalists, the Palestinian prime minister's office said it was not aware of the directive, and that it would follow up. There was no sign of the order either being enforced or officially repudiated, and journalists simply ignored it. In 2004, the Palestinian Journalist Syndicate, a journalists' union controlled by the PNA, ordered reporters in the Gaza Strip not to cover protests by militants or any internal Palestinian clashes.

Continuing a trend from the previous year, journalists were regularly warned against using certain video footage. In mid-September, the Al-Aqsa Martyrs' Brigade, a faction associated with Fatah, held a press conference outlining its political goals and strategies for the future. Shortly after the conference ended, Fatah warned journalists not to broadcast the footage.

LEBANON

In the popular uproar that followed the assassination of former Prime Minister Rafiq al-Hariri in February 2005, Lebanon's press, already among the most vibrant in the Arab world, hoped for greater freedom. But a series of bomb attacks on journalists who dared criticize Syria and its Lebanese allies quickly demonstrated that the old order had not been overthrown.

Thousands of Lebanese packed Beirut's Martyrs' Square to protest the murder, in what the press dubbed the "Cedar Revolution." Syria, which was also under intense international pressure, eventually withdrew its 14,000 troops from Lebanon at the end of April. During its 25-year-long rule, Damascus and its Lebanese allies had placed severe restrictions on the Lebanese media, forbidding criticism of the Syrian presence.

Some journalists believed that criticism of Syrian officials and politicians linked to Damascus, such as Lebanese President Emile Lahoud, would be possible. "The gloves are now off," said one journalist. He and his colleagues soon learned, however, that it was the enemies of press freedom who were geared up for a fight.

On June 2, prominent columnist Samir Qassir of *Al-Nahar* newspaper was killed outside his home in East Beirut by a bomb placed in his car. Qassir, 45, a leading figure in the Democratic Left movement, wrote extensively about the need for Lebanese independence. He challenged the security order in Lebanon and highlighted the inability of Syrian President Bashar al-Assad to bring about real political reform. Journalists were outraged by Qassir's murder, and saw it as a warning that critical coverage of Syria was still off-limits. Syrian troops and security services may have withdrawn, but many journalists believe a shadowy network working for Damascus and its allies remained, and that it continues to pose a threat to journalists and press freedom. Editors said Qassir's death produced widespread fear and self-censorship. For some time, Syrian journalists who had traditionally published in Lebanese newspapers were especially wary and submitted fewer articles than before.

For several weeks after the killing, some journalists thought the threat to their safety had diminished, and editors said the murder may even have spurred some writers to become outspoken. But on September 25, an attempt on the life of May Chidiac, a political talk-show host with the Lebanese Broadcasting Corporation, reignited journalists' fears. Chidiac, a strong critic of Syria, lost an arm and a leg when a bomb exploded under the driver's seat of her car near the port city of Jounieh. Just 10 days earlier, Ali Ramez Tohme, who had published a book on al-Hariri, escaped a similar attack. He was not in his car when it blew up.

Qassir's friend Elias Khoury, the cultural editor of *Al-Nahar*, has started the Samir Qassir Cultural Foundation, which aims to defend press freedom in the region. CPJ and human rights lawyers in Lebanon are pushing to have the United Nations Security Council assign Qassir's case to UN chief investigator Detlev Mehlis, who is in charge of the al-Hariri murder investigation. Qassir's family, including his wife, prominent Al-Arabiya journalist Gisele Khoury, have brought his case before a French court, and a French judicial investigation is under way. Qassir had French and Lebanese citizenship.

The year ended with another assassination. Gebran Tueni, *Al-Nahar*'s managing director and columnist, was killed by a bomb that targeted his armored vehicle in east Beirut. Tueni was a member of parliament and harsh critic of Syrian policies. He was killed on December 12—the day he returned home from Paris, where he had spent considerable time because of fears for his safety.

Self-censorship remained a problem because of a lack of faith in the independence of the Lebanese judiciary, editors say. The country's press law restricts criticism that incites "sectarian grudges" and forbids "attacking foreign kings and heads of state." On July 21, two Lebanese journalists—Zahi Wehbe and *Al-Mustaqbal* director Tawfiq Khattab—were indicted on charges of libeling Lahoud. Libel is still a criminal offense punishable by prison, although no journalists have been jailed in several years.

The indictment was apparently brought against the journalists for an article that appeared on June 7 in *Al-Mustaqbal*, which is owned by Hariri, just five days after Qassir's death. In the article, titled "His Excellency, the Murderer," Wehbe wrote, "The general has not, and will not, understand that the people cannot be terrorized... Your Excellency the murderer. Enough. Go." Lahoud is often referred to as "the general" in the press. The *Al-Mustaqbal* article did not mention Lahoud by name. In an Associated Press article, Wehbe said the piece was aimed at "all killers in Lebanon." If convicted, Wehbe could face up to two years in prison. Khattab could face up to three years.

Meanwhile, Murr Television is reportedly set to reopen early in 2006. The station, owned by Christian opposition politician Gabriel Murr, was closed in September 2002 for violating a ban on airing propaganda during elections. Some observers suspect the closure was due in part to its criticism of Syria.

MOROCCO

Morocco's independent press has grown bigger and bolder in recent years, challenging taboos against criticizing the monarchy and questioning Morocco's claim to Western Sahara. In March, journalists welcomed a promise by Minister of Communications Nabil Benabdallah to end imprisonment as a punishment for offenses under the kingdom's stringent press laws. The minister's pledge, however, did not translate into immediate progress. In fact, the media were quickly disabused of the idea that the country might increase press freedom when, shortly after Benabdallah's announcement, authorities filed a string of criminal defamation suits against journalists. One editor was handed an unprecedented 10-year ban on practicing journalism as a result of a defamation prosecution.

The Association of Relatives of Saharawi Victims of Repression, a previously unknown group whose spokesman is a government employee, sued independent journalist Ali Lmrabet for defamation after he wrote an article for the Madrid-based daily *El Mundo* that referred to the Saharawi people in the Algerian city of Tindouf as refugees, contradicting the Moroccan government's position that they are prisoners of the rebel Polisario Front. The Polisario, which are fighting for the independence of neighboring Western Sahara, operate mostly out of Algeria.

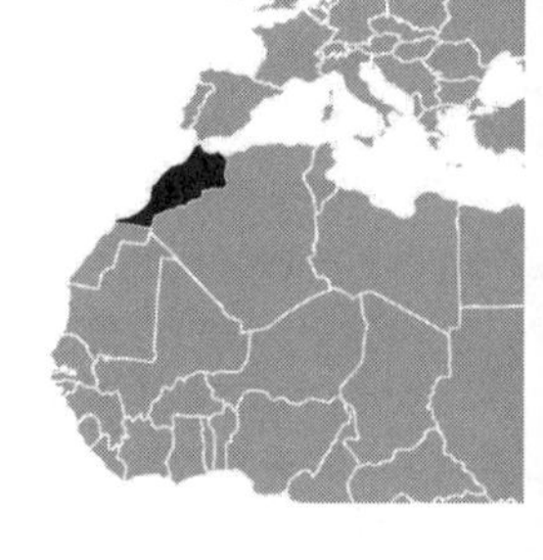

Although neither the association nor its spokesman, Ahmed Khier, was mentioned in the article, the criminal court convicted Lmrabet in April and barred him from working for any Moroccan publication for 10 years. The prosecution appealed, calling the sentence too lenient. In June, an appeals court ordered Lmrabet to publish the court's verdict daily for three weeks in the Arabic-language daily *Ahdath Al Maghribiya*, at his own expense.

No local journalist contacted by CPJ had heard of either The Association of Relatives of Saharawi Victims of Repression or Khier before January 2005, when Lmrabet applied for a license to launch a satirical weekly, *Demain Libéré*. Local journalists told CPJ that the organization might have been created or possibly revived in response to Lmrabet's application.

Lmrabet had been sentenced to three years in prison in 2003 for publishing cartoons lampooning the monarchy in the satirical weeklies *Demain* (in French) and *Douman* (in Arabic), both of which he edited. He had also published an interview with Abdullah Zaaza, a critic of the monarchy who advocated self-determination for the people of Western Sahara. Lmrabet received a royal pardon and was released from jail in January 2004 after serving nine months of his sentence.

But on January 18, 2005, shortly after Lmrabet applied for a license for *Demain Libéré*, the Ministry of Justice suspended the Oujda-based weeklies *Al-Sharq* and *Al-Hayat Al-Maghribiya* for three months in a move that local journalists saw as a warning to Lmrabet. The papers' editors had been jailed along with Lrambet in the 2003 press crackdown and later pardoned.

Authorities used the criminal defamation laws again in June against Abdelaziz Koukas, editor of the Arabic-language *Al-Ousbouia Al-Jadida*. He was charged with insulting the monarchy after the weekly ran a front-page interview with Nadia Yassine, the daughter of Abdelsalam Yassine, who is head of the banned Islamist group Al-Adl Wal Ihsan. The interview quoted Yassine as saying that the monarchy was the wrong form of government for Morocco. After Koukas was charged, the authorities stopped pursuing the case. Local journalists believed the authorities wanted to avoid further negative international attention in the wake of the Lmrabet case.

In August, Ahmed Benchemsi and Karim Boukhari, managing director and editor, respectively, of the independent weekly *Tel Quel*, were convicted of defamation and given two-month suspended prison sentences. The charges stemmed from a satirical article they had published earlier in the summer about Member of Parliament Hlima Assali, in which they referred to her former career as a dancer. In Arab culture, calling a woman a "dancer" could have negative connotations. Benchemsi, who was in the United States when the trial took place, told CPJ that the proceedings were highly irregular, with the judge announcing the verdict before the defense lawyer presented his case. The court ordered the magazine to pay one million dirhams (US$109,000) in damages to the MP. This would put a serious financial strain on any Moroccan publication. The journalists have appealed the verdict.

In late October, *Tel Quel* was convicted in another defamation suit, this time involving the head of a local child-relief agency, and ordered to pay 900,000 dirhams (US$96,000) in damages. The case stemmed from the paper's publication of a report that police were looking into the possible embezzlement of funds at the agency. The case led Benchemsi to declare that a judicial campaign was afoot against the newspaper. "The intention to kill us has become clear and unambiguous," he wrote, noting that other Moroccan newspapers that ran the same report had not faced charges.

Moroccan journalists told CPJ that journalists and editors working outside the major cities were subject to harassment by local officials. Brahim Fillali, publisher of the French- and Arabic-language biweekly *Ici et Maintenant*, in the southern town of Ourzazate, has been repeatedly summoned by police since publishing articles critical of local officials. Unidentified attackers also burned the newspaper's offices. Police have failed to investigate the attack, according to local journalists.

Local and foreign journalists covering Western Sahara are also subject to official harassment. The government tries to discourage coverage of the Polisario or of those advocating self-determination for Western Sahara. Journalists are strongly encouraged to travel with official government escorts. Local journalists told CPJ that during protests in May in the Saharan city of Laayoune, several local and foreign reporters were expelled by authorities or prevented from entering the city.

SAUDI ARABIA

Responding to international critics who linked Saudi terrorism to the lack of basic liberties in the kingdom, the government has loosened its shackles on the domestic press since the September 11, 2001, attacks, with local journalists seizing the initiative to produce more daring reports.

Saudi newspapers now publish news accounts that would have been unthinkable five years ago. Stories on crime, drug trafficking, and the security forces' battles with armed extremists have become regular fare. Saudi columnists publish probing articles about extremists' use of religious summer camps to indoctrinate Saudi youth and authorities' tolerance of extremists in schools. They write essays arguing for the right of women to drive cars.

But progress has been uneven, and enterprising coverage of central political issues such as the actions of the royal family, the influence of the religious establishment, and government corruption remain strictly off-limits. "Criticism goes always to the lower end of the [ladder], especially if the official has power," noted one Saudi academic who was once banned from writing in the press because of his political criticisms. "And if the official is a prince, it means [that] he never makes mistakes. Have you ever heard or read anything public criticizing the ministry of [the] interior?... The same thing applies to the ministry of defense and ministry of foreign affairs," he told CPJ.

For a short period after the Riyadh suicide bombings of May 2003, the country's newspapers were filled with introspective coverage about the roots of terrorism in the kingdom. But the already-narrow margin of freedom to criticize the role of the country's powerful religious establishment in fostering extremism has shrunk further under pressure from religious conservatives and their allies in the government, journalists said.

In 2005, the government allowed CPJ to conduct its first fact-finding mission to Saudi Arabia. For two weeks in July, CPJ met with journalists, writers, and intellectuals to examine the state of press freedom. While pro-government editors painted a positive portrait of the media, independent-minded writers, including those who have faced reprisals from the government, expressed frustration at the web of official—and unofficial—restrictions faced by journalists.

While noting recent gains for the press, journalists also described an efficient system of government controls that brings unpublicized pressure on editors and reporters to rein in independent journalism. Spearheaded by Interior Minister Prince Nayef bin Abdel Aziz, the leading powerbroker for the country's media, government officials routinely send directives to newspapers to suspend publication of outspoken writers. Editors, who are approved by the government, comply and often unilaterally sanction critical writers and censor news to stay in the government's good graces. Interior Ministry agents frequently pressure writers through phone calls, issuing admonishments and warnings.

They have forced journalists and critics to sign agreements pledging not to write in the press or to criticize the government. Some writers and intellectuals have been banned indefinitely from writing in the press. These include Abdel Mohsen Mussalam, whose poem against corruption in the judiciary briefly landed him in jail when it was published in a local newspaper three years ago; female writer Wajeaha al-Howeidar, who has been outspoken about social problems and the limited rights of women in the kingdom; and Hassan Maliki, a religious critic who has censured Wahhabism, Saudi Arabia's official brand of Islam.

While most press controls are administered out of sight, officials occasionally resort to more transparent methods. In January, Mohamed al-Oshen, editor-in-chief of the Riyadh-based Islamist weekly *Al-Mohayed*, was reportedly detained without charge for several weeks after publishing articles that attacked the Saudi government, including criticism that it had not taken a more active role in advocating the release of Saudi prisoners held by U.S. authorities at Guantánamo Bay, Cuba. The German news agency Deutsche Presse Agentur reported that al-Oshen, who has two brothers at Guantánamo, is also a member of the legal defense team for Saudi detainees.

Another major source of pressure against journalists is the religious establishment, which broadly consists of clerics and activists. These groups were active in protesting news coverage through phone calls and faxes to newsrooms. They also pressed the government to retaliate against critical journalists. In one case in July, television talk-show host Abdel Rahman al-Hussein, who works for state-run Saudi Television Channel 3, was demoted after his weekly talk show featured a discussion with Saudi teens who criticized the country's powerful religious police, the mutawaeen. The station's director told al-Hussein he had received phone calls from unidentified religious conservatives complaining about the program, and that al-Hussein had been dropped by the station because his show was insulting to the mutawaeen. Al-Hussein was reinstated several days later, following the intervention of Information Minister Iyad Madani.

Religious activists also used the courts against critics in the media. In March, then–Crown Prince Abdullah bin Abdel Aziz overturned a Sharia court ruling sentencing Hamzah al-Muzeini, a linguistics professor at King Saud University and an outspoken critic of religious extremism, to four months in prison and 200 lashes. The case was unique in that legal complaints against writers and journalists are handled through the Saudi Arabian Ministry of Information, outside the jurisdiction of religious courts. Al-Muzeini had been taken to court by an Islamist professor who alleged that al-Muzeini had insulted him in an exchange conducted on the opinion pages of two local newspapers. Al-Muzeini had attacked what he called the infiltration of Saudi universities by religious radicals, who had banned music, dance, and the teaching of female students by male professors. During the trial, the judge also accused al-Muzeini of offending Islamic religious scholars in other articles he had written.

Abdullah's intervention not only quashed the verdict against al-Muzeini but also nullified several other cases pending against writers indicted in religious courts, effectively setting a precedent barring religious courts from being used as a weapon against journalists by religious conservatives.

But the Saudi government doesn't always side with journalists against the religious establishment. Writers continue to be suspended, dismissed, and harassed by the Interior Ministry in response to calls from religious leaders. In November, the government ordered Saudi editors not to cover the case of Muhammad al-Harbi, a Saudi high school teacher viciously harassed by fellow teachers who objected to his criticisms of religious extremism.

Many reporters contend that a significant degree of responsibility for the media's failings lies with Saudi editors, who too often cater to the wishes of authorities and who rarely attempt to expand the margins of freedom in the country's newspapers. "Freedom has been given to us for a long time, but some editors don't take it," remarked the deputy editor of one major newspaper. "Some editors are more pro-government than the government itself."

Critics say that editors have also failed to use the newly established Saudi Journalists Association (SJA), composed of the country's leading editors, to push for greater freedom. The SJA was licensed by the government in 2003 as the first association of its kind in the country, and it held its first elections in 2004. Although a positive development on paper, it has since been largely inactive, and journalists are skeptical about its role as a positive force for a free press. Few journalists know its precise agenda. Its ineffectiveness has been evident through its silence in the face of job dismissals and the harassment or banning of outspoken writers. The association could play a positive role, for example, by protesting attacks on press freedom when the government takes action against writers. But, to date, it has shown little interest in doing this.

For all the restrictions on local media, Saudi citizens still have access to an array of alternative media sources. The country has one of the highest penetration rates for residential satellite dishes in the region—over 90 percent, according to one study—which means that most citizens can circumvent local media controls and view any of the dozens of satellite news stations that broadcast in the region The government strictly censors the Internet for both morally and politically sensitive material, although Web-savvy users can easily evade the restrictions. Although uncensored debate is absent from the local press, Saudi intellectuals and journalists carry on rich discussions about politics and religion on both the Internet and satellite-TV programs.

TUNISIA

Some Tunisian journalists had hoped that an influx of world business, media, and human rights figures attending a United Nations conference in Tunis in November might prompt the government to relax its grip on the local media. Instead, President Zine Al-Abidine Ben Ali's 18-year-old administration ran true to form, stifling the critical press and preventing a fledgling journalists' union from holding its first conference.

Three journalists went on hunger strikes in 2005, two of them to protest their detention, one in jail and one under virtual house arrest. Tunisia, one of the most efficient police states in the region, found itself in the spotlight as an unprecedented number of international groups sent fact-finding missions and wrote reports on press freedom in the run-up to the World Summit for the Information Society (WSIS), a U.N.–sponsored gathering seeking to establish international regulations for the Internet. Three fact-finding missions undertaken in January, May, and September by the Tunisian Monitoring Group, which operates under the umbrella of the International Freedom of Expression Exchange, concluded that attacks on freedom of expression and association and the media "have escalated since January 2005."

International attention did not deter attacks on the press. Just days before the WSIS began in the capital, reporter Christophe Boltanski of the French daily *Libération* reported that he was beaten, blinded with pepper spray, and stabbed by four men near his hotel in the otherwise heavily guarded diplomatic quarter. The attackers took his cell phone, notebook, and personal belongings as nearby police ignored his cries for help. Boltanski, who was in Tunis to investigate human rights abuses in advance of the summit, had just published an article that described plainclothes police assaulting human rights activists. As the WSIS unfolded, a number of instances of police surveillance, harassment, and property confiscation were reported by press and human rights advocates.

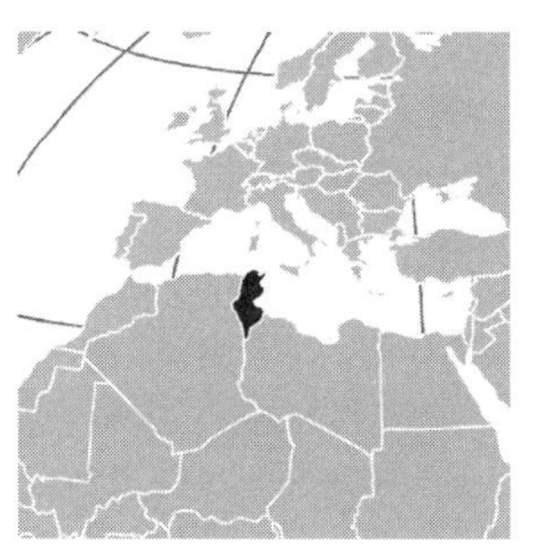

The government, which used a range of Soviet-style techniques to keep the media in check, dismissed foreign criticism of its media policy, saying that freedom of the press in Tunisia "is a tangible reality." Independent journalists said they were harassed by plainclothes police. Their phone lines were monitored and often arbitrarily cut. Charges were fabricated against them and heard by courts under the thumb of the executive branch. Mohamed Fourati, a freelance journalist, appeared before the Court of Appeals in the southern city of Gafsa, on June 29 and again on September 21, on fabricated charges of "belonging to an unauthorized association," even though he had twice been acquitted of the charge. On October 26, the Gafsa Court of Appeals also acquitted Fourati.

In October, Ambeyi Ligabo, special rapporteur on the promotion and protection of the right to freedom of opinion and expression for the U.N. Commission on Human Rights, called on Tunisia to relax press restrictions. Voicing alarm over the lack of dialogue between the authorities and the media, Ligabo urged the government to lift restrictions on independent journalism and to adopt legislation for "the decriminalization of defamation and related offenses." In a press release issued on October 14, Ligabo urged Tunisian authorities to "guarantee full access to information for media professionals, as well as for ordinary citizens," to ensure that "all media workers can exercise their profession without any impediment or restriction."

The authorities questioned the sources of Ligabo's information, calling them "neither independent nor credible." They claimed that "nobody can be imprisoned in Tunisia because of his opinions or journalistic activities."

Yet Hamadi Jebali, former editor of the now-defunct *Al-Fajr*, the weekly newspaper of the banned Islamist Al-Nahda party, has been serving a 16-year prison sentence since 1991 for "defamation" and "belonging to an illegal organization plotting to change the nature of the state." In April, he went on a hunger strike until the government ended the solitary confinement that had been imposed on him and other political prisoners for more than a decade. On September 15, Jebali began a second hunger strike in protest of inhumane prison conditions. He ended it on October 21 after authorities promised to look into his case.

Abdallah Zouari, a former *Al-Fajr* reporter, went on hunger strikes in February and September to protest his virtual house arrest since his release from prison in 2002. Sentenced to 11 years in prison by a military court in 1992 for "belonging to an illegal organization" and planning "to change the nature of the state," Zouari is under virtual house arrest in the southern city of Zarzis, more than 300 miles (500 kilometers) from his wife and children. He is prevented from working or using public Internet cafes.

The third journalist to resort to a hunger strike was Lotfi Hajji, head of the Tunisian Journalists Syndicate (SJT). On October 18, he embarked on a fast with a group of seven human rights and political activists to defend press and political freedoms. Police began harassing Hajji in May 2004, when he helped set up the SJT. Hajji was interrogated in May 2005 after the release of an SJT report about attacks on the press in Tunisia. Hajji said he was warned that the Tunisian authorities did not recognize the SJT, even though it had been set up in accordance with Tunisian law. In August, Hajji was questioned again by police and told that the government had decided to bar the SJT from holding its first congress, which was scheduled for September 7 in Tunis. The congress was supposed to elect the group's first board of directors. Hajji was also told that the group could not hold a seminar, planned for the same week, that would have brought together journalists from across North Africa.

At the same time, journalists working for both state-controlled and privately owned media were summoned by managers and editors and asked to choose between their jobs and the SJT. Hajji was denied a national press card and accreditation as correspondent for the Arabic satellite-TV channel Al-Jazeera.

Other independent journalists regarded as being close to opposition parties were also denied press credentials. Official figures indicate that the government has issued 960 cards. Nearly 80 percent of Tunisian journalists work for state-owned media. The private media are kept on a tight leash by the Tunisian External Communication Agency, which controls advertising and other forms of government support to the media.

The privately owned press is sometimes used to smear dissidents and independent journalists, such as Sihem Ben Sedrine, editor of the online magazine *Kalima*, and reporter Mohamed Krichene of Al-Jazeera. Editors are often instructed by high-ranking officials to tarnish the image of democracy advocates or independent journalists. In May, for instance, an insulting and obscene campaign was launched against Ben Sedrine by three privately owned papers, *Ashourouq*, *As-sarih*, and *Al-hadath*. They presented her as a "prostitute," a "creature of the devil," a "hateful viper," and an "agent of the Zionists and Freemasons." One of the smear campaigners, Abdelhamid Riahi of *Ashourouq*, was later decorated by the president.

On October 6, Tunisian dailies ran a front-page message from the state-run Tunisian Journalists Association thanking Ben Ali for "the support he has given to journalists to help them carry out their noble mission under the best conditions." This came at the same time that the media, with the exception of the beleaguered opposition papers *Al-Mawkif* and *Al-Tariq al-Jadid*, had for weeks turned a blind eye to the hunger strikes of Jebali, Zouari, and Hajji, and to a series of unprecedented attacks on freedom of association and expression that included the closure of the office of the Association of Tunisian Judges in July and the banning of the Tunisian League of Human Rights conference in September.

In July, the authorities allowed the establishment of the private radio station Radio Jawhara. Independent journalists saw this as an attempt to spread the illusion of media pluralism ahead of the U.N.-sponsored conference. They noted that the station was owned by a businessman close to the president.

YEMEN

Yemen's press found itself on the defensive as a string of chilling attacks occurred against a backdrop of armed conflict, economic upheaval, and public protests. The release of imprisoned editor Abdel Kareem al-Khawaini was a bright spot in an otherwise troubled year that saw harassment and violent attacks against journalists on the rise.

President Ali Abdullah Saleh pardoned al-Khawiani, editor of the opposition weekly *Al-Shoura*, in March. Al-Khawiani spent nearly seven months in jail for publishing opinion articles that condemned the government's fight against Hussein Badreddin al-Hawthi, a rebel cleric who led a three-month uprising in northern Saada before being killed. Al-Khaiwani's plight drew condemnation from local journalists and international press freedom advocates, who together waged a months-long campaign seeking the editor's release. In February, a CPJ delegation headed by Pulitzer Prize–winning columnist Clarence Page and former *Philadelphia Inquirer* and *New York Times* managing editor Gene Roberts met with Yemen's ambassador to the United States, Abdulwahab Abdulla al-Hajjri, to express alarm at al-Khawaini's imprisonment. The delegation pointed out that Saleh had promised to abolish prison penalties for journalists just three months before al-Khaiwani's jailing.

Al-Khawiani's release gave some impetus to government efforts to reform the tough press law that sets prison penalties. The Ministry of Information said in April that it had drafted amendments to the law, and Parliament was completing details in late 2005. Yemeni press reports said the measure could abolish prison sentences for most press offenses, but it could also create a host of new restrictions and fines.

In many instances, however, legal harassment was not the most pressing fear for journalists. Police, security forces, armed men, and bodyguards for local officials attacked reporters in several documented cases. In a shocking case reported in August, four men seized Jamal Amer, editor of the weekly *Al-Wasat*, and bundled him into a waiting car. Amer said the men punched him, accused him of getting funding from the U.S. and Kuwaiti embassies, and warned him about defaming unspecified "officials." Amer was released about four hours later. He said he believed a car used in the abduction belonged to the Yemeni Republican Guard, a special military division headed by Saleh's son, based on the numeric configuration of its license plate. Amer's newspaper has been a harsh critic of the Yemeni government and frequently publishes stories about corruption, nepotism, and government misconduct. One story named relatives of government officials who had received government scholarships to study abroad.

Orchestrated attacks against journalists were reported throughout the year. In January, assailants lobbed hand grenades and opened fire on the Sana'a office housing the news Web site *Al-Motamar*, which belongs to the ruling General People's Congress. Religious extremists were suspected in the attack, but no arrests were made. In July, Haji al-Jehafi, editor of the weekly newspaper *Al-Nahar*, was wounded when a letter bomb addressed to him exploded. Al-Jehafi said he had received threats from "an influential social figure" criticized in *Al-Nahar*, the English-language weekly *Yemen Times* reported. Yemeni journalists complained that officials showed little interest in preventing or seriously investigating such attacks.

Press conditions worsened in July when rioting erupted in Sana'a after the government withdrew fuel subsidies. Reporters for pan-Arab satellite stations and other journalists were arrested while covering the unrest, and officials warned news organizations not to print or broadcast images of the rioting. An Associated Press reporter said police had confiscated his camera, and satellite broadcasters confirmed that Yemeni officials had prohibited them from using state facilities to send their reports.

Elsewhere in the country, fighting persisted in the northwest city of Saada, where rebels led by al-Hawthi's father continued to battle the Yemeni army. Journalists said access to the region was difficult due to the violence and army blockades. Some foreign reporters who sought entry encountered resistance from authorities. On April 3, Yemeni authorities detained freelance journalists James Brandon, a Briton, and Shane Bauer, an American; brothers Munif and Munaf Damesh, who were working as fixers; and the Dameshes' uncle, Naif Damesh, who was the group's driver. The five were detained at an army checkpoint as they were leaving Saada. Brandon and Bauer were released 12 hours later, but their fixers were held for several weeks without charge or access to legal counsel and their families.

As the year came to a close, reporters continued to be harassed and violently attacked. In September, Yemeni air force officials detained reporter Khaled al-Hammadi and held him for two days in the town of Marib, in eastern Yemen, al-Hammadi told the UAE-based *Gulf News* in an interview. The officials had been angered over an article he had written describing crashes involving military planes. Al-Hammadi, who reports for the London-based daily *Al-Quds al-Arabi*, was released after pledging not to write about the military without permission, the paper said.

The following month, Mujeeb Suwailih, a cameraman for the pan-Arab news channel Al-Arabiya, and Najib Al-Sharabi, a news correspondent for the Saudi-owned satellite channel Al-Ekhbariyya, were beaten by Yemeni security forces while covering a strike by employees of a public textile factory over unpaid wages in Sana'a. Suwailih was struck repeatedly after he refused to hand over his camera, suffering internal bleeding, three broken ribs, and severe bruising on his legs, according to Al-Arabiya. The Yemeni Ministry of Interior said it would investigate, but no officer was immediately held responsible.

BAHRAIN

- In February, Bahraini authorities detained blogger Ali Abdel Imam and two technicians working with him. Abdel Imam is the founder and editor of *bahrainonline*, which features a blog with commentary about Bahrain, as well as a discussion forum. The three were charged with violating the press, communications, and penal codes. They were released in mid-March, but the case was not closed.

KUWAIT

- In January, Adel Aidan, a correspondent working for the Arabic news channel Al-Arabiya, was detained by authorities shortly after the station aired a disputed report of clashes between Kuwaiti government forces and militants. According to press reports quoting Aidan's lawyer, the journalist was charged with "reporting false news that undermines the country's position internally and abroad." Aidan was released four days later.
- In February, during a meeting with Kuwaiti newspaper editors, Prime Minister Sheikh Sabah al-Ahmed al-Sabah threatened either to suspend or to shut down any newspaper that publishes information related to the government's fight against religious extremists

LIBYA

- In June, the body of Libyan journalist Dayf al-Ghazal al-Shuhaibi was found in a Benghazi suburb. He had been missing since May 21. A former reporter for the government-owned daily *Azahf al-Akhdar*, al-Ghazal had recently been critical of government officials and the official media in articles written for the London-based online publications *Libya Alyoum* and *Libya Jeel*. He was briefly detained and questioned about his online writings by Libyan security agents in April. Justice Minister Ali Hasnaoui said al-Ghazal had been shot in the head and that his death was being investigated as murder.

MAURITANIA

- In March, freelance journalist Mohamed Ould Lamine Mahmoudi and two anti-slavery activists were detained after they interviewed a woman in southern Mauritania who claimed that she had been kept as a slave by a family in a nearby town. A local source told CPJ that the three were charged with fabricating information and tarnishing Mauritania's image. An appeals court ordered their release in April.

SUDAN

- In June, Sudanese justice officials canceled the license of Sudan's English-language daily, *The Khartoum Monitor*. The *Monitor* has been harassed by authorities repeatedly over the years. The newspaper's more recent problem with its license can be traced to its publication of articles on slavery more than two years ago. The license was restored in July by order of President Omar Hassan al-Bashir, according to press reports.
- In May, U.S. freelance photographer Brad Clift was released after two weeks' detention by Sudanese authorities. Sudanese security forces detained Clift while he was taking photographs at a camp for internally displaced persons outside Nyala, the capital of South Darfur state. He was accused of working without a proper permit, but charges were not filed against him. Clift was held under house arrest at the U.S. Agency for International Development office.

TURKEY

- On October 12, Turkish-Armenian journalist Hrant Dink was convicted of "insulting and weakening Turkish identity through the media." An Istanbul court sentenced Dink, the editor-in-chief of the bilingual Turkish-Armenian weekly *Agos*, to a six-month suspended term. He planned to appeal. The charges arose from articles published in 2004 dealing with the collective memory of the Armenian massacres of 1915–17 under the Ottoman Empire. Turkish law, even with recent legal reforms, allows for journalists to be criminally prosecuted and imprisoned for their work. Dink was prosecuted under a provision of the new penal code that states: "A person who insults Turkishness, the Republic, or the Turkish Parliament will be punished with imprisonment ranging from six months to three years." Turkish authorities did not elaborate on what they considered insulting in Dink's work. Dink, who founded *Agos* in 1996, was sentenced the same week talks began on Turkey's application to join the European Union.

UNITED ARAB EMIRATES

- In June, Bassma al-Jandaly, a reporter with the English-language daily *Gulf News*,was detained briefly and harassed at the Dubai airport. Al-Jandaly was told that she was wanted in the neighboring emirate of Sharjah, where police claimed that an article she had written in February had interfered with an investigation. The article concerned a Sharjah woman who was wounded by a knife-wielding man who had apparently attacked other women. Al-Jandaly was released from airport custody after a few hours.

47 JOURNALISTS KILLED IN 2005

Kidnappers in Iraq, car bombers in Beirut, and hit men in the Philippines made murder the leading cause of work-related deaths among journalists worldwide, a CPJ analysis found. Forty-seven journalists were killed in 2005, more than three-quarters of whom were murdered to silence them or to punish them for their work. That compared with 57 deaths in 2004, just under two-thirds of which were murders.

Iraq, the most dangerous place for journalists in 2005, also became the deadliest conflict for the media in CPJ's 24-year history. A total of 60 journalists were killed on duty in Iraq from the beginning of the U.S.-led invasion in March 2003 through the end of 2005. The toll surpassed the 58 journalists killed in the Algerian conflict from 1993 to 1996.

CPJ's annual survey confirmed another trend—those who murder journalists usually go unpunished. Slayings were carried out with impunity about 90 percent of the time in 2005, a figure consistent with data collected for more than a decade, CPJ found. Less than 15 percent of journalist murders since 1992 have resulted in the arrest and prosecution of those who ordered the killings.

Although the 2005 toll reflected a decline from the previous year, it was still well above the annual average of 34 deaths that CPJ documented over the past 10 years. In fact, 104 journalists were murdered in 2004 and 2005, making it the deadliest two-year period since the war in Algeria raged a decade ago.

Iraq accounted for 22 deaths in 2005, or nearly half of the year's total, CPJ found. Even in this conflict zone, murder was the leading cause and accounted for more than 70 percent of deaths. The prevalence of targeted killings reflected the evolving threat in Iraq, where crossfire had been the leading cause of death the previous year. Fatal abductions emerged as a particularly disturbing trend as at least eight journalists were kidnapped and slain in 2005, compared with one fatal abduction the previous year.

Iraqi journalists bore the brunt of these attacks as it became increasingly hazardous for foreign reporters and photojournalists to work in the field. American freelancer Steven Vincent was the only foreign journalist to be killed in Iraq in 2005; five foreigners died there a year earlier.

At least three journalists were killed as a result of fire from U.S. forces, compared with six such deaths in 2004. U.S. forces' fire killed 13 journalists between March 2003 and the end of 2005.

The Philippines, where outspoken radio journalists have been murdered in alarming numbers, was the second deadliest place in 2005. CPJ documented four murders in the Philippines, a decline from the eight recorded in 2004. The drop was due in part to more concerted national law enforcement, CPJ's analysis found.

Six countries recorded two deaths each. Prominent Lebanese columnists Samir Qassir and Gebran Tueni of the daily *Al-Nahar*—both of whom were renowned for their biting criticism of the Syrian government and its influence over Lebanon—were

JOURNALISTS KILLED IN CONFLICTS:
The five deadliest conflicts in CPJ's 24-year history

Conflict	Killed
IRAQ (2003-05)	60
ALGERIA (1993-96)	58
COLOMBIA (1986-2005)	52
BALKANS (1991-95)	36
PHILIPPINES (1983-87)	36

killed in separate car bombings in Beirut. A third Lebanese journalist was maimed in another car bombing. The other countries with two killings were Russia, Bangladesh, Pakistan, Sri Lanka, and Somalia.

The Americas showed a marked improvement with four confirmed deaths, down from eight a year earlier. Some journalists in the region ascribed the drop to increased self-censorship by journalists, a phenomenon that CPJ found prevalent in Colombia and Mexico.

Two journalists also went missing in 2005, one in an extremely hazardous area for the media, the Mexican border with the United States. Alfredo Jiménez Mota, who reported on drug trafficking and organized crime for the daily *El Imparcial*, disappeared in the city of Hermosillo in the northwestern state of Sonora in April.

Elyuddin Telaumbanua, a reporter for the Indonesian newspaper *Berita Sore*, also went missing during the year. Details about missing journalists are available on CPJ's Web site, *www.cpj.org*.

CPJ considers a journalist to be killed on duty if the person died as a result of a hostile action, including retaliation for his or her work; in crossfire while covering a conflict; or while reporting in dangerous circumstances such as a violent street demonstration.

CPJ continues to investigate the cases of 11 other journalists killed in 2005 to determine whether their deaths were related to their journalistic work. CPJ staff has compiled detailed information on journalists killed around the world since 1992. Statistical information is available at *www.cpj.org*.

JOURNALISTS KILLED: MOTIVE CONFIRMED

AZERBAIJAN: 1

Elmar Huseynov, *Monitor*
March 2, Baku

Huseynov, founder and editor of the opposition weekly news magazine *Monitor*, was gunned down in his apartment building in the capital, Baku.

Huseynov was shot several times while walking up the stairwell of his building on his way home from work, according to local reports. The shooting occurred at approximately 9 p.m., and the editor died at the scene, the Baku-based independent news agency Turan reported.

The attack appears to have been well-planned. Chingiz Sultansoy, deputy director of the Baku Press Club, told CPJ in a telephone interview that a light at the entrance of the apartment building was not working, and that several telephones in the area had been disconnected at the time of the shooting.

Huseynov's family said the editor had received several threats and was concerned about his security, Sultansoy said. Eynulla Fatullayev, an investigative reporter with *Monitor*, told CPJ he believed that Huseynov's murder was related to his work.

Monitor has long angered officials with its hard-hitting commentary. The magazine has been targeted with several lawsuits in retaliation for its critical reporting, and journalists working for the publication have faced a steady stream of harassment from government officials.

In April, the National Security Ministry identified several ethnic Azerbaijanis living in neighboring Georgia as suspects, but the ministry did not describe any motive or provide any evidence linking them to the crime. Georgian authorities refused to extradite the suspects due to the lack of evidence. Huseynov's family and colleagues criticized authorities for not looking into work-related motives.

BANGLADESH: 2

Sheikh Belaluddin, *Sangram*
February 11, Khulna

Belaluddin, a correspondent with the conservative Bengali-language daily *Sangram*, died of injuries sustained in a bomb attack six days earlier. The device exploded at around 9:15 p.m. outside the press club in the southwestern city of Khulna. The bomb, hidden in a bag hanging from a motorcycle, detonated as Belaluddin approached the vehicle.

Three other journalists were hurt, but their injuries were not life-threatening. On February 8, three days after the blast, Khulna journalists observed a news blackout and formed a human chain at the press club to protest the bombing. Across the country, journalists took to the streets to condemn the attack, demanding that authorities find and punish those responsible.

After Belaluddin died, editors from across the political spectrum formed a group called the Forum to Protect Journalists. The group rallied in the capital, marched to the National Press Club, and called for justice in the murders of journalists.

In July, a former leader of Islami Chhatra Shibir, the Islamic fundamentalist political party Jamaat-i-Islami's student wing, confessed to taking part in the deadly bombing. Just three weeks later, though, the suspect was freed on bail.

Gautam Das, *Samakal*
November 17, Faridpur

Das, a reporter for the Dhaka-based daily *Samakal*, was found strangled in his office in the town of Faridpur, 40 miles (64 kilometers) west of the Bangladeshi capital, according to news reports.

A colleague called police after repeated telephone calls to Das went unanswered and the door of the *Samakal* bureau in Faridpur remained locked at midday, according to the local advocacy group Media Watch. At 2 p.m., police broke down the door of the office to find Das' body inside, with fractures to the legs and hand and nylon rope around his neck, according to a statement by the group.

Although colleagues were not aware of any specific threat against the reporter, they said that Das had recently written about sensitive topics such as the activities of Islamic militant groups, according to Media Watch. Sumi Khan, a reporter for *Samakal*, said that Das was known for his reporting on crime and corruption, including coverage of illegal activities by members of the ruling Bangladesh Nationalist Party. The Associated Press reported that Das had recently written about local government officials accused of taking bribes in exchange for construction contract awards.

Two days later, journalist groups around the country protested the killing and criticized the government for not doing more to protect the press.

On November 19, police arrested Tamjid Hossain Babu, the son of a local MP, in connection with Das' murder, according to *The Daily Star*. Local journalists said police arrested three other suspects.

COLOMBIA: 1

o

Julio Hernando Palacios Sánchez
Radio Lemas, January 11, Cúcuta

Two armed motorcyclists shot Palacios, 55, a veteran radio news host, as he drove to work around 5:30 a.m. in the city of Cúcuta, in the unstable northeastern region near the Venezuelan border. Palacios, who hosted the morning program "Radio Periódico El Viento" on Radio Lemas, was shot three times in the chest, said the local police chief, Col. José Humberto Henao.

Despite his wounds, Palacios drove back home and his family took him to a local hospital. He died two hours after arriving at San José Hospital in Cúcuta, Henao told CPJ. He did not speculate about a motive. Local police offered a reward for information leading to the capture of the gunmen.

Palacios was a controversial and outspoken journalist who devoted a segment of his program to denouncing local corruption, sources told CPJ. Local journalists said that Palacios had made enemies because of his tough talk against corruption; they said they believed the murder was connected to his work.

Palacios received anonymous threats in October 2004, sources told CPJ. The Cúcuta-based daily *La Opinión* said local police gave Palacios a security manual and suggested he change his daily routine.

He survived an attack nine years earlier when assailants hurled a grenade into his office that failed to explode, The Associated Press reported. Palacios was a political conservative known for supporting President Àlvaro Uribe.

ECUADOR: 1

o

Julio Augusto García Romero
La Bocina and *Punto de Vista*
April 19, Quito

Photographer García Romero died after inhaling tear gas while covering a demonstration against then-President Lucio Gutiérrez. Protesters were moving toward the Palacio de Carondelet, the seat of the executive branch, when police fired water cannons and tear gas grenades into the crowd.

The Chilean-born García Romero, 58, was taking photographs when he collapsed, the Guayaquil-based daily *El Universo* reported. He was taken to Red Cross headquarters in Quito, where he arrived with symptoms of asphyxia. Later, he suffered cardiorespiratory arrest and was transferred to a nearby hospital, where he was pronounced dead, according to Jonny Franco, spokesman for the Ecuadoran Red Cross.

García Romero worked for the small Chilean news agency La Bocina, *El Universo* said. Local sources told CPJ he also worked for the weekly *Punto de Vista*. He lived in Ecuador for about 20 years.

Protests in Ecuador increased in frequency after April 1, when Supreme Court magistrates—appointed by Gutiérrez and his allies in Congress—dismissed corruption charges against two former presidents and a former vice president. Gutiérrez was later forced from office and faced prosecution himself.

HAITI: 1

o

Robenson Laraque, Tele Contact
April 4, Petit-Goâve

Laraque, a reporter with the private radio station Tele Contact, died in a Cuban hospital from injuries suffered while covering a March 20 clash between U.N. troops and members of the disbanded Haitian military in the city of Petit-Goâve.

The confrontation began after the ex-soldiers occupied the police station in the southwestern city. The Associated Press reported that three people, including a Sri Lankan peacekeeper, died in the gun battle.

Laraque and several colleagues were on

the nearby balcony of Tele Contact's offices, when the journalist was struck by two shots to the head and neck, the AP said.

Laraque was taken to a hospital in Port-au-Prince, Haiti's capital, where he received initial care. The injuries were so severe that he was transferred to Santo Domingo, in the Dominican Republic, and later to Cuba.

Wilner Saint-Preux, a journalist for Tele Contact, told CPJ that Laraque and other station reporters were trying to cover the skirmish. Witnesses reported that the shots appeared to have been fired by U.N. peacekeepers, Saint-Preux said. Fritz Ariel Nelson, a Tele Contact editor, said witnesses reported that Laraque was holding a microphone at the time.

David Beer, the U.N. civilian police commissioner in Haiti, told CPJ that the shooting was under investigation. "We take this very seriously," he said in an interview shortly after the journalist's death. "We are trying to determine what happened and which side the bullet came from."

Col. El Ouafi Boulbars, spokesman for the U.N. forces in Haiti, told CPJ in late October that the inquiry was continuing.

The United Nations Stabilization Mission in Haiti operates under a U.N. mandate that grants it the authority to "ensure a secure and stable environment within which the constitutional and political process in Haiti can take place" and to "protect civilians under imminent threat of physical violence."

IRAQ: 22

ooooooooooooooooooooooo

Raeda Wazzan, Al-Iraqiya
February 25, Mosul

Wazzan, a news anchor with the Iraqi state TV channel Al-Iraqiya who was kidnapped on February 20, was found dead five days later on a roadside in Mosul, where the journalist had lived and worked, according to press reports citing her husband. She had been shot in the head repeatedly. Gunmen had also kidnapped Wazzan's 10-year-old son, but he was released days later.

Wazzan's husband said that his wife had received several death threats with demands that she quit her job, The Associated Press reported. The station, funded by the Iraqi government, also came under mortar attack the previous week, injuring three technicians, according to press reports. The AP reported that al-Qaeda's affiliate in Iraq claimed responsibility for the attacks in Internet postings, but those claims could not be independently verified.

Hussam Sarsam, Kurdistan TV
March 14, Mosul

Sarsam, a cameraman working with Kurdistan TV, a station affiliated with the Kurdistan Democratic Party, was kidnapped and shot by suspected insurgents.

Sarsam was abducted on March 13 in front of Mosul University. The following day his captors returned him to the same location, where they killed him in front of a number of pedestrians, several Iraqi sources told CPJ.

Colleagues and a family member said burn marks were found on Sarsam's upper body, an indication of possible torture. The family member told CPJ that the cameraman's Kurdistan TV identification cards and a media card issued by U.S.-backed coalition forces were placed on his corpse by his killers.

Sarsam had worked with Kurdistan TV since January 2004. CPJ sources said Sarsam had videotaped confessions of insurgents held by Iraqi police in Mosul that were aired on a program on Kurdistan TV called "Al-Irhab ala Haqiateh" (Terrorism Exposed). His colleagues and a family member suspected his murderers were motivated by his filming of the detainee confessions.

Ahmed Jabbar Hashim, *Al-Sabah*
April 1, Baghdad

Hashim, a reporter working for the Baghdad-based daily *Al-Sabah*, part of the U.S.-backed Iraq Media Network, was kidnapped on March 25 by an unidentified armed group. His decapitated body was discovered on April 1.

Mohammad Abdul Jabbar, editor-in-chief of the newspaper, told CPJ that he didn't know the precise reason for the kidnapping and murder. However, insurgents have frequently targeted journalists working for U.S.-backed news outlets in Iraq. Some journalists familiar with the case told CPJ that Hashim might have been killed because he had also done work for U.S. media. Eight armed men in three cars ambushed the journalist while he was taking his daily route home. They decapitated him and sent a recording of the killing to *Al-Sabah* as a warning.

Fadhil Hazem Fadhil, Al-Hurriya
Ali Ibrahim Issa, Al-Hurriya
April 14, Baghdad

The two Al-Hurriya television journalists were killed in twin suicide bombings while on their way to an assignment. The station's Baghdad director, Nawrooz Mohamed, told CPJ that producer Fadhil and cameraman Issa were en route to an event honoring the new president, Jalal Talabani.

Mohamed told CPJ that the journalists were traveling in a car with a reporter and a driver when the bombs exploded outside the Interior Ministry. The reporter and driver were injured, he said. Mohamed said that the journalists were not targets of the attacks, which The Associated Press said took the lives of at least 18 people.

Saman Abdullah Izzedine, Kirkuk TV
April 15, Kirkuk

Unidentified assailants gunned down Izzedine, a news anchor for the Patriotic Union of Kurdistan-backed Kirkuk TV as he was driving on the main highway from Kirkuk to Baghdad. Kurdish journalists in Kirkuk said that Izzedine's car was fired on by a group of armed men driving in a black Nissan. After Izzedine was shot, his attackers threw his body onto the road and left the scene, the journalists reported.

Kurdish journalists said Kirkuk TV's anti-insurgent stance has made it vulnerable to attack from armed groups, and they believe Izzedine, a prominent personality on Kirkuk TV, was targeted for his work.

Ahmed al-Rubai'i, *Al-Sabah*
Mid-April, Baghdad

Al-Rubai'i, a reporter and editor at the U.S.-backed daily *Al-Sabah* who also worked in the media department of the Iraqi National Assembly, was abducted and apparently murdered by unknown perpetrators in Baghdad. The circumstances of his abduction and apparent murder are not clear. No body was found.

Iraqi officials told the journalist's family that al-Rubai'i had been murdered, colleagues said. *The Washington Post* reported on June 6 that "police arrested several members of a criminal gang who admitted to killing several people. Rubai'i's press pass was found among the identity cards in their possession." *The Post* said the detainees told Iraqi police that al-Rubai'i had been beheaded, although his body was not recovered. CPJ could not corroborate this account.

The Iraqi National Guard and Interior Ministry told *Al-Sabah* staffers that the perpetrators belonged to the militant group Tawhid and Jihad, and they killed al-Rubai'i because he was a "traitor." Al-Rubai'i worked as a reporter for *Al-Sabah*. He took a second job as a media officer for the National Assembly five months before his death, staff said.

Saleh Ibrahim, Associated Press Television News, April 23, Mosul

Ibrahim was killed by gunfire near the city's al-Yarmouk Circle, the scene of an earlier explosion that he and his brother-in-law, AP photographer Mohamed Ibrahim, had gone to cover, according to The Associated Press.

A journalist at the scene, whose name was withheld, told the AP that the Ibrahims had arrived at the scene together after the 2:30 p.m. blast and that U.S. forces were in the area. The journalist told the AP that gunfire broke out and both men were struck, although the report did not indicate who fired on them.

Saleh Ibrahim was taken to a local hospital, where he died shortly after arrival. Mohamed Ibrahim, treated for shrapnel wounds, was detained at the hospital by U.S. troops and released the following day. The AP, citing Mosul's deputy police chief, said a U.S. patrol was the target of the earlier explosion.

Ahmed Adam, *Al-Mada*
Najem Abed Khudair, *Al-Mada*
May 15, Latifiyah

Adam and Khudair, reporters with the private Iraqi newspaper *Al-Mada*, were murdered on a road in Latifiyah, a town about 25 miles (40 kilometers) south of Baghdad after leaving the office of their newspaper in Baghdad.

A colleague told CPJ that they were killed after meeting with newspaper staff in Baghdad and getting assignments for the week. The journalists were on the way home to Karbala, their hometown, when armed men ambushed their car. The colleague told CPJ that the journalists' throats were slit and their bodies were left on the side of the road. At least four other journalists were killed after being ambushed on roads in the area south of Baghdad. Initial press reports said that the journalists were traveling with a driver, who was also killed.

Jerges Mahmood Mohamad Suleiman
Nineveh TV, May 31, Mosul

Suleiman, a news anchor at Nineveh TV, was shot by unidentified assailants in late May. Nineveh TV is part of the U.S.-backed Iraqi Media Network. The Associated Press said the shooting occurred on May 31.

Co-workers said Suleiman worked for the station for just 20 days before he was killed. He was shot as he approached Nineveh TV's offices, about 220 yards (200 meters) from the building. Colleagues said Suleiman had not received any prior threats, but they suspect he was targeted because he was an employee of Nineveh TV. Insurgents have frequently targeted Nineveh TV's offices with gunfire and mortars.

Maha Ibrahim, Baghdad TV
June 25, Baghdad

Ibrahim, a news producer for the Iraqi television station Baghdad TV, was shot by U.S. forces as she drove to work with her husband, who was a fellow employee, Iraqi journalists and colleagues at Baghdad TV told CPJ.

Staff at the Baghdad TV station said Ibrahim's car was hit as U.S. troops attempted to disperse a crowd from a Baghdad road. They said Ibrahim was wounded in the abdomen and that she died on arrival at a local hospital. Ibrahim's husband survived the shooting. Baghdad TV is a local television station affiliated with the Iraqi Islamic Party.

Ahmed Wael Bakri, Al-Sharqiyah
June 28, Baghdad

Bakri, a director and news producer for the local television station, Al-Sharqiyah, was killed by gunfire as he approached U.S. troops, according to Ali Hanoon, a station director. Hanoon said Bakri was driving from work to his in-laws' home in southern Baghdad at the time.

U.S. soldiers fired at the car 15 times, and Bakri died later at Yarmouk Hospital, Hanoon said. The Associated Press, citing another colleague and a doctor who treated the journalist, reported that Bakri failed to pull over for a U.S. convoy while trying to pass a traffic accident.

The U.S. embassy in Baghdad issued a statement of condolence to the family and the station, the BBC reported.

Khaled al-Attar, Al-Iraqiya
July 1, Mosul

Al-Attar, an Iraqi television producer for the state news channel Al-Iraqiya, was killed in Mosul after being kidnapped earlier in the day.

Ghazi al-Faisal, a supervisor at the Al-Iraqiya station in Mosul, said al-Attar helped produce a number of programs, including a satirical look at the Iraqi government. Al-Attar also appeared on camera. Al-Faisal said that he was unaware of any threats to al-Attar, but noted that the station's employees have been targeted.

Al-Faisal said that al-Attar was working when he was kidnapped shortly after noon. His bullet-ridden body was found later in the day near a local mosque. Insurgents increasingly targeted Al-Iraqiya and its journalists because of the station's ties to the U.S.-supported Iraqi government. Insurgents killed at least three other employees of the station and its affiliates since 2004, and the offices of the station and its affiliates have repeatedly come under mortar attack.

Adnan al-Bayati, TG3
July 23, Baghdad

Al-Bayati, a freelance producer and translator who worked for the television station TG3, was murdered by three gunmen at his home in al-Adhamiya neighborhood. The men knocked on al-Bayati's door and opened fire when he answered, killing him in front of his wife and baby daughter, said TG3 journalist Giovanna Botteri, who worked closely with al-Bayati.

Al-Bayati was not politically active and had no known personal disputes with any Iraqi factions, according to his colleagues. Botteri and other Italian media believe al-Bayati was targeted because of his work for TG3. The Web site *Articolo 21* said that "al-Bayati fell victim to revenge attacks by Sunni terrorist groups who do not let Iraqis work with foreigners, especially with Western news media, above all Italian media."

Italian journalists in Iraq have been at risk. On February 4, journalist Giuliana Sgrena of the Rome-based daily *Il Manifesto* was kidnapped and held captive for a month. In August 2004, Italian freelance journalist Enzo Baldoni was kidnapped and murdered by a militant group in Najaf.

Al-Bayati, who was born in Diyala, northwest of Baghdad, spoke fluent Italian and spent five years in Italy earning a college degree. He also did some work for the television stations Rai, Mediaset and TG3, and for the magazine *Panorama*.

Steven Vincent, Freelance
August 3, Basra

Vincent, who had written for a number of U.S. publications and was working on a book, was abducted along with his interpreter, Noor al-Khal, on August 2. They were taken by armed men driving what initial reports described variously as a government pickup truck or police car.

Vincent's body was riddled with bullets, his hands were tied with plastic wire, and his neck was wrapped in red cloth, *The New York Times* reported. Al-Khal was seriously wounded and was hospitalized.

In an opinion article published in *The Times* on July 31, Vincent said police in Basra had fallen under the sway of Shiite religious groups, and he strongly criticized British authorities in charge of police training for tolerating such influence.

Vincent's work also appeared in *The Christian Science Monitor* and the *National Review*. A resident of New York City, he had been in Basra for several months working on a book about the Iraqi port city. Vincent was the first U.S. journalist to be murdered in Iraq.

The reason for Vincent's murder remains unclear. Some speculated he was killed in retaliation for his sensitive reporting on Shiite religious groups in Basra. Others said his close relationship with al-Khal may have run against religious sensibilities and led to his murder.

Rafed Mahmoud Said al-Anbagy
Diyala TV and Radio
August 27, Baaquba

Al-Anbagy, a 36-year-old news anchor and director at Diyala, part of the U.S.–backed Iraq Media Network, was shot dead in Za'toun neighborhood in the city of Baaquba, east of Baghdad, while covering a football match, sources at the broadcaster told CPJ.

Al-Anbagy was interviewing one of the team's coaches when gunmen opened fire, killing both men. Al-Anbagy was shot in the head. Diyala sources said they believe al-Anbagy was killed because of his on-air criticism of insurgent groups and former Baathists. The sources said al-Anbagy had received several death threats for his reporting.

Waleed Khaled, Reuters
August 28, Baghdad

Khaled, 35, a soundman for Reuters, was shot by U.S. forces several times in the head and chest as he drove with cameraman Haidar Kadhem to investigate a report of clashes between armed men and police in Baghdad's Hay al-Adil district, Reuters reported.

Reuters quoted an Iraqi police report as saying, "A team from Reuters news agency was on assignment to cover the killing of two policemen in Hay al-Adil; U.S. forces opened fire on the team from Reuters and killed Waleed Khaled, who was shot in the head, and wounded Haider Kadhem."

Kadhem, the only known eyewitness, was wounded and was held by U.S. forces at an undisclosed location for three days. Kadhem told reporters at the scene that he heard gunfire and saw a U.S. sniper on the roof of a nearby shopping center. Lt. Col. Steve Boylan, a U.S. military spokesman in Iraq, said Kadhem was detained "due to inconsistencies in his story."

Hind Ismail, *As-Saffir*
September 17, Mosul

Ismail, a 28-year-old reporter for the daily *As-Saffir*, was kidnapped in the northern city of Mosul, local journalists told CPJ. Police in the southern suburb of al-Muthana found her body the next morning with a single bullet wound to the head.

"Hind was a very active reporter in Mosul," *As-Saffir* Deputy Editor Slayhe al-Jowiree said. "We respected her very much in her pursuit to uncover the truth."

The Baghdad-based *As-Saffir* took a strong pro-democracy editorial position and ran a campaign to educate Iraqis on the importance of the new constitution, local journalists said. It criticized insurgent attacks against Iraqi civilians, calling them terrorist operations.

Staff members believe insurgents targeted the newspaper because it supported the new Iraqi constitution, urged citizens to vote, and frequently covered press conferences held by the Iraqi police. The day before her abduction, Hind had covered a police press conference.

A close colleague told CPJ that Ismail was tortured by her captors and forced to reveal the names of other staffers at the newspaper. The torture session was filmed and later viewed by a staff member of the newspaper, the colleague said. The day after Ismail's death, insurgents circulated a list of newspaper staff and posted it on the walls of mosques in Mosul, according to the colleague. On September 20, *As-Saffir* journalist Firas Maadidi was also killed.

Fakher Haider, *The New York Times*
September 19, Basra

Several men claiming to be police officers seized Haider from his home in al-Asmaey neighborhood on the night of September 18. His body was found the next day in the southwestern Al-Kiblah neighborhood with a gunshot to the head, according to his family. He also had bruises on his back, *The New York Times* said in a statement.

Haider, 38, who reported for *The Times* for more than two years, also worked for Merbad TV in Basra, the *Guardian* of London, *National Geographic*, and other publications. He was married with three small children.

The Times reported that before his murder, Haider "had just filed a report on clashes between British forces in the area and members of a militia that has infiltrated the Basra police force but is loyal to the radical Shiite cleric Moqtada al-Sadr."

Firas Maadidi, *As-Saffir* and *Al-Masar*
September 20, Mosul

Maadidi, 40, Mosul bureau chief for *As-Saffir* and chief editor of the local daily *Al-Masar*, was killed by unidentified gunmen in the al-Noor neighborhood, *As-Saffir* Deputy Editor Slayhe al-Jowiree told CPJ. Maadidi was shot six times, including twice to the head.

As-Saffir, based in Baghdad, took a strong pro-democracy editorial stance and ran a campaign to educate Iraqis on the importance of the new constitution, local journalists said. It said insurgent attacks against Iraqi civilians were terrorist operations.

"We are an independent newspaper serving the Iraqi people, and we have no political or factional affiliations," Jowiree told CPJ. The murder came just days after the slaying of Hind Ismail, a 28-year-old reporter for *As-Saffir*.

Mohammed Haroon, *Al-Kadiya*
October 19, Baghdad

Unidentified gunmen killed Haroon, a controversial journalist, as he was driving in Baghdad. Haroon, 47, publisher of the weekly newspaper *Al-Kadiya* who also served as secretary-general of the Iraqi Journalists Syndicate, was shot four times, according to CPJ sources.

In the weeks before his death, he told colleagues that he had been threatened, told to resign his position at the syndicate, and lower his public profile, CPJ sources said. The syndicate is among a small number of professional press associations in Iraq. In his weekly columns for *Al-Kadiya*,

Haroon often accused Iraqi journalists of collaborating with U.S. intelligence, according to CPJ sources. Haroon had once worked for newspapers overseen by Uday Hussein, son of the former Iraqi president, those sources said.

LEBANON: 2

oo

Samir Qassir, *Al-Nahar*
June 2, Beirut

Columnist Qassir was killed in a car bombing outside his home in Beirut's Ashrafiyeh neighborhood. Qassir, well-known throughout the region for supporting democratic reform, died when a bomb exploded under the driver's seat of his Alfa Romeo. Qassir's murder prompted mass demonstrations in Beirut.

In his popular newspaper column, Qassir vigorously criticized the Syrian government, its Lebanese allies, and Syria's 29-year military and political presence in Lebanon. He was threatened and harassed for his outspoken writing.

In 2001, Lebanese security agents confiscated Qassir's passport in response to his editorials criticizing the Lebanese army and security services. His passport was eventually returned, but authorities said they were investigating the legality of his Lebanese citizenship.

Gebran Tueni, *Al-Nahar*
December 12, Beirut

Tueni, *Al-Nahar* columnist and managing director, was killed by a car bomb in East Beirut. Tueni, 48, who also served as a member of parliament, was a fierce critic of the Syrian government and its policies in Lebanon.

A parked car exploded as Tueni's armored vehicle drove past. The blast killed three other people and injured 32. Tueni was killed the day after he returned from Paris, where he had spent considerable time because of safety concerns. The Lebanese opposition blamed the attacks on Syria, which denied them.

The bombing came on the day that the United Nations Security Council received a report on a U.N. investigation into the February 14, 2005, assassination of former Prime Minister Rafiq al-Hariri.

Since al-Hariri's murder and the launch of the U.N. inquiry, prominent *Al-Nahar* columnist Samir Qassir was killed in one car bombing and Lebanese Broadcasting Corp. talk show host May Chidiac was seriously wounded in another.

Tueni was a prominent opposition politician and was active in the protests following al-Hariri's assassination which helped prompt Syria to withdraw from Lebanon.

Tueni was well-known for his *Al-Nahar* columns. He helped break an important press taboo in 2000 when he wrote a front-page letter to Bashar al-Assad, son and heir apparent to Syrian president Hafez al-Assad. The letter called for the redeployment and withdrawal of Syrian troops in Lebanon under the 1990 Taif Accords that ended Lebanon's civil war. Although Tueni's letter triggered a public outcry from some newspapers and Lebanese officials, other writers followed his lead.

LIBYA: 1

o

Daif al-Gahzal al-Shuhaibi, Freelance
June 2, outside Benghazi

Al-Ghazal's body was found in a suburb of Benghazi. He had gone missing on May 21, according to several sources. Al-Ghazal was a former journalist for the government-owned daily *Azahf al-Akhdar* and was a contributor to the London-based Web sites *Libya Alyoum* and *Libya Jeel*.

Justice Minister Ali Hasnaoui said al-Ghazal was shot in the head and the death was being investigated as a murder.

Al-Ghazal, who was a member of the governing Revolutionary Committees, had recently been critical of government officials and the official media in articles for the London-based Web sites. Al-Ghazal wrote an open letter in February, announcing his intention never to write for official media again and saying he was "protesting the attacks...journalists have faced while trying to reveal the truth." Al-Ghazal publicly criticized Libyan officials in his other articles on *Libya Alyoum* and *Libya Jeel*, accusing them of corruption and "stealing the public's money." A source close to al-Ghazal told CPJ that the journalist was briefly detained and questioned by Libyan security agents in April.

MEXICO: 1

o

Dolores Guadalupe García Escamilla
Stereo 91, April 16, Nuevo Laredo

Crime reporter García Escamilla died from injuries she suffered in an April 5 shooting in front of her radio station in the border city of Nuevo Laredo. García Escamilla was hospitalized in critical condition after being struck by nine shots to the abdomen, pelvis, arms, and legs as she arrived at work, Stereo 91 News Director Roberto Gálvez Martínez told CPJ. She hosted the program "Punto Rojo" for Stereo 91 XHNOE in Nuevo Laredo, a violence-plagued city of 500,000 in the state of Tamaulipas.

The attack occurred about a half hour after the station aired a report by García Escamilla on the slaying of a Nuevo Laredo defense lawyer, Gálvez Martinez said. An unidentified assailant approached García Escamilla after she parked her car in front of the station just before 8 a.m., firing 14 times in all, the Mexican press reported.

García Escamilla, an experienced reporter who had worked for several media outlets in the city, had covered crime for Stereo 91 since 2001. Gálvez Martinez told CPJ that García Escamilla's car was torched in early January in front of her house. He said no motive was established for the arson, although press reports speculated that it stemmed from her reporting.

Several news reports later included speculation that García Escamilla had links to one of the criminal groups fighting to control the drug trade in Nuevo Laredo, but the evidence was inconclusive. Investigators, who initially said the murder appeared to be connected to her reporting, said later that they had not disregarded other motives.

NEPAL: 1

o

Maheshwar Pahari, *Rastriya Swabhiman*
October 4, Pokhara

Imprisoned reporter Pahari died after being denied proper medical treatment by authorities. Pahari, 30, who worked for the weekly *Rastriya Swabhiman*, died of multiple illnesses in a hospital in Pokhara, 80 miles (130 kilometers) northwest of Kathmandu, according to local journalist groups.

Local doctors had recommended Pahari be transferred to Kathmandu for better treatment, and members of the Federation of Nepalese Journalists (FNJ) in Pokhara offered to pay to send him, the FNJ said. But officials refused, citing security concerns. He was provided treatment at the local hospital only after repeated appeals by his wife, Durga Pahari, local journalists told CPJ.

Pahari was detained by security forces in the village of Khorako Mukh, in western Nepal's Kaski district on January 2, 2004. He was held incommunicado for several months. Local journalists believe that his detention was linked to his journalistic work. Pahari maintained close contacts in the Maoist rebel movement, and some sources told CPJ that security forces might have detained him to gather information about the leadership of the insurgency against King Gyanendra.

Pahari was held under an antiterrorism law that has been used to jail journalists since it was introduced in November 2001. Authorities released and re-arrested him four times after January 2004 in order to comply with that law, which limits detention without trial to six months. In May, he was released from a Kaski jail and arrested before he could leave the compound, local human rights and media advocacy groups reported.

PAKISTAN: 2

oo

Allah Noor, Khyber TV
Amir Nowab (also known as **Mir Nawab**)
Associated Press Television News
and *Frontier Post*
February 7, Wana

Gunmen in the capital of the remote South Waziristan tribal area fatally shot Nowab, also known as Nawab, a freelance cameraman for Associated Press Television News and a reporter for the *Frontier Post* newspaper, and Noor, who was working for Peshawar-based Khyber TV.

The journalists were on their way back from the town of Sararogha, where they were covering the surrender of suspected tribal militant Baitullah Mehsud.

A car overtook the journalists' bus at around 7:30 p.m. near the town of Wana, and assailants opened fire with AK-47 assault rifles, according to The Associated Press, which quoted Mahmood Shah, chief of security for Pakistan's tribal areas bordering Afghanistan.

Two other journalists riding in the bus were injured. Anwar Shakir, a stringer for Agence France-Presse, was wounded in the back during the attack, according to news reports. Dilawar Khan, who was working for Al-Jazeera, received minor injuries.

Days later, an unknown group calling itself "Sipah-e-Islam" (Soldiers of Islam) took responsibility for the killings in a letter faxed to newspapers. It accused some journalists of "working for Christians" and of "being used as tools in negative propaganda...against the Muslim mujahedeen."

Local journalists blamed officials for not doing more at the time of the murders. They said no attempt was made to stop the gunmen's vehicle even though the attack took place in an area under government control. They also said no real investigation into the murders took place.

The Pakistani military launched a major offensive against suspected al-Qaeda fighters in South Waziristan, a semiautonomous tribal region, in early 2004. Access to areas of the fighting is increasingly restricted for all journalists, and threats from militants make reporting conditions very dangerous, local sources say.

PHILIPPINES: 4

oooo

Marlene Garcia-Esperat

Midland News and DXKR

March 24, Tacurong

A gunman walked into columnist Marlene Garcia-Esperat's house in the city of Tacurong, and shot her in front of her family. Garcia-Esperat died at the scene from a single bullet wound to her head, police told reporters. The gunman and his accomplice escaped from the scene on a motorcycle.

An anti-graft columnist for the *Midland Review* in the southern island of Mindanao, Garcia-Esperat, 45, was under police protection as a result of death threats. Local news reports said that on the day of the shooting she let her two guards leave early for the Easter holiday.

The Philippine National Police Chief, General Arturo Lomibao told reporters "the motive is work-related as media practitioner." In a radio interview, George Esperat said that his wife had "made many enemies because of her exposés" and that she had received death threats via text message. He also suggested Garcia-Esperat's murder was connected to a corruption story that she wrote, accusing a police officer of involvement in illegal logging activity. Tacurong Police Chief Raul Supiter said that no motive had been ruled out, according to the Philippines-based MindaNews news service.

On April 11, police announced the arrest of four suspects, including an army sergeant. The four were said to confess their involvement, according to local reports. Newspapers reported several possible leads as to the mastermind; those reports included allegations that two officials from the Mindanao Department of Agriculture, Osmeña Montañer and Estrella Sabay, plotted Garcia-Esperat's murder. The officials denied the accusations, but one of the defendants, Randy Barua, a former bodyguard for Sabay, told police that he hired the gunmen at the behest of Montañer and Sabay, the *Philippine Daily Inquirer* reported.

Murder charges were brought against the two officials, but a judge dismissed them on August 31 because of what he termed insufficient and conflicting evidence. The Esperat family lawyer, Nena Santos, told the *Manila Standard* that the dismissal was "highly questionable and suspicious," and that it was a "miscarriage of justice." Santos said the judge made the decision the day before being transferred to another jurisdiction, and the court clerk did not announce the ruling until September 20.

Press freedom groups protested the dismissal of charges against the accused masterminds. The four initial defendants also complained to President Gloria Macapagal Arroyo. Gerry Cabayag, identified as the gunman, said he was afraid of retribution from the two agriculture officials, the *Inquirer* reported.

A chemist by training, Garcia-Esperat began her work exposing corruption in the early 1990s. During her tenure as ombudsman for the Department of Agriculture, she filed legal actions against several officials accusing them of graft, according to the *Inquirer*. She also spent two years in the witness protection program due to her ombudsman discoveries.

Garcia-Esperat became a full-time journalist in 2004 after growing frustrated with the government's tepid reaction to corruption, she told the *Inquirer* in an earlier interview. She started hosting a program on local radio station DXKR in 2001, and began her column "Madame Witness" at the end of 2002. Garcia-Esperat was also a longtime source for many journalists.

Klein Cantoneros, DXAA
May 4, Dipolog City

Cantoneros, a "block-time" radio broadcaster known for hard-hitting commentary, died after being shot as many as seven times by motorcycle-riding gunmen in Dipolog City on the southern island of Mindanao.

Cantoneros, 32, who frequently criticized local officials for alleged corruption and illegal gambling on his talk radio program on DXAA-FM, was returning home at around 1:30 a.m. when he was attacked by as many as three gunmen, according to local news reports.

Cantoneros was clutching his own .45-caliber pistol when he was found, and he appeared to have fired back at his attackers, the news Web site *ABS-CBN* quoted police as saying. Cantoneros' colleague, Robert Baguio, told radio station DZBB that the journalist identified his assailants before undergoing surgery, according to the Inquirer News Service. He died at around 11 p.m.

Cantoneros' colleagues told reporters that the journalist had received several death threats, some by text message, *ABS-CBN* reported. Journalists said that Cantoneros was likely murdered in retaliation for his bold commentary about local politicians.

Cantoneros began hosting his popular program, "Nasud, Pagmata Na" (People, Wake Up), in 2004. Prior to joining the station, he did public relations for political candidates.

A special task force dedicated to solving Cantoneros' murder was formed in

May, headed by Dipolog City Philippine National Police Chief Tomas Hizon. In September, police arrested a suspect after a witness identified him as one of three gunmen. Another witness confirmed the identification. The suspect has denied involvement.

"Block-timing" is a controversial practice in which the broadcaster leases airtime from a station owner. These commentators solicit their own commercial sponsors; critics say they are more likely to abuse their power and engage in questionable practices.

Cantoneros died two days after CPJ named the Philippines the most murderous country for journalists in the world.

Philip Agustin, *Starline Times Recorder*, May 10, Paltic

Agustin, editor and publisher of the local weekly *Starline Times Recorder*, was killed by a single shot to the back of the head, according to local news reports. Police said a gunman fired through an open window in the home of Agustin's daughter and then fled on a motorcycle driven by an accomplice. The murder occurred in the village of Paltic, about 70 miles (112 kilometers) northeast of Manila.

A special edition of the *Starline Times Recorder* dedicated to corruption and illegal logging in the nearby town of Dingalan was scheduled to come out on May 11. Valentino Lapuz, a member of the local council who witnessed the shooting, said in an interview with GMA television that the newspaper linked the local mayor to missing government money. Mayor Jaime Ylarde denied wrongdoing.

Agustin's family told police that his articles about local corruption and official inaction against the illegal logging trade were the likely motives for his murder, according to the *ABS-CBN* news Web site.

Witnesses in May identified three suspects. The alleged gunman, Reynaldo Morete, arrested on May 14, identified Ylarde as the mastermind, according to local press reports and the Center for Media Freedom and Responsibility, a press freedom organization. The other suspects remained at large.

The mayor was not immediately charged and repeatedly denied any involvement in the killing.

Rolando "Dodong" Morales
DXMD, July 3, Polomolok

The radio commentator was ambushed and shot at least 15 times by a gang of motorcycle-riding assailants while driving home on the southern island of Mindanao. Morales, who died at the scene, had just finished hosting his weekly program on radio DXMD in General Santos City.

Danilo Mangila, the local police chief, told reporters that Morales was riding a motorcycle with a companion on a highway leading to the town of Polomolok when eight assailants on four motorcycles stopped him and opened fire at around 6 p.m. The gunmen surrounded Morales and continued shooting even after he fell to the ground, witnesses told police. Morales' companion was wounded, according to local news reports.

Police compiled a list of possible suspects

in mid-July that included several police officers assigned to Polomolok, the Inquirer News Service reported.

Police cited Morales' crusading anti-drug commentaries as the likely motive for his murder, but Chief Inspector Rex Anongos, head of the Polomolok police, told the MindaNews wire service that police had not ruled out personal motives for the killing.

In August, police in General Santos City arrested and filed murder charges against two suspects in Morales' murder, including the alleged mastermind.

Morales, 43, hosted a weekly "blocktime" program called "Voice of the Village" on Radyo Agong, a Radio Mindanao Network affiliate, and he was known for his tough commentaries, Mangila said. He accused local politicians of corruption and involvement in the illegal drug trade. Morales, who had been broadcasting since 2003, was active with a neighborhood anticrime task force and reported its findings on the air, the Center for Media Freedom and Responsibility reported. The *ABS-CBN* news Web site reported that Morales also accused local officials of involvement in summary executions.

Morales worked as an inspector at the Dole pineapple plantation and held local office before starting his radio work, CMFR reported.

Morales' wife, Floreta, told the *Philippine Daily Inquirer* that her husband had received several death threats by text message beginning in November 2004 because of his crusade against illegal drugs. She said that he continued to broadcast despite the threats "because it was a public service," and that he worked at the radio station on a volunteer basis.

Emir Bariquit, program director of DXMD Radyo Agong told the Inquirer News Service that Morales was likely killed for his fiery commentary. Bariquit said he saw a threatening letter sent to Morales a few months ago, warning the commentator to halt his criticism of local officials and illegal drugs.

RUSSIA: 2

oo

Pavel Makeev, Puls
May 21, Azov

Makeev's body was found beside a road on the outskirts of the Rostov region town shortly after the 21-year-old cameraman arrived to film illegal drag racing. Authorities initially classified the death as a traffic accident, but colleagues believed Makeev was killed to prevent his reporting, according to CPJ interviews.

The body, which had multiple bruises and fractures, was found in a ditch around 1 a.m. The road connecting Azov with the town of Bataysk is the site of drag races organized by local young people, which draw large crowds and illegal betting. Residents said the races had been going on for years, but police had not stopped them.

Makeev had gone to film a race for a report for the Puls television station. Colleague Sergei Bondarenko told CPJ he gave Makeev a ride to the site at 11:30 p.m. on May 20. Bondarenko said he left an hour later. "Pavel said he wanted to shoot some more. He assured me that he could get a taxi or ask somebody for a ride to come back home," Bondarenko said.

Police discovered a pool of blood on the road 50 feet (15 meters) from Makeev's body, according to local reports and CPJ interviews, indicating the body might have been dragged to the ditch. No tire marks were found on the pavement.

Makeev's video camera and cell phone were missing. Police said they discovered the car that allegedly hit Makeev, but no arrests were reported.

The investigation was transferred to the Rostov regional prosecutor's office. "Investigators do not consider Makeev's professional activity to be a possible motive for the crime," Elena Velikova, press secretary for the prosecutor, told CPJ. But at least two journalists told CPJ that they believed Markeev's death was linked to his work. They noted that reporters who have tried to cover drag racing have often been threatened.

Aleksei Sklyarov, Puls general director, told CPJ that racers would not want to see Makeev report on an illegal event. Grigory Bochkaryov, Rostov expert for the Moscow-based press freedom organization Center for Journalism in Extreme Situations, told CPJ that traffic police often accept bribes in exchange for allowing the drag races. In a report following Makeev's death, Puls said the drag races typically attract large crowds, and it asked why no witnesses had come forward.

Makeev's colleagues conducted their own investigation because Rostov prosecutors would not discuss the case and closed the investigation, claiming an "absence of evidence of a crime," Sklyarov told CPJ. Eyewitnesses told the journalists that a drag racing vehicle struck Makeev, and that a suspected race organizer threw Makeev's camera into a nearby river after watching its footage, Sklayrov said.

After additional inquiries by CPJ, Rostov prosecutor Vasily Afanasiev said in September that his office had reopened the case.

Magomedzagid Varisov

Novoye Delo, June 28, Makhachkala

Machine gun-toting assailants opened fire on Varisov's sedan at around 9 p.m., as he was returning home with his wife and driver. Varisov sustained multiple bullet wounds and died at the scene. His wife was not injured; the driver was hospitalized with injuries, according to local press reports.

The Kirovsky district prosecutor's office said Varisov's journalism was the most likely motive, local reports said.

For the past three years, Varisov wrote analytical articles for the Makhachkala-based *Novoye Delo*, Dagestan's largest weekly. Rumina Elmurzayeva, editor of *Novoye Delo*, told CPJ that Varisov had his own page devoted to political analysis, which was often critical of the Dagestan opposition. Varisov wrote that the opposition was trying to destabilize the republic and topple the regional government. Varisov also wrote about organized crime and terrorism, local reports said.

Varisov headed the Republican Center for Strategic Initiatives and Political Technologies, a center for political analysis in

Makhachkala, Elmurzayeva told CPJ. Varisov was considered a leading expert on the North Caucasus region, and his expertise was sought by many Russian journalists, she said.

In the most recent issue of *Novoye Delo,* Varisov examined a Russian army unit's June 4 sweep in the Chechen border town of Borozdinovskaya, in which one person was killed and 11 others were reported missing. Ethnic Avars, fearing for their lives, left Borozdinovskaya by the hundreds and crossed into neighboring Dagestan, local reports said.

"Varisov criticized Chechen authorities in his article for failing to protect the safety of Borozdinovskaya residents and appealed to Dagestan authorities to do right by them," Elmurzayeva told CPJ.

For the past year, Varisov had spoken of threats against him and had written about those threats in articles for *Novoye Delo,* Elmurzayeva said. Varisov complained that unknown individuals were following him, and he unsuccessfully sought protection from Makhachkala law enforcement authorities, she said.

A combat unit in Makhachkala killed three suspects during a separate operation on October 25, Elmurzayeva told CPJ. Local prosecutors closed their case shortly afterward, she said.

SERBIA & MONTENEGRO: 1

o

Bardhyl Ajeti, *Bota Sot*
June 25, outside Pristina

Ajeti, 28, a reporter for the Albanian-language daily *Bota Sot,* died in an Italian hospital on June 25, three weeks after being shot in Kosovo, Agence France-Presse reported.

Ajeti was driving from Kosovo's capital, Pristina, to the eastern Kosovo town of Gnjilane on June 3 when at least one attacker shot at him from a passing car, according to the Kosova Journalists Association, a local union. Ajeti fell into a coma after being shot and was evacuated to a hospital in Milan where he died, AFP reported.

Police spokesman Refki Morina said that Ajeti was shot in the head at close range but did not disclose any possible motives, according to The Associated Press.

Baton Haxhiu, president of the Kosova Journalists Association, told CPJ that Ajeti wrote daily editorials for *Bota Sot,* which is allied with the governing Democratic League of Kosovo party. He often criticized opposition party figures in his editorials, Haxhiu told CPJ.

The Temporary Media Commissioner, Kosovo's internationally supervised media regulator, said in a June 6 statement that Ajeti filed a complaint with the office on May 17 saying that his life had been threatened.

In summer 2002, *Bota Sot* and Ajeti supported international authorities who arrested former members of the Kosova Liberation Army (KLA) as part of a broader anticrime campaign, according to the London-based Institute for War & Peace Reporting. Ajeti later criticized nationalist Albanian protestors for demanding that international forces release the arrested members of the KLA.

Several journalists from Kosovo told CPJ that Ajeti was in the process of leaving *Bota Sot* to establish a rival newspaper.

SIERRA LEONE: 1

o

Harry Yansaneh, *For Di People*
July 28, Freetown

A judicial inquest found that a May attack on Yansaneh, acting editor of the daily *For Di People*, contributed to his death from kidney failure more than two months later. Yansaneh had accused Member of Parliament Fatmata Hassan of ordering the May 10 attack, which she denied.

The extent of Yansaneh's injuries was not clear at the time of the attack, and he was not hospitalized. The inquest found that Yansaneh's death was "accelerated by the beating" and called it a case of involuntary manslaughter.

A magistrate ordered the arrest of Hassan, three of her children, and two other men for suspected manslaughter. Hassan, an MP for the ruling Sierra Leone People's Party, Olu Campbell, and Reginald Bull were detained on August 26. All three were released on bail on August 30. Police said they planned to seek the extradition of Hassan's two sons and a daughter from the United Kingdom.

Prior to the attack, Hassan had sought to evict *For Di People* and five other independent newspapers from the offices they had rented from her late husband for many years. *For Di People*'s offices were also vandalized.

Yansaneh had taken over as senior editor following the imprisonment of *For Di People*'s editor and publisher, Paul Kamara, in October 2004. Kamara was convicted of "seditious libel" and sentenced to two years in jail for articles that criticized President Ahmad Tejan Kabbah.

The government ordered the inquest under strong local and international pressure.

SOMALIA: 2

o o

Kate Peyton, BBC
February 9, Mogadishu

Peyton, a BBC producer, was shot outside her hotel in the Somali capital. Peyton underwent surgery at a local hospital but died later of internal bleeding, according to the BBC.

News reports said Peyton was shot outside the Sahafi Hotel, where she had arrived just hours earlier to begin a series of reports on the strife-torn country. Several foreign reporters were based at the heavily guarded hotel.

Agence France-Presse quoted witnesses as saying that assailants targeted Peyton before speeding off in a white sedan. The vehicle was later found abandoned in a central Mogadishu neighborhood, Mohammed Warsame Doleh, the acting police chief, told AFP.

Peyton's attackers were believed to be two independent militiamen, according to the National Union of Somali Journalists, which conducted its own investigation into the slaying. No official legal action was taken.

The BBC said Peyton had spent the last 10 years in Africa and was based in Johannesburg. She had worked for the BBC since 1993 and had also worked as a producer and trainer for the South African Broadcasting Corporation in Johannesburg.

Foreign reporters had just returned to Mogadishu, where efforts were under way to install a transitional reconciliation government. Local sources said Peyton may have been targeted to discourage foreigners and maintain a climate of insecurity.

Violence and lawlessness are rife in Somalia, which has had no effective central government since the fall of dictator Siad Barre in 1991.

Duniya Muhyadin Nur, Capital Voice June 5, Afgoye

Muhyadin was shot to death while covering a protest in Afgoye, about 18 miles (30 kilometers) from Mogadishu. Muhyadin, 26, was a reporter for the Mogadishu-based radio station Capital Voice, owned by the HornAfrik media company.

She was covering a blockade by commercial drivers on the Mogadishu-Afgoye road, according to HornAfrik Co-Director Ahmed Abdisalam Adan. The drivers were protesting the proliferation of militia roadblocks. While they were attempting to stop private traffic, a gunman fired into Muhyadin's taxi, Abdisalam told CPJ. The bullet passed through the front seat and hit Muhyadin, who died instantly.

CPJ sources said the gunman was the assistant of a protesting trucker from the same sub-clan as his victim. Following negotiations, he paid compensation to her family, according to Somali tradition.

Somalia has had no functioning central government since the collapse of the Siad Barre regime in 1991. Militia leaders have carved the country into rival fiefdoms, many of them riddled by violence. In May, veteran HornAfrik journalist Abdallah Nurdin was wounded by an unidentified gunman.

SRI LANKA: 2

oo

Dharmeratnam Sivaram, *TamilNet* and *Daily Mirror*, April 29, Colombo

Sivaram was abducted on the night of April 28 and found dead the next morning from gunshot wounds to the head.

Four unidentified men forced Sivaram into a jeep as he left a restaurant directly across from the Bambalapitya police station in the capital, according to witness accounts. Police told The Associated Press that they received an anonymous call early the next morning giving the location of Sivaram's body in Talangama, several miles outside of Colombo. The *TamilNet* news Web site reported that his body was found in a high-security area behind a parliament building.

A founding member and contributor to *TamilNet* and a military and political columnist for the English-language *Daily Mirror*, Sivaram wrote sympathetically about the rebel group the Liberation Tigers of Tamil Eelam (LTTE). Police searched his house twice last year looking for weapons but did not find anything.

The LTTE split into two warring factions in 2004 after a rebel leader known as Colonel Karuna broke away to form his own rival army in eastern Sri Lanka. A cycle of violence has escalated from the east throughout the country, with the warring Tamil factions going on killing sprees that target each other's alleged supporters, including journalists.

A pro-LTTE Tamil lawmaker, Amirthanathan Adaikkalanathan, told The Associated Press that Sivaram's last article for the Tamil-language daily *Virekasari* criticized the rebel leader Karuna. Sivaram had received death threats in recent weeks, according to exiled Tamil journalists.

Relangi Selvarajah
Sri Lanka Rupavahini Corp.
August 12, Colombo

Popular Tamil broadcaster Selvarajah and her husband, a political activist, were killed by unidentified gunmen in Colombo on the same day that Lakshman Kadirgamar, Sri Lanka's foreign minister, was assassinated. Political leaders blamed the rebel Liberation Tigers of Tamil Eelam (LTTE) for all three killings, charges the LTTE denied.

The attackers shot Selvarajah, 44, and her husband, Senathurai, in the office where they ran a travel agency. Sri Lanka's *Sunday Times* reported that the LTTE had criticized Selvarajah for broadcasting anti-LTTE programs.

Selvarajah was a radio and television host for 20 years, presenting news programs for the state-run Sri Lanka Broadcasting Corporation (SLBC) and more recently for the Sri Lanka Rupavahini Corp., according to the Free Media Movement, a local press freedom organization.

Local newspapers reported that Selvarajah also produced the SLBC program "Ithaya Veenai," a program known for criticizing the LTTE, and allegedly funded by the opposition Tamil political party, the Eelam People's Democratic Party.

Selvarajah's husband was affiliated with the formerly militant and now mainstream group, the People's Liberation Organization of Tamil Eelam (PLOTE), according to local news reports and sources. PLOTE is critical of the LTTE; the LTTE accuses PLOTE of attacking its members, according to The Associated Press.

Sri Lanka's *Daily Mirror* quoted police as saying that they suspected the couple may have been murdered because of Selvarajah's anti-LTTE programs. But their connection to PLOTE also raised the possibility that their killing may have been part of a larger cycle of violence and could be connected to the April murder of well-known pro-LTTE Tamil journalist Dharmeratnam Sivaram, local sources told CPJ. Sivaram was a former member of PLOTE who defected to the LTTE.

Political and ethnic factions began a series of revenge killings across the country last year when a Tamil rebel leader known as Colonel Karuna split from the LTTE.

The government declared a state of emergency on August 13 and President Chandrika Kumaratunga accused the LTTE of killing Kadirgamar, a critic of the LTTE.

JOURNALISTS KILLED: MOTIVE UNCONFIRMED

BELARUS: 1

Vasily Grodnikov, *Narodnaya Volya*
October 17, Minsk

Grodnikov, a freelancer for the Minsk opposition newspaper, was found dead in his apartment with a head wound.

Grodnikov's brother, Nikolai Grodnikov, said the journalist was murdered because of his work for *Narodnaya Volya*, Agence France-Presse reported. He said his brother had survived an attack in January, but he gave no details.

Narodnaya Volya Editor-in-Chief Yosif Seredich said that Grodnikov, 66, wrote mostly about social issues and had no links to the authorities or the opposition, the independent news agency Belapan reported.

Authorities had harassed *Narodnaya Volya* in retaliation for its criticism of President Aleksandr Lukashenko. State-run kiosks were not permitted to sell the newspaper. Authorities had recently ended its printing contract, forcing it to use a printer in the neighboring Russian city of Smolensk.

Nikolai Grodnikov said, "There was a lot of blood on the walls, the floor, the window... Everything in the house was turned over." The journalist's niece, Natalya Grodnikov, said that there was no sign of robbery or forced entry.

The Interior Ministry said that Grodnikov had died of a stroke, the independent Moscow daily *Gazeta* reported. However, an autopsy at the Minsk Regional Clinical Hospital concluded that the cause of death was head trauma. The Minsk regional prosecutor's office was investigating the death, Belapan reported.

DEMOCRATIC REPUBLIC OF CONGO: 1

Franck Kangundu, *La Référence Plus*
November 3, Kinshasa

Kangundu, a veteran political affairs journalist at the independent daily *La Référence Plus*, was shot shortly after midnight by unidentified assassins who accosted him at his home in the capital, Kinshasa. The attackers also killed Kangundu's wife, Hélène Mpaka.

The Kinshasa-based press freedom organization Journaliste en Danger (JED) reported that several masked men approached Kangundu in front of his house, forced their way in, and shot his wife as she tried to escape. When Kangundu offered them money and his car if they would let him go, the assailants replied that they had been "sent to kill him," according to witnesses interviewed by JED whose names were withheld. The assailants took the journalist's mobile phone before leaving.

Kangundu, 52, worked for *La Référence Plus* for more than 10 years and was well-respected by his colleagues, local journalists said. He covered a variety of topics for the newspaper, including the sometimes acrimonious relations between political parties in the DRC's power-sharing government, as well as business and economic issues.

A delegation of journalists met on November 7 with Vice President Azerias Ruberwa to demand an independent inquiry. The meeting was held after 1,000 journalists and other media workers took part in a silent demonstration through the streets of Kinshasa. The government said it had detained suspects and promised a full inquiry.

HAITI: 1

Jacques Roche, *Le Matin*
July 14, Port-au-Prince

Roche, cultural editor with the Port-au-Prince-based daily *Le Matin*, was kidnapped on July 10 and found dead four days later in a slum in Haiti's capital. His body was handcuffed, riddled with bullets, and mutilated, according to international press reports.

The journalist was taken from his car in the Port-au-Prince neighborhood of Nazon, the Haitian press reported. Roche, who was also a poet, hosted a local television station show for the 184 Group, a coalition of civil society organizations that opposed former President Jean-Bertrand Aristide. His captors demanded US$250,000 in ransom, The Associated Press said.

The *St. Petersburg Times* reported that the kidnappers who seized Roche sold the journalist to a gang that wanted him dead for sympathizing with an anti-Aristide group. Franck Séguy, a colleague at *Le Matin*, told CPJ that there is wide speculation that Roche may have been killed because of his television work for the 184 Group.

Judge Jean Peres Paul, who is in charge of the investigation, told CPJ that three suspects had been identified and faced preliminary charges. He said he couldn't comment on the possible motive or disclose the identities of the suspects. Published reports said that on July 21 Haitian authorities arrested the Rev. Gerard Jean-Juste, a prominent Roman Catholic priest and figure in the Lavalas party of ousted President Aristide. Authorities accused him of involvement in Roche's slaying. The priest was jailed but not immediately charged. Aristide supporters said the priest's detention was politically motivated. Amnesty International labeled Jean-Juste a "prisoner of conscience."

IRAQ: 1

Abdul-Hussein Khazal, Al-Hurra
February 9, Basra

Khazal, 40, and his son were gunned down outside their home around 8 a.m., Al-Hurra said in a statement. Khazal, who joined the U.S.-funded television station in April 2004, also worked as a correspondent for the U.S.-funded radio station Radio Sawa, the station said.

Al-Hurra News Director Mouafac Harb told CPJ that the station was investigating the incident and was not aware of any threats against Khazal stemming from his work.

Agence France-Press reported that a previously unknown group calling itself The Imam al-Hassan al-Basri Brigades claimed responsibility for the shooting in a statement posted on an Islamic Web site. Agence France-Presse said the posting accused Khazal of being a member of the Badr Brigades, a Shiite militia affiliated with Supreme Council for Islamic Revolution in Iraq.

The Associated Press reported that Khazal was a member of the rival Shiite political party Dawa, worked as an editor for a local newspaper, and served as a press officer for the Basra city council.

In an interview with CPJ, Harb disputed reports of Khazal's Shiite political affiliations and said the reporter "was killed because he was a journalist."

MEXICO: 1

o

Raúl Gibb Guerrero, *La Opinión*
April 8, Poza Rica

Gibb Guerrero, 53, owner and director of the daily newspaper in the eastern state of Veracruz, was killed in an apparent ambush in the city of Poza Rica at about 10 p.m., according to press reports. Four unidentified gunmen fired at least 15 shots at Gibb Guerrero as he was driving home to Papantla, according to those reports.

Struck by eight shots, three to his head, Gibb Guerrero lost control of his vehicle and crashed. He was pronounced dead at the scene. The assailants fled in two cars, according to the local press.

Earlier that night, Gibb Guerrero was in the city of Martínez de la Torre, where a new edition of *La Opinión* was launched, the Mexican press reported. Gibb Guerrero had received anonymous death threats days before the attack, but he didn't express great concern over them, a *La Opinión* editor told CPJ on condition of anonymity.

In October, federal agents raided the home of Gibb Guerrero's sister, seizing a grenade, several pistols, and a large stash of ammunitions, The Associated Press reported. A few days later, a second home was raided and the personal secretary of the director's sister was charged with arms possession.

Investigators told CPJ that Gibb Guerrero's slaying could have been motivated by personal factors, but did not rule out professional possibilities.

PHILIPPINES: 4

oooo

Arnulfo Villanueva, *Asian Star Express Balita*, February 28, Naic

Villanueva, 43, a columnist for the community newspaper, was found shot on a road in the town of Naic, just south of Manila. A local village official found his body, according to the Manila-based Center for Media Freedom and

Responsibility (CMFR).

Villanueva had criticized local officials in connection with illegal gambling, according to CMFR, but police did not determine a motive.

Ricardo "Ding" Uy, DZRS
November 18, Sorsogon City

Radio announcer Uy, known for his leftist political activities, was killed by a gunman outside his home in Sorsogon City, Sorsogon province, 230 miles (375 kilometers) southeast of Manila.

Uy, 49, was president of the Media Reporters Association and provincial coordinator of Bayan Muna (People First), a leftist political party. Uy was shot five times by an assailant who fled with an accomplice on a motorcycle, according to Deutsche Presse Agentur. He died soon after at a nearby hospital. In an interview with the *ABS-CBN* news Web site, Bayan Muna Deputy Secretary General Roberto de Castro said that Uy received threats before he was killed. De Castro said Uy was known as a critic of the army.

Robert Ramos, *Katapat*
November 20, Cabuyao

Ramos, 39, a reporter for the weekly tabloid, was shot twice in the head outside a market in Cabuyao, Laguna province, 30 miles (48 kilometers) south of the capital, Manila. Ramos was waiting for a ride home from work when two motorcycle-riding assailants shot him, according to police reports cited in the local media. He was pronounced dead at the scene.

On December 1, police identified two brothers as suspects in the murder. Police said the suspects believed the reporter had tipped off authorities that they sold pirated DVDs and CDs from a shop in Cabuyao. Authorities had raided the shop and confiscated merchandise on November 17. It was not immediately clear whether Ramos worked on a story connected to pirated merchandise.

George Benaojan, DYBB and *Bantay Balita*, December 1, Cebu

An unidentified gunman killed radio and newspaper journalist Benaojan in the central city of Cebu before fleeing in a taxi. Benaojan, 27, died at a local hospital shortly afterward, according to international news reports.

Benaojan was talking to a man in a market when the gunman approached and shot the journalist in the mouth, neck, and chest, according to news reports. A bystander was injured by a stray bullet. Witnesses reported seeing the gunman in the area several hours before the attack, according to news reports.

Local police told reporters that Benaojan had been receiving death threats; they were reviewing his commentaries and columns to investigate possible motives. Benaojan had reported on alleged corruption in the local customs bureau for DYBB and *Bantay Balita,* a publication distributed among customs personnel. Benaojan was known for reporting on official corruption.

Benaojan survived an attack in August 2004 when three men ambushed him and two colleagues. Benaojan told reporters that he returned fire.

The journalist also ran several businesses, according to news reports.

THAILAND: 2

oo

Pongkiat Saetang, *Had Yai Post*
February 14, Had Yai

Unidentified gunmen shot Pongkiat, editor of the semimonthly newspaper *Had Yai Post,* near a market in Had Yai, in southern Thailand's Songkhla province.

Two assailants shot Pongkiat twice in the back while he was riding his motorcycle near Thungsao Market at around 8:30 a.m., *The Nation* quoted police as saying. The Bangkok-based Southeast Asian Press Alliance reported that Pongkiat was pronounced dead at the scene, and the gunmen fled by motorcycle.

Pongkiat, 54, was known for his outspoken commentary on local politics. His critical reporting on Had Yai politicians had prompted threatening phone calls, his wife told reporters.

Local police inspector Lt. Col. Samart Boonmee said that police had not ruled out other possible motives, including personal conflicts, according to local news reports.

The Thai Journalists Association and the Southern Journalists Association of Thailand, to which Pongkiat belonged, condemned the murder and called on Thai national police to conduct a fair and open investigation into the case.

Santi Lamaneenil, *Pattaya Post*
November 2, outside Pattaya

Santi was found with multiple gunshot wounds to the head in the back of his car outside the beach resort of Pattaya, according to news reports.

Santi, owner of the local *Pattaya Post,* was also a freelance contributor to Channel 7 television and newspapers including *Khaosod*. Police told reporters that the murder could be related to his reporting, but they had not ruled out other motives. Santi had recently reported on illegal operations in late-night entertainment venues, police told local reporters.

Santi's body was found blindfolded and his hands tied with the cord of a mobile phone battery charger on the morning of November 2. Initial autopsy reports showed that he had been dead for about 10 hours, according to local news reports.

Jongrak Juthanond, the local police chief, told the *Bangkok Post* that investigators believe there were at least three assailants. The journalist's wife told police that Santi had stayed with relatives intermittently in recent months for fear of abduction or attack, according to local news reports.

JOURNALISTS KILLED: A STATISTICAL PORTRAIT 1996 – 2005

DEADLIEST COUNTRIES

Iraq: 60
Colombia: 28
Philippines: 26
Russia: 23
Sierra Leone: 16
India: 15
Bangladesh: 12
Serbia and Montenegro: 10
Afghanistan: 10
Mexico: 9
Algeria: 9

DEMOGRAPHIC TRAITS

Female journalists: 19
Photographers, camera operators: 67
Radio journalists: 62
U.S. journalists: 9

DEATHS BY CIRCUMSTANCE

Murder: 237 (70.3 percent)
Crossfire in war: 67 (19.9 percent)
Reporting in other dangerous circumstances: 33 (9.8 percent)

DEATHS BY YEAR:

2005: 47
2004: 57
2003: 40
2002: 20
2001: 37
2000: 24
1999: 36
1998: 24
1997: 26
1996: 26
Total: 337

MURDER'S BACK STORY

Murders with impunity: 202 (85.2 percent of murders) *
Kidnapped before murdered: 29 (12.2 percent of murders)
Threatened before murdered: 61 (25.7 percent of murders)

* Cases in which those who ordered killings have not been arrested and prosecuted.

METHODOLOGY

CPJ applies strict journalistic standards when investigating a death. We consider a case "confirmed" only when we are reasonably certain that a journalist was murdered in direct reprisal for his or her work; in crossfire during war; or while carrying out a dangerous assignment. We do not include journalists who are killed in accidents—such as car or plane crashes—unless it was caused by hostile action (for example, if a plane were shot down or a car crashed trying to avoid gunfire). For this statistical portrait, CPJ used only cases in which the motive was confirmed to be work-related.

If the motives are unclear, but it is possible that a journalist was killed because of his or her work, CPJ classifies the case as "unconfirmed" and continues to investigate to determine the motive.

JOURNALISTS IN PRISON IN 2005

China, Cuba, Eritrea, and Ethiopia were the leading jailers of journalists in 2005, together accounting for two-thirds of the 125 editors, writers, and photojournalists imprisoned around the world, according to CPJ's annual census.

The United States, which held journalists in detention centers in Iraq and Guantánamo Bay, Cuba, rose to sixth among countries jailing journalists, just behind Uzbekistan and tied with Burma.

"Antistate" allegations, including subversion, divulging state secrets, and acting against the interests of the state, were the most common charges used to imprison journalists. Seventy-eight journalists were jailed under such charges, many by the Chinese and Cuban governments.

A sudden and far-reaching crackdown on the Ethiopian press fueled an increase in the number of journalists jailed worldwide, according to CPJ's census of those held on December 1, 2005. The global tally was three more than the 122 imprisoned journalists in CPJ's 2004 census. Twenty-four countries imprisoned journalists in 2005, reflecting an increase from the 20 nations included in the 2004 census.

For the seventh consecutive year, China was the world's leading jailer of journalists, with 32 imprisoned. Fifteen, or nearly half, of the cases in China involved Internet journalists; more than three-quarters of the cases were brought under vague "antistate" laws.

Cuba ranked second, with 24 reporters, writers, and editors behind bars, most of them jailed in the country's massive March 2003 crackdown on dissidents and the independent press. Eritrea was the leader among African countries, with 15 journalists in prison, many of them held incommunicado in secret jails for reasons the government would not fully explain.

Neighboring Ethiopia imprisoned 13 journalists, all of whom were swept up by authorities seeking to quell dissent amid civil unrest in November. Ethiopian police blocked most private newspapers from publishing; raided newspaper offices, confiscating computers, documents, and other materials; and issued a "wanted list" of editors, writers, and dissidents.

Uzbekistan ranked fifth among countries, with six journalists in prison. Burma and the United States followed, with five apiece. U.S. detention centers in Iraq were holding four journalists, while the U.S. Naval Base at Guantánamo Bay held one.

Other trends and details that emerged in CPJ's analysis:

- Forty-one journalists whose work appeared primarily on the Web or in other electronic forms were in jail, accounting for just under one-third of the cases worldwide.
- Nine were charged with criminal defamation, the second most common allegation used to imprison journalists.

- Another five were jailed for reporting what governments called "false" information.
- No charge was publicly disclosed in 11 cases. The United States and Eritrea each account for five such cases.
- The longest-serving journalists in CPJ's census were Chen Renjie and Lin Youping, who were jailed in China in July 1983 for publishing a pamphlet titled *Ziyou Bao* (Freedom Report). Co-defendant Chen Biling was later executed.

JOURNALISTS IN JAIL *as of December 1, 2005, by country:*

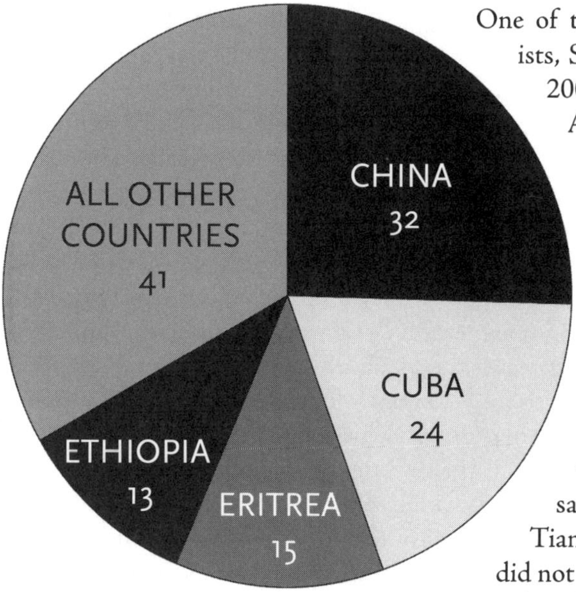

One of the imprisoned Chinese journalists, Shi Tao, was honored with CPJ's 2005 International Press Freedom Award. A freelance journalist for Internet publications and an editor of the business daily *Dangdai Shang Bao*, Shi is serving a 10-year sentence for "leaking state secrets abroad." Shi was imprisoned in November 2004 for posting online notes detailing the government's instructions on how the news media were to cover the 15th anniversary of the military crackdown in Tiananmen Square. The government did not classify the instructions as secret until after the fact.

CPJ's list is a snapshot of journalists incarcerated at midnight on December 1, 2005. It does not include those who were imprisoned and released throughout the year; accounts of their cases can be found at *www.cpj.org*.

CPJ considers any journalist deprived of his or her liberty by a government to be imprisoned. Journalists remain on CPJ's list until the organization determines with reasonable certainty that they have been released.

Journalists who either disappear or are abducted by nonstate entities such as criminal gangs, rebels, or militant groups are not included on the imprisoned list. Their cases are classified as "missing" or "abducted." Details of these cases are also available on CPJ's Web site.

125 JOURNALISTS IMPRISONED AS OF 12/1/2005

AFGHANISTAN: 1

o

Ali Mohaqqiq Nasab
Haqooq-i-Zan (Women's Rights)
IMPRISONED: October 1, 2005

The attorney general ordered editor Nasab's arrest on blasphemy charges after the religious adviser to President Hamid Karzai, Mohaiuddin Baluch, filed a complaint about his magazine. "I took the two magazines and spoke to the Supreme Court chief, who wrote to the attorney general to investigate," Baluch told The Associated Press.

The allegedly blasphemous articles questioned the use of harsh punishments under traditional Islamic law, such as amputating the hands of thieves as punishment for stealing and publicly stoning those accused of adultery, according to international news accounts.

Nasab was convicted in Kabul's Primary Court on October 22 and sentenced to two years in prison. Judge Ansarullah Malawizada said that his ruling was based on recommendations from the conservative Ulama Council, a group of the country's leading clerics. "The Ulama Council sent us a letter saying that he should be punished, so I sentenced him to two years' jail," Malawizada told the AP.

In a report shown on Afghan state television, Nasab rejected the conviction: "I do not accept the verdict by the court. It is a forced and illegal court." Nasab said that he was not allowed to have a lawyer to help in his defense. Held in Kabul's central jail, Nasab was under threat from other inmates because of the nature of the charges, local sources said. Journalists said that his conviction had a chilling effect on reporting, especially on religious issues.

Writings considered anti-Islamic are prohibited under a revised media law signed in March 2004, but the law is vaguely worded and local journalists are uncertain what constitutes a violation. The revised law also stipulates that journalists can only be detained with the approval of a 17-member commission of government officials and journalists. Yet police did not obtain approval from the commission before arresting Nasab.

On October 19, Minister of Information and Culture Sayed Makhdum Raheen did convene a hearing of the media commission, which found Nasab not guilty. "We found there was no blasphemy in the articles at all," Raheen said in an interview with *The New York Times*. The commission's recommendations, however, were nonbinding.

On December 21, an appeals court reduced Nasab's sentence and ordered him released.

ALGERIA: 3

ooo

Djamel Eddine Fahassi
Alger Chaîne III
IMPRISONED: May 6, 1995

Fahassi, a reporter for the state-run radio station Alger Chaîne III and a contributor to several Algerian newspapers, including the now-banned weekly of the Islamic Salvation Front, *Al-Forqane*, was abducted near his home in the al-Harrache suburb of the capital, Algiers, by four well-dressed men carrying walkie-talkies. According to eyewitnesses who later spoke with his wife, the men called out Fahassi's name and then pushed him into a waiting car. He has not been seen since, and Algerian authorities have denied any knowledge of his arrest.

Prior to Fahassi's "disappearance," Algerian authorities had targeted him on at least two occasions because his writing criticized the government. In late 1991, he was arrested after an article in *Al-Forqane* criticized a raid conducted by security forces on an Algiers neighborhood. On January 1, 1992, the Blida Military Court convicted him of disseminating false information, attacking a state institution, and disseminating information that could harm national unity.

He received a one-year suspended sentence and was released after five months. On February 17, 1992, he was arrested a second time for allegedly attacking state institutions and spreading false information. He was transferred to the Ain Salah Detention Center in southern Algeria, where hundreds of Islamic suspects were detained in the months following the cancellation of the January 1992 elections.

In late January 2002, Algerian Ambassador to the United States Idriss Jazairy responded to a CPJ query, saying a government investigation had not found those responsible for Fahassi's abduction. The ambassador added that there was no evidence of state involvement.

Aziz Bouabdallah, *Al-Alam al-Siyassi*
IMPRISONED: April 12, 1997

Bouabdallah, a reporter for the daily *Al-Alam al-Siyassi*, was abducted by three armed men from his home in the capital, Algiers. According to Bouabdallah's family, the men stormed into their home and, after identifying the journalist, grabbed him, put his hands behind his back, and pushed him out the door and into a waiting car. An article published in the daily *El-Watan* a few days after his abduction reported that Bouabdallah was in police custody and was expected to be released soon.

In July 1997, CPJ received credible information that Bouabdallah was being held in Algiers at the Châteauneuf detention facility, where he had reportedly been tortured. But Bouabdallah's whereabouts are currently unknown, and authorities have denied any knowledge of his abduction.

In late January 2002, Algerian Ambassador to the United States Idriss Jazairy responded to a CPJ query, saying a government investigation had not found those responsible for Bouabdallah's abduction. The ambassador added that there was no evidence of state involvement.

Mohamed Benchicou, *Le Matin*
IMPRISONED: June 14, 2004

Benchicou, publisher of the French-language daily *Le Matin*, was sentenced to two years in prison after being convicted of violating the country's currency laws in 2003. The sentence was widely viewed as retaliation for *Le Matin*'s critical editorial line against the government.

The case was launched in August 2003, after *Le Matin* alleged that Interior Minister Yazid Zerhouni had tortured detainees while he was a military security commander in the 1970s. Benchicou, a frequent government critic, further angered officials in February 2004, when he published a book titled *Bouteflika, An Algerian Fraud*.

Dozens of other cases are pending against Benchicou, including lawsuits alleging that he defamed Bouteflika in articles published in *Le Matin*.

BURMA: 5

ooooo

U Win Tin, Freelance
IMPRISONED: July 4, 1989

U Win Tin, former editor-in-chief of the daily *Hanthawati* and vice chairman of Burma's Writers' Association, was arrested and sentenced to three years of hard labor on the spurious charge of arranging a "forced abortion" for a member of the opposition National League for Democracy (NLD). One of Burma's most well-known and influential journalists, U Win Tin helped establish independent publications during the 1988 student democracy movement. He was also a senior leader of the NLD and a close adviser to opposition leader Daw Aung San Suu Kyi.

In 1992, he was sentenced to an additional 10 years for "writing and publishing pamphlets to incite treason against the state" and "giving seditious talks," according to a May 2000 report by the Defense Ministry's Office of Strategic Studies. On March 28, 1996, prison authorities extended U Win Tin's sentence by another seven years after they convicted him, along with at least 22 others, of producing clandestine publications—including a report describing the horrific conditions at Rangoon's Insein Prison, to the U.N. special rapporteur for human rights in Burma.

U Win Tin was charged under Section 5(e) of the Emergency Provisions Act for having "secretly published antigovernment propaganda to create riots in jail," according to the Defense Ministry report. His cumulative sentence was 20 years of hard labor and imprisonment.

Now 75, the veteran journalist is said to be in extremely poor health after years of maltreatment in Burma's prisons—including a period when he was kept in solitary confinement in one of Insein Prison's notorious "dog cells," formerly used as kennels for the facility's guard dogs. He suffers from a degenerative spine disease, as well as a prostate gland disorder. The journalist has had at least two heart attacks and spent time in the hospital twice in 2002: once following a hernia operation, and again in connection with a heart ailment.

According to a report in *Le Monde*, a Burmese army officer asked U Win Tin to sign a document in early 2003 that would have freed him from prison if he agreed to stop his political work, but the journalist refused.

Burma's ruling military junta has announced several amnesties for political prisoners over the last few years, but U Win Tin has not been among those released. According to the Thailand-based Assistance Association for Political Prisoners in Burma, he remained in prison in 2005.

Maung Maung Lay Ngwe
Pe-Tin-Than
IMPRISONED: September 1990

Maung Maung Lay Ngwe was arrested and charged with writing and distributing publications that "make people lose respect for the government." The publications were titled, collectively, *Pe-Tin-Than* (Echoes). CPJ has not been able to confirm his legal status or find records of his sentencing.

Aung Htun, Freelance
IMPRISONED: February 1998

Aung Htun, a writer and activist with the All Burma Federation of Student Unions, was arrested in February 1998 for writing a seven-volume book documenting the history of the Burmese student movement. He was sentenced to a total of 17 years in prison, according to a joint report published in December 2001 by the Thailand-based Assistance Association for Political Prisoners in Burma and the Burma Lawyers Council. Aung Htun was sentenced to three years for violating the 1962 Printer and Publishers Registration Act, seven years under the 1950 Emergency Provisions Act, and another seven years under the 1908 Unlawful Associations Act. He is jailed at Tharawaddy Prison.

In August 2002, Amnesty International issued an urgent appeal on Aung Htun's behalf saying that the journalist required immediate medical attention. Amnesty reported that Aung Htun "has growths on his feet which require investigation, is unable to walk, and suffers from asthma."

Tha Ban, a former editor at *Kyemon* newspaper who was arrested with Aung Htun, was released from Insein Prison in the capital, Rangoon, on July 12, 2004, after serving more than six years of his seven-year prison sentence. According to the BBC, Tha Ban was released from prison after signing a pledge not to participate in politics.

Thaung Tun (also known as Nyein Thit)
Freelance
IMPRISONED: October 1999

Thaung Tun, an editor, reporter, and poet better known by his pen name, Nyein Thit, and Aung Pwint, a videographer, editor, and poet, were arrested separately in early October 1999. CPJ sources said they were arrested for making independent video documentaries that portrayed life in Burma, including footage of forced labor and hardship in rural areas. Aung Pwint worked at a private media company that produced videos for tourism and educational purposes, but he also worked with Thaung Tun on documentary-style projects. Their videotapes circulated through underground networks.

The two men were tried together, and each was sentenced to eight years in prison, according to CPJ sources. Thaung Tun was jailed at Moulmein Prison, according to the Thailand-based Assistance Association for Political Prisoners in Burma. Aung Pwint was initially jailed at Insein Prison but was later transferred to Tharawaddy Prison, according to CPJ sources.

CPJ honored the two journalists in 2004 with International Press Freedom Awards for their courage and commitment to press freedom. Aung Pwint was released on July 6, 2005, but Thaung Tun remained behind bars.

Ne Min (also known as **Win Shwe**)
Freelance
IMPRISONED: May 7, 2004

Ne Min, a lawyer and former stringer for the BBC, was sentenced to a 15-year prison term by a special court in the infamous Insein Prison in the capital, Rangoon, along with four other former political prisoners who also received lengthy prison sentences, according to the Assistance Association for Political Prisoners in Burma (AAPPB), a prisoner assistance group based in Thailand.

Military intelligence officers arrested the five men in February for allegedly passing information to unlawful organizations outside Burma, according to the AAPPB. The four others were Maung Maung Latt, Paw Lwin, Ye Thiha, and Yan Naing.

In 1989, Ne Min, who is also known as Win Shwe, was charged with "spreading false news and rumors to the BBC to fan further disturbances in the country," and the "possession of documents including antigovernment literature, which he planned to send to the BBC," according to the official Rangoon radio. He was sentenced to 14 years of hard labor by a military tribunal near Insein Prison and served nine years.

Exiled Burmese journalists say it is likely that Ne Min, who is thought to be in his mid-50s, continued to provide news and information to exiled and international news sources after his release from prison in 1998. The media in Burma are strictly controlled and censored, and most Burmese get their news from international radio.

The convictions came just 10 days before the opening of the National Convention, called by Burma's ruling junta to frame a new constitution as part of a so-called seven-step plan to democracy. The National League for Democracy, the main opposition political party, boycotted the convention, and foreign reporters were not issued visas to cover the event. Local journalists said the harsh sentences were meant as a warning and were part of an overall increase in intimidation and pressure on the media in Burma.

CAMBODIA: 1

Mam Sonando, Sombok Khmum
IMPRISONED: October 11, 2005

Police detained Mam Sonando, owner and manager of Sombok Khmum (Beehive Radio), at his home outside the capital, Phnom Penh, after Prime Minister Hun Sen filed criminal defamation charges.

On October 17, Hun Sen filed a second charge against Sonando, accusing him of broadcasting illegal information.

The prime minister cited a September interview with Sean Peng Se, an expert on Cambodia's borders, who questioned Cambodia's border agreement with Vietnam. The prime minister later threatened to prosecute others who criticize his government. "This is no joke," Deutsche Presse Agentur quoted him as saying.

A government spokesman told the U.S. government–funded Voice of America that Sonando was jailed for "professional mistakes" because the report on the border agreement gave only one side of the story. If convicted, Sonando faces up to one year in jail. Cambodia's court of appeal denied bail on November 3, and Sonando was being held in Phnom Penh's crowded Prey Sar Prison. He can be held for up to six months without bail under Cambodian law.

The popular FM station is the only source of independent news broadcasting in Cambodia. It leases airtime to Voice of America and the U.S. government-funded Radio Free Asia. The leases are another source of conflict with the government, which has periodically banned the rebroadcast of foreign-sourced news.

Sonando, a former opposition politician, was arrested in 2003 and spent two weeks in jail on charges of incitement, discrimination, and disseminating false news in connection with anti-Thai riots that swept Phnom Penh early that year. The riots followed comments attributed to popular Thai actress Suwanan Konying that Cambodia's famed Angkor Wat Temple should belong to Thailand. She denied making the comments. CPJ sources who witnessed the riots did not believe that the radio station was a direct cause of the violence.

CHINA: 32

Chen Renjie, *Ziyou Bao*
Lin Youping, *Ziyou Bao*
IMPRISONED: July 1983

In September 1982, Chen, Lin, and Chen Biling wrote and published a pamphlet titled *Ziyou Bao* (Freedom Report), distributing about 300 copies in Fuzhou, Fujian province. They were arrested in July 1983 and accused of making contact with Taiwanese spy groups and publishing a counterrevolutionary pamphlet. According to official government records of the case, the men used "propaganda and incitement to encourage the overthrow of the people's democratic dictatorship and the socialist system." In August 1983, Chen Renjie was sentenced to life in prison, and Lin Youping was sentenced to death with reprieve. Chen Biling was sentenced to death and later executed.

Fan Yingshang, *Remen Huati*
SENTENCED: February 7, 1996

In 1994, Fan and Yang Jianguo printed more than 60,000 copies of the magazine *Remen Huati* (Popular Topics). The men had allegedly purchased fake printing authorizations from an editor of the *Journal of European Research at the Chinese Academy of Social Sciences*, according to official Chinese news sources.

CPJ was unable to determine the date of Fan's arrest, but on February 7, 1996, the Chang'an District Court in Shijiazhuang City sentenced him to 15 years in prison for "engaging in speculation and profiteering." Authorities termed *Remen Huati* a "reactionary" publication. Yang escaped arrest and was not sentenced.

Hua Di, Freelance
IMPRISONED: January 5, 1998

Hua, a permanent resident of the United States, was arrested while visiting China and charged with revealing state secrets. The charge is believed to stem from articles that Hua, a scientist at Stanford University, had written about China's missile defense system.

On November 25, 1999, the Beijing No. 1 Intermediate People's Court held a closed trial and sentenced Hua to 15 years in prison, according to the Hong Kong-based Information Center for Human Rights and Democracy. In March 2000, the Beijing High People's Court overturned Hua's conviction and ordered that the case be retried. This judicial reversal was extraordinary, particularly for a high-profile political case. Nevertheless, in April 2000, the Beijing State Security Bureau rejected a request for Hua to be released on medical parole; he suffers from a rare form of male breast cancer.

On November 23, 2000, after a retrial, the Beijing No. 1 Intermediate People's Court issued a modified verdict, sentencing Hua to 10 years in prison. News of Hua's sentencing broke in February 2001, when a relative gave the information to foreign correspondents based in Beijing. In late 2001, Hua was moved to Tilanqiao Prison in Shanghai, according to CPJ sources.

Gao Qinrong, Xinhua News Agency
IMPRISONED: December 4, 1998

Gao, a reporter for China's state news agency, Xinhua, was jailed for reporting on a corrupt irrigation scheme in drought-plagued Yuncheng, Shanxi province. Xinhua never carried Gao's article, which was finally published on May 27, 1998, in an internal reference edition of the official *People's Daily* that is distributed only among a select group of party leaders. But by fall 1998, the irrigation scandal had become national news, with reports appearing in the Guangzhou-based *Nanfang Zhoumo* (Southern Weekend) and on China Central Television. Gao's wife, Duan Maoying, said that local officials blamed Gao for the flurry of media interest and arranged for his prosecution on false charges.

Gao was arrested on December 4, 1998, and eventually charged with crimes including bribery, embezzlement, and pimping, according to Duan. On April 28, 1999, he was sentenced to 12 years in prison after a closed, one-day trial. He was being held in a prison in Qixian, Shanxi province, according to CPJ sources.

In September 2001, Gao wrote to Mary Robinson, then the United Nations high commissioner for human rights, and asked her to intercede with the Chinese government on his behalf. Gao has received support from several members of the Chinese People's Political Consultative Conference of the National People's Congress, who issued a motion at its annual parliamentary meeting in March 2001 urging the Central Discipline Committee and Supreme People's Court to reopen his case. But by late 2005, there had been no change in his legal status.

Yue Tianxiang
Zhongguo Gongren Guancha
IMPRISONED: January 1999

The Tianshui People's Intermediate Court in Gansu province sentenced Yue to 10 years in prison on July 5, 1999. The journalist was charged with "subverting state power," according to the Hong Kong-based Information Center for Human Rights and Democracy. Yue was arrested along with two colleagues—Wang Fengshan and Guo Xinmin—both of whom were sentenced to two years in prison and have since been released. According to the Hong Kong-based daily *South China Morning Post*, Yue, Guo, and Wang were arrested in January 1999 for publishing *Zhongguo Gongren Guancha* (China Workers Monitor), a journal that campaigned for workers' rights.

With help from Wang, Yue and Guo started the journal after they were unable to get compensation from the Tianshui City Transport Agency following their dismissal from the company in 1995. All three men reportedly belonged to the outlawed China Democracy Party, a dissident group, and were forming an organization to protect the rights of laid-off workers. The first issue of *Zhongguo Gongren Guancha* exposed extensive corruption among officials at the Tianshui City Transport Agency. Only two issues were ever published.

Wu Yilong, *Zaiye Dang*
IMPRISONED: April 26, 1999

Mao Qingxiang, *Zaiye Dang*
IMPRISONED: June 1999

Zhu Yufu, *Zaiye Dang*
IMPRISONED: September 1999

Wu, an organizer for the banned China Democracy Party (CDP), was detained by police in Guangzhou on April 26, 1999. In June, near the 10th anniversary of the brutal crackdown on pro-democracy demonstrations in Tiananmen Square, authorities detained CDP activist Mao. Zhu and Xu Guang, also leading CDP activists, were detained in September. The four were later charged with subversion for, among other things, establishing a magazine called *Zaiye Dang* (Opposition Party) and circulating pro-democracy writings online.

On October 25, 1999, the Hangzhou Intermediate People's Court in Zhejiang province conducted what *The New York Times* described as a "sham trial." On November 9, 1999, all of the journalists were convicted of subversion. Wu was sentenced to 11 years in prison. Mao was sentenced to eight years, and Zhu to seven years. Their political rights were suspended for three years each upon release. Xu was sentenced to five years in prison, with a two-year suspension of political rights.

In December 2002, Mao was transferred to a convalescence hospital after his health had sharply declined as a result of being confined to his cell. Zhu, who has also been confined to his cell and forbidden from reading newspapers, was placed under tightened restrictions in 2002 after refusing to express regret for his actions, according to the New York-based advocacy group Human Rights in China. Xu was released from Zhejiang's Qiaosi Prison in September 2004.

Xu Zerong, Freelance
IMPRISONED: June 24, 2000

Xu was arrested in the city of Guangzhou and held incommunicado for 19 months before being tried by the Shenzhen Intermediate Court in January 2002. He was sentenced to 10 years in prison on charges of "leaking state secrets," and to an additional three years on charges of committing "economic crimes."

Xu, an associate research professor at the Institute of Southeast Asian Studies at Zhongshan University in Guangzhou, has written several freelance articles about China's foreign policy and co-founded a Hong Kong-based academic journal *Zhongguo Shehui Kexue Jikan* (China Social Sciences Quarterly). Xu is a permanent resident of Hong Kong.

Chinese officials have said that the "state secrets" charges against Xu stem from his use of historical materials for his academic research. In 1992, Xu photocopied four books published in the 1950s about China's role in the Korean War, which he then sent to a colleague in South Korea, according to a letter from the Chinese government to St. Antony's College, Oxford University. (Xu earned his Ph.D. at St. Antony's College, and since his arrest, college personnel have actively researched and protested his case.) The Security Committee of the People's Liberation Army in Guangzhou later determined that these documents should be labeled "top secret."

The "economic crimes" charges are related to the "illegal publication" of more than 60,000 copies of 25 books and periodicals since 1993, including several books about Chinese politics and Beijing's relations with Taiwan, according to official government documents.

Some observers believe that the charges against Xu are more likely related to an article he wrote for the Hong Kong-based *Yazhou Zhoukan* (Asia Weekly) news magazine revealing clandestine Chinese Communist Party support for Malaysian communist insurgency groups in the 1950s and 1960s. Xu was arrested only days before the article appeared in the June 26, 2000, issue. In the article, Xu accused the Chinese Communist Party of hypocrisy for condemning the United States and other countries for interfering in China's internal affairs by criticizing its human rights record. "China's support of world revolution is based on the concept of 'class above sovereignty'...which is equivalent to the idea of 'human rights above sovereignty,' which the U.S. promotes today," Xu wrote.

An appeal by Xu's family was rejected.

Jiang Weiping, Freelance
IMPRISONED: December 4, 2000

Jiang, a freelance journalist, was arrested after he published a number of articles in the Hong Kong-based magazine *Qianshao* (Frontline), a Chinese-language monthly focusing on mainland affairs. The stories exposed corruption scandals in northeastern China.

Jiang wrote the *Qianshao* articles, which were published between June and September 1999, under various pen names. His coverage exposed several major corruption scandals involving high-level officials. Notably, Jiang reported that Shenyang Vice Mayor Ma Xiangdong had lost nearly 30 million yuan (US$3.6 million) in public funds gambling in Macau casinos. Jiang also revealed that Chinese Trade Minister Bo Xilai had covered up corruption among his friends and family during his years as Dalian mayor.

Soon after these cases were publicized in *Qianshao* and other Hong Kong media, central authorities detained Ma. He was accused of taking bribes, embezzling public funds, and gambling overseas and was executed for these crimes in December 2001. After Ma's arrest, his case was widely reported in the domestic press and used as an example in the government's ongoing fight against corruption. However, in May 2001, Jiang was indicted for "revealing state secrets."

The Dalian Intermediate Court held a secret trial in September 2001. On January 25, 2002, the court formally sentenced Jiang to eight years in prison on charges including "inciting to subvert state power" and "illegally providing state secrets overseas." This judgment amended an earlier decision to sentence Jiang to nine years. During the January sentencing, Jiang proclaimed his innocence and told the court that the verdict "trampled on the law," according to CPJ sources. Jiang immediately appealed his sentence to the Liaoning Province Higher People's Court. On December 26, 2002, the court heard the appeal and, while upholding Jiang's guilty verdict, reduced his sentence to six years, according to the California-based Dui Hua Foundation, which has been in direct contact with the Chinese government about the case. A court official told The Associated Press that, "We just thought that his criminal records were not as serious as previously concluded."

According to CPJ sources, Jiang has a serious stomach disorder and has been denied medical treatment. Held in a crowded cell in unsanitary conditions early in his prison term, he also contracted a skin disease. His wife, Li Yanling, was repeatedly interrogated and threatened following her husband's arrest. In March 2002, the local public security bureau brought her in for questioning and detained her for several weeks.

An experienced journalist, Jiang had worked until May 2000 as the northeastern China bureau chief for the Hong Kong-based newspaper *Wen Hui Bao*. He contributed freelance articles to *Qianshao*. In the 1980s, he worked as a Dalian-based correspondent for Xinhua, China's official news agency.

In November 2001, CPJ honored Jiang with its annual International Press Freedom Award. In February 2002, CPJ sent appeals to Chinese President Jiang Zemin from almost 600 supporters—including CBS news anchor Dan Rather, civil rights leader Jesse Jackson, and former U.S. Ambassador to China Winston Lord—demanding Jiang's unconditional release. That month, U.S. President George W. Bush highlighted Jiang's case in meetings with Jiang Zemin during a state visit to China.

In May 2005, CPJ learned about a deterioration in the health care and prison conditions provided to Jiang. Prison authorities had barred Jiang from making phone calls for a period of months and denied him permission to read books, according to CPJ sources. The reasons for the severe measures were not disclosed. Relatives who visited Jiang at the end of April reported a visible deterioration in his health.

Yang Zili, *Yangzi de Sixiang Jiayuan*
Xu Wei, *Xiaofei Ribao*
Jin Haike, Freelance
Zhang Honghai, Freelance
IMPRISONED: March 13, 2001

Yang, Xu, Jin, and Zhang were detained on March 13 and charged with subversion on April 20. On May 29, 2003, the Beijing Intermediate Court sentenced Xu and Jin to 10 years in prison each on subversion charges, while Yang and Zhang were sentenced to eight years each on similar charges.

The four were active participants in the Xin Qingnian Xuehui (New Youth Study Group), an informal gathering of individuals who explored topics related to political and social reform and used the Internet to circulate relevant articles.

Yang, the group's most prominent member, published a Web site, *Yangzi de Sixiang Jiayuan* (Yangzi's Garden of Ideas), which featured poems, essays, and reports by various authors on subjects such as the shortcomings of rural elections. Authorities closed the site after Yang's arrest.

When Xu, a reporter with *Xiaofei Ribao* (Consumer Daily), was detained on March 13, 2001, authorities confiscated his computer, other professional equipment, and books, according to an account published online by his girlfriend, Wang Ying. Wang reported that public security officials also ordered *Xiaofei Ribao* to fire Xu. The newspaper has refused to discuss his case with reporters, according to The Associated Press.

The Beijing No. 1 Intermediate People's Court tried all four on September 28, 2001. Prosecutors focused predominantly on the group's writings, including two essays circulated on the Internet called "Be a New Citizen, Reform China" and "What's to Be Done?" According to the indictment papers, these articles demonstrated the group's intention "to overthrow the Chinese Communist Party's leadership and the socialist system and subvert the regime of the people's democratic dictatorship." In November 2003, the Beijing Supreme People's Court rejected an appeal filed by a lawyer for Yang, Xu, Jin, and Zhang. In the appeal, the defense noted that three key witnesses who testified for the prosecution against the four men have since retracted their original testimony.

Tao Haidong, Freelance
IMPRISONED: July 9, 2002

Tao, an Internet essayist and pro-democracy activist, was arrested in Urumqi, the capital of the Xinjiang Uighur Autonomous Region (XUAR), and charged with "incitement to subvert state power." According to the Minzhu Luntan (Democracy Forum) Web site, which had published Tao's recent writing, his articles focused on political and legal reform. In one essay, titled "Strategies for China's Social Reforms," Tao wrote that "the Chinese Communist Party and democracy activists throughout society should unite to push forward China's freedom and democratic development or else stand condemned through the ages."

Previously, in 1999, Tao was sentenced to three years of "re-education through labor" in Xi'an, Shaanxi province, according to the New York-based advocacy group Human Rights in China, because of his essays and work on a book titled *Xin Renlei Shexiang* (Imaginings of a New Human Race). After his early release in 2001, Tao began writing essays and articles and publishing them on various domestic and overseas Web sites.

In early January 2003, the Urumqi Intermediate Court sentenced Tao to seven years in prison. His appeal to the XUAR Higher Court later in 2003 was rejected.

Zhang Wei
Shishi Zixun and *Redian Jiyao*
IMPRISONED: July 19, 2002

Zhang was arrested and charged with illegal publishing after producing and selling two underground newspapers in Chongqing, in central China. According to an account published on the Web site of the Chongqing Press and Publishing Administration, a provincial government body that governs all local publications, beginning in April 2001, Zhang edited two newspapers, *Shishi Zixun* (Current Events) and *Redian Jiyao* (Summary of the Main Points), which included articles and graphics he had downloaded from the Internet.

Two of Zhang's business associates, Zuo Shangwen and Ou Yan, were also arrested on July 19, 2002, and indicted for their involvement with the publications. Zuo printed the publications in neighboring Sichuan province, while Ou managed the publications' finances. At the time of their arrests, police confiscated 9,700 copies of *Shishi Zixun*.

The official account of their arrests stated that the two publications had "flooded" Chongqing's publishing market. The government declared that "the political rumors, shocking 'military reports,' and other articles in these illegal publications misled the public, poisoned the youth, negatively influenced society, and sparked public indignation." Zhang, Zuo, and Ou printed more than 1.5 million copies of the publications and sold them in Chongqing, Chengdu, and other cities.

On December 25, 2002, the Yuzhong District Court in Chongqing sentenced Zhang to six years in prison and fined him 100,000 yuan (US$12,000), the amount that police said he had earned in profits from the publications. Zuo was sentenced to five years and fined 50,000 yuan (US$6,000), while Ou was sentenced to two years in prison.

Abdulghani Memetemin
East Turkistan Information Center
IMPRISONED: July 26, 2002

Memetemin, a writer, teacher, and translator who had actively advocated for the Uighur ethnic group in the northwestern Xinjiang Uighur Autonomous Region, was detained in Kashgar, a city in Xinjiang, on charges of "leaking state secrets."

In June 2003, Kashgar Intermediate People's Court sentenced him to nine years in prison, plus a three-year suspension of political rights. Radio Free Asia provided CPJ with court documents listing 18 specific counts against Memetemin, including translating state news articles into Chinese from Uighur; forwarding official speeches to the Germany-based East Turkistan Information Center (ETIC), a news outlet that advocates for an independent state for the Uighur ethnic group; and conducting original reporting for the center. The court also accused him of recruiting additional reporters for ETIC, which is banned in China.

Memetemin did not have legal representation at his trial and has not been in contact with his wife or children since his arrest. His harsh punishment reflected the intense suppression of information in Xinjiang.

Cai Lujun, Freelance
IMPRISONED: February 21, 2003

Cai was arrested at his home in Shijiazhuang, Hebei province. In October 2003, the Shijiazhuang Intermediate People's Court sentenced him to three years in prison on subversion charges.

Cai, 35, had used pen names to write numerous essays distributed online calling for political reforms. His articles included "Political Democracy Is the Means; A Powerful Country and Prosperous Citizenry Is the Goal"; "An Outline for Building and Governing the Country"; and "The Course of Chinese Democracy."

Following the November 2002 arrest of Internet essayist Liu Di, Cai Lujun began to publish online essays under his own name calling for Liu's release and expressing his political views. Liu was released on November 28, 2003.

Luo Changfu, Freelance
IMPRISONED: March 13, 2003

Public security officials arrested Luo at his home in Chongqing municipality and charged him with "subversion." On November 6, 2003, the Chongqing No. 1 Intermediate Court sentenced him to three years in prison.

Luo, 40, is an unemployed factory worker. Before his arrest, he had actively campaigned for the release of Internet essayist Liu Di, who was arrested in November 2002 and released on bail a year later. Luo had written a series of articles calling for Liu's release and protesting the Chinese government's censorship of online speech. His essays also called for political reforms in China.

In the 1980s, Luo was sent to a re-education-through-labor camp for three years for his dissident activities, according to the New York-based organization Human Rights in China.

Luo Yongzhong, Freelance
IMPRISONED: June 14, 2003

Luo, who has written numerous articles that have been distributed online, was detained in Changchun, Jilin province. On July 7, he was formally arrested. On October 14, the Changchun Intermediate Court sentenced him to three years in prison and two years without political rights upon his release, which is scheduled for June 13, 2006.

In sentencing papers, which have been widely distributed online, the court stated that between May and June 2003, Luo wrote several essays that "attacked the socialist system, incited to subvert state power, and created a negative influence on society."

Several specific articles were cited as evidence, including "At Last We See the Danger of the Three Represents!"—a reference to a political theory formulated by former President Jiang Zemin—and "Tell Today's Youth the Truth about June 4," a reference to the military crackdown on peaceful pro-democracy protesters in June 1989. According to the court papers, the articles were published on online forums including *Shuijing Luntan* (Crystal) Web site.

Luo has also written a number of articles advocating the rights of people with disabilities.

Huang Jinqiu, *Boxun News*
IMPRISONED: September 13, 2003

Huang, a columnist for the U.S. -based dissident news Web site *Boxun News*, was arrested in Jiangsu province. Huang's family was not officially notified of his arrest until January 2004. The Changzhou Intermediate People's Court sentenced him on September 27, 2004, to 12 years in prison on charges of "subversion of state power," plus four years' deprivation of political rights.

Huang worked as a writer and editor in his native Shandong province, as well as in Guangdong province, before leaving China in 2000 to study journalism at the Central Academy of Art in Malaysia. While he was overseas, Huang began writing political commentary for *Boxun News* under the pen name "Qing Shuijun." He also wrote articles on arts and entertainment under the name "Huang Jin." Huang's writings reportedly caught the attention of the government in 2001. Huang told a friend that authorities had contacted his family to warn them about his writing, according to *Boxun News*.

In January 2003, Huang wrote in his online column that he intended to form a new opposition party, the China Patriot Democracy Party. When he returned to China in August 2003, he eluded public security agents just long enough to visit his family in Shandong province. In the last article he posted on *Boxun News*, titled "Me and My Public Security Friends," Huang described being followed and harassed by security agents.

Huang's appeal was rejected in December 2004. Huang's lawyer told CPJ in early 2005 that the journalist had been mistreated in prison and was in poor health.

Kong Youping, Freelance
IMPRISONED: December 13, 2003

Kong, an essayist and poet, was arrested in Anshan, Liaoning province. He had written articles online that supported democratic reforms and called for a reversal of the government's "counterrevolutionary" ruling on the pro-democracy demonstrations of 1989, according to the Hong Kong-based Information Center for Human Rights and Democracy.

Kong's essays included an appeal to democracy activists in China that stated, "In order to work well for democracy, we need a well-organized, strong, powerful, and effective organization. Otherwise, a mainland democracy movement will accomplish nothing." Several of his articles and poems were posted on the *Minzhu Luntan* (Democracy Forum) Web site.

In 1998, Kong served time in prison after he became a member of the Liaoning province branch of the China Democracy Party, an opposition party. On September 16, 2004, the Shenyang Intermediate People's Court sentenced Kong to 15 years in prison.

Yu Huafeng, *Nanfang Dushi Bao*
Li Minying, *Nanfang Dushi Bao*
IMPRISONED: January 2004

The Dongshan District Court in Guangzhou, Guangdong province, sentenced Yu, *Nanfang Dushi Bao* deputy editor-in-chief and general manager, to 12 years in prison on corruption charges. Li, former editor of *Nanfang Dushi Bao*, was sentenced to 11 years for bribery in a related case. Li also served on the Communist Party Committee of the Nanfang Daily Group, the newspaper's parent company. In an appellate trial held on June 7, 2004, Li's sentence was reduced to six years in prison, while Yu's sentence was reduced to eight years.

Nanfang Dushi Bao (Southern Metropolis News) became popular for its aggressive investigative reporting on social issues and wrongdoing by local officials. The paper broke news that a young graphic designer, Sun Zhigang, was beaten to death in March 2003 while being held in police custody in Guangzhou. Public outcry over Sun's death led to the arrest of several local government and police officials.

On December 26, 2003, *Nanfang Dushi Bao* reported a suspected SARS case in Guangzhou, the first new case in China since the epidemic died out in July 2003. The government had not yet publicly released information about the case when the newspaper's report was published. Editors and reporters who worked on the SARS story were reprimanded. Yu was detained on January 14, 2004, according to a report in the official English-language *China Daily*.

According to a March 19 report in the official Xinhua News Agency, Yu was convicted of embezzling 580,000 yuan (US$70,000) and distributing the money to members of the paper's editorial committee. The court also accused Yu of paying Li a total of 800,000 yuan

(US$97,000) in bribes while Li was editor of *Nanfang Dushi Bao*. Li was accused of accepting bribes totaling 970,000 yuan (US$117,000).

Both men maintain that the money was acquired legally and was distributed in routine bonus payments to the staff. Chinese journalists familiar with the case have told CPJ that evidence presented in court did not support the corruption charges.

In recent years, government authorities have made moves to consolidate control over the Nanfang Daily Group, which owns a number of China's most independent and popular newspapers, including *Nanfang Zhoumo* (Southern Weekend) and *Ershiyi Shiji Jingji Baodao* (21st Century Economic Herald). In March 2003, *Ershiyi Shiji Huanqiu Baodao* (21st Century World Herald), also owned by the Nanfang Daily Group, was closed after it ran a series of sensitive stories, including an interview with a former secretary of Mao Zedong who called for political reforms.

In June 2005, more than 2,000 journalists in China signed an open letter to the Guangdong High People's Court appealing for the release of Yu and Li.

Zhao Yan, *The New York Times*
IMPRISONED: September 17, 2004

Zhao, a news assistant at *The New York Times* Beijing bureau and a former reporter for Beijing-based *Zhongguo Gaige* magazine, was detained in Shanghai.

On September 21, 2004, Zhao's family received a notice from the Beijing State Security Bureau accusing Zhao of "providing state secrets to foreigners," according to international news reports. Prosecutors issued a formal arrest warrant for Zhao on October 20, 2004, but they did not specify the alleged actions leading to his arrest. That month, then–U.S. Secretary of State Colin Powell expressed concern about Zhao's case to Foreign Minister Li Zhaoxing. Li responded that it was an internal matter.

The detention followed an article in *The New York Times* revealing Jiang Zemin's plan to retire from the position of chairman of the Central Military Commission. The September 7 article preceded the official announcement of the final transfer of leadership to Hu Jintao on September 19 and cited unnamed sources with ties to leadership.

Zhao's associates speculated that the journalist came under investigation because of the leak. *The New York Times* said that Zhao—who worked as a researcher for *The Times* and not as a reporter—did not provide any state secrets to the newspaper and was not involved in the September 7 story. A confidential state security report obtained by *The Times* said that a high-level inquiry targeting Zhao was initiated after the September 7 article appeared.

Before joining *The Times*, Zhao was a well-known investigative journalist who reported on farmers' rights issues for the Beijing-based *Zhongguo Gaige* (China Reform) magazine. He had been the frequent target of local police harassment and interrogation for his stories, which included reporting on a local official's alleged misappropriation of compensation for thousands of people displaced by the Taolinkou reservoir in Hebei province. Zhao has also worked as an activist for farmers' rights.

In April 2005, police informed Zhao's lawyer Mo Shaoping that a new accusation of fraud had been leveled against the journalist, allowing authorities to set back the clock on the legal investigation period for Zhao's case and to continue detaining him without trial. Authorities deprived Zhao of any contact with a lawyer for roughly nine months after his detention.

In December, Zhao was indicted on a charge of leaking state secrets, which could result in a prison term of 10 years or more. He was also indicted on a lesser count of fraud. Zhao's lawyers were not given immediate access to the indictment, and authorities did not disclose any supporting details for the charges. Zhao was expected to stand trial in early 2006.

Shi Tao, Freelance
IMPRISONED: November 24, 2004

Officials from the Changsha security bureau detained Shi near his home in Taiyuan, Shanxi province, on November 24, 2004, several months after he e-mailed notes detailing the Propaganda Department's instructions to the media about coverage of the anniversary of the crackdown at Tiananmen Square. Authorities confiscated his computer and other documents and warned his family to stay quiet about the matter.

On December 14, authorities issued a formal arrest order, charging Shi with "leaking state secrets." On April 27, 2005, the Changsha Intermediate People's Court found Shi guilty and sentenced him to a 10-year prison term.

The state-run Xinhua News Agency reported that Shi had been found guilty of posting online his notes about a government document that was read to his publication's editorial staff in April 2004. Xinhua said that his report had been picked up by several overseas Web sites, and that the National Administration for the Protection of State Secrets later certified the contents as state secrets.

Shi is the former editorial director of *Dangdai Shang Bao*, a newspaper based in Changsha, Hunan province. On April 20, 2004, he e-mailed to a U.S.-based online editor, Cary Hung, his notes from the propaganda ministry's instructions to the newspaper regarding the return of overseas dissidents to China to mark the 15th anniversary last year of the military crackdown on pro-democracy demonstrators at Tiananmen Square.

Hung is editor of the New York-based *Minzhu Luntan* (Democracy Forum), a dissident news Web site that is banned in China, and *Minzhu Tongxun* (Democracy Communication), an e-mail-based information network. Shi's notes were distributed through *Minzhu Tongxun* and later posted on other Web sites.

Shortly before Shi's trial, Guo Guoting, who was originally set to act as Shi's defense lawyer, received notice that his license to practice law had been suspended. Guo told CPJ at the time that he believed the punitive action was related to the lawyer's defense of controversial freedom of expression cases like Shi's.

Guo's replacement, defense lawyer Tong Wenzhong, was never granted access to the contents of the "state secrets" that Shi was accused of leaking, said Shi Hua, the journalist's brother. Tong was told only the title of the material, and its government designation as "secret." Nevertheless, Tong entered a guilty plea on Shi's behalf on March 11.

Shi changed his plea to not guilty in a written appeal submitted to the Hunan Province High People's Court. On June 2, the court rejected Shi's appeal without giving the journalist a hearing.

Shi's mother, Gao Qinsheng, has alleged "serious procedural defects" in the proceeding, the human rights group Human Rights in China reported. Gao filed a request for review with the Hunan Province High People's Court on August 21, sources confirmed to CPJ. Shi's current lawyer, Mo Shaoping, filed a brief in support of the request.

Mo's brief argues that the court did not hear arguments in Shi's defense, nor did it respond, as required by law, to the evidence that was presented. The appeal hearing was not open to the public, which is in violation of the criminal procedure law, the brief said.

Shi's verdict, which was leaked to the public, revealed that the U.S.-based Internet company Yahoo had given Chinese authorities information about Shi's e-mail account that was used to convict him.

In November 2005, CPJ honored Shi with its annual International Press Freedom Award.

Zheng Yichun, Freelance
IMPRISONED: December 3, 2004

Zheng, a former professor, was a regular contributor to overseas online news sites including *Dajiyuan* (Epoch Times). He wrote critically about the Communist Party and its control of the media. He was imprisoned in Yingkou, in Liaoning province.

Yingkou Ribao reported on February 24, 2005, that authorities had officially arrested Zheng on suspicion of inciting subversion. Zheng's family was warned not to publicize his arrest, and they remained silent until state media reported it.

Zheng was initially tried by Yingkou Intermediate People's Court on April 26, 2005. No verdict was announced. On July 21, he was tried again on the same charges. As in the April 26 trial, proceedings lasted just three hours. Though officially "open" to the public, the courtroom was closed to all observers except close family members and government officials. Zheng's supporters and a journalist were prevented from entering, according to a local source.

Prosecutors cited dozens of articles written by the journalist, and listed the titles of several essays in which he called for political reform, increased capitalism in China, and an end to the practice of imprisoning writers.

On September 20, the court sentenced Zheng to seven years in prison, to be followed by three years' deprivation of political rights.

Sources familiar with the case believe that Zheng's harsh sentence may be linked to Chinese leaders' objections to the *Dajiyuan* series "Nine Commentaries on the Communist Party," a widely read and controversial look at Chinese Communist Party history and current practices.

Zheng is diabetic, and has not received adequate treatment in prison, according to his brother.

Zhang Lin, Freelance
IMPRISONED: January 29, 2005

Zhang, a political essayist who wrote regularly for overseas online news sites, was detained on his return to Bengbu in central China's Anhui province after traveling to Beijing to mourn the death of Zhao Ziyang, the ousted general secretary of the Communist Party.

Scheduled for release after 15 days of administrative detention, Zhang was instead put in "criminal detention" on suspicion of "endangering state security." The allegations were linked to essays by Zhang that were critical of the Communist Party and called for political reform and democracy in China. On March 19, 2005, Zhang's wife, Fang Caofang, received notice that he had been formally arrested on allegations of inciting subversion.

The indictment against him, filed on May 23, accused Zhang of using the Internet and overseas radio transmissions "to openly disseminate language that misrepresents and denigrates the national authorities and the socialist system, and which incites subversion of state power and the overthrow of the socialist system under Article 105 of China's criminal law," according to a translation by the New York-based group Human Rights in China.

On June 21, Zhang pleaded not guilty to the charges filed against him. His trial at the Intermediate People's Court of Bengbu in central China's Anhui province concluded within five hours, defense lawyer Mo Shaoping told CPJ.

The defense argued that the six articles and one interview cited by the prosecution were protected free expression. Zhang's wife believes that his imprisonment is also connected to essays he wrote about protests by unemployed workers and official scandals, according to Agence France-Presse.

On July 28, the court convicted Zhang and sentenced him to five years in prison. Zhang's appeals were rejected twice. He was detained at Bengbu No. 1 Detention Center.

Zhang began a hunger strike on September 1, was hospitalized briefly, and returned to the detention center, according to local sources. He waged the hunger strike for 28 days to protest his unjust sentence and the harsh conditions of his detention center.

Prison officials subjected him to long hours of forced labor and refused to allow him to read newspapers or other material, according to his lawyer. Zhang was forced to make Christmas ornaments before the hunger strike made him too weak to work, according to a CPJ source.

Ching Cheong, *The Straits Times*
IMPRISONED: April 22, 2005

Ching, a veteran Hong Kong reporter who was the China correspondent for the Singapore daily *The Straits Times*, has been held without access to a lawyer since April 22. His wife, Mary Lau, said that Ching was detained in Guangzhou while attempting to obtain a transcript of interviews of the ousted leader Zhao Ziyang. Zhao died after spending 15 years under house arrest for opposing the military crackdown at Tiananmen Square in 1989.

In May, after learning privately from a mainland government official that her husband would be charged with "stealing core state secrets," Lau decided to go public with the news of her husband's detention, according to *The Washington Post*. Though Lau and *The Straits Times* had known since April that Ching was detained, they were warned by authorities not to report the detention, and stayed silent in an effort to obtain his release through diplomatic means, *The Post* reported.

A week later, the Chinese Foreign Ministry responded to news reports about the journalist's imprisonment by stating that Ching had admitted his involvement in espionage. Authorities did not provide evidence for the accusation, and Ching's employers and family were unable to contact him directly to seek his version of events, or to provide him with legal counsel. Ching was held under house arrest in Beijing.

Foreign Ministry spokesman Kong Quan denied that Ching's detention was related to his efforts to gain access to the interviews conducted by Zong. "I can tell you plainly that Ching's case is not connected to Zhao Ziyang at all... The key thing is that Ching himself admitted to his illegal activities," said Kong, according to Reuters.

On August 5, Xinhua News Agency reported that Ching had been formally arrested on suspicion of spying for Taiwan. The report said that Ching was accused of collecting millions of Hong Kong dollars between early 2000 and March 2005 for the purpose of "setting up channels of espionage in Hong Kong and the island" on the instructions of Taiwan's National Security Bureau. Authorities allege that Ching used the name Chen Yuanchun to buy information on "China's political, economic, and especially military affairs," including some classified as "top secret," and passed it on to Taiwanese intelligence, harming national security.

If charged and convicted for this crime, Ching could receive the death penalty under Chinese law.

Ching has been a reporter for the Singapore daily since 1996. He was formerly a reporter for *Wen Wei Po*, a Hong Kong newspaper with links to the Communist Party. In 1989, he resigned in protest of the government's military crackdown at Tiananmen Square. Ching holds a British overseas national passport and is a legal resident of Singapore.

Li Jianping, Freelance
IMPRISONED: May 27, 2005

Authorities detained Li on May 27 in Zibo, a city in northeastern China's Shandong province, and formally arrested him for defamation on June 30, according to *ChinaEForum*, a U.S.-based dissident news forum.

Local police had summoned the journalist to the police station days before detaining him, Li's wife told the editors of *ChinaEForum*. She also said that government-employed Internet-control personnel had searched his computer.

Li wrote frequently for overseas news Web sites banned in China, such as *Boxun News*, *Epoch Times*, *China Democracy* and *ChinaEWeekly*. Some of his articles directly criticized Chinese Communist Party leadership, including former and current Chinese presidents Jiang Zemin and Hu Jintao. Just days before his detention, Li wrote a strongly critical analysis of Hu Jintao's policy toward Taiwan, posted on *ChinaEWeekly* on May 17. It was unclear which of his articles led to his detention.

In August, Li was formally indicted on charges of inciting subversion, a charge that usually results in a prison term of several years.

Yang Maodong (also known as **Guo Feixiong**), Freelance
IMPRISONED: September 12, 2005

Freelance writer Yang Maodong, commonly known by his pen name Guo Feixiong, was detained in mid-September after reporting on attempts by villagers in Taishi village, Guangdong province, to oust a village chief. Guo was formally arrested on October 4 by the Panyu District Public Security bureau in Guangzhou after being accused of "sending news overseas" and "gathering crowds to disturb public order."

Guo, a prolific writer, also worked as a legal analyst for the Beijing-based Shengzhi law firm. He had been advocating for villagers in Taishi attempting to stage a recall campaign of their village chief, whom they accused of corruption. The protests grew into a national crisis when mobs that appeared to be employed by the local government beat foreign journalists and Chinese activists and threatened local villagers. Guo was detained a day after 1,000 riot police stormed the government office to remove local villagers who had been protesting there.

Guo gave information on Taishi to foreign journalists, and he wrote detailed reports on the situation through the online *Yannan* bulletin board. The site was later shut down by the government for its coverage.

Guo was held at the Panyu District Detention Center and went on a hunger strike after being detained.

A Panyu city government spokesman, quoted in the official English-language newspaper *China Daily*, said Guo "called upon the villagers to appeal and stage hunger strikes...kept himself updated on the 'latest developments' in Taishi village, and then tried all means to exploit foreign media and Web sites to spread distorted reports and rumors." The official also accused Guo of illegally collecting money from the villagers.

Guo was freed on December 27, and prosecutors told him he would not be indicted, according to international news reports. Officials did not explain the decision to release him without charge, a step that was considered highly unusual. Guo was quoted by Reuters as saying, "The pressure from public opinion was too great. They can't shut the door on the world and ignore public opinion anymore." Guo added that the allegations against him were baseless. About the same time, authorities also released several villagers who had been held in connection with the protests, according to press reports.

CUBA: 24

oooooooooooooooooooooooo

Alejandro González Raga, Freelance
IMPRISONED: March 18, 2003

González Raga, an independent freelance journalist based in central Camagüey province, was tried and convicted under Article 91 of the penal code, which imposes lengthy prison sentences or death for those who act against "the independence or the territorial integrity of the state." In April 2003, he was sentenced to a 14-year prison term, which he is serving in Canaleta prison in central Ciego de Ávila province.

Alfredo Pulido López, El Mayor
IMPRISONED: March 18, 2003

Pulido López, director of the independent news agency El Mayor in central Camagüey province, was tried under Article 91 of the penal code, which imposes lengthy prison sentences or death for those who act against "the independence or the territorial integrity of the state." In April 2003, he was sentenced to 14 years in prison and taken to the Combinado del Este prison in Havana, hundreds of miles from his home. In August 2004, he was transferred to Kilo 7 Prison, in his native Camagüey province.

The journalist's wife, Rebeca Rodríguez Souto, told CPJ that he looked pale and very thin during her visits in 2005. He has suffered from severe headaches, neck pain, respiratory problems, high blood pressure, and other medical problems, she said.

Iván Hernández Carrillo, Patria
IMPRISONED: March 18, 2003

Hernández Carrillo, a journalist with the independent news agency Patria in western Matanzas province, was tried under Law 88 for the Protection of Cuba's National Independence and Economy, which imposes up to 20 years in prison for committing acts "aimed at subverting the internal order of the nation and destroying its political, economic, and social system." In April 2003, he was sentenced to 25 years in prison, which he is serving at Cuba Sí Prison in eastern Holguín province, hundreds of miles from his home.

Hernández Carrillo was originally placed in the Holguín Provincial Prison. In 2003, prison officials placed Hernández Carrillo in a punishment cell after he complained of illness. He waged two hunger strikes, in 2003 and 2004, to protest inadequate food and medicine and to call attention to threats made against him by other prisoners and prison officials. He was transferred to Cuba Sí Prison in August 2004.

José Gabriel Ramón Castillo
Instituto Cultura y Democracia Press
IMPRISONED: March 18, 2003

Ramón Castillo, director of the independent news agency Instituto Cultura y Democracia Press, was tried under Article 91 of the penal code, which imposes lengthy prison sentences or death for those who act against "the independence or the territorial integrity of the state." In April 2003, he was sentenced to a 20-year prison term and was sent to Villa Clara Provincial Prison in central Cuba, hundreds of miles from his home.

In July 2004, prison officials searched Ramón Castillo's cell and confiscated his notes, a diary, and letters, according to the Miami-based *CubaNet* Web site.

Ramón Castillo suffers from a heart condition, liver problems, and high blood pressure, according to his brother, Jorge Ramón Castillo. With his health deteriorating, Ramón Castillo was transferred to the Carlos J. Finlay military hospital in Havana in November 2004. In February 2005, Ramón Castillo was transferred to Boniato Prison in his native Santiago de Cuba province, in eastern Cuba. There, he shared a cell with two common criminals.

In 2005, his brother said, Ramón Castillo began suffering from a sleep disorder and severe anxiety. A Catholic, Ramón Castillo has not had access to a priest or other religious guidance.

José Luis García Paneque, Libertad
IMPRISONED: March 18, 2003

García Paneque, director of the independent news agency Libertad in eastern Las Tunas province, was tried under Article 91 of the penal code, which imposes lengthy prison sentences or death for those who act against "the independence or the territorial integrity of the state." In April 2003, he was sentenced to 24 years in prison, which he is now serving at Las Mangas Prison in eastern Granma province.

Originally placed at Guamajal Prison in central Villa Clara province, he was transferred a number of times before being taken to the Combinado del Este Prison in Havana for a medical checkup. His wife, Yamilé Llanes, said he had been suffering from diarrhea for a full year and had lost at least 30 pounds before getting treatment. He was finally diagnosed with an intestinal ailment.

In June 2005, Llanes told CPJ that her husband was suffering from malnutrition, his weight having dropped from 190 pounds to about 120 pounds. She said his blood pressure was very low, and he was still having bouts of diarrhea. Llanes said he was not getting the high-protein diet he needed.

Julio César Gálvez Rodríguez
Freelance
IMPRISONED: March 18, 2003

Gálvez Rodríguez, a Havana-based independent freelance journalist, was tried under Law 88 for the Protection of Cuba's National Independence and Economy, which imposes up to 20 years in prison for committing acts "aimed at subverting the internal order of the nation and destroying its political, economic, and social system." In April 2003, he was sentenced to 15 years in prison. He was being held at Combinado del Este Prison in Havana.

Gálvez Rodríguez suffers from several ailments, including high blood pressure, liver problems, high cholesterol, and urinary problems. These illnesses have either arisen or worsened during his imprisonment, according to his wife, Beatriz del Carmen Pedroso. From February 26 to July 9, 2004, Gálvez was hospitalized and underwent gallbladder surgery. Pedroso has told CPJ she was very worried about her husband's health, including his increased anxiety.

Léster Luis González Pentón

Freelance

IMPRISONED: March 18, 2003

González Pentón, an independent journalist based in central Villa Clara province, was tried under Article 91 of the penal code, which imposes lengthy prison sentences or death for those who act against "the independence or the territorial integrity of the state." He was sentenced to 20 years in prison in April 2003. He was transferred a number of times before being taken to a military hospital in Havana.

His mother, Mireya de la Caridad Pentón, told CPJ that he was diagnosed with chronic gastritis, sinusitis, and lower back pain, she said. In addition, she said, his imprisonment and the separation from his young daughter had caused him anxiety.

Miguel Galván Gutiérrez

Havana Press

IMPRISONED: March 18, 2003

Galván Gutiérrez, a journalist with the independent news agency Havana Press, was tried under Article 91 of the penal code, which imposes lengthy prison sentences or death for those who act against "the independence or the territorial integrity of the state." In April 2003, he was sentenced to 26 years in prison, which he was serving at Agüica Prison in western Matanzas province.

In May 2004, Galván Gutiérrez was moved from solitary confinement to a cell with hardened criminals, according to the Miami-based *CubaNet* Web site. In a phone call from prison, he told his family that prison officials had threatened him and were inciting other prisoners to attack him, *CubaNet* reported.

Omar Rodríguez Saludes

Nueva Prensa Cubana

IMPRISONED: March 18, 2003

Rodríguez Saludes, director of the independent news agency Nueva Prensa Cubana, was tried under Article 91 of the penal code, which imposes lengthy prison sentences or death for those who act against "the independence or the territorial integrity of the state." In April 2003, he was sentenced to 27 years in prison. He was transferred a number of times before being placed at the Toledo Prison in Havana.

Rodríguez Saludes was in good health but complained about the poor quality of prison food, his wife, Ileana Marrero Joa, told CPJ in June 2005. He was sharing a prison cubicle with hardened prisoners.

Pedro Argüelles Morán

Cooperativa Avileña de Periodistas Independientes

IMPRISONED: March 18, 2003

Argüelles Morán, director of the independent news agency Cooperativa Avileña de Periodistas Independientes in central Ciego de Ávila province, was tried under Law 88 for the Protection of Cuba's National Independence and Economy, which imposes up to 20 years in prison for committing acts "aimed at subverting the internal order of the nation and destroying its political, economic, and social system." In April 2003, he received a 20-year prison term, which he was serving at Canaleta Prison in central Ciego de Ávila province.

Argüelles Morán had been moved from prison to prison several times. His wife, Yolanda Vera Nerey, told CPJ in November 2004 that Argüelles Morán suffered from inflammation in his left knee. He was hospitalized in February 2005 after his liver was found to be inflamed. Vera Nerey said he developed emphysema in prison, and eye problems had worsened to the point of near blindness. Vera Nerey said that he continued to suffer from inflammation in his knees and legs, and that a doctor diagnosed him with arthritis.

Ricardo González Alfonso, Freelance
IMPRISONED: March 18, 2003

González Alfonso, an independent freelance journalist and Cuba correspondent for the Paris-based press freedom organization Reporters Without Borders, was tried under Article 91 of the penal code, which imposes lengthy prison sentences or death for those who act against "the independence or the territorial integrity of the state." In April 2003, he was sentenced to a 20-year prison term. González Alfonso is also the president of the independent journalists' association Sociedad de Periodistas Manuel Márquez Sterling.

González Alfonso was first placed in Kilo 8 Prison in central Camagüey province, hundreds of miles from his home. He spent seven months in solitary confinement there. In November 2003, he was transferred to a cell with hardened criminals who harassed him. González Alfonso went on a two-week hunger strike in December 2003 to demand his transfer to another unit within the prison where he could be with other political prisoners. As punishment for the strike, prison officials placed him in a small cell with no running water that was lit 24 hours a day. He remained there until late December 2003.

González Alfonso has had numerous health problems. He suffered from high blood pressure, and a cyst was found in his throat. In July 2004, González Alfonso was admitted to the Amalia Simoni Hospital in the city of Camagüey, where he was diagnosed with hepatitis. A prison transfer later, González Alfonso was taken to the hospital in Combinado del Este Prison in January 2005 for gallbladder surgery. His surgical wounds didn't properly heal and he developed a lingering bacterial infection, according to his wife, Álida Viso Bello.

Víctor Rolando Arroyo Carmona
Unión de Periodistas y Escritores de Cuba Independientes (UPECI)
IMPRISONED: March 18, 2003

Arroyo, a journalist with the independent news agency Unión de Periodistas y Escritores de Cuba Independientes (UPECI) in western Pinar del Río province, was tried under Article 91 of the penal code, which imposes lengthy prison sentences or death for those who act against "the independence or the territorial integrity of the state." In April 2003, he received a 26-year prison sentence. He was placed at the Guantánamo Provincial Prison in eastern Guantánamo province, hundreds of miles from his home.

In December 2004, Arroyo was taken to the Combinado del Este Prison in Havana for a medical checkup. According to the Miami-based *CubaNet* Web site, which quoted his wife, Elsa González Padrón, he was diagnosed with pulmonary emphysema and other ailments.

On September 8, 2005, Arroyo went on a hunger strike to protest mistreatment, his sister Blanca Arroyo told CPJ. He was subsequently taken to the prison hospital. Arroyo's wife learned of the hunger strike from family members of other dissidents at the Guantánamo Provincial Prison, Blanca Arroyo said. González, who hadn't seen Arroyo for four months, made the long journey from her home in Pinar del Río on September 21, but she was forced to wait several days before getting permission to visit.

González was finally able to see her husband for about 10 minutes on October 2, Blanca Arroyo said. The following morning, Arroyo was taken to a hospital in neighboring Holguín province. His wife reported that he looked weak, his voice was barely audible, and his skin had a yellow cast, Blanca Arroyo said. He ended his hunger strike the same day, after receiving assurances from authorities that he would get better treatment in Holguín, his sister said. But on October 13, after 10 days in the hospital, Arroyo was transferred back to Holguín Provincial Prison, his wife told CPJ.

Adolfo Fernández Saínz, Patria
IMPRISONED: March 19, 2003

Fernández Saínz, a journalist with the independent news agency Patria, was tried under Law 88 for the Protection of Cuba's National Independence and Economy, which imposes up to 20 years in prison for committing acts "aimed at subverting the internal order of the nation and destroying its political, economic, and social system." In April 2003, he was sentenced to 15 years in prison. He was placed at the Holguín Provincial Prison in eastern Holguín province, hundreds of miles from his home.

In 2003 and 2004, Fernández Saínz waged at least three hunger strikes to protest inadequate food and medicine, along with the mistreatment of fellow prisoners. Julia Núñez Pacheco, the wife of Fernández Saínz, told CPJ in 2004 that she was very concerned that the hunger strikes and poor prison food had taken a great toll on her husband. In December 2004, Fernández Saínz was taken to the Combinado del Este Prison for a medical checkup, which revealed he had several ailments, including emphysema, a hernia, high blood pressure, and a small kidney cyst.

Joana Fernández Núñez, the journalist's daughter, told CPJ in 2005 that his family was very worried that he had lost about

25 pounds. When his family sought to give him some pork during a January 6, 2005, visit, prison officials initially barred the delivery and relented only after a long, heated argument, she said.

Fernández Saínz waged another hunger strike in August 2005, to protest the mistreatment of imprisoned dissident Arnaldo Ramos Lauzurique. Fernández Saínz began the strike after learning that Ramos Lauzurique had been beaten by a prison officer and placed in a punishment cell, according to Fernández Núñez.

Alfredo Felipe Fuentes, Freelance
IMPRISONED: March 19, 2003

Fuentes, an independent freelance journalist based in western Habana province, was tried under Article 91 of the penal code, which imposes lengthy prison sentences or death for those who act against "the independence or the territorial integrity of the state." In April 2003, he was sentenced to a 26-year prison term. He was placed at Guamajal Prison in central Villa Clara province, hundreds of miles from his home.

His wife, Loyda Valdés González, told CPJ in May 2004 that her husband was fed broth and foul-smelling ground meat for months. As a result, he lost a lot of weight, some of which he recovered after spending a month at a hospital in the city of Santa Clara. In 2005, Fuentes shared a prison unit with around 60 inmates convicted of common crimes.

Fabio Prieto Llorente, Freelance
IMPRISONED: March 19, 2003

Prieto Llorente, an independent freelance journalist based in western Isla de la Juventud Special Municipality, was tried under Law 88 for the Protection of Cuba's National Independence and Economy, which imposes up to 20 years in prison for committing acts "aimed at subverting the internal order of the nation and destroying its political, economic, and social system." In April 2003, he was sentenced to 20 years in prison. He was eventually jailed at Kilo 8 Prison in central Camagüey province, hundreds of miles from his home.

The transfer to Kilo 8 caused Prieto Llorente to sink into depression because it was difficult for his family to visit, according to his sister, Clara Lourdes Prieto Llorente. Prieto Llorente, who was placed in a damp and poorly lit cell on his arrival at Kilo 8, suffered from hemorrhoids, high blood pressure, back pain, and emphysema, family members said.

Prieto Llorente waged a hunger strike in August 2004. He was harassed for protesting his conditions, according to *CubaNet*. Ramona Mirta Llorente, the journalist's mother, told CPJ that he has had to endure solitary confinement and the withholding of family mail.

Héctor Maseda Gutiérrez
Grupo de Trabajo Decoro
IMPRISONED: March 19, 2003

Maseda Gutiérrez, a journalist with the independent news agency Grupo de Trabajo Decoro, was tried under Article 91 of the penal code, which imposes lengthy prison sentences or death for those who act against "the independence or the territorial integrity of the state;" and under Law 88 for the Protection of Cuba's National Independence and Economy, which imposes up to 20 years in prison for committing acts "aimed at subverting the internal order of the nation and destroying its political, economic, and social system." In April 2003, he received a 20-year prison term, which he was serving at La Pendiente Prison in central Villa Clara province.

In July 2003, Maseda Gutiérrez's wife, Laura Pollán, told CPJ that he had been diagnosed with skin rashes triggered by prison conditions. Pollán said that prison authorities would not allow her to bring clean sheets and medicine to her husband.

In August 2004, Maseda Gutiérrez was transferred to a cell with repeat offenders, according to Pollán. He was concerned that prison authorities would encourage the hardened prisoners to harass him. Pollán said she appealed to Cuban authorities to grant him amnesty, but government officials did not respond to her request.

On January 17, 2005, Pollán said, she was summoned to a State Security Department (DSE) office in Havana, blamed for her husband's attitude, and threatened with imprisonment for "defaming" the DSE. She was told to keep quiet about her husband's situation and to cooperate with the DSE. Pollán has regularly hosted relatives of imprisoned journalists and dissidents at her house. She told CPJ she believed the government was trying to force her to adopt a lower profile.

On January 26, Maseda Gutiérrez was transferred to a high-security unit within the Villa Clara Provincial Prison, also in Villa Clara province. In a January 29 letter from prison that Pollán made available to CPJ, Maseda Gutiérrez wrote that his transfer was "a sort of punishment" and the "worst violation yet committed against me." He complained about the harsh treatment there, which included being handcuffed whenever he was taken outside, to make a phone call, or to visit prison doctors.

José Ubaldo Izquierdo

Grupo de Trabajo Decoro

IMPRISONED: March 19, 2003

Ubaldo Izquierdo, a journalist with the independent news agency Grupo de Trabajo Decoro in western Habana province, was tried under Article 91 of the penal code, which imposes lengthy prison sentences or death for those who act against "the independence or the territorial integrity of the state." In April 2003, he was sentenced to 16 years in prison. After a transfer, he was jailed at Guanajay Prison in western Habana province.

Juan Carlos Herrera Acosta

Agencia de Prensa Libre Oriental

IMPRISONED: March 19, 2003

Herrera Acosta, a journalist with the independent news agency Agencia de Prensa Libre Oriental in eastern Guantánamo province, was tried under Law 88 for the Protection of Cuba's National Independence and Economy, which imposes up to 20 years in prison for committing acts "aimed at subverting the internal order of the nation and destroying its political, economic, and social system." In April 2003, he received a 20-year prison term.

In August 2003, Herrera Acosta joined imprisoned journalists Manuel Vázquez Portal and Normando Hernández González and other jailed dissidents at Boniato Prison in a one-week hunger strike. As punishment for his involvement, he was transferred to Kilo 8 Prison in central Camagüey province, hundreds of miles from his home.

In October 2004, the Miami-based organization Directorio Democrático Cubano, quoting Herrera Acosta's wife, Ileana Danger Hardy, said that prison officials badly beat the journalist that month.

In a June 2005 interview with CPJ, Danger Hardy said her husband suffered from a heart condition and high blood pressure. Since his imprisonment, she said, his ailments have worsened, and he appeared very thin during a June 8 visit. A couple of weeks before, on May 23, a prison official dragged him across a hospital hall while he was handcuffed, causing cuts to his hands, she reported. Danger Hardy said her husband has wounded himself several times to protest prison conditions and mistreatment.

Mijaíl Bárzaga Lugo
Agencia Noticiosa Cubana
IMPRISONED: March 19, 2003

Bárzaga Lugo, a journalist with the independent news agency Agencia Noticiosa Cubana in Havana, was tried under Law 88 for the Protection of Cuba's National Independence and Economy, which imposes up to 20 years in prison for committing acts "aimed at subverting the internal order of the nation and destroying its political, economic, and social system." In April 2003, he was sentenced to 15 years in prison, and was placed at Villa Clara Provincial Prison in central Villa Clara province, hundreds of miles from his home.

Normando Hernández González
Colegio de Periodistas Independientes de Camagüey
IMPRISONED: March 19, 2003

Hernández González, director of the independent news agency Colegio de Periodistas Independientes de Camagüey, was tried under Article 91 of the penal code, which imposes lengthy prison sentences or death for those who act against "the independence or the territorial integrity of the state." In April 2003, he was sentenced to 25 years in prison.

In April 2003, he was sent to Boniato Prison in eastern Santiago de Cuba province. In August, Hernández González joined imprisoned journalist Manuel Vázquez Portal and other jailed dissidents at Boniato Prison in a one-week hunger strike. As punishment for his involvement in the strike, Hernández González was sent to Kilo 5 1/2 Prison in Pinar del Río at the opposite end of the island.

In May 2004, Hernández González waged another hunger strike to protest his transfer to a cell with hardened criminals at Kilo 5 1/2. After a family visit that month, Reyes said her husband looked very thin, haggard, and pale.

In January 2005, a doctor found that Hernández González was exposed to tuberculosis but was not infected, said his wife, Yaraí Reyes. She said her husband's overall health has worsened and he has lost weight during his imprisonment.

Omar Ruiz Hernández
Grupo de Trabajo Decoro
IMPRISONED: March 19, 2003

Ruiz Hernández, a journalist with the independent news agency Grupo de Trabajo Decoro in central Villa Clara province, was tried under Article 91 of the penal code, which imposes lengthy prison sentences or death for those who act against "the independence or the territorial integrity of the state." In April 2003, he received an 18-year prison term.

In April 2003, Ruiz Hernández was sent to the Guantánamo Provincial Prison in eastern Guantánamo province, hundreds of miles from his home. In March 2004, his wife, Bárbara Maritza Rojo Arias, told CPJ that he was stressed, was having chest pain, and was suffering from high blood pressure. Because his prison cell was poorly lit, his eyes became irritated whenever he was exposed to sunlight, Rojo Arias said.

In August 2004, Ruiz Hernández was transferred to Canaleta Prison in central Ciego de Ávila Province.

In December 2004, Ruiz Hernández was taken to the hospital at Combinado del Este Prison in Havana for a medical checkup. He was diagnosed with severe high blood pressure and was found to have a dilated aorta. Soon after, he was returned to Canaleta Prison.

In May 2005, Ruiz Hernández was taken to a small and poorly ventilated cell after he refused to stand at attention when a prison officer walked past, Rojo Arias told CPJ. During three days there in intense heat, his blood pressure increased. Rojo Arias said that her husband's diet was very poor and he depended on the food she brought for him in her visits to the prison. In November 2005, he was taken to Nieves Morejón Prison in central Sancti Spíritus Province.

Pablo Pacheco Ávila
Cooperativa Avileña de Periodistas Independientes
IMPRISONED: March 19, 2003

Pacheco Ávila, a journalist with the independent news agency Cooperativa Avileña de Periodistas Independientes, was tried under Law 88 for the Protection of Cuba's National Independence and Economy, which imposes up to 20 years in prison for committing acts "aimed at subverting the internal order of the nation and destroying its political, economic, and social system." In April 2003, he was sentenced to 20 years in prison, which he began serving at Agüica Prison in western Matanzas province, hundreds of miles from his home. In August 2004, he was moved to Morón Prison in Ciego de Ávila, his native province.

In March 2005, his wife, Oleivys García Echemendía, told CPJ that Pacheco Ávila suffered from high blood pressure, severe headaches, inflammation in both knees, and acute gastritis. His knee problems had worsened to the point that he could barely walk, García Echemendía said.

Oscar Mario González
Grupo de Trabajo Decoro
IMPRISONED: July 22, 2005

González, a journalist with the independent news agency Grupo de Trabajo Decoro, was arrested about a block from his home in Havana, according to colleague Ana Leonor Díaz.

Authorities did not immediately say why González was detained or file any charges against him publicly. Díaz said González might have been detained in connection with a police crackdown that began July 22, when opposition activists planned to hold an antigovernment protest outside the French Embassy in Havana.

Several leaders of the protest group, the Assembly to Promote Civil Society in Cuba (APSC), were detained before they could join other protesters. In all, at least 29 people were detained; most were released without charge.

In May, González covered the APSC congress for Grupo de Trabajo Decoro. The unprecedented two-day congress brought together 200 activists and guests to discuss ways to create a democratic society in Cuba. At the time, Cuban authorities detained and expelled at least five foreign journalists who had traveled to Cuba to cover the meeting.

A police investigator told the journalist's relatives that he would be prosecuted under Law 88 for the Protection of Cuba's National Independence and Economy, Diaz reported. The law sets penalties of up to 20 years in prison for anyone who commits "acts that in agreement with imperialist interests are aimed at subverting the internal order of the nation and destroy its political, economic, and social system."

As of December 1, Cuban authorities had yet to formally charge González. He was being held by police in Havana.

Albert Santiago Du Bouchet Hernández
Havana Press
IMPRISONED: August 6, 2005

Du Bouchet Hernández was arrested on August 6, tried three days later, and handed a one-year jail term—all without the knowledge of his family, who learned of his detention only after he smuggled a note out of prison. Du Bouchet Hernández is director of the independent news agency Havana Press, which sends reports to the Miami-based Web site *Nueva Prensa Cubana*.

Du Bouchet Hernández was detained on a reporting trip to Artemisa, 38 miles (60 kilometers) from Havana, according to his wife, Bárbara Pérez Araya. He was charged with "disrespecting" the local chief of police and resisting arrest. He was sent to the Melena del Sur prison in Habana province after his conviction.

Pérez Araya told CPJ said her husband did not have access to a lawyer before or during the trial, that the charges were fabricated, and that his trial was "a sham."

Du Bouchet Hernández covered the congress of the Assembly to Promote Civil Society (APSC) in May 2005. The two-day gathering, unprecedented in Cuba, brought together 200 opposition activists and guests to discuss ways to create a democracy in Cuba.

Pérez Araya said state security agents warned Du Bouchet Hernández in May and July to stop work or face imprisonment. They ordered him to appear at a police station on the opening day of the APSC meeting, but he ignored the summons and covered the conference.

Neither Pérez Araya nor her husband has received a copy of the court ruling. She said her husband has not been able to sleep well in jail. She took him sedatives and other medication, but he was not allowed to receive most of them.

DEMOCRATIC REPUBLIC OF CONGO: 1

o

Patrice Booto

Le Journal and *Pool Malebo*

IMPRISONED: November 2, 2005

Security forces arrested Booto, publisher of the thrice-weekly *Le Journal* and its sister publication, *Pool Malebo*. Booto was detained at a police station in the capital, Kinshasa, according to the local press freedom organization Journaliste en Danger (JED).

On November 10, Booto was transferred to the state security court, where he was charged the following day with publishing "false rumors." He was questioned about articles published in the two newspapers in mid-September that claimed the government had given a large sum of money to Tanzanian education agencies while Congolese teachers were on strike for more pay.

Le Journal and *Pool Malebo* were suspended for three months in September by the independent but officially sanctioned High Authority on Media (HAM), over the same reports. Some local sources suspected that the HAM's action was the product of political pressure.

Representatives from JED were able to meet with the jailed journalist on November 9. He said he had been forced at gunpoint to reveal his source for the story and that the source was arrested, JED reported. The name of the source was not revealed.

ERITREA: 15

ooooooooooooooo

Zemenfes Haile, *Tsigenay*

IMPRISONED: January 1999

Haile, founder and manager of the private weekly *Tsigenay*, was detained by Eritrean authorities and sent to Zara Labor Camp in the country's lowland desert. Authorities accused Haile of failing to complete the national service program, but sources told CPJ that the journalist completed the program in 1994.

Near the end of 2000, Haile was transferred to an unknown location. CPJ sources said he was released from prison in 2002 but was sent to the army to perform national service. CPJ sources believe that Haile's continued deprivation of liberty is part of the government's general crackdown on the press, which began in September 2001.

Ghebrehiwet Keleta, *Tsigenay*
IMPRISONED: July 2000

Keleta, a reporter for the private weekly *Tsigenay,* was kidnapped by security agents on his way to work sometime in July 2000 and has not been seen since. The reasons for Keleta's arrest remain unclear, but some CPJ sources believe that Keleta's continued detention is part of the government's general crackdown on the press, which began in September 2001.

Amanuel Asrat, *Zemen*
Medhanie Haile, *Keste Debena*
Yusuf Mohamed Ali, *Tsigenay*
Mattewos Habteab, *Meqaleh*
Temesken Ghebreyesus, *Keste Debena*
Said Abdelkader, *Admas*
Dawit Isaac, *Setit*
Seyoum Tsehaye, Freelance
Dawit Habtemichael, *Meqaleh*
Fesshaye "Joshua" Yohannes, *Setit*
IMPRISONED: September 2001

In the days following September 18, 2001, Eritrean security forces arrested at least 10 local journalists. The arrests came less than a week after authorities abruptly closed all privately owned newspapers, allegedly to safeguard national unity in the face of growing political turmoil in the tiny Horn of Africa nation.

International news reports quoted presidential adviser Yemane Gebremeskel as saying that the journalists could have been arrested for avoiding military service. Sources in the capital, Asmara, however, said that at least two of the detained journalists, freelance photographer Tsehaye and Mohamed Ali, editor of *Tsigenay,* were legally exempt from national service. Tsehaye was reportedly exempt as an independence war veteran, while Mohamed Ali was apparently well over the maximum age for military service.

CPJ sources said the suspension and subsequent arrests of independent journalists were part of a full-scale government effort to suppress political dissent in advance of December 2001 elections, which the government canceled without explanation.

On March 31, 2002, the 10 jailed reporters began a hunger strike to protest their continued detention without charge, according to local and international sources. In a message smuggled from inside the Police Station One detention center in Asmara, the journalists said they would refuse food until they were either released or charged and given a fair trial. Three days later, nine of the strikers were transferred to an undisclosed detention facility. According to CPJ sources, Swedish national Isaac was sent to a hospital, where he was treated for post-traumatic stress disorder, a result of alleged torture while in police custody.

During a July 2002 fact-finding mission to Asmara, a presidential official told a CPJ delegation that only "about eight" news professionals were being held in detention facilities, whose locations he refused to disclose.

Swedish diplomats have worked to win Isaac's freedom. He was released for a medical checkup on November 19, 2005, and allowed to phone his family and a friend in Sweden. Isaac was returned to jail two days later, according to CPJ sources.

Selamyinghes Beyene, *Meqaleh*
IMPRISONED: Fall 2001

Beyene, a reporter for the independent weekly *Meqaleh*, was arrested sometime in the fall of 2001. CPJ was unable to confirm the reasons for his arrest, but Eritrean sources believe that his detention was part of the government's general crackdown on the press, which began in September 2001. In 2002, he was taken to do military service and was still performing his national service requirement, according to CPJ sources.

Hamid Mohammed Said
Eritrean State Television
Saleh Aljezeeri, Eritrean State Radio
IMPRISONED: February 15, 2002

During a July 2002 fact-finding mission to the capital, Asmara, CPJ delegates confirmed that around February 15, Eritrean authorities arrested Said, a journalist for the state-run Eritrean State Television (ETV); Saadia Ahmed, a journalist with the Arabic-language service of ETV; and Aljezeeri, a journalist for Eritrean State Radio.

Ahmed was released, according to CPJ sources, although the date is unclear.

The reasons for their arrests are unclear, but CPJ sources in Eritrea believe that their continued detention was related to the government's general crackdown on the press, which began in September 2001.

ETHIOPIA: 13

○○○○○○○○○○○○○

Dawit Kebede, *Hadar*
Feleke Tibebu, *Hadar*
IMPRISONED: November 2, 2005

Zekarias Tesfaye, *Netsanet*
Dereje Habtewolde, *Netsanet*
Fassil Yenealem, *Addis Zena*
Wosonseged Gebrekidan, *Addis Zena*
Andualem Ayle, *Ethiop*
Nardos Meaza, *Satanaw*
Mesfin Tesfaye, *Abay*
Wenakseged Zeleke, *Asqual*
IMPRISONED: November 9–14, 2005

Serkalem Fassil, *Menilik*, *Asqual* and *Satanaw*
Iskinder Nega, Freelance
IMPRISONED: November 27, 2005

Sisay Agena, *Ethiop* and Ethiopian Free Press Journalists Association
IMPRISONED: November 29, 2005

In a massive crackdown on the private press following antigovernment protests, authorities arrested at least 13 editors and publishers in the capital, Addis Ababa. Police prevented most private newspapers from publishing; raided newspaper offices, confiscating computers, documents and other materials; and forced much of the remaining press into hiding. The journalists were jailed along with dozens of opposition and civil society leaders. On November 9, Prime Minister Meles Zenawi threatened to charge detainees with treason, which is punishable by death in

Ethiopia.

The crackdown began amid clashes between security forces and opposition supporters who accused Zenawi of rigging polls in May that returned him to power. More than 40 people were killed in a week of violence, which began on November 1.

Starting on November 5, the government released a list of people it planned to prosecute for attempting to "violently undermine the constitutional order in the country."

The list identified 17 publishers and editors of eight private, Amharic-language weekly newspapers, in addition to opposition leaders, the heads of the Ethiopian Teachers' Association, and local representatives of the international charity Action Aid. It also included the president of the Ethiopian Free Press Journalists' Association (EFJA), Kifle Mulat. State media distributed photographs of many of these journalists and called on the public to tell police their whereabouts.

Security and intelligence agents arrested nine of the targeted journalists, many of whom were in hiding. Four more turned themselves in after their names were listed.

The detained journalists were not immediately charged. Several appeared in court, along with dozens of detained opposition leaders, trade unionists, and others arrested in the crackdown. They were denied bail, and their detentions were extended while police investigated their supposed activities, according to local and international news reports.

IRAN: 2

oo

Akbar Ganji, *Sobh-e-Emrooz* and *Fath*
IMPRISONED: April 22, 2000

Ganji, a leading investigative reporter for the now-defunct reformist daily *Sobh-e-Emrooz* and a member of the editorial board of the now-defunct, pro-reform daily *Fath*, was prosecuted in Iran's Press Court and its Revolutionary Court.

The case in the Press Court stemmed from Ganji's investigative articles about the 1998 killings of several dissidents and intellectuals that implicated top intelligence officials and former President Hashemi Rafsanjani. In the Revolutionary Court, Ganji was accused of promoting propaganda against the Islamic regime and threatening national security in comments he made at an April 2000 conference in Berlin on the future of the reform movement in Iran.

The result of the case in the Press Court remains unclear, but on January 13, 2001, the Revolutionary Court sentenced Ganji to 10 years in prison, followed by five years of internal exile. In May 2001, after Ganji had already served more than a year in prison, an appellate court reduced his punishment to six months.

The Iranian Justice Department then appealed that ruling to the Supreme Court, arguing that the appellate court had committed errors in commuting the original 10-year sentence. The Supreme Court overturned the appellate court's decision and referred the case to a different appeals court. On July 16, 2001, that court sentenced Ganji to six years in jail. According to the state news agency IRNA, the ruling was "definitive," meaning that it cannot be appealed.

Mojtaba Saminejad, Freelance
IMPRISONED: February 12, 2005

On June 2, 2005, Saminejad, a 25-year-old blogger, was sentenced to two years in prison for "insulting the supreme leader." He has not been allowed to appeal the ruling and the specifics of the case have not been disclosed. The prosecution is widely believed to be the result of his Web logs, which were critical of the Iranian government. He is in Gohar Dashat Prison outside Tehran.

Saminejad was jailed in February, when Tehran's chief prosecutor summoned him for a court hearing. He had been detained previously, in November 2004, after reporting the arrests of three fellow bloggers on his Web site.

He was also charged with "insulting the prophets," which is punishable by death, but a Tehran court cleared him of that count in June.

IRAQ: 4

oooo

Abdul Ameer Younis Hussein
CBS News
IMPRISONED: April 5, 2005

Hussein, an Iraqi cameraman working for CBS News, was taken into custody after being wounded by U.S. forces' fire on April 5 while he filmed clashes in Mosul in northern Iraq. CBS News reported at the time that the U.S. military said footage in the journalist's camera led them to suspect he had prior knowledge of attacks on coalition forces. Agence France-Presse also cited U.S. officials as saying the journalist "tested positive for explosive residue."

No charges have been made public and the evidence used to hold him remains classified. *The New York Times* reported that the U.S. military referred Hussein's case to Iraqi justice officials who reviewed Hussein's file but declined to prosecute him. Nevertheless, Hussein remained in U.S. custody.

U.S. military officials have made unspecific accusations that Hussein was "engaged in anti-coalition activity," and that he had been "recruiting and inciting Iraqi nationals to violence against coalition forces and participating in attacks against coalition forces." Military officials did not provide any evidence to support these accusations.

CBS, CPJ, and other groups sought information about the detention but were unable to obtain further details.

Samir Mohammed Noor, Reuters
IMPRISONED: May 2005

Noor, a freelance television cameraman working for Reuters, was arrested by Iraqi troops at his home in the northern town of Tal Afar in May 2005 and ordered detained indefinitely by the U.S.-Iraqi Combined Review and Release Board, which oversees detentions in Iraq.

A U.S. military spokesman told the news

agency that Noor was determined to be "an imperative threat to the coalition forces and the security of Iraq." U.S. officials did not specify the basis for the accusation. Reuters said he was held at Camp Bucca in southern Iraq.

Ali al-Mashhadani, Reuters
IMPRISONED: August 8, 2005

Al-Mashhadani, a freelance photographer and cameraman for Reuters news agency, was held incommunicado and without explanation by U.S. forces since his detention on August 8. Al-Mashhadani was taken from his home in Ramadi during a general sweep of the neighborhood by U.S. Marines who became suspicious after seeing pictures on his cameras, Reuters quoted his family as saying.

He was placed in Abu Ghraib Prison. Reuters reported that the U.S.–Iraqi Combined Review and Release Board, which oversees detentions in Iraq, determined that al-Mashhadani posed a "threat" and ordered his continued detention. U.S. officials told Reuters that al-Mashhadani would be denied access to counsel or family for 60 days, but would be granted a review of his case within 180 days. Officials did not publicly substantiate the basis for his continued detention.

Majed Hameed
Al-Arabiya and Reuters
IMPRISONED: September 15, 2005

Hameed, a reporter working with the Dubai-based broadcaster Al-Arabiya and a freelancer for Reuters, was arrested along with several other men at a gathering that followed the funeral of a relative in Anbar province.

Both Reuters and Al-Arabiya have said his arrest appears connected to footage found on his camera by U.S. troops. U.S. officials did not explain the basis for his detention. According to Al-Arabiya, Hameed was held at a U.S. facility in western Anbar province.

LIBYA: 1

o

Abdel Raziq al-Mansouri, Freelance
IMPRISONED: January 12, 2005

Al-Mansouri, a 52-year-old Internet writer, was arrested in the city of Tobruk in apparent reprisal for Internet writings that were critical of the Libyan government.

The U.S.-based Human Rights Watch, which visited al-Mansouri in Abu Selim prison in May, reported that al-Mansouri wrote about 50 articles on the United Kingdom-based Web site *Akhbar-Libya*. Human Rights Watch said Libyan security agents questioned al-Mansouri about his writings and confiscated his computer, papers, and computer disks. A brother said security agents told him that al-Mansouri had confessed to "writing articles online that criticized the state of Libya."

Libyan security officials maintained that al-Mansouri was arrested for having a gun without a license. On October 19, a court sentenced al-Mansouri to one and a half years in prison on the weapons charge. After the sentence was passed, al-Mansouri's family wrote to the government to protest the verdict and to state its belief that the sentence was a result of his Internet writings, according to Human Rights Watch.

MALDIVES: 3

ooo

Ahmed Didi, *Sandhaanu*
IMPRISONED: February 5, 2002

Didi, Mohamed Zaki, and Ibrahim Luthfee—businessmen who founded, edited, and wrote for the Dhivehi-language Internet publication *Sandhaanu*—were arrested along with their secretary, Fathimath Nisreen.

All four were held in solitary confinement for five months until their sentencing on July 7, 2002. After a summary three-day trial, they were convicted of defamation, incitement to violence, and treason. Didi, Luthfee, and Zaki were sentenced to life imprisonment and one year of banishment for defamation, and Nisreen received a 10-year prison sentence, with a one-year banishment for defamation. The four were sent to Maafushi Prison, which is known for its harsh conditions, 18 miles (29 kilometers) south of the capital, Malé.

Before *Sandhaanu* was effectively closed in early 2002, the Web site attracted a large audience by local standards, according to Luthfee. The independent publication criticized the government for alleged abuse of power and called for political reform.

Although the Maldivian government claims that the four received a fair trial, Luthfee told CPJ that officials denied the defendants' requests for legal representation at the time of the trial.

A Maldivian government representative in London sent a statement to the BBC in 2003 claiming that the charges against Didi, Luthfee, Nisreen, and Zaki were "purely criminal" because their publication was not officially registered, and that the four were convicted of inciting people "to violence...against a lawfully elected government."

Luthfee told CPJ that the case against them was politically motivated, and that it was intended as a warning to others who criticize the government. Since Maldivian authorities control the media, Luthfee says it is impossible to write anything critical about the government in the official press. Therefore, Didi, Luthfee, and Zaki decided to launch their independent publication online from Malaysia, where Zaki immigrated from Mali in 1990. Because they were concerned about government surveillance inside the Maldives, Didi and Luthfee sent the text of *Sandhaanu* to Zaki in Malaysia in PDF files to upload and distribute from there.

On May 19, 2003, Luthfee escaped from custody while receiving medical treatment in Sri Lanka and received asylum outside the region. In the wake of prison riots in September 2003, Maldivian President Maumoon Abdul Gayoom pledged to reform his county's prison system.

In December 2003, Zaki and Didi's prison sentences were reduced to 15 years; Nisreen's sentence was halved to five years, and she was banished to Feeali Island, south of Malé. All three were on medical leave when police and the National Security Service rearrested them in an August 2004 crackdown on pro-democracy reformists. After a massive tsunami struck the Maldives in December 2004, Nisreen's remaining term was postponed. Zaki, who suffers from back and kidney problems, was released in August 2005.

Mohamed Nasheed (Colonel)
Abdullah Saeed (Fahala)
Minivan Daily
IMPRISONED: October 13, 2005

Nasheed, known as Colonel, a columnist and political activist with the opposition publication *Minivan Daily*, and Saeed, also known as Fahala, a longtime journalist who is also affiliated with the opposition Maldivian Democratic Party (MDP), were summoned by police for questioning on October 13, 2005, and were kept in detention.

The state-run media reported on September 20 that several staff members of *Minivan Daily*, including Colonel and Fahala, were under investigation for writing critical articles about the government. Colonel was also accused of taking part in a pro-democracy rally in August 2005. Police accused Fahala of possessing a large quantity of drugs at the time of his questioning at the police station, the online version of *Minivan Daily* reported. Staffers at the paper accused the police of planting the drugs on Fahala.

The two journalists have been transferred from the police station to the Dhoonidhoo detention center.

A speech by Colonel titled "(President) Gayoom will do anything to stay in power" was reported in *Minivan Daily*, and the paper cited that as the likely motivation for his arrest.

The Maldives has tightly restricted media, with little independent journalism. President Maumoon Gayoom has come under pressure in recent years to make democratic reforms and open up the press environment. After applying for more than a year, *Minivan Daily* was finally granted a license and allowed to start publishing in July 2005, a significant step. The paper is affiliated with the opposition MDP.

Minivan Daily said that the government stepped up its case against the paper after the August arrest of MDP activist Mohamed Nasheed, known as Anni. The paper investigated his arrest on terrorism charges after he made a critical speech against the president in July and published documents calling into question the legitimacy of the state's case against him.

The paper said that the journalists are innocent and that other journalists from the paper are now at risk of arrest. *Minivan Daily* reported that if the journalists are prosecuted, the newspaper's license will be revoked.

MOROCCO: 1

o

Anas Tadili, *Akhbar al-Ousboue*
IMPRISONED: April 15, 2004

Tadili, editor of the weekly *Akhbar al-Ousboue*, was detained shortly after publishing an April 2004 article alleging that Economics Minister Fathallah Oualalou was homosexual. In September 2004, he was convicted of defamation and sentenced to one year in prison.

Tadili's original sentence concluded in September 2005, but another sentence then took effect. On April 15, 2005, while he was in jail, Tadili was found guilty of breaking currency laws and sentenced to an additional four months in jail. The alleged currency violation had occurred several years earlier, but the case was revived in 2004 after the Oualalou article was published. Tadili's supporters believe the currency case was brought in retaliation for the article.

NEPAL: 1

o

Tej Narayan Sapkota, *Yojana*

IMPRISONED: November 24, 2003

Sapkota, a former editor of the newspaper *Yojana*, was seized by two plainclothes security forces personnel from the Sarbottam printing press office in Kathmandu, according to Amnesty International. He was kept in police custody until his transfer to jail.

Sapkota is charged with murder under the controversial Terrorist and Disruptive Activities Ordinance (TADO). The ordinance allows suspects to be held without charge or trial for renewable periods of six months. Sapkota's case has come up for hearing eight times and the government has failed to present its evidence on each occasion. Sapkota strongly denies the murder charge against him.

A delegation of CPJ and Federation of Nepalese Journalists (FNJ) representatives visited Sapkota in October 2005 in Nakkhu jail on the outskirts of Kathmandu. When the delegation inquired about Sapkota at the prison gate, the chief guard replied, "Oh, you mean the terrorist."

Through a wire mesh barrier, Sapkota said that he had been blindfolded for five consecutive months following his arrest, and was beaten every day. His treatment improved when he was transferred to jail, he said. He was well-fed, received frequent medical attention, and was allowed access to a lawyer and communication with human rights activists and colleagues.

Sapkota and his lawyer said that they believe that authorities intend to hold him indefinitely under TADO. FNJ believes that Sapkota was being held to obtain information on Maoist sources.

NIGER: 1

o

Salifou Soumaila Abdoulkarim

Le Visionnaire

IMPRISONED: November 12, 2005

Abdoulkarim, director of the private newspaper *Le Visionnaire*, was placed in "preventive detention" at police headquarters in the capital, Niamey, after State Treasurer Siddo Elhadj brought a criminal defamation suit against him. Abdoulkarim was transferred to prison on November 17 and denied bail pending his trial.

Abdoulaye Massalaki, president of Niger's journalist union, told CPJ that preventive detention for journalists charged with defamation is allowed under Niger's 1999 press law.

Elhadj brought the suit over an article in *Le Visionnaire* that accused him of embezzling 17 billion CFA francs (US$30 million) in government funds. On December 2, a Niamey court sentenced Abdoulkarim to two months in jail.

NIGERIA: 1

o

Owei Kobina Sikpi, *Weekly Star*

IMPRISONED: October 11, 2005

Sikpi, publisher of the tabloid *Weekly Star* in the southern city of Port Harcourt, was arrested by agents of the State Security Service (SSS) over an article in the previous week's edition that accused a local official of money laundering, the paper's editor, Obinna Ahiaidu, told CPJ.

Sikpi was arrested along with four printing press staff as the *Weekly Star* was going to press, according to Ahiaidu. The four were released the same day, but Sikpi was held at the SSS office in Port Harcourt. He was later transferred to the city's central prison. Security agents who raided the newspaper's premises also impounded its 4,000-copy print run.

On October 17, Sikpi was brought before Port Harcourt High Court and charged with several counts of publishing false information, according to international news reports and a CPJ source. He was denied bail.

Sikpi was charged in relation to an article that accused the state governor of involvement in money laundering. He was also charged over articles published in May and June relating to separatist militia in the oil-rich Niger delta and the presence of former Liberian president Charles Taylor in Nigeria.

RWANDA: 1

o

Jean Léonard Rugambage, *Umuco*

IMPRISONED: September 7, 2005

Rugambage, a reporter for the twice-monthly newspaper *Umuco*, was jailed in the central town of Gitarama and accused of participating in the 1994 genocide, although several local sources told CPJ they believe he was jailed for his journalistic work. His arrest came soon after he wrote an article for the August 25 edition of *Umuco* that accused officials of the semi-traditional "gacaca" courts in the Gitarama region of corruption, mismanagement, and manipulating witnesses.

Gacaca courts, in which suspects are judged by their peers with no recourse to a defense lawyer, were set up to try tens of thousands of genocide suspects who have been languishing in overcrowded jails since 1994. The genocide left some 800,000 ethnic Tutsis and moderate Hutus dead in less than three months. Human rights activists and independent observers have raised concern that the courts have given rise to false accusations in some cases.

CPJ sources said accusations that Rugambage participated in the genocide were based on contradictory and vague testimony by a small number of witnesses. They said the testimony was not given until after Rugambage's articles appeared. One witness testified to a gacaca court in Rugambage's home village that he took part in a murder; other witnesses said he may have participated in looting and distributing arms, the sources said.

Rugambage was not present at these hearings. A prisoner has written a letter stating that Rugambage was not present during the murder for which he was accused.

In November, Rugambage was found in contempt of a gacaca court and sentenced to a year in prison after he protested that the presiding judge was biased. Rugambage said the judge refused to consider defense evidence or testimony, according to CPJ sources. The underlying charges were still pending.

Umuco, which is based in Kigali and publishes mainly in Kinyarwanda, has been targeted for its criticism of the authorities.

In August, Editor Bonaventure Bizumuremyi was twice held by police for questioning following an article on police corruption and a story that called for the release of jailed opposition leader and former president Pasteur Bizimungu. In mid-September, police seized copies of *Umuco* and summoned Bizumuremyi several times for questioning.

SOMALIA: 1

o

Ahmed Mohammed Aden
Gedonet Online and Jubba FM
IMPRISONED: November 28, 2005

Reporter Aden was jailed in the southern city of Kismayo following an online story claiming that the Jubba Valley Alliance had been importing arms in violation of a U.N. arms embargo, the National Union of Somali Journalists (NUSOJ) reported.

The Jubba Valley faction, which controls Kismayo, accused him of posting "false information" in an article on the *Gedonet Online* Web site, according to NUSOJ. Aden also works for private radio station Jubba FM in Kismayo and is a prominent member of NUSOJ.

Somalia has had no functioning central government since the collapse of the Siad Barre regime in 1991. A Transitional Federal Government (TFG) established under a 2004 peace accord remains divided between factions based in the town of Jowhar and the capital, Mogadishu. Jubba Valley Alliance leader Barre "Hirale" Aden Shire is reconstruction minister in the TFG.

Aden was freed without charge on December 2, NUSOJ reported.

TAJIKISTAN: 1

o

Jumaboy Tolibov, Freelance
IMPRISONED: April 24, 2005

Tolibov, an independent journalist from northern Tajikistan, was detained on April 24 in the capital of Dushanbe, at the direction of Ayni district prosecutor Sabit Azamov. Tolibov was later transferred to the Ayni district remand center in the northern region of Sogd, according to local reports.

On July 28, a Shahristan District Court judge sentenced Tolibov to two years in a prison colony on charges of hooliganism, trespassing, and abusing his office as a local government administrator, according to local and international reports.

Nuriddin Karshiboyev, head of the National Association of Independent Media of Tajikistan (NANSMIT), a press freedom group, said his organization believed the charges were fabricated in retaliation for Tolibov's published work.

Tolibov, who is also chairman of the legal department in Ayni's local government, wrote commentaries in the ruling party newspaper *Minbar i Halq* and the parliamentary newspaper *Sadoi Mardum* that were highly critical of the district prosecutor's office. In three articles published in late 2004, Tolibov alleged that Azamov assaulted him and reproached local authorities for refusing to investigate. Tolibov said the attack occurred when he was seeking information from the prosecutor's office earlier in the year.

The articles included "A barbarian prosecutor" and "Who supports a barbarian prosecutor?" in *Minbar i Halq*, and "Who will protect us?" in *Sadoi Mardum*.

Marat Mamadshoyev, a NANSMIT correspondent who monitored the 13-day trial, said the verdict came in the face of contradictory witness statements. Mamadshoyev also said several key witnesses who allegedly filed complaints against Tolibov were not present in court and instead submitted written testimony.

After the defense appealed, the Supreme Court partially overturned the conviction and ordered Tolibov's release, according to local reports. In its October 11 ruling, the Supreme Court threw out Tolibov's conviction for trespassing and abuse of office, and it reduced a conviction on hooliganism to a lesser charge of insult. The court also reduced Tolibov's punishment from two years in prison to one year of corrective labor; the court accepted the imprisonment already served as the equivalent of a year of corrective labor. The ruling was issued two days before U.S. Secretary of State Condoleezza Rice visited Tajikistan.

But the prosecutor general's office in Dushanbe, moved immediately to block Tolibov's release. Under the Tajik Code of Criminal Procedure, the prosecutor can suspend implementation of a Supreme Court decision by filing a letter of appeal. Sabbargun Kurbanova, spokesman for the prosecutor general's office, told CPJ that it wanted to "check the rationale behind Tolibov's release." Tajik authorities finally released Tolibov from prison on December 16.

TUNISIA: 2

○○

Hamadi Jebali, *Al-Fajr*
IMPRISONED: January 1991

On August 28, 1992, a military court sentenced Jebali, editor of *Al-Fajr*, the now-defunct weekly newspaper of the banned Islamic Al-Nahda party, to 16 years in prison. He was tried along with 279 others accused of belonging to Al-Nahda. Jebali was convicted of "aggression with the intention of changing the nature of the state" and "membership in an illegal organization."

During his testimony, Jebali denied the charges and presented evidence that he had been tortured while in custody. Jebali has been imprisoned since January 1991, when he was sentenced to one year in jail after *Al-Fajr* published an article calling for the abolition of military courts in Tunisia. International human rights groups monitoring the mass trial concluded that the proceedings fell far below international standards of justice.

Jebali waged hunger strikes in 2005 to protest his imprisonment.

Mohamed Abbou, Freelance
IMPRISONED: March 1, 2005

Abbou, a human rights lawyer, was arrested by Tunisian secret police on March 1. On April 28, he was handed a prison sentence of three and a half years because of an Internet article that allegedly "defamed the judicial process" and was "likely to disturb public order."

Abbou wrote for a banned Tunisian news Web site, *Tunisnews*, comparing torture in Tunisia's prisons with that of Iraq's infamous Abu Ghraib. An appeals court upheld the verdict on June 10.

TURKEY: 1

Memik Horuz,
Ozgur Gelecek and *Isci Koylu*
IMPRISONED: June 18, 2001

Horuz, editor of the leftist publications *Ozgur Gelecek* and *Isci Koylu*, was arrested and later charged with "membership in an illegal organization," a crime under Article 168/2 of the penal code. Prosecutors based the case against Horuz on interviews he had allegedly conducted with leftist guerrillas, which *Ozgur Gelecek* published in 2000 and 2001.

The state also based its case on the testimony of an alleged former militant who claimed that the journalist belonged to the outlawed Marxist-Leninist Communist Party. Horuz was convicted on June 18, 2002, and sentenced to 12 years and six months in prison.

UNITED STATES NAVAL BASE, GUANTÁNAMO BAY: 1

Sami Muhyideen al-Haj, Al-Jazeera
IMPRISONED: December 15, 2001

Al-Haj, a 35-year-old Sudanese national and assistant cameraman for Al-Jazeera, was detained by Pakistani forces after he and an Al-Jazeera reporter attempted to re-enter southern Afghanistan at the Chaman border crossing in Pakistan, station officials said.

Al-Jazeera said it sought information

from Pakistan, Afghanistan, and United States. It learned of his detention—first at a U.S. detention camp in Afghanistan and later at the U.S. military facility in Guantánamo Bay—from letters he sent to the station and to his wife in care of Al-Jazeera, beginning in April 2002. Initial letters identified him as detainee #JJJSDE, Al-Jazeera said.

Youssef al-Shouli, the reporter who was with al-Haj at the border, told CPJ that the cameraman was stopped by order of Pakistani intelligence. He said a Pakistani intelligence official said that there was a problem with al-Haj's passport. Al-Shouli was not detained.

Al-Haj's lawyer, Clive Stafford Smith, told CPJ in October 2005 that his client was being held at Guantánamo as an accused "enemy combatant." Smith said no specific allegations had been lodged and his client denied any wrongdoing. Al-Jazeera condemned the detention and said it fully supported al-Haj. Station representatives said al-Haj had worked for another Qatar television station before joining Al-Jazeera.

U.S. Navy Lt. Cmdr. Chris Loundermon, a spokesman for the U.S. Southern Command, which administers the Guantánamo military facility, would not provide any information about al-Haj, nor would he confirm the journalist's detention. He said the information constituted confidential intelligence.

The Guardian of London reported in September 2005 that U.S. military interrogators allegedly tried to recruit al-Haj as a spy. Interrogators allegedly told him he would be released if he agreed to inform U.S. intelligence authorities about the satellite news network's activities. In an interview with CPJ, Smith repeated the allegation. He said interrogators had been "trying to get Sami to become an informant against Al-Jazeera."

UZBEKISTAN: 6

oooooo

Muhammad Bekjanov, *Erk*
Yusuf Ruzimuradov, *Erk*

IMPRISONED: March 15, 1999

Bekjanov, editor of *Erk*, a newspaper published by the banned opposition party Erk, and Ruzimuradov, an employee of the paper, were sentenced to prison terms of 14 years and 15 years, respectively, at an August 1999 trial in the capital, Tashkent.

They were convicted of publishing and distributing a banned newspaper containing slanderous criticism of President Islam Karimov; participating in a banned political protest; and attempting to overthrow the regime. In addition, the court found them guilty of illegally leaving the country and damaging their Uzbek passports.

Both men were tortured during their six-month pretrial detention in the Tashkent City Prison, according to CPJ sources. Their health deteriorated as a result of prison conditions.

According to human rights activists in Tashkent, on November 27, 1999, Bekjanov was transferred to "strict-regime" Penal Colony 64/46 in the city of Navoi in central Uzbekistan. He lost considerable weight and, like many prisoners in Uzbek camps, suffered from malnutrition. Local sources told CPJ that Ruzimuradov was being held in "strict-regime" Penal Colony 64/33 in the village of Shakhali near the town of Karshi.

In May 2003, the 49-year-old Bekjanov was interviewed for the first time since his imprisonment by a local correspondent for the London-based Institute for War & Peace Reporting (IWPR) and a local stringer for The Associated Press. The interview took place in the Tashkent Prison Hospital, where he was being treated for tuberculosis, which he contracted while in detention.

Bekjanov described daily torture and beatings that resulted in a broken leg and loss of hearing in his right ear, according to IWPR. The journalist and opposition activist said he intends to resume his political activities after he is released from prison in 2012. "I will do what I used to do," Bekjanov told the AP.

By 2005, Bekjanov was placed at Prison Colony 64/62 in the city of Kagan in the Bukhara region and Ruzimuradov was serving his term at a prison colony in the Navoi region, Erk party Secretary-General Atanazar Arifov told CPJ. Arifov said that the wives and children of both journalists fled to the United States.

Gayrat Mehliboyev, Freelance
IMPRISONED: July 24, 2002

Mehliboyev was arrested at a bazaar in the capital, Tashkent, for allegedly participating in a rally protesting the imprisonment of members of the banned Islamist opposition party Hizb ut-Tahrir. When police searched Mehliboyev's bed in a local hostel, they allegedly found banned religious literature that prosecutors later characterized as extremist in nature, according to international press reports.

Mehliboyev, who was unemployed at the time, admitted in court that he had studied the ideas of Hizb ut-Tahrir, but denied possessing the religious material police allegedly found in the hostel.

He had written several articles on religious issues for the government-funded Tashkent newspapers *Hurriyat* and *Mohiyyat* during 2001 and graduated from the journalism faculty at Tashkent State University in 2002, according to local press reports.

Mehliboyev was held in pretrial detention for more than six months before his trial began on February 5, 2003. Prosecutors presented as evidence of Mehliboyev's alleged religious extremism a political commentary he had written for the April 11, 2001, edition of *Hurriyat*. The article questioned whether Western democracy should be a model for Uzbekistan and said that religion was the true path to achieving social justice. Prosecutors claimed that the article contained ideas from Hizb ut-Tahrir.

A Tashkent-based representative of Human Rights Watch monitored the trial and told CPJ that several times during the proceedings, Mehliboyev said he was beaten in custody, but the court ignored his comments. Mehliboyev's brother, Shavkat, said the defendant was forced to confess to having connections to Hizb ut-Tahrir.

The Shaikhantaur Regional Court sentenced the 23-year-old Mehliboyev to seven years in prison on February 18, 2003, after convicting him of anticonstitutional activities, participating in extremist religious organizations, and inciting religious hatred, according to local and international press reports.

Mehliboyev appealed the case. On March 14, 2005, the Tashkent City Court reduced his sentence to six and a half years in prison, the Tashkent-based Independent Group for Human Rights Defenders reported.

Ortikali Namazov
Pop Tongi and *Kishlok Khayoti*
IMPRISONED: August 11, 2004

Namazov, editor of the state newspaper *Pop Tongi* (Dawn of the Pop District) and correspondent for the state newspaper *Kishlok Khayoti* (Agricultural Life), was imprisoned while standing trial on embezzlement charges. He was later convicted of the charges—which local sources say were politically motivated—and sentenced to five and a half years in prison.

The 53-year-old journalist was charged with embezzling 14 million som (US$13,500) from *Pop Tongi*. The charges were filed after he wrote a series of articles about alleged abuses in local tax inspections and collective-farm management.

Namazov denied embezzling the money and said the charges were fabricated. After his trial began on August 4, 2004, Namazov complained that the judge was biased and was not allowing him to speak in his defense. Authorities took him into custody on August 11, before a verdict was reached.

The Turakurgan District Criminal Court convicted Namazov on August 16, a verdict condemned by local journalists and press freedom activists.

Mutabar Tadjibaeva, a local human rights activist who monitored the trial, told CPJ that local authorities harassed the journalist's family during the August trial, cutting his home telephone line and firing his daughter from her job as a school doctor.

Namazov was serving his sentence at a prison in the eastern Namangan region, the Tashkent-based Ozod Ovod press freedom group reported.

Sobirdjon Yakubov, *Hurriyat*
IMPRISONED: April 11, 2005

Yakubov, 22, was detained in the capital, Tashkent, on suspicions of religious extremism, according to local and international press reports. Three days later, he was criminally charged with "undermining the constitutional order," Alisher Sharafutdinov, deputy minister of the interior, announced at a press conference in the capital.

The formal charge was based on Yakubov's alleged religious activities. The government did not describe those purported actions in detail, but local reports cited Yakubov's alleged participation in an illegal Islamic organization.

Yakubov's colleagues said the charge was politicized and he was being punished for writing about Islam and advocating democratic reforms, according to press reports. He had recently visited the holy city of Mecca and published a series of articles about his pilgrimage, titled "A Journey to Dreamland," local reports said.

Yakubov's colleagues speculated that authorities might also have targeted him for a March article about slain Ukrainian journalist Georgy Gongadze. In the article, Yakubov said Gongazde's death "became a driving force [for Ukrainians] to realize the necessity of democratic reforms and freedom." According to some of Yakubov's colleagues, Uzbek authorities might have interpreted that as a call for a governmental change, local reports said.

The Tashkent-based news Web site *Uznews* reported that Yakubov called the *Hurriyat* newsroom on April 11 to inform his colleagues of his detention, but for four days police denied holding him.

Shukhrat Soipov, a lawyer representing Yakubov, said in September that the journalist was being held in the main Tashkent police prison and that prosecutors were investigating, the Tashkent-based Ozod Ovod press freedom group reported. Soipov said prison officials would not allow the journalist's family to visit Yakubov in prison.

Nosir Zokirov, Radio Free Europe/ Radio Liberty (RFE/RL)
IMPRISONED: August 26, 2005

An Uzbek court sentenced Zokirov, an Uzbek reporter who has worked for RFE/RL's local language service, to six months in prison for insulting a security officer, the U.S. government-funded radio service said.

Zokirov was summoned to court in the eastern city of Namangan on August 26 on charges of insulting a National Security Service (SNB) officer in a telephone call, RFE/RL said in a statement. Zokirov was detained, tried without counsel or witnesses, sentenced, and imprisoned—all on August 26.

The charge stemmed from an August 6 phone call Zokirov made to the Namangan SNB office to protest government pressure on poet Khaidarali Khomilov. In an earlier interview with Zokirov, the poet criticized the government's May 13 crackdown in nearby Andijan. Security forces killed hundreds of antigovernment demonstrators in the city that day, according to independent accounts.

In the aftermath of the massacre, Zokirov and other reporters working for foreign media faced harassment. Zokirov's land and cell phone lines were cut on May 17. His mobile service provider told Zokirov the line was shut down on "higher orders," RFE/RL said.

Zokirov appealed the conviction. On September 19, the Namangan Appeals Court examined the appeal for 15 minutes and issued a ruling upholding the conviction, the Tashkent-based Arena Committee for Freedom of Speech and Expression reported.

VIETNAM: 3

ooo

Nguyen Khac Toan, Freelance
IMPRISONED: January 8, 2002

Toan was arrested at an Internet café in the capital, Hanoi. He had reported on protests by disgruntled farmers and then transmitted his reports via the Internet to overseas pro-democracy groups. Authorities later charged him with espionage. On December 20, 2002, Toan was sentenced to 12 years in prison, one of the harshest sentences given to a Vietnamese democracy activist in recent years.

Toan served in the North Vietnamese army in the 1970s. After becoming active in Vietnam's pro-democracy movement, he began to write articles using the pen name Veteran Tran Minh Tam.

During the National Assembly's December 2001 and January 2002 meeting, large numbers of peasants gathered in front of the meeting hall to demand compensation for land that the government had confiscated during redevelopment efforts. Toan helped the protesters write their grievances to present to government officials. He also wrote several news reports about the demonstrations and sent the articles to overseas pro-democracy publications.

Toan's trial took less than one day, and his lawyer was not allowed to meet with him alone until the day before proceedings began.

The day after Toan was sentenced, the official Vietnamese press carried reports stating that he had "slandered and denigrated executives of the party and the state by sending electronic letters and by providing information to certain exiled Vietnamese reactionaries in France." He was being held in B14 Prison, in Thanh Tri District, outside Hanoi.

In March 2005, Toan was allowed to write to his mother after almost a year of being deprived of the right to communicate with his family, according to his letter, in which he called for the aid of international statesmen and the media in protesting his unjust imprisonment.

Pham Hong Son, Freelance
IMPRISONED: March 27, 2002

Son, a medical doctor, was arrested after he posted an essay online about democracy. Authorities also searched his home and confiscated his computer and several documents, according to the Democracy Club for Vietnam, an organization based in both California and Hanoi, Vietnam's capital.

Prior to his arrest, Son translated into Vietnamese and posted online an essay titled "What Is Democracy?" The article first appeared on the U.S. State Department's Web site. Son had previously written several essays promoting democracy and human rights, all of which appeared on Vietnamese-language online forums.

After Son's arrest, the government issued a statement claiming that his work was "antistate," according to international press reports.

On June 18, 2003, the Hanoi People's Court sentenced Son to 13 years in prison, plus three years of administrative detention, or house arrest.

The trial was closed to foreign diplomats and correspondents. Son's wife, Vu Thuy Ha, was also barred from the courtroom, except when she was called to testify. On appeal in 2003, the Hanoi Supreme Court reduced Son's prison sentence to five years.

In August 2004, Son's wife, Vu Thuy Ha, told the U.S. government-funded Radio Free Asia that her husband was in very poor health and suffered from a hernia.

By July 2005, a U.S.-based Vietnamese dissident group, the People's Democracy Party (PDP), reported that Son had been coughing up blood. Son remained incarcerated in 2005 despite several amnesties of political prisoners by the Vietnamese government during the past year.

Nguyen Vu Binh, Freelance
IMPRISONED: September 25, 2002

Security officials searched Binh's home in Vietnam's capital, Hanoi, before arresting him, said CPJ sources. Police did not disclose the reasons for the writer's arrest, although CPJ sources believe that his detention may be linked to an essay he wrote criticizing border agreements between China and Vietnam.

In a trial on December 31, 2003, the Hanoi People's Court sentenced Binh on espionage charges to seven years in prison, followed by three years of house arrest upon release. Binh's wife was the only family member allowed in the courtroom. Foreign diplomats and journalists were barred from the trial.

Following the proceedings, the official Vietnam News Agency reported that Binh was sentenced because he had "written and exchanged, with various opportunist elements in the country, information and materials that distorted the party and state policies." He was also accused of communicating with "reactionary" organizations abroad.

Binh is a former journalist who worked for almost 10 years at *Tap Chi Cong San* (Journal of Communism), an official publication of Vietnam's Communist Party. In January 2001, he left his position there after applying to form an independent opposition group called the Liberal Democratic Party.

Since then, Binh has written several articles calling for political reform and criticizing government policy. In August 2002, he wrote an article titled "Some Thoughts on the China-Vietnam Border Agreement," which was distributed online.

In late July 2002, Binh was briefly detained after submitting written testimony to a U.S. Congressional Human Rights Caucus briefing on freedom of expression in Vietnam. Authorities then required him to report to the local police station daily. He was also subjected to frequent daylong interrogation sessions.

In 2002, Vietnamese authorities cracked down on critics of land and sea border agreements signed by China and Vietnam as part of a rapprochement following the 1979 war between the two countries. Several writers have criticized the government for agreeing to border concessions without consulting the Vietnamese people.

CPJ INTERNATIONAL PRESS FREEDOM AWARDS

Since 1991, CPJ has honored several journalists from around the world with its annual International Press Freedom Awards. Recipients have shown extraordinary courage in the face of enormous risks, bravely standing up to tyrants who refuse to allow free discussion in order to hide corruption or keep the world from witnessing their deeds. These journalists have endured terrible difficulties, including jail or physical violence, simply for working to uncover and report the truth, or because they have expressed opinions that the leaders of their countries deem to be dangerous. Here are the 2005 awardees:

Galima Bukharbaeva, UZBEKISTAN

Bukharbaeva drew international attention to the Uzbek government's authoritarian policies, earning a reputation as one of Central Asia's most outspoken journalists. Her work for the London-based Institute for War & Peace Reporting focused on sensitive issues such as police torture, repression of Islamic activists, and state-sponsored abuses against journalists and human rights activists. As a result, Bukharbaeva was placed under police surveillance, denied press accreditation, and threatened with prosecution. The government organized Soviet-style "protests" in the capital, Tashkent, denouncing her as a traitor.

Bukharbaeva was one of the few journalists to witness and report on the May 13 massacre in the northeastern Uzbek city of Andijan. A bullet tore through her backpack, piercing her notebook and press pass, when troops opened fire on demonstrators.

As a result of her reporting, state media accused her of "conducting open information warfare against the state." Facing government reprisals, she fled the country and resettled in New York City, where she undertook studies at the Columbia University Graduate School of Journalism.

Beatrice Mtetwa, ZIMBABWE

Mtetwa, a prominent media lawyer, has defended many journalists in Zimbabwe who have been detained and harassed. In a country where the law is used as a weapon against independent journalists, Mtetwa has defended journalists and argued for press freedom, all at great personal risk.

This year, Mtetwa won acquittals for Toby Harnden and Julian Simmonds, journalists with *The Sunday Telegraph* of London, who were arrested outside a polling place in Zimbabwe during the April 2005 parliamentary election. The government of President Robert Mugabe, which severely restricted independent coverage of the vote, had charged them with working without accreditation.

Reuters

Mtetwa worked on behalf of the *Daily News*, Zimbabwe's sole independent daily newspaper until it was closed by the government in 2003. She has continued to defend the newspaper's journalists, many of whom face criminal charges for their work.

In October 2003, Mtetwa was arrested on specious allegations of drunken driving. She was taken to a police station, where she was held for three hours, beaten and choked, then released without charge. Although she was unable to speak for two days as a result of the assault, she returned to the police station on the third day, with medical evidence in hand, to file charges against her assailants.

Lúcio Flávio Pinto, BRAZIL

Pinto reports from the lawless and isolated Amazon region of Brazil, one of the most dangerous beats in Latin America. As publisher and editor of *Jornal Pessoal* in the northern state of Pará, he covers an area that is almost twice the size of Texas and is home to corrupt ranchers and land speculators.

He has reported on drug trafficking, environmental devastation, and political and corporate corruption. In return, he has been threatened and subjected to a wave of spurious lawsuits. A powerful local media owner, who is also a politician, attacked Pinto in a restaurant in January, beating and kicking him. The assailant's bodyguards provided cover during the assault.

Writing columns and directing coverage in his semimonthly paper, Pinto has challenged the self-dealing and domination of a prominent media company. In retaliation, the company's principals have unleashed a barrage of legal complaints.

Judges, politicians, and business owners have also filed criminal and civil complaints against Pinto, who has exposed illegal corporate appropriation of timber-rich land, as well as corruption involving land titles.

Shi Tao, CHINA

Shi was sentenced to 10 years in prison for "leaking state secrets abroad." Shi worked as an editor for *Dangdai Shang Bao* (Contemporary Trade News), a newspaper in the city of Changsha, in Hunan province. He also wrote essays calling for political reform that were posted on overseas news Web sites that are banned in China.

He was arrested in November 2004 for posting notes from a directive issued by China's Propaganda Department that told the media how to cover the 15th anniversary of the military crackdown in Tiananmen Square.

Shi's imprisonment highlighted the government's intense efforts to control the Internet, the only alternative to China's officially sanctioned print and broadcast media. The government monitors Internet content, blocks Web sites, requires bloggers to register their identities, and solicits the help of companies doing business in China. In this case, the U.S. Internet giant Yahoo helped authorities identify Shi through his e-mail account.

Nearly half of the 32 journalists imprisoned in China in 2005 were jailed for work distributed on the Internet. Many had written for Chinese-language Web sites hosted overseas.

INTERNATIONAL PRESS FREEDOM AWARD RECIPIENTS 1991-2004

1991

Byron Barrera, *La Época*, Guatemala
Bill Foley and Cary Vaughan, United States
Tatyana Mitkova, TSN, former Soviet Union
Pius Njawe, *Le Messager*, Cameroon
IMPRISONED: Wang Juntao and Chen Ziming, *Economics Weekly*, China

1992

Muhammad al-Saqr, *Al-Qabas*, Kuwait
Sony Esteus, Radio Tropic FM, Haiti
David Kaplan, ABC News, United States
Gwendolyn Lister, *The Namibian*, Namibia
Thepchai Yong, *The Nation*, Thailand

1993

Omar Belhouchet, *El Watan*, Algeria
Nosa Igiebor, *Tell*, Nigeria
Veran Matic, Radio B92, Yugoslavia
Ricardo Uceda, *Sí*, Peru
IMPRISONED: Doan Viet Hoat, *Freedom Forum*, Vietnam

1994

Iqbal Athas, *The Sunday Leader*, Sri Lanka
Daisy Li Yuet-wah, Hong Kong Journalists Association, Hong Kong
Aziz Nesin, *Aydinlik*, Turkey
In memory of staff journalists, *Navidi Vakhsh*, Tajikistan
IMPRISONED: Yndamiro Restano, freelance, Cuba

1995

Veronica Guerin, *Sunday Independent*, Ireland
Yevgeny Kiselyov, NTV, Russia
Fred M'membe, *The Post*, Zambia
José Rubén Zamora Marroquín, *Siglo Veintiuno*, Guatemala
IMPRISONED: Ahmad Taufik, Alliance of Independent Journalists, Indonesia

1996

J. Jesús Blancornelas, *Zeta*, Mexico
Yusuf Jameel, *Asian Age*, India
Daoud Kuttab, Internews Middle East, Palestinian Authority Territories
IMPRISONED: Ocak Isik Yurtcu, *Ozgur Gundem*, Turkey

1997

Ying Chan, *Yazhou Zhoukan*, United States
Shieh Chung-liang, *Yazhou Zhoukan*, Taiwan
Victor Ivancic, *Feral Tribune*, Croatia
Yelena Masyuk, NTV, Russia
Freedom Neruda, *La Voie*, Ivory Coast
IMPRISONED: Christine Anyanwu, *The Sunday Magazine*, Nigeria

1998

Grémah Boucar, Radio Anfani, Niger
Gustavo Gorriti, *La Prensa*, Panama
Goenawan Mohamad, *Tempo*, Indonesia

Pavel Sheremet, ORT, *Belorusskaya Delovaya Gazeta*, Belarus
IMPRISONED: Ruth Simon, Agence France-Presse, Eritrea

1999

María Cristina Caballero, *Semana*, Colombia
Baton Haxhiu, *Koha Ditore*, Kosovo
Jugnu Mohsin and Najam Sethi, *The Friday Times*, Pakistan
IMPRISONED: Jesús Joel Diáz Hernández, Cooperativa Avileña de Periodistas Independientes, Cuba

2000

Steven Gan, *Malaysiakini*, Malaysia
Zeljko Kopanja, *Nezavine Novine*, Bosnia-Herzegovina
Modeste Mutinga, *Le Potentiel*, Democratic Republic of Congo
IMPRISONED: Mashallah Shamsolvaezin, *Asr-e-Azadegan* and *Neshat*, Iran

2001

Mazen Dana, Reuters, West Bank
Geoff Nyarota, *The Daily News*, Zimbabwe
Horacio Verbitsky, freelance, Argentina
IMPRISONED: Jiang Weiping, *Qianshao*, China

2002

Ignacio Gómez, "Noticias Uno," Colombia
Irina Petrushova, *Respublika*, Kazakhstan
Tipu Sultan, freelance, Bangladesh
IMPRISONED: Fesshaye Yohannes, *Setit*, Eritrea

2003

Abdul Samay Hamed, Afghanistan
Aboubakr Jamai, *Le Journal Hebdomadaire* and *Assahifa al-Ousbouiya*, Morocco
Musa Muradov, *Groznensky Rabochy*, Russia
IMPRISONED: Manuel Vázquez Portal, Grupo de Trabajo Decoro, Cuba

2004

Alexis Sinduhije, Radio Publique Africaine, Burundi
Svetlana Kalinkina, *Belorusskaya Delovaya Gazeta*, Belarus
In memory of Paul Klebnikov, *Forbes Russia*, Russia
IMPRISONED: Aung Pwint and Thaung Tun, freelance, Burma

CPJ BURTON BENJAMIN AWARD

Since 1991, CPJ has given the Burton Benjamin Memorial Award to an individual in recognition of a lifetime of distinguished achievement for the cause of press freedom. The award honors Burton Benjamin, the late CBS News senior producer and former CPJ chairman, who died in 1988. In 2005, CPJ honored the late ABC News anchor and correspondent Peter Jennings.

2005

Peter Jennings
ABC News

AP

Before his death in August 2005, Peter Jennings' career was intertwined with the major events of the past four decades. He reported on the building of the Berlin Wall in 1961 and its demolition in 1989. He established the first American television news bureau in the Arab world in 1968 and drew on his knowledge of the region to inform his reporting in both U.S. wars in Iraq. He reported on the civil rights movement in the southern United States during the 1960s and the struggle for equality in South Africa in the 1970s and 1980s.

Jennings was one of the first reporters to go to Vietnam in the 1960s, and he reported from Bosnia in the 1990s. He was on the scene when the independent political movement Solidarity was born in a Polish shipyard, and he was in Hungary, Czechoslovakia, East Germany, Romania, and the Soviet Union to record the fall of communism.

In the week following the September 11, 2001, attacks, Jennings anchored more than 60 hours of news coverage, providing a reliable and reassuring voice during a time of crisis. He also earned a reputation for raising complex issues. His special series, "Peter Jennings Reporting," focused on vital international affairs such as the tense relations between India and Pakistan, the crisis in Haiti, and the drug trade in Central and South America. He also tackled important domestic issues such as abortion, gun control, and health care.

Jennings was named anchor and senior editor of "World News Tonight" in 1983. In more than 20 years in that position, he was honored with almost every major award given to television journalists.

BURTON BENJAMIN MEMORIAL AWARD RECIPIENTS 1991-2004

1991

Walter Cronkite
CBS News

1992

Katharine Graham
The Washington Post Company

1993

Ted Turner
CNN

1994

George Soros
Open Society Institute

1995

Benjamin C. Bradlee
The Washington Post

1996

Arthur Ochs Sulzberger
The New York Times

1997

Ted Koppel
ABC News

1998

Brian Lamb
C-SPAN

1999

Don Hewitt
CBS News

2000

Otis Chandler
Times Mirror Company

2001

Joseph Lelyveld
The New York Times

2002

Daniel Pearl
The Wall Street Journal

2003

John F. Burns
The New York Times

2004

John S. Carroll
Los Angeles Times

CONTRIBUTORS

CPJ is extremely grateful to the individuals, foundations, and corporations whose generosity made our press freedom work possible in 2005:

ABC News
David Abramowicz
Advance Publications/*Star-Ledger*
Ronald Allen
Marcia and Franz Allina
ALM Media Inc.
Altria Group Inc.
James S. Altschul
American Express
Alfred Andersson
Andrews McMeel Publishing
Argus Media Inc.
Irwin Arieff
David Armon and Maureen Fitzpatrick-Armon
The Associated Press
The Atlantic Philanthropic Service Co.
Robert Bazell
Alex Belida and Patricia Reber
The Belo Foundation
Lucy Benson
Tobias and Eva Bermant
N.S. Bienstock Inc.
Mary Billard/Barry Cooper
Molly Bingham
The Morton and Jane Blaustein Foundation Inc.
Bloomberg
Malcom Borg
Kimberly G. Braswell
Bridgewater Fieldwater Foundation
Meredith and Tom Brokaw
Jerry Bruckheimer Television
Brunswick Group LLC
BusinessWeek
William Cafritz
José F. Carreno
Virginia H. Carter
CBS
CBS News
CCS Fund Raising Co. LLC
Cisco Systems Inc.
Citigroup Inc.
CNBC
CNN
CNN.com
Andrew H. Cohn
Columbia University Graduate School of Journalism
Condé Nast Publications
Continental Airlines
Ann Cooper
Carole Cooper and Richard Leibner
Cox Newspapers Inc.
Credit Suisse First Boston
Walter Cronkite
Crowell & Moring LLP
Tom Curran
Walter Dear
Debevoise & Plimpton LLP
Elizabeth DeMarse
Dianne Doctor
Dow Jones & Company
Dow Jones Foundation
Stanley Eisenberg
Gail and Richard Elden
Ernst and Young
Ethics and Excellence in Journalism Foundation
Factiva
Elizabeth Farnsworth
Jeremy Feigelson and Eugenie Allen
Robert and Emily Fenichel
Forbes Inc.
Forbes Magazine
Ford Motor Company

Judy Foreman
Fox News
Max Frankel and Joyce Purnick
The Freedom Forum/Newseum
Josh Friedman and Carol Ash
Ruth Friendly
Rose Gallagher
Gannett Co. Inc
Micah Garen and Marie-Hélène Carleton
Anne Garrels and Vint Lawrence
GE Energy Financial Services
Robert Giles
Eric Goldberg
Goldman Sachs and Co.
James C. and Toni K. Goodale
Cheryl Gould
Harold R. Grueskin
William S. Grueskin
Edwin Guthman
The Mark Haas Foundation
Robert Haiman
Mohammad Hajizadeh
Ruth Ann and William F. Harnisch
Hearst Corporation/Hearst Newspapers
Drue Heinz Trust
Sharon Held and Ian Hague
Cherie Henderson
Nicola Hewitt
Peter Heydon
Kathleen E. Hunt
Alberto Ibargüen
Gwen Ifill
Steven L. Isenberg
Alex S. Jones
Eason Jordan
Kahn Charitable Foundation
Andrew Katell
David A. Katz
Mr. and Mrs. George Keller
Jim Kelly
Saundra Keyes
Gay and Donald Kimelman
Kevin Klose
John S. and James L. Knight Foundation
Jane Kramer
Kruger Inc.
Kwittken and Company LLC
The LaFetra Foundation
Landmark Publishing Group
Thomas and Carolyn Langfitt Family Foundation
Esther and David Laventhol
Lazard Frères
Stuart Leavenworth
Vladimir Lenskiy
Robert L. Lenzner
Frankie F.L. Leung Esq.
The Leon Levy Foundation
Tony Lewis
Steven Liesman
Steve and Amy Lipin
Los Angeles Times
The Malayala Manorama Co. Ltd.
Jimena P. Martinez and Michael J. Hirschhorn
Joaquin Martinez
Kati Marton
Michael Massing
C. Tyler Mathisen
Robert R. McCormick Tribune Foundation
Mike and Debra McCurry
MediaNews Group Inc.
Merrill Lynch & Co. Inc.
Merrill Lynch & Co. Foundation Inc.
Geraldine Fabrikant Metz and Robert T. Metz
MN Newspaper Guild/Typographical Union - CWA
Victor and Anne Navasky
NBC News
NBC Universal
New York Daily News
The New York Times Company
The New York Times Company Foundation
Department of Journalism, Faculty of Arts and Science, New York University
The New Yorker

Samuel I. Newhouse Foundation Inc.
Newsday
Newsweek Inc
Nieman Foundation for Journalism
The North Jersey Media Group Foundation Inc.
Open Society Institute
William A. Orme and Deborah Sontag
Susan and Peter Osnos
James Ottaway
The Overbrook Foundation
Charles L. Overby
Clarence Page
Mark Palermo
PARADE Publications
Park Foundation
Michael Parks
Norman Pearlstine
St. Petersburg Times
Jan and Barry Petersen
Pew Charitable Trusts
Stone Phillips
The Playboy Foundation
Erwin Potts
Prudential Financial Inc.
Lisa Ramaci
Dan Rather
Tom Redburn
Reuters Group PLC
Robert Rivard
Susan and Gene Roberts
David and Laura Ross
Charles Rowe
Sandra Mims Rowe
William Ruane
Russert Family Foundation
Robert J. Samuelson
David and Rachel Schlesinger
Irene Schneider
Scripps Howard Foundation
Neal Shapiro and JuJu Chang
Christine M. Simone
Skadden, Arps, Slate, Meagher & Flom
Slate Magazine
Kathleen M. Sloane
Sony Corporation of America
The Star-Ledger employees
David Starr
Paul E. Steiger
Jean Stein
Patty Stonesifer
Straus Newspapers
The Street.com/CNBC
Paul C. Tash
David Thompson
Time Inc.
Time Magazine
Time Warner Inc.
Audrey and Seymour Topping
Garry and Jane Trudeau
UBS
Verizon
Viacom
The Svetlana and Herbert M. Wachtell Foundation
Robert C. Waggoner
The Wall Street Journal
Ed Wallace and Pamela Falk
The Washington Post Company
Weil, Gotshal & Manges
Reid H. Weingarten
Davis Weinstock and Elizabeth Hawes Weinstock
John D. Weis
Jacob Weisberg
Martin and Lois Whitman
Matthew Winkler
Robert and Colleen Wood
William D. Zabel
Anonymous (10)

We also extend our gratitude to the many individuals and organizations who supported CPJ with gifts under $250, not listed here due to space limitations.

MEMORIAL CONTRIBUTIONS

The Committee to Protect Journalists is grateful to the friends and family of the following people, in whose names generous contributions were made.

In memory of Mark Fineman: Marcia and Tom Little

In memory of Paul Klebnikov: Henri Cauvin and Rachel L. Swarns, Michael Hirschorn

In memory of Lars-Erik Nelson: Benjamin Buchwald, Nathan Buchwald, Brian Moss, Mary Santarcangelo

In memory of Jack Prescott Smith: Patricia Olson

In memory of Scott Shuger: Emanuel and Marjorie Massing

In memory of Joseph R. Slevin: Susan Blaustein and Alan Berlow

GIFTS IN HONOR

In honor of John M. Arthur: Rosamond Dean

In honor of Judy Miller: Eric Hursh

In honor of Chip Mitchell: Elizabeth Tisel

In honor of Norman Pearlstine: The American Society of Magazine Editors

In honor of Stephen Salyer and Susan Moeller: Elaine and Hirschel Abelson, Deborah Kalb, Marvin Kalb, Dorothy Moeller, Judith O. and Robert E. Rubin, Melinda Ward, Bert Wells and Laura Walker

In honor of Frank Smyth: Holland + Knight Charitable Foundation

In honor of John Temple: *The Columbus Dispatch*

Some of the vital resources that help make our work possible are in-kind services and contributions. CPJ thanks the following for their support in 2005:

ABC, Associated Press Television News, AP/Wide World Photos, BBC, CBS, Debevoise & Plimpton, Patrice Fletcher, Lester Holt, Alan Ives, Megan Marcus, Michele Mathison, Gordon Miller, Tendai Musiya, NBC, Reuters/ITN, Mercedes Sayagues

Continental Airlines is the preferred carrier of the Committee to Protect Journalists.

CPJ AT A GLANCE

How did CPJ get started? A group of U.S. foreign correspondents created CPJ in response to the often brutal treatment of their foreign colleagues by authoritarian governments and other enemies of independent journalism.

Who runs CPJ? CPJ has a full-time staff of 23 at its New York headquarters, including area specialists for each major world region. CPJ has a Washington, D.C., representative, and consultants stationed around the world. A 35-member board of prominent journalists directs CPJ's activities.

How is CPJ funded? CPJ is funded solely by contributions from individuals, corporations, and foundations. CPJ does not accept government funding.

Why is press freedom important? Without a free press, few other human rights are attainable. A strong press freedom environment encourages the growth of a robust society, which leads to stable, sustainable democracies and healthy social, political, and economic development. CPJ works in more than 120 countries, many of which suffer under repressive regimes, debilitating civil war, or other problems that harm press freedom and democracy.

How does CPJ protect journalists? By publicly revealing abuses against the press and by acting on behalf of imprisoned and threatened journalists, CPJ effectively warns journalists and news organizations where attacks on press freedom are occurring. CPJ organizes vigorous public protests and works through diplomatic channels to effect change. CPJ publishes articles and news releases; special reports; a magazine, *Dangerous Assignments*; and *Attacks on the Press*, the most comprehensive annual survey of press freedom around the world.

Where does CPJ get its information? CPJ has full-time program coordinators monitoring the press in Africa, the Americas, Asia, Europe and Central Asia, and the Middle East and North Africa. They track developments through their own independent research, fact-finding missions, and firsthand contacts in the field, including reports from other journalists. CPJ shares information on breaking cases with other press freedom organizations through the International Freedom of Expression Exchange, a global e-mail network.

When would a journalist call upon CPJ? *In an emergency.* Using local and foreign contacts, CPJ can intervene whenever local and foreign correspondents are in trouble. CPJ is prepared to notify news organizations, government officials, and human rights organizations immediately of press freedom violations. *When traveling on assignment.* CPJ can advise journalists covering dangerous assignments. *When covering the news.* Attacks against the press are news, and they often serve as the first signal of a crackdown on all freedoms. CPJ is uniquely situated to provide journalists with information and insight into press conditions around the world.

HOW TO REPORT AN ATTACK ON THE PRESS

CPJ needs accurate, detailed information in order to document abuses of press freedom and help journalists in trouble. CPJ corroborates the information and takes action on behalf of the journalists and news organizations involved. Anyone with information about an attack on the press should contact CPJ. Call collect if necessary. Our number is (212) 465-1004. Sources may also e-mail to the addresses below, or send a fax to (212) 465-9568.

What to report:

Journalists who are:

- Arrested
- Censored
- Harassed
- Killed
- Threatened
- Wrongfully expelled
- Assaulted
- Denied credentials
- Kidnapped
- Missing
- Wounded
- Wrongfully sued for libel or defamation

News organizations that are:

- Attacked, raided, or illegally searched
- Closed by force
- Materials confiscated or damaged
- Censored
- Transmissions jammed
- Wrongfully sued for libel or defamation

CPJ needs accurate, detailed information that includes:

- Background, including the journalists and news organizations involved.
- Date and circumstances.

Contact information for regional programs:

Africa: (212) 465-9344, x112 E-mail: africa@cpj.org
Americas: (212) 465-9344, x120 E-mail: americas@cpj.org
Asia: (212) 465-9344, x140 E-mail: asia@cpj.org
Europe and Central Asia: (212) 465-9344, x101 E-mail: europe@cpj.org
Middle East and North Africa: (212) 465-9344, x104 E-mail: mideast@cpj.org

What happens next:

Depending on the case, CPJ will:

- Investigate and confirm the report, sending a fact-finding mission if necessary.
- Pressure authorities to respond.
- Notify human rights groups and press organizations around the world, including IFEX, Article 19, Amnesty International, Reporters Sans Frontières, PEN, International Federation of Journalists, and Human Rights Watch.
- Increase public awareness through the press.
- Publish advisories to warn other journalists about potential dangers.

CPJ STAFF

Executive Director Ann Cooper
Deputy Director Joel Simon
Editorial Director Bill Sweeney
Director of Development and Outreach John Weis
Director of Finance and Administration Lade Kadejo
Senior Editor Robert Mahoney
Journalist Assistance Coordinator Elisabeth Witchel
Washington, D.C., Representative Frank Smyth
Webmaster and Systems Administrator Mick Stern
Development Associate Elena Snyder
Executive Assistant and Board Liaison Maya Taal
Receptionist and Office Manager Janet Mason

REGIONAL PROGRAMS

AFRICA

Program Coordinator Julia Crawford
Research Associate Alexis Arieff

THE AMERICAS

Program Coordinator Carlos Lauría
Senior Research Associate Sauro González Rodríguez

ASIA

Program Coordinator Abi Wright
Research Associate Kristin Jones
Program Consultant Shawn W. Crispin

EUROPE AND CENTRAL ASIA

Senior Program Coordinator Alex Lupis
Research Associate Nina Ognianova
Program Consultant Masha Yulikova

MIDDLE EAST AND NORTH AFRICA

Senior Program Coordinator Joel Campagna
Research Associate Ivan Karakashian
Program Consultant Kamel Eddine Labidi

INDEX BY COUNTRY

5/17 Arr. 7:15 am 5/18
AA Nwk → Roma
To Villa on 19th

Fly out on Mon. Sun. night in Roma

Duckworths →